Humanistic Studies in the Communication Arts

George N. Gordon, General Editor

ETHICS AND THE PRESS

Readings in Mass Media Morality

H|S
—+—
C|A

Humanistic Studies in the Communication Arts

ETHICS AND THE PRESS

Readings in Mass Media Morality

Edited, with special introductory notes and bibliography by

JOHN C. MERRILL
University of Missouri

and

RALPH D. BARNEY
Brigham Young University

COMMUNICATION ARTS BOOKS

HASTINGS HOUSE, PUBLISHERS
New York 10016

LIBRARY OF CONGRESS CATALOGING IN PUBLICATION DATA
Main entry under title:

Ethics and the press.

   (Humanistic studies in the communication arts)
(Communication arts books)
   Bibliography: p.
   Includes index.
   1. Journalistic ethics—Addresses, essays, lectures.
I. Merrill, John Calhoun, 1924-   II. Barney,
Ralph D.
PN4756.E8   174'.9'097   75-17981

ISBN 0-8038-1923-4 Cloth Edition
ISBN 0-8038-1924-2 Paper (text) Edition

Published simultaneously in Canada by
Saunders of Toronto, Ltd., Don Mills, Ontario

Printed in the United States of America
Designed by Al Lichtenberg

CONTENTS

Part Two: ETHICAL PROBLEMS

PREFACE

IN RECENT YEARS journalists and journalism students have turned increasingly to the scientists—especially the behavioral scientists—for their insights and their methods. They have put their faith in sophisticated audience analysis techniques, and in a multitude of theoretical models to help them define and direct their activities. And at the same time they have become enamored with a proliferation of electronic and computerized gadgets which have thrust themselves into the newsrooms. *How* their journalism is done—the *methodology* of their craft—has distracted their attention from the *motivations* and *consequences* of their work. Morality, if it is considered at all, has taken a kind of peripheral position to the mechanisms of technology and an obsession with methodology.

The Watergate Affair, however, may have been a turning point. Journalism students are more concerned with morality—at least with press morality; and they, among many others, are questioning the ethical foundations of journalism. There is a growing insistence that more emphasis be placed on journalistic philosophy. This is a hopeful sign.

Basic problems of journalism are, and always have been, philosophical—and mainly ethical, even when the chief concern has been with epistemology. So it is rather strange that since the early 1930's little attention has been given to journalistic ethics—at least in a systematic way. Few books and articles have focused on the subject, whereas the literature of the 20's and 30's was filled with discussions of morality.

It may well be, however, that a groundswell of criticism of the media, probably beginning in the 1940's with the Commission on Freedom of the Press

("Hutchins Commission"), and continuing into the 1960's and 1970's with the Pentagon Papers, the Cuban Missile Crisis, the Vietnam and Watergate problems, and the Middle East confrontations, has resulted in a heightened awareness of the importance of ethics in journalism.

At any rate, an interest in journalistic ethics is beginning to reappear in journalism education programs, in textbooks and other literature related to mass communications. And one hears increasing reference to press ethics in public speeches and lectures—and even at newspaper and broadcasting conventions and conferences. Names of philosophers are slowly filtering into journalism classes: Kant, Spinoza, Nietzsche, Hobbes, Sartre, and Dewey are beginning to share time with Katz, Lasswell, Osgood, Deutsch, Doob, Parsons, and Lerner. Sociological and psychological emphases, though still potent, are beginning—albeit slowly—to be joined by philosophical emphases in journalism.

Basic philosophical foundations of American journalism are not—and probably never have been—very strong. Journalists today, however, seem to be especially frustrated in the area of ethics; they flail about in a marshland of ethical subjectivism with little to support them. They have actually thought very little about theories of ethics and know almost nothing about the history of moral philosophy. Modern journalists are increasingly pulled between what they consider their "rights" as journalists (editorial self-determinism, for instance) and their responsibility to society or to various persons or groups within that society. Dennis J. Chase, in an excellent article in *The Quill* ("The Aphilosophy of Journalism," Sept., 1971), puts it this way:

> With nothing fixed, with everything continually evolving, the editor is free to unleash his reporters at whatever strikes his fancy. There is never an obligation to inquire about the function of a newspaper, or to define a newspaper's chief commodity: news.

There are, of course, many ethical areas of "non-concern" in journalism other than the "news-defining" area mentioned by Chase. Daniel P. Moynihan gives a good example of one such area in an article on the presidency and the press (*Commentary*, March, 1971); he refers to the common press practice of reporting "leaks" (unattributed "stories") without giving the source of such anonymous information.

Moynihan poses these "ethical questions": Who is the leaker? Why does he want the story leaked? Other questions also suggest themselves: Why does the reporter want to publicize this anonymous leak? Do the people have a right to know the source of the leak? Can they adequately judge the validity or importance of the story without the source? Can they be anything but pawns in the leaker-reporter game without some means of verification? And on and on.

Perhaps many ethical questions are considered unimportant to journalists because they realize that they are a part of an intrinsically unsystematic craft and that the public generally realizes this and tolerates a tremendous amount of error and sloppiness (technical *and* ethical) on the part of the press. For one thing, news media naturally distort reality; it is the nature of abstracting from that reality and creating verbal and pictorial representations for second-hand consumption. The reader, the listener and the viewer each recognizes this and resigns himself to it. The noted Italian journalist, Luigi Barzini, has written in the *Encounter* magazine of London (Jan., 1968) of the audience member: "Everything, he discovers, has been touched up and simplified, often as unrecognisable to him as the picture taken from a plane of an intricate jungle, filled with wild beasts, colourful birds, and monstrous flowers, is to the traveller on foot."

In addition to such basic problems suggested by the above quotation, there are others which are more in the journalist's power to control. For example, the simple (or complex) matter of integrity. John Dean, the former counsel to President Nixon who served a jail sentence for his role in the Watergate coverup, admitted that his "ambition got in the way of" his integrity. Such a statement, perhaps, also fairly sums up some of the problems of ethics for journalists. In an important pivotal role in their society, journalists have the potential, at least collectively, for massive influence on the direction the society takes, for they make available to the public the information upon which decisions are based.

In their critical positions, journalists find themselves buffeted by, or the target of, special influence groups who have strong vested interests in determining the direction the public decision-making process will take. These vested interests range from a government administration in power (at any level) that is concerned with perpetuating itself in that position to special interest groups devoted to influencing public opinion at home to lever legislators into favoring special legislative measures.

As a result of this pressure imbalance, it often appears that society (more properly, those who actively work to influence opinions) makes unethical conduct an activity to be rewarded, rather than despised. Thus, it sometimes appears difficult to make a case *for* ethical behavior in the face of an unfeeling public and the very real rewards that are available for those who keep silent, or—in the case of journalists—who apply a little extra selectivity in the publication of the information at their disposal.

It may be axiomatic that virtually all pressures a journalist receives are designed to persuade him in favor of a narrow vested interest. Almost none of the pressures take the larger view of the "public good," except for holding the enrichment of the vested interest as in the public good. Therefore, the major bulwark a journalist has to bolster his resolve to public good is a bulwark that lies within himself. It is the realization that ultimately ethics is a personal matter.

In addition to the many ethical problems arising from the natural inclination to oversimplification and falsification in journalism to which Luigi Barzini alluded earlier and those which result from submitting to various public pressures, there are hundreds of other mundane and recurring ethical problems to which journalists must (or should) address themselves every day. A few of these—and they should be approached seriously, systematically, and rationally by any humanistically inclined journalist—follow:

What about the ethics of a network paying a well-known newsmaker for a television interview? Of a newsman honoring off-the-record statements? How much emphasis should be given to social disorders—riots, etc.—and on their leaders? Should juvenile names be used in newsstories? Should rape victims be named in stories? Is the creation of news by the media themselves ethical?

Should truth be the overriding ethical principle or standard of a news medium, or the individual journalist? Is it ethical for the reporter to speculate on motives or consequences in a newsstory? Is it ethical to quote someone out of context or to tamper—however mildly—with direct quotations? Is it ethical to "stage" newspictures? Is it ethical for journalists to accept gifts from, or to go on junkets sponsored by, persons or institutions about which they report?

We have, in the present book of readings, sought to spotlight many such ethical questions and to suggest many others which the reader may think about and discuss. A rather large number of ethical positions are treated in the pages which follow, and we will not attempt to pass judgment on the rightness or wrongness of these positions; rather, we simply make them available in one volume as a catalyst for thought and discussion. The articles in Part One are mainly concerned with more generalized ethical discussions—and might be called "meta-ethical" in nature. Those in Part Two are more specifically concerned with particular ethical problems faced in everyday journalism.

Journalistic ethics can be called the branch of philosophy which aids journalists in determining what is right to do. It is ultimately concerned with providing moral principles or norms for journalistic action; as such it might be considered a normative science of conduct. Perhaps "art" would really be a better term, for it is actually very "unscientific" because there is a reluctance to prescribe for the individual *any one* system of ethics. At the very least, journalistic ethics—or at least we believe—should provide the journalist with a kind of "catalogue" of ethical positions from which he may choose. This will make him ethically "aware" or "concerned" and at the same time will permit him to retain a sense of autonomy. And this should give him a humanistic ground of being and foundation of action.

Journalistic ethics, we believe, should set forth guidelines, rules, norms, codes—at least, broad principles or maxims—that will lead, not *force,* the journalist to be more humane and not necessarily more "human." We sincerely hope that this book of readings will aid in this objective.

JOHN C. MERRILL, Ph.D.
University of Missouri—Columbia

RALPH D. BARNEY, Ph.D.
Brigham Young University

April, 1975

FOREWORD

I AM ABLE to think at the moment of no more pertinent and ironic issue facing the communication arts, particularly that of journalism in its many manifestations, than the matter of ethical principles.

It is pertinent because we have recently lived through a period when, from every side, problems concerning nearly all practice and policy in modern communications have been written bold on the handpress of history: the Vietnam war, Pentagon papers, Commissions on Violence and Pornography, the Watergate extravaganza and the state and fate of the economies of the West. It is ironic because our heads have been pushed into this bold type by a recent cataclysm—the first of its pith in our national experience—at the highest levels of government, resulting in a pardoned ex-President and assorted cabinet officers facing jail sentences, all relics of a shattered federal administration that was overtly and ostensibly *more* concerned with the ethics of editorial and reportorial journalism than any other in two generations.

In this latter respect, I feel unsettled writing a Foreword to an anthology whose sometimes-hero, bobbing up and down between and on its pages, is none other than the disgraced and dishonored ex-Vice President of the United States, Spiro Agnew.

That Agnew himself had apparently neither read nor remembered his Aristotle is merely quirky, not ironic, because the ancient Athenian's advice might well have saved Agnew from the ignomy of a *nollo contendere* plea and, for better or worse, his job as well. Aristotle understood that ethical behavior related not to how one *acted* in given circumstances but to his ongoing *habits* of doing the right thing. The Agnew that the reader will meet in the pages ahead is a figure whose *acts,* calls to accountability in political matters of the masscom establishment, are gently and circumspectly praised and faulted, even by his antagonists. Would that his *habits* had been equally as "happy," in the precise word of Aristotle, who wisely equates the pursuit of the ethical life, in fact, with the achievement of happiness.

Lest these considerations be Greek to the working newspaperman, journalism professor and/or student who picks up this volume, what I mean is that this book, in my opinion, is being published at a time when we today look forward to more and deeper humanistic consideration of the professional *rights* and *wrongs* that mass communicators must learn to live by as a consequence of their preferred status in society than ever before in history. There is, of course, nothing *new* about concerns centering upon the morals and ethics of journalists and broadcasting pundits. The Canons of Journalism of the (then) American Society of Newspaper Editors go back to 1923; the years since then have been punctuated by Blue Books, White Papers and Codes of Ethics and Commission Reports (some rigidly professional and others "Lucely" academic). To swing full circle, newspaper reports of the ASNE meetings in April 1975 indicate a proposal to amend the Canons by loosening their definition of "freedom" and dropping the section on "decency," the first changes made in them in more than half a century. But most students of mass communications in our time and place have all too often arched an eyebrow and smiled cynically at the pragmatic dissonance between what has been written and what has been done within that ever growing social technostructure some of us call "the press" and others refer to ominously as "the media." And working journalists, I am afraid, have often laughed at them.

Granted that it is hyperbolic to claim that this technostructure—or any part of it—has in knightly solitude disengaged us from Southeast Asia, toppled a corrupt administration or, for that matter, simply forced us to celebrate our bicentennial year with new appreciation of the genius of our system of checks and balances. The articles and essays in this book, taken together, explain precisely why journalists, like everybody else, tend to enjoy patting themselves on the back and so sentimentally cherish their presumed role as the "fourth estate." But these essays also demonstrate that journalists can be mercilessly honest in appraising their own roles in the scheme of things, if and when they feel the time is ripe.

What *has* occurred in the past few years is that more and more of our plain citizens—and more and more journalists as well—are reflecting critically about the "skill and power," in Kinglake's words, of the people who address them in print and on the airwaves as purveyors of news. Agnew was merely a catalytic moment and Watergate a precipitating accident that hurried, I think, the inevitable crystallization among the many ideas that Walter Lippmann, A. J. Liebling and others had been spreading to the few for decades. Let us remember that we are living in the age of Ralph Nader and gods of ecology and consumerism who are requesting, if not demanding, ever more severe ethical accountability from many and various sectors of our culture, not only its editorial desks but from its salesmen, bankers, lawyers, teachers and others.

I suppose there is also something ironic about all of this panting after professional propriety in a period of rising crime statistics, permissive personal morality and the fragmentation of honored artistic traditions. As one's hair falls out or turns white, however, he or she either learns to live with paradox, goes raving mad or sends a bullet through the soft palate of the mouth. We should, I suppose, console ourselves by thanking the Fates that time and circumstance have conspired, at least, to prod journalists and students of journalism to self-appraisals long overdue in their select domains and pray silently that they possess a power of example equal to the force they have already and recently demonstrated they are competent to apply by exhortation.

That Professors Merrill and Barney have compiled this provocative collection of contents and discontents with the ethical sides of the documentation of our era is, it seems to me, serendipitous. Both editors of this book have track records as tough-minded realists who appreciate the work-a-day problems that newsmen and women face in the maelstrom of their professional lives, and they enjoy few illusions and swallow fewer myths about the inherent virtues of public opinion. On the other hand, they are idealistic enough to sense and identify a moral flame both in the press and its consumers that may gutter at times but is responsive to the interests of journalism's ethically sensitive community today. More important, they are also aware of the obligation of all teachers of journalism to construct a viable moral substructure for the young men and women who are preparing to pursue this well established profession to-morrow—the practice of which, come to think of it, is quite a bit older than most of today's medical sciences.

Philosophical training is not necessary to comprehend well the challenge we face in using our freedoms wisely and responsibly, lest those same freedoms destroy us utterly. The recent crisis of government through which we have lived has, if it has done nothing else, made this bitter point quite clear to all but the insensitive or stupid.

George N. Gordon, Ph.D.
Hofstra University

June, 1975

Part One

Ethical

Foundations

JOURNALISM (media studies, mass communication) is a rapidly expanding course of study in colleges and universities. Hordes of young people are pouring into journalism education; the majority of them are intelligent, concerned and idealistic students, and as such, often seem rather surprised at the lack of emphasis given to philosophical foundations in their media studies. They are particularly impressed by the place "on the sidelines" to which ethics has been relegated in many journalism programs.

The first article which follows ("Great Media Rush of 1970's") by John Phelan deals with this increased interest in journalism and describes some of the directions it is taking. Certainly this article reinforces the philosophical concern mentioned above by insisting that journalism education provide an experience both "humane and scientific" in order to meet the needs of an increasingly complex society.

In the second article ("Ethics and Journalism"), John Merrill brings the discussion specifically to ethics, presenting ethical theories that are easily adapted to basic journalistic moral orientations. He deals mainly with the distinction between teleological and deontological ethical systems, and notes the increasing popularity of relativistic morality.

Edmund Opitz in "Instinct and Ethics" next continues Merrill's discussion of ethical theories with an explication of "humanistic" and "theistic" positions in morality; he calls for a new perspective which avails itself of the strong points of both positions. He also presents a very interesting thesis: "The moral code plays a role in the life of man comparable to the role of instinct in the

1

lower organism, in that each functions to relate the inner nature of the respective organism to the full range of its environment.'' The Rev. Mr. Opitz proceeds to describe an ethical code for man which has interesting potential for the journalist.

Getting back to relating ethics more specifically to journalism, Gene Gilmore and Robert Root (''Ethics for Newsmen'') next present an interesting overview of basic concerns. They discuss such important topics as freedom and responsibility, reportorial objectivity, press pluralism, Christian backgrounds of American journalism, and pragmatic considerations in press morality.

One of the key terms in a discussion of journalistic ethics is ''responsibility.'' Wilbur Schramm suggests, in his piece on quality in mass communication, that the public should have a greater impact on the mass media; he presents specific suggestions for the audiences in making the media more responsible and in improving their quality generally.

In the article ''Masscom as Guru,'' W. H. Ferry offers a thoughtful discussion of social and cultural responsibilities of the mass media. He suggests that ''masscom'' (shorthand for ''mass communication'') might be less concerned about ever-increasing profits and more about ''fundamental obligations.'' Masscom's failures and weaknesses (e.g., delighting in shoddy and mind-dulling information, and the use of dishonest commercials) are discussed, and Ferry firmly denies that they are ''an inevitable concomitant of affluence and literacy.''

Edward Jay Epstein, in the next article (''Some Truths about Truths'') develops a timely and interesting discussion of epistemological (and ethical) problems connected with finding, and objectively reporting, news. The focus is ever on ''truth'' in journalism, and Epstein maintains that journalists are caught in a dilemma—either serving as messengers for some interest or recasting the message into their own version. Digging deeper into the epistemological and ethical problems exposed by Epstein is Donald McDonald in ''Is Objectivity Possible?'' He does a thorough job of covering almost every possible area of concern with ''journalistic objectivity'' in his article that has become almost a classic on the subject.

Paul Weaver, in ''The New Journalism and the Old,'' discusses two kinds of journalism coexisting with some difficulty today: the so-called ''objective'' (old) and ''adversary'' (new) journalism. The resulting state for the press, Weaver contends, is a kind of ''institution in limbo'' and the ethical (and other) implications for journalism are dealt with in considerable depth.

Michael Novak next, in his ''Why the Working Man Hates the Press,'' turns the critical spotlight on journalists and the media, revealing many of the reasons the average citizen distrusts them. One of the main reasons, he says, is that the journalists have gained enormous powers the working man does not have: thus—a new cynicism has arisen as a kind of defense against such power. Not only have the media helped to develop a public more critical of government, but also they have made the people cynical about journalism itself.

Novak not only exposes the roots of this public cynicism, but offers suggestions as to how it may be lessened.

In the final article of Part One, John Merrill suggests a philosophical stance (which he calls "Apollonysian") that would synthesize the orientations that Paul Weaver called "old" and "new" journalism into a kind of moderate "middle way." What he is suggesting is a philosophical foundation of freedom, commitment and rationality upon which the journalist can build his ethical system—a kind of scientifically oriented existentialism, if you will, to keep the journalist from straying too far toward the extremes.

John M. Phelan:

The Great Media Rush of the 1970's

HIGHER EDUCATION, like the economy, has come upon hard times. The distinguished quarterly, *Daedalus,* has devoted its last two bulging issues to an anthology of almost uniformly gloomy observations about the future of all institutions of higher learning—particularly in the private sector. Cutbacks in grants, stagflationary shrinkage of endowments, lack of long-range planning in the past, loss of prestige and purpose, and simple lack of interest on the part of current high school students in pursuing university degrees, which they feel lead to cultural enrichment and actual poverty, are some of the causes cited. In New York State, a recent study shows that there are just too many colleges and universities for an ever ebbing pool of available students. Within this bleak landscape, there is an especially barren sector, that of the humanities and liberal arts, forsaken for more practical training in currently employable skills.

It is ironic that we have come to such a pass at a time when Daniel Bell, along with other sophisticated observers, sees the birth of a knowledge-oriented society.

There are at this time, however, some booming university departments and

Professor Phelan is chairman of the communications department of Fordham University in New York City. This article is reprinted here from *America,* Vol. 132, No. 5 (Feb. 8, 1975), with permission of *America,* 1975; all rights reserved © America Press, 106 W. 56 St., New York, N.Y. 10019.

4 | *John M. Phelan*

professional schools. Chief among these is the growing number of communication and journalism departments. Why do students flock to these departments? What do they learn? How can the answers to these questions illumine
some of the possible solutions to the higher education recession?

Why do they come?

There is a wealth of superficial surmise surrounding this question: Because
students want to be television anchor-persons when they grow up so they can
tell the entire country what is going on, and can get to dress well, and get paid
more than the President of the United States (over the table). Because students
can neither read nor write, and disc jockeys, who cater to the illiterate, are both
glamorous and rich. Because cheeky reporters can insult governors and gen-
erals and get paid for that. Because Socrates is dead, and the sophists have
reappeared at communication schools during the final decline of the West.

Well. It is undeniable that most of us, adult and adolescent, make career
decisions within a penumbra of egoistic fantasy, but the decisions are maintained in the hard light of rational motivation. Having observed and befriended
hundreds of undergraduate communication students over the past decade, I
would say the interest and motivation are constant, but now more widespread. I
offer here what I believe to be the principal factors of serious motivation for engaging in communication study: quest for community, idealistic values and
thirst for knowledge.

The quest for community is basic to all of us. It is also fundamental to the
purpose of the university, whose very name suggests unity and whose history
and definition, until very recently, was that of a community of scholars. Confined to a campus in space, the university offered initiation into the widest historical and geographic community available—the 3,000-year tradition and heritage of Western civilization. With its common stock of ideas and ideals, it
provided a universe of discourse and a place for conversation, a calendar of festivals and reasons for celebration. More parochially, it was a locus for generations to get to know one another over a period of what is now derided as lock-
step progression for four years. Community and personal identity could coexist.

The well-documented explosion of population, mass education, mass culture and mass money brought about the rise of the multiversity, obsession with
professional preparation and commuter campuses peopled by the lonely crowd.
In the last 25 years, the disintegration of neighborhoods, and the necessary mobility of corporate employees, have made one's job or profession the principal
source of social satisfaction (or dissatisfaction). Thus, students have lost community at the new multiversity, and they look ahead to careers that rarely offer
entrance into a community. This vacuum leads to a twofold desire for communication studies.

First, by design and circumstance, the media have rushed in to fill this
yearning for community. Our calendar of festivals is *TV Guide*. We have been
formed into what Daniel Boorstin terms "consumer communities," like the

Pepsi Generation, the Cosmopolitan woman or flavor cravers. Our universe of discourse is replaced with a daily list of topics—"the news." The community characters that once provided us with gossip and diversion are replaced by that fluid troop of interchangeable celebrities on talk and game shows. Secondly, as the media sell the image of community to us, they also present themselves as happy families of news teams.

It is no wonder, then, that young people desire to participate actively in the world that they perceive by joining the media.

For sound commercial reasons, the media interface in a maze of cross-promotions: films promote paperbacks promote records promote TV series promote films. At its worst, we have a vacuous hall of mirrors, and at its best, we have exposure to the surface of the significant that leads to greater knowledge in science (*Nova*, NASA coverage), art (*Civilisation*), history (*America*) and politics (local and national investigative reporting).

It is, therefore, no surprise that youthful talent seeks to test itself in the forum of the media at its best and to create the *60 Minutes*, the *Hallmark Hall of Fame* of the 1980's.

I think only a cynic would call this interest in media study the latest form of running away to join the circus. Creatures of the media, children wish to join the working professionals whose work they have observed and admired. They want to belong in order to contribute, and they simply want to belong. If the world of the media is often crass and superficial, so was the world of the village and small town, so were Hollywood and Broadway and even the Algonquin set of former decades, to say nothing of the counterculture of the 1960's. In fact, the tinsel and troubles of our times have most often been exposed as such by the media themselves—from Watergate and Vietnam to the Man in the Gray-Flannel Suit and Sammy Glick.

This critical function of the media leads to idealistic values as a motivation for joining the media. Adolescents and young adults are critical of most of what they observe. They are drawn to the media as critics of the institutions they themselves find fault with. Both are often naive and priggish critics.

Last spring, at Fordham University, a young woman indulged in a long tirade against the unmitigated evils of the federal government and contrasted them with the pure goodness of the media. Mike Wallace, the distinguished CBS correspondent for whose benefit this performance was chiefly intended, listened patiently, then calmly pointed out that he agreed with much of the substance, if not the inflated rhetoric, of Spiro Agnew's celebrated catalog of media shortcomings. Communication study may attract the critical instincts of the young, at first, as a base to construct a platform from which to declaim, but subsequent exposure to working professionals and competent academics tempers their zeal, and helps them see the mote in their own eye. Further, the brightest and most critical media students often turn their most severe gaze on the communication establishment, much as medical students are sharply critical of the medical establishment. If we are, indeed, in a knowledge-oriented society, the communication industries are in no position to make serious errors of judgment or lapses from ethical standards. Too much is at stake.

The framers of the First Amendment saw the press as a necessary check and balance to government itself—as a watchdog against abuses of power. That mandate was recently vindicated in large measure. Yet the role and the responsibility of the press must now extend beyond big government to big business, big labor, local government and such politico-scientific matters as environmentalism, energy, land use, economic policy, health care, demography—all the "crisis" and "explosion" questions that the public and its representatives must face for the immediate and forseeable future. To meet this mammoth mandate, the press has become the media: a protean collection of print, broadcast and film forms for a cataract of headlines, reports, studies, statistical analysis, opinions, forecasts and retrospectives. As the outpouring of matter has multiplied, so have the sources, beyond established publishers, broadcasters and studios, to foundations, commissions, agencies, research corporations, as well as to less well-connected and occasionally radical sources like the Network Project.

There is an explosive need for humane information-processing in this technical society. It is much more sophisticated a task than the fedora-clamped heads of *The Front Page* could ever conceive of. The young sense this, for all their naiveté about scoops and other holdovers from the dark ages of communications. They must know what questions to put to experts and leaders. They must know how to evaluate and how to present the answers accurately. They have a thirst for knowledge, but for them it is not knowledge for its own sake. It is knowledge as social service, and they feel they can learn how to learn this at a communications department.

What do they learn?

They learn about the media. They learn through the media. They learn how to use the media.

First, they learn about the media in historical context and within the intellectual discipline of the social sciences. Journalism has a long history here and abroad that is intimately interwoven with the politics of nations and the culture of cities. Journalism and the media have structures and functions within and around our major institutions of law, business and belief. Mass media and public opinion can be grasped only after a painstaking examination of the social organization and psychology of individuals, groups, classes and their symbols. Historical context, after all, is the intellectual form of community, and its teaching has been the unifying purpose of the university.

Second, they learn through the media. The media thrive on crisis and controversy, and it is from current issues that enduring ideas can be imparted. The voluminous literature on authority and freedom, the individual and society, personality and culture can be approached from current questions about, for instance, population growth and control, corruption in government, multinational corporations and world trade. At a university, there is a richness of resources from which students can draw a depth of understanding from the past, incited by their passion for the immediate. The specific communication concern with censorship, for example, provokes investigation into the entire matter of social control that takes us back to Socrates.

Third, they learn how to use the media. For some reason, the basic endowment of the educated—active and passive literacy—becomes more desirable for students if it is linked with production for the media. A book editor or news director at times can demand more polish and precision than a professor of English could hope for, because his demands are tied to the realistic requirements of publication. Students who might have opted for communication because they felt it soared above (or crawled beneath) the drudgery of prose composition, in favor of the instant word-with-picture, are disabused of this illusion shortly after contact with any communication program that is not merely therapeutic.

It is for these reasons, then, that I believe communications departments are attractive to so many students. They provide a door into a community, an arena for critical values, a source of knowledge about the past in the present and for the future. While communications departments provide, in many students' eyes, the most accessible avenue toward satisfying careers, in educators' plans they serve as an ideal conduit for the traditional values of college education: civil sensibility, critical intellect, sense of history, love of language.

There is no law demanding that education must be either theoretical or practical, either of intellectual substance or of commercial value. If neither the humanities nor the sciences were related to current concerns and genuine experience, they could not be either humane or scientific. Perhaps the cry for "relevance" masked the complaint that many college courses were of neither practical nor theoretical value, but rather were creatures of the internal organizational needs of graduate schools and professional associations.

In the last 10 years, graduate communication programs have increased and multiplied. Let us hope that their internal needs do not destroy an excellent vehicle for liberal education suited for useful careers and intelligent living in what can truly be a knowledge-oriented society.

John C. Merrill:

Ethics and Journalism

WHEN WE ENTER the area of journalistic ethics, we pass into a swampland of philosophical speculation where eerie mists of judgment hang low over a boggy terrain. In spite of the unsure footing and poor visibility, there is no reason not to make the journey. In fact, it is a journey well worth taking for it brings the matter of morality to the individual person; it forces the journalist, among others, to consider his basic principles, his values, his obligations to himself and to others. It forces him to decide for himself how he will live, how he will conduct his journalistic affairs, how he will think of himself and of others, how he will think, act and react to the people and issues surrounding him.

Ethics has to do with duty—duty to self and/or duty to others. It is primarily individual or personal even when it relates to obligations and duties to others. The quality of human life has to do with both solitude and sociability. We do right or wrong by ourselves in that part of our lives lived inwardly or introvertedly and also in that part of our lives where we are reacting and responding to other persons. This duality of individual and social morality is implicit in the very concept of ethics. The journalist, for example, is not simply writing for the consumption of others; he is writing as *self*-expression, and he puts himself and his very being into his journalism. What he communicates is in a very real way what he himself *is*. He pleases or displeases himself—not just those in his audience. What he does to live up to some standard within him not only affects the activities and beliefs of others, but in a very real way, the very essence of his own life.

A concern for ethics is important. The journalist who has this concern obviously cares about good or right actions; such a concern indicates an attitude which embraces both freedom and personal responsibility. It indicates also that the journalist desires to discover norms for action that will serve him as guiding principles or specific directives in achieving the kind of life which he thinks most meaningful and satisfying. Ethical concern is important also for it forces the journalist to commitment, to thoughtful decision among alternatives. It

This is a portion of Chapter 8 from Dr. Merrill's *The Imperative of Freedom* (New York: Hastings House, Publishers, 1974). Reprinted by permission.

leads him to seek the *summum bonum,* the highest good in journalism, thereby heightening his authenticity as a person and journalist.

What characterizes most journalists today is a lack of commitment and consistency, a lack of a coherent life plan. Before any journalist chooses any particular ethics he must decide whether or not to be ethical: this is the first and most important choice facing him. However, it may well be, as Sartre and other Existentialists have believed, that "not to choose is already to have chosen"; that the "refusal to choose the ethical is inevitably a choice for the nonethical." [1] There is a tendency today to identify as "ethics" any personal decision to act; anything I want to do, I do—therefore, it is ethical for me to do it. Hazel Barnes points out that this is exactly parallel to what has happened to "religion." She says that "an age which is willing to apply the term 'religion' to communism, aesthetic awe, devotion to one's fellow man, and allegiance to impartial demands of pure science has no difficulty in labeling any guiding motif or choice a personal ethics." [2] If one accepts this position he is really saying that nobody is really nonreligious or nonethical; all meaning will have been drained from the concepts "religious" and "ethical" if nobody can be non-religious or non-ethical.

Ethics is that branch of philosophy that helps journalists determine what is right to do in their journalism; it is very much a normative science of conduct, with conduct considered primarily as self-determined, voluntary conduct. Ethics has to do with "self-legislation" and "self-enforcement"; although it is, of course, related to *law,* it is of a different nature.[3] Although law quite often stems from the ethical values of a society at a certain time (i.e., law is often reflective of ethics), law is something that is socially determined and socially enforced. Ethics, on the other hand, is personally determined and personally enforced—or should be. Ethics should provide the journalist certain basic principles or standards by which he can judge actions to be right or wrong, good or bad, responsible or irresponsible.

It has always been difficult to discuss ethics; law is much easier, for what is legal is a matter of law. What is ethical transcends law, for many actions are legal, but not ethical. And there are no "ethical codebooks" to consult in order to settle ethical disputes. Ethics is primarily personal; law is primarily social. Even though the area of journalistic ethics is swampy and firm footing is difficult, as was mentioned earlier, there are solid spots which the person may use in his trek across the difficult landscape of life.

First of all, it is well to establish that ethics deals with *voluntary* actions. If a journalist has no control over his decisions or his actions, then there is no need to talk of ethics. What are voluntary actions? Those which a journalist could have done differently had he wished. Sometimes journalists, like others, try to excuse their wrong actions by saying that these actions were not personally chosen but *assigned* to them—or otherwise forced on them—by editors or other superiors. Such coercion may indeed occur in some situations (such as a dictatorial press system) where the consequences to the journalist going against an order may be dire. But for an American journalist not to be able to "will" his journalistic actions—at least at the present time—is unthinkable; if he says that he is not so able and that he "has to" do this—or—that, he is only exhibiting his ethical weakness and inauthenticity.

The journalist who is concerned with ethics—with the quality of his actions—is, of course, one who wishes to be virtuous. Just what a virtuous person, is, however, is somewhat circular and gets us back to the question: What is a moral or ethical person? However, the nature of virtue is not really so relative or vague if we have any respect for the great thinkers of history; there has been considerable commonality of meaning among philosophers generally, even though "virtue" has been comceptualized in terms containing considerable semantic noise.

The "Virtuous" Journalist

The virtuous journalist is one who has respect for, and tries to live by, the cardinal virtues which Plato discusses in *The Republic*.[4] First is *wisdom,* which gives "direction" to the moral life and is the rational, intellectual base for any system of ethics. Wisdom is part natural and part acquired, combining knowledge and native abilities; it largely comes form maturing, from life experiences, from contemplation, reading, conversing and study. Second, there is *courage,* which keeps one constantly pursuing his goal, the goal which wisdom has helped him set for himself. Courage is needed to help the journalist resist the many temptations which would lead him away from the path which wisdom shows.

The third virtue is *temperance,* the virtue that demands reasonable moderation or a blending of the domination of reason with other tendencies of human nature. It is this virtue, giving harmony and proportion to moral life, which helps us avoid fanaticism in pursuit of any goal. And, last, there is *justice,* distinguished from the other cardinal virtues in that it refers more specifically to man's social relations. Justice involves considering a man's "deservingness"; each man must be considered, but this does not mean that each man has to be treated like every other—for example, justice would not require that every person elected to a city, state or national office receive equal attention on television or the same amount of space in a newspaper. Equal treatment simply does not satisfy deservingness—does not imply "just" coverage.

One sign of virtue in journalism may well be a deep loyalty to truth. At least the pursuit of truth by the journalist surely takes wisdom, courage, temperance and justice. John Whale, an editorial writer for the *Sunday Times* of London, contends that at the base of journalistic ethics is an allegiance to truth. It is the authenticity of the information contained in the story that is the journalist's chief ethical concern, according to Whale. What methods should a journalist use in trying to get at this "truth"? Whale answers: *Only those methods which the journalist would be willing to publish as part of the story.* This is one reason why Whale and many others (including me) are opposed to the passage of "shield laws." What is far more important than keeping a source's name secret, Whale maintains, is whether what he said is true. It is hard to verify truth if the source's name is hidden from the public. This allegiance to truth, not to some person (source) who reveals information, is what is important. Too often those who reveal information and elicit the journalist's promise not to identify them have motives other than a desire to let the truth come out. Virtue in journalism, believes Whale, has to do with getting as much truth as possible into the story—and, of course, the source of the information is *part of* the "truth" of the story.[5]

The desire to search out and present the truth does, indeed, seem to be one of the moral foundations of libertarian journalism.[6] Most journalists think of truth as they do of objectivity—as temporary, splintered and incomplete. Accuracy, fairness, balance, comprehensiveness are generally related to objectivity by the journalist—and, therefore, have to do with truth.

Naturally, the main problem with such truth is that it must be considered in context with editorial determinism. *What* truth—or what parts of what truth—will a journalistic medium choose to present? "All the news that's fit to print," replies *The New York Times,* proclaiming to all that certain matters (even if *truthful* or contributing to the truth) which are not considered "fit" will not be printed. Therefore, *The Times* is explicitly saying what all journalists believe and practice: truth is what journalists consider fit to call truth, just as news is what they decide is news—nothing more and nothing less.

Moral philosophers have at least given us a wide variety of alternative standards for determining virtuous actions. In general, these ethical standards boil down to two main ones: *teleological* theories and *deontological* theories. The first consider the moral rightness or wrongness of an action as the good that is produced. The second, on the other hand, hold that something other than (but sometimes, perhaps, in addition to) consequences determine which actions are morally right or good.

Teleological theories. Teleologists look at the consequences of an act; they consider consequences and only consequences as determining the moral rightness or wrongness of actions. Teleologists differ among themselves only as to whose good it is that one ought to try to promote. Egoists, for example, hold that one should always do what will promote his own greatest good; this view was held by Epicurus, Hobbes and Nietzsche, among others. Utilitarians—or ethical socialists—take the position that an act or rule of action is right or good if and only if it is, or probably is, conducive to the greatest possible balance of good over evil everywhere. Some utilitarians (e.g., Jeremy Bentham and J. S. Mill) have been hedonists in their view of good being connected with the greatest happiness (pleasure) to the greatest number.

Ethical egoism, one of the teleological theories, holds that it is the duty of the individual to seek his own good. This stance has a great deal to say for itself; for if we regard the moral end as perfection, it is likely that we can do very little to achieve the perfection of anybody other than ourselves. A man may influence to some degree the activities of others, but he can *control* only his own activities. This is somewhat related to Kant's "duty ethics" whereby man is urged to seek his own perfection by being obligated to a rationally accepted principle or maxim. Self-perfection is the goal of a moral life.

The universal or social ethics of utilitarianism, on the other hand, holds that every person should seek the good of his group, community, nation—or world—as a whole. It claims, in a way, to combine the true elements of egoism and altruism—as the good of the group or community will include, of course, the agent's own good. Its appeal is that it sets no narrow limits on the range of moral obligations. One form of utilitarianism, the extreme *altruistic* stance, emphasizes the seeking of good of other individuals with no regard for the agent's own good; this is the stance of self-sacrifice, with the emphasis being entirely on *others*.

The social (utilitarian) ethical theory enthrones others—the group, collective or society generally—and sees the good as that which benefits the life of the group or the society. This is usually the ethics of collective altruism, and has been expressed generally in terms of the utilitarian principle that good conduct is that which results in the greatest good to the greatest number. There are two practical problems with this theory: (1) the problem of determining what is really good for most people, and (2) the problem posed by equating "good" with majority opinion or action. The journalist, for instance, in deciding whether or not to present a story, has no sound way of knowing which action will result in the greatest good to the greatest number of people. He can only guess—and hope. The second problem above leads the journalist to a kind of "give them what they want" ethical stance, abdicating personal commitment (and personal reason) for the social determinism of "vote-morality."

Deontological theories. These theories are quite different from the teleological ones just discussed for they hold that something other than consequences determine which actions are morally right. Some deontologists say the important thing is the motive of the agent; Kant, for example, contends that an action is justified if the intentions of the doer are good, regardless of the consequences that might ensue from the action. A deontologist believes that producing the greatest possible happiness to the greatest possible number has nothing (or may have nothing) to do with the morality of the action. He also believes that personal satisfaction or gain is irrelevant to ethical action. He sees an action being right or obligatory simply because of some fact about it or because of its own nature.

Probably the best example of a deontologist is Immanuel Kant, and his basic principle or rule—the Categorical Imperative—lies at the base of his ethical system: "Act only on that maxim which you can at the same time will to be a universal law." Kant is here offering this "imperative" as the necessary principle for determining what more specific and concrete ethical rules we should adopt to guide our behavior. He is saying, in effect, that a person is acting ethically only if he is—or would be—willing to have everyone act on his maxim. Or, said another way, a person is acting ethically if he would be willing to see his rule applied by everyone who is in a similar situation.

If we ask "Which actions are right" we are really asking for some way to identify right actions. Utilitarians (teleologists) would reply: Those which maximize utility or which do the greatest service for the greatest number, or something like that. Kant and other deontologists would claim that those actions are right which pass the test of some personal and rationally accepted imperative. For Kant, for example, virtue has nothing to do with pleasure or with any other "consequences."

If consequences and states such as happiness are not important in determining ethical actions, then what is relevant must be something to do with basic maxims or principles. For the deontologists what is important is the principle from which the action has been performed; and the test applied to the maxim must be something independent of consequence. The Categorical Imperative is not really a specific maxim from which one acts—rather it is a principle or general rule which will allow a journalist (or anyone else) to test all maxims from which he acts. It is a kind of "super-maxim" which serves to guide thinking about specific rules to be applied in specific cases. If a journalist accepts the Categorical Imperative, then it is unnecessary for him to carry around in his head (or on a printed Code or Creed) specific rules or guidelines to follow. These he formulates on the basis of his "super-maxim" as the various occasions arise. If these guidelines for each case pass the test of the Categorical Imperative, then his action based on that "super-maxim" is ethically sound, and the journalist may be considered virtuous.

Although Kant's philosophy has profoundly influenced Western thought, it is obvious that at least among modern intellectuals his strict and absolutist "duty ethics" has lost considerable appeal and force. A kind of relativism or situationism is in ascendency, an ethics which has a great appeal to those who like to think of themselves as "rational." This new situationism is a kind of synthesis emerging from the clash of ethical legalism, on one hand, and ethical antinomianism on the other. It will be discussed in the following section.

The Appeal of Relativism

The ethics of "law," of "duty" and "absolute obligation" is a little strong for most thinkers. So this *legalistic* stance in ethical thinking has been confronted by its opposite: what has been called *antinomianism*. The rebel against Kantianism and other legalistic ethics has accepted what might actually be considered by some as a "non-ethics"—a completely open kind of morality which is against any rules. The antinomian has, in effect, tossed out all basic principles, precepts, codes, standards and laws which might guide his conduct. Just as the legalist tends toward absolutist or universal ethics, the antinomian tends toward anarchy or nihilism in ethics. He is against standards; he thinks he needs no *a priori* guidelines, directions or moral rules. He is satisfied to "play it by ear," making ethical judgments and decisions intuitively, spontaneously, emotionally, and often irrationally. He is a kind of Existentialist—or very closely related—in that he has great faith that personal, existential instincts will give the ethical direction needed.

The antinomian in journalism is usually found in the free-wheeling ranks of rebellious journalism where an anti-Establishment stance is considered healthy. The antinomian journalist affronts mainstream journalism, making his ethical decisions as he goes—almost subconsciously—about his daily activities. His ethical (or nonethical) system might be called "whim ethics," and his confrontation with mainstream journalism is not very potent or successful because it is weakened considerably by a lack of rational force.

From the clash of these two ethical "extremes"—legalism and antinomianism—a kind of synthesis has developed which has a potent impact on ethical thinking. It is usually known as *situation ethics*.[7] Although it is related to code or legalistic ethics more closely than it is to antinomian ethics in most of its characteristics, it does synthesize certain strains of both orientations. Like code ethics, it is basically rational, and like antinomian ethics it is relativistic and is not tied securely to absolute principles. Situation ethics begins with traditional legalistic ethics but is willing to deviate from these basic principles when rationality and the situation call for it.

The journalistic situationist may well be the one who believes that he should tell the truth *as a basic principle,* or that he should not generally distort his story, but who will, after due consideration of the situation in which he finds himself, conclude that it is all right to distort *this particular story,* or even to lie. Do the circumstances in this case warrant a departure from basic—generally held—moral guidelines: this is the rational question which always confronts the situationist. He is one, then, who takes special situations into consideration in making his ethical decisions; he is a relativist to be sure, but a rational relativist, one who *thinks* before breaking a basic ethical rule.

One who subscribes to what may be called "Machiavellian ethics" is one type of situationist. Maurice Cranston has pointed out that Machiavelli believed that persons (statesmen, at least) should not allow their relationships with other states always to be governed by the same ethical scruples that govern their dealings with private persons. His ethics, however, were really absolutist, says Cranston; he accepted one true morality, but he believed the ruler should sometimes disregard it. As Machiavelli says in *The Prince,* the ruler "should not depart from what is morally right if he can observe it, but should know how to adopt what is bad when he is obliged to."[8] Machiavelli does not contend that the bad is anything other than bad; he only contends that bad things are to be done only sparingly—and then only in a concealed manner, if possible.

Journalists like to point out Machiavellianism in others (especially in government officials), but they themselves very often operate under this variant of situation ethics. They usually contend they believe in absolutes (such as giving their audiences all the pertinent facts or not changing or distorting quotes from a source), yet they depart from these principles when they think that "in this special case" it is reasonable to do so. They normally talk about their belief in "letting the people know" but they determine innumerable exceptions to this principle—times when they will not (because of the circumstances of the special situation) let the people know. And, of course, they are not very interested in letting the people know that they are not knowing.

The press is much more interested, of course, in pointing out Machiavellian situationism in government officials. This is natural and it is very healthy for the press to do this, for certainly our government is filled with myriads of Machiavellian functionaries busy justifying to themselves (and sometimes to others) their departure from basic moral principles. It is interesting to note how closely members of the Nixon Administration—especially some of his closest "advisors"—followed Machiavellian situationism in rationalizing the many unethical practices connected with the Watergate Affair which got world-wide airing in 1973. Not only did these officials seem to know that what they had done was wrong or unethical, but they felt that it would be best if they kept these things secret. Certainly they were not inclined to reveal them until the press and the Congress (and the courts) forced their disclosure.

Very little has been written about journalistic ethics beyond certain repetitious phrases appearing in "codes" and "creeds" designed largely for framing and hanging as wall trappings. Perhaps one reason for this is that most editors, publishers, news directors and other journalists simply write the whole subject of ethics off as "relative," giving little or no importance to absolute or universal journalistic principles. A newspaper friend put it succinctly recently when he said that he looked at ethics as "just the individual journalist's way of doing things." Certainly a free journalist has the right to consider ethics in this way, but such a relativistic concept relegates ethics to a kind of "nothingness limbo" where anything any journalist does can be considered ethical. Or, said another way, what one journalist does can be considered just as ethical as what any other journalist does.

If we throw out absolute theories of ethics (exemplified by Kant), then a discussion of morality becomes merely a discussion of preferences, arbitrary choices, detached judgments—none of which establishes obligation. The statement "this was the right journalistic decision" means no more than "I liked this decision"—just as one might say "I liked the view of the ocean." One form of relativism in ethics contends that a journalistic practice in Context A may be quite good—ethical—while if practiced in Context B it might be bad or unethical. In other words, it would be all right to submit to government censorship without objection in the Soviet Union but not all right to submit to government censorship in the United States. Or, taking this further, it would be all right to submit to censorship in the United States "under certain conditions" but wrong to do this under other conditions. Circumstances dictate the ethics; contexts determine "rightness" or "wrongness," say the relativists.

Often I have heard, for instance, that in Mexico journalists often accept bribes to supplement their meagre incomes; I am also informed that many journalists also work for a newspaper part-time and for some politician as a sort of private "press agent"—therefore having a conflict of interest. And, I am told, that this is all right in Mexico—maybe not in the United States—but quite "acceptable" (therefore ethical?) in Mexico where the conditions are different. The relativist's position here is: If it's good in a particular society, it's good, and if it's bad, it's bad—there is really no objective or universal principle. Also I hear from Soviet journalists that close party-government control of what goes into the press and over the air-waves is quite "ethical" in the Soviet Union; it is not only "all right" that this happens—it is actually the best situation, the most moral.

The situationist positions mentioned above can be considered a part of "subjectivist" ethics for what one does in a certain situation is determined *subjectively* by the individual at the time when an ethical decision is demanded. The temper of the times has thrust the subjectivist into a dominant moral position—at least from the point of being in the majority. And for many persons today if the majority believe something ethical, then it is ethical. These are the days of the subjectivist—the relativist and situationist. These are the days when it is considered unenlightened to make a value judgment, to take a stand, to feel a sense of "duty" or have a commitment. These are the days of the person who believes one opinion is as good as another and that one man's moral standards are as good as his neighbor's. These are the days of the "we-are-probably-both-right" school of thinking, the days of the tolerant men—the "adapters"—who feel no impulse to speak out loudly and clearly on moral standards.

Although the relativistic position is indeed intriguing due to its aura of individualism (and therefore seeming to enhance the theme of this book), I must reject it. In fact, at the risk of making a value judgment, I will even say that it is not really an ethical position at all; rather it is a "non-ethics" or an "anti-ethics." When the matter of ethics is watered down to subjectivism, to situations or contexts, it loses all meaning as ethics. If every case is different, if every situation demands a different standard, if there are no absolutes in ethics, then we should scrap the whole subject of moral philosophy and simply be satisfied that each person run his life by his whims or "considerations" which may change from situation to situation. . . .

NOTES

[1] Hazel Barnes, *An Existentialist Ethics,* p. 7.
[2] *Ibid.,* p. 5.
[3] For a good discussion of law, taking the position that "a sentiment of respect for law is a rational

one," see Bertrand Russell, *Human Society in Ethics and Politics* (New York: Mentor Books, 1962), p. 28 f.

[4] Cf. Josef Pieper, *The Four Cardinal Virtues* (Notre Dame University Press, 1966). Pieper uses the term "prudence" for "wisdom" and the term "fortitude" for "courage," but retains the terms "justice" and "temperance" as used by Plato.

[5] John Whale, in a lecture, Journalism School, University of Missouri, July 19, 1973.

[6] See a good discussion of journalistic truth in Ch. 13 ("Ethics for Newsmen") in Gene Gilmore and Robert Root, *Modern Newspaper Editing* (Berkeley, Calif.: The Glendessary Press, 1971), pp. 242–43.

[7] See John Merrill and Ralph Lowenstein, *Media, Messages, and Men,* pp. 251–55—section on the "Ethical Dialectic".

[8] Maurice Cranston, "Ethics and Politics," *Encounter* (London), Vol. 38, No. 6, June, 1972.

Edmund A. Opitz:

Instinct and Ethics

NEARLY EVERYONE is a moralist these days, and a moralist in popular carica-ture is one who always views with alarm. Even the self-proclaimed immoralists of our time fall into this category, for they denounce as "intolerant" any and all who look askance at their weird "beat" deviations. Disagreements are sharp at all levels, among the viewers with alarm, but the primary breach is between those who hold that the ultimate sanction for ethical standards must be sought in a supernatural order, and—on the other hand—those who assert that within the social and natural orders we may find the ingredients for a viable ethic. The first position is theistic; the latter humanistic.

The humanists, if we may be permitted this term for the second group, admit that the moral code which prevailed in the West until two or three gener-ations ago was widely believed to have had its origin and sanction in religion. But, as they view the matter, the transcendent dimension has such a weak hold upon modern man that to insist on a metaphysical source of moral values in these times is to weaken ethics by tying it to a dead horse. Moral values, they

The Rev. Mr. Opitz is a member of the staff of The Foundation for Economic Education. This ar-ticle is Chapter 10 of his *Religion and Capitalism.* Copyright © 1970 by Arlington House, New Rochelle, N.Y. All rights reserved; reprinted here with permission.

assert, are autonomous if they are anything; let them therefore stand on their own feet. Detach ethics from religion, they urge, in order that men may be virtuous for the sake of happiness! Men should not do right in a vain effort to please some deity, or because they believe that God has arbitrarily commanded certain actions and forbidden others.

These nontraditionalists tout a "scientific" or "rational" ethic. The opposite of "rational" in this context is not "irrational"; it is "theistic," "customary," or "received." No one would admit that his own ethical system or moral code is irrational, and it is obvious to everyone who has checked into the matter that there have been and are ethicists of several schools who are powerful reasoners. Every philosopher relies on reason, and not only rationalists; however, reason does tell some men that reason is not the exclusive route to knowledge of the complex reality that environs us.

A distinction which arises at this point seems to elude many. It is a distinction between reason as a means for achieving a norm, and reason itself as the norm. Perhaps the point may be clarified by analogy. "How do you propose to go to Boston?" is a question which demands answers in two distinct categories. "By car" is one answer, which informs us that the means of transportation is not train, plane, foot, or horse. Having settled this point, we still need further information before the question can be regarded as answered. "By way of the Taconic, north, to the western end of the Massachusetts Turnpike, then east." This gives us the route, so that we know that the car will not proceed up the Merritt or over the New England Thruway.

Now take the serious question, "How shall we validate ethical norms?" Those who answer, "By reason," are really uttering a mere truism. "We're going to think about it," they are saying. And everyone who thinks about these or any other matters is using his reason. This is our only means for figuring things out, and it is not a means belonging exclusively to rationalists; it is the common means employed by everyone who philosophizes. Using this means, we seek for answers to the question of how to validate ethical norms. This has to do with the realm where the sanctions may find anchorage, whether within nature and society, or in a realm beyond the natural and social orders. Reason is our tool for operating on the problem posed; it is not itself the answer.

Experts at Debate

There are dogmatists on both sides of this controversy, and the skilled among them can and do expose weaknesses in their opponent's position. The humanist might charge his opposition as follows: The moral code is an acquired characteristic; it has to be learned anew by each generation. It is difficult enough to establish this code theoretically, even if we treat it as self-evidently useful to society and necessary for harmony in human relationships. Why, then, compound these difficulties and force things out of focus by involving ethics with metaphysics? The uncertain, in this or any other area, is shored up by relating it to the certain; but when you hook ethics up with metaphysics, you relate it to the even more uncertain, to the dubious! We don't need a transcendent sanction in order to validate or prove a down-to-earth ethic.

To which the theist might respond: If you appeal to Nature to sanction human conduct, you haven't looked very far into Nature. Not even Kropotkin with his mutual aid theories denied the Darwinian struggle for existence; he merely desired to point out that it was not the whole story. But it is part of the story, and a large enough part so that we are justified in saying that Nature gives a mandate to the powerful, the fleet, the unscrupulous to live off the weaker, the slower, the innocent. And if you think to draw your ethical sanctions from society, whose society are you talking about? A society of head-hunters? Nazi society? Communist society? The Great Society? As a matter of fact, if a significant number of people can be made to believe that moral conduct is merely that which is sanctioned by the society in which they live, then morality is subverted into merely customary behavior and mere legality. Furthermore, you are confusing sanctions with consequences. An ethical code resides somewhere behind the sanctions advanced to validate it, and the consequences cited to justify it. If the code is put into practice, the consequences may well be personal happiness, interpersonal harmony, and a prosperous society. But these results do not constitute a set of sanctions; the sanctions are on the other side of the code, in the realm of philosophy. Once we are intellectually convinced that our moral code is valid, then muster enough will power to practice it, then—and only then—do we get a bonus in the form of well-being in society. But you have the thing turned around! So much for the preliminary give and take.

A Way Through the Dilemma

Evidently, each side has a case which might be spelled out at length. Is it a deadlock, or do we have here an instance of an impasse due to the hardening of the categories on either side to the point where their usefulness as conceptual tools has been impaired? And, if this is so, is there a way between the horns of the dilemma? There might be such a breakthrough if we could—by adopting a new perspective—pose and develop a thesis which might avail itself of certain strong points in both positions. Here's such a thesis: The moral code plays a role in the life of man comparable to the role of instinct in the lower organisms, in that each functions to relate the inner nature of the respective organism to the full range of its environment.

The recently published *Harper Encyclopedia of Science* says that "the scientific study of instinct has increased greatly in recent years, and the concept itself has regained an academic respectability it has not had since the time of Darwin." At the forefront of this research, much of it under field conditions, are Tinbergen, Lorenz, Thorne and Barrends; Europeans all. "It now seems clear," the entry continues, "that instinct and intelligence are two quite different ways by which animals meet life's problems. Instincts are essentially prefabricated answers.'' In a word, an organism's instinctual equipment adapts it optimally to its normal environment. Animals—along with birds, insects, and fish—are equipped with a kind of internal servomechanism, or automatic pilot, which keeps them effortlessly on the beam. Instincts align the animal with the forces of life, or with the laws of its own nature. Organism and environment are thus kept ''in play'' with each other—except when environmental changes are so catastrophic that the automatic adjustment equipment fails, the organism perishes, and perhaps a species becomes extinct.

The very perfection of automatic, instinctual adjustment may prove the undoing of organisms relying on this device; when survival depends on a creative response to novel environmental changes, something other than instinct is needed. This is, of course, intelligence. Instinct is not a mere precursor of intelligence, nor is intelligence an outgrowth of instinct; they are radically different. In order for intelligence in man to have an opportunity to flourish, the instincts had to be suppressed.

The Absence of Instincts

Human beings are virtually without specific instincts. There is no servomechanism in men which automatically keeps the human organism or the species within the pattern laid down for human life. Men have to figure things out and, by enormous effort, learn to conform their actions to the relevant norms in the various sectors of life. This absence of instincts in man constitutes the ground for man's radical inner freedom, the freedom of his will. Animal lives are fixed to run in narrow, constricted channels; they obey the will of God willy-nilly. Men, however, vary enormously from each other at birth, and the differences widen as individuals mature each into his specialized individuality. And each person has the gift of a freedom so radical that he can deny the existence of the creative forces which produced him. This freedom of his makes it not only possible but mandatory that man take a hand in the fashioning of his own life. No man *creates* himself, but every man *makes* himself, using the created portions of his being as his resources. this is what it means to say that man is a responsible being.

A magnificent animal like Man o' War is not a natural horse; he is the product of generations of human breeders and trainers of horses. They are mainly responsible for his superiority, not he. Of all the orders of creation only man is a responsible being; everything else, every horse, dog, lion, tiger, and shark is what it is. Only man is, in any measure, responsible for what he is. Man makes himself, and therefore each person is morally responsible for himself. This is possible because man has escaped from the strait jacket of instinct.

Let me quote from a once well-known Dreiser novel, *Sister Carrie,* which appeared in 1900. ''Among the forces which sweep and play throughout the universe, untutored man is but a wisp in the wind. Our civilization is but a wisp in the wind, scarcely beast, in that it is no longer wholly guided by instinct;

scarcely human, in that it is not yet wholly guided by reason. On the tiger no responsibility rests. We see him aligned by nature with the forces of life—he is born into their keeping and without thought he is protected. We see man far removed from the lairs of the jungles, his innate instincts dulled by too near approach to free will, his free will not sufficiently developed to replace his instincts and afford him perfect guidance. He is becoming too wise to hearken always to instincts and desire; he is still too weak to always prevail against them.''

Dreiser makes full use of a novelist's liberties here, but his pointer is in the right direction. Something within the tiger causes it to obey the laws of its inner nature unconsciously and easily, and, by so doing, the beast is in harmony with outer nature as well. But man's case is radically different. Does he have a true nature deep within him, visible when the environmentally imposed camouflages are peeled off? And, if so, what are its mandates? Once man knows the laws of his own being, how shall he muster sufficient will power to obey them while avoiding distractions and temptations that emanate from other facets of his complex nature?

My thesis is that the role played by instinct in the lower order—keeping the organism on target—is assumed in man by the ethical code. Animals have instincts but no morals; men have morality but no instincts. An animal's instincts guarantee that he will neither disobey nor deviate from the law of his being; a fish does not seek the dry land, a robin does not try to burrow in the ground, a gibbon does not yearn to swing on the North Pole. But man fulfills the law of his being only with the utmost difficulty—if then—and the only means at his disposal to align him with the forces of life is his ethical code. It is this code, and this alone, which may provide him with a life-giving, life-enhancing regimen.

A Single Ethical Code

Let me anticipate two quibbles. Instinct is sometimes contrasted with intelligence, and it is the latter, some say, on which man must rely. Or reason, as Dreiser suggests above. This is a play on words. We rely on intelligence to improve transportation, but we actually ride in automobiles or airplanes, which are the end result of applying intelligence to the problem of getting from here to there. Similarly, it is intelligence that discovers, analyzes, frames, and selects the ethical code. Which brings up the second quibble. Why *the* ethical code? Are there not many conflicting codes? Well, no—to be dogmatic! There is a hard core of similarity, almost identity, in every one of the world's developed moral codes. This is the *Tao,* the Way, referred to by the great ethical and religious teachers in all cultures. Without it, man ceases to be man. (For an expansion of this point the interested reader is referred to C. S. Lewis' *The Abolition of Man.*)

This begins to move us away from the humanistic ethics referred to earlier.

Do we need to part company, and if so, by how much? The two most prominent schools of naturalistic ethics are the utilitarians and the pragmatists. It was John Stuart Mill who invented the name and argued the case for the former. He described it as "the creed which accepts as the foundation of morals, utility, or the Greatest Happiness Principle." It "holds that actions are right in proportion as they tend to promote happiness, wrong as they tend to produce the reverse of happiness. By happiness is intended pleasure, and the absence of pain; by unhappiness, pain, and the privation of pleasure."

Pleasure and happiness are desirable indeed, and we wish more of them for everyone, But to equate "pleasure producing" with "right" at the outset of a proposed ethical inquiry is to beg the question. There is undoubtedly a connection here, for doing the right thing has a high degree of correlation with happiness, but the connection is along the lines of the intelligence-automobile illustration above. It is as if the utilitarian were asked, "What is the temperature of this room?" and he answered, "I feel chilly." Now there is some relation between this question and the answer, but the answer is not directly responsive to the question. It evades the question, implying that there is no way of finding out the temperature. There is no thermometer, perhaps. Mill and the utilitarians do not really get at the ethical question. They think they are talking about ethics when, in fact, they are discussing something else. Similarly, the pragmatists.

Why Does It Work?

The pragmatists are mainly concerned with workability; it's right if it works. Here is a map of the New England states. The pragmatist follows it and drives to Boston without getting lost. "Wherein lies the virtue of this map?" you ask him. "This map is good because it works; it got me to where I wanted to go." "Why," you pursue, "do you suppose this map got you to your destination?" "That," says out pragmatist, "is a metaphysical question of the sort I cannot be bothered with." So, we have to answer the question for him. The map "worked" because it was not just any old map; it was a map which corresponded to the terrain over which our pragmatist traveled.

An eminent British philosopher of a generation or two ago, W. P. Sorley, neatly wraps up and disposes of utility-workability theories. "It may be allowed," he writes, that the "relation between theory and practice does not necessitate the pragmatic explanation that the truth of the theory simply consists in its practical utility. The correspondence between theory and practice can also be explained on the view that the knowledge proves itself useful in its applications because it is true: the utility does not make it true; its truth is the ground of its utility. The former explanation is open to the fatal objection that it tends to discredit itself; for, according to it, the truth of the view that truth consists in utility must consist in the utility of this view. It would be difficult to show any practical utility which the explanation posesses; but if we did succeed in showing such utility, it would be formulated in yet another proposition, whose truth again would have to consist in some practical end supposed to be served by it, and so on indefinitely. But if the truth of the proposition does not consist in or depend upon its utility, then we may hold that its utility depends upon its truth: it is useful because it expresses reality or real relations in the form of knowledge, and this brings them within the range, and possibly within the power, of the human mind.''

Objective Moral Values

And now what about the weaknesses in the case for the theistic ethics, as the case is usually put? Fundamental to this position is the conviction that moral norms and standards are as much a part of the ultimate nature of things as the fact of the specific gravity of water. It might be convenient, at times, if water had other characteristics, but wishing won't alter the facts. Likewise, moral values. Honesty is right, and most of the time it may also be the best policy. But there are times when dishonesty would pay, where honesty makes us mighty uncomfortable; there is a conflict between what I want to do and what I know I ought to do. In order to maintain the integrity of the moral life, the ethicist champions the view that moral values are "out there," objective, as impervious to human tampering as any other fact of nature. Emphasis on their objectivity seems to imply that moral values are alien to human nature, and, if alien, hostile to man. If they are equated with God's will, God comes to seem an Oriental despot inflicting arbitrary and perverse rules upon his creatures for his pleasure and their frustration. This syndrome is, of course, a caricature.

Moral values are said to be objective in the sense that their validity is part of the system and order of the universe, of that same universe which is manifested also in persons. Neither is alien to the other, because both are part of the same reality. Sorley goes a step further. "The objective moral value is valid independently of me and my will, and yet it is something which satisfies my purpose and completes my nature." The ethical code may come into conflict with our superficial self on occasion, precisely because it takes its orders from our real self. Inner conflicts are a part of living, and we encounter them in all the ventures of life.

Take any sport played to win. It becomes a day and night preoccupation, with hours given over day after day for years to strenuous workouts. But this is only the visible part of the story. There is also a perpetual conflict with the impulse that wants to break training, to goof off, to lead a more normal life. Then there is the agony of the contest itself where the will to win takes over and pushes the athlete beyond his powers of conscious endurance into collapse the moment after his victory. His deepest will had attached itself to a regimen for optimum functioning, overcoming the continuous static and rebellion from other facets of his personality. Similar experiences are encountered in the intellectual life, and in the moral life.

Check out the latter with a medieval theologian. Thomas Aquinas says: ''If virtue were at odds with man's nature, it would not be an act of the man himself, but of some alien force subtracting from or going beyond the man's own identity." Go back to St. Paul. The Gentiles do not have the Mosaic law, he writes in his Epistle to the Romans, but "they show the work of a law written in their hearts." And Moses himself, as recorded in Deuteronomy, commends the keeping of God's commandments in order that there shall be flourishing life. "Choose life," he says. Where is this commandment, he asks rhetorically; is it up in heaven or beyond the sea? No, he declares, "the word is very nigh unto thee, in thy mouth and in thy heart, that thou mayest do it." What are we to understand Thomas, Paul, and Moses to be saying? Are they saying that to obey God's will for us is equivalent to following the laws of our own being? It's pretty close to that. And that is precisely what an animal's instincts do for him. The difference is that we are free to ignore or disobey the laws of our being, whereas no animal has that power.

Tested by Time, the Human Potential Emerges

In the course of several thousand generations of human beings a slow deposit has accumulated as the result of individuals here and there successfully realizing a portion of the human potential. The recipes they left behind, tested and winnowed over the centuries, form the hard core of the ethical code. This is not a presciption for a life of power-seeking, or one of money-making, or a life devoted to fun and games, or to fame. These things are not intrinsically evil, but an inordinate attachment to any one of them breaks training, so to speak. Proper use of them, on the other hand, is part of life's schooling process.

What are we being schooled for? A clear-cut positive answer to this question is impossible, for it outruns human experience. But a pretty clear hint comes through when we contemplate the alternatives. Wealth, pleasure, power, and even knowledge, when sought as ends in themselves, begin to send up signals that they are, in reality, only means to ends beyond themselves. The space scientists "build redundancy" into their capsules, more of everything than normal requirements would ever demand. Man, too, is overbuilt, in that each person has a wide range of potencies and a reservoir of untapped energy at his disposal, more than any of us ever use. Nor is man left on dead center with all this latent power. He has a chart containing the salient landmarks, and this chart is the ethical code. Let him begin to use this chart and the pieces fall into place, bits of the great design begin to emerge, the person fulfills his destiny. "The event is in the hands of God."

Gene Gilmore and Robert Root:

Ethics for Newsmen

A RASPING VOICE on the police radio near the city desk announces at 11:38 P.M. that a car has smashed into a utility pole off Hathaway Boulevard. Moments later the sirens of an ambulance from City Hospital scream by below the newsroom. The city editor dispatches a reporter, and within minutes the facts begin to fit into the mosaic of a story. Editors start making decisions, of space, display—and ethics.

The driver, in "critical" condition with a possible concussion, is Oscar Ragsdeal, forty-eight years old, according to the police. His address checks out in the city directory, which lists him as an administrative vice president of First National Bank. Good story. There were two in the car, the second hospitalized in "fair" condition. The police are working on the identification.

So far there appear to be no serious problems. Straight-forward story: serious accident, prominent man, maybe two—probably front page and no argument. But then the ethical complications begin.

The reporter at the hospital calls again with details on the skid and says he is still trying to get the girl's name.

A woman?—probably Mrs. Ragsdeal. Unlikely, the reporter says, because this girl is in her late twenties. Oh yes, he adds, there were a couple of broken whiskey bottles in the wreckage. "Looks like Oscar had something going," says the cynical newsman—but that is his personal, not his professional editorial comment.

The injured woman turns out to be Mrs. Sally Hinslaw, twenty-eight, who has been working in a First National branch since the death of Captain Hinslaw in Vietnam. Ragsdeal is the brother of the Ragsdeal who is advertising manager of the big department store at the corner. The women's editor reminds the city editor that Mrs. Hinslaw is the one who is such a close friend of their publisher's second daughter, in the Junior League and all; yes, these are the Hinslaws of the old mining family who are always in the parties reported on the women's page.

Dr. Gilmore is a professor in the College of Communications, University of Illinois; the late Dr. Root was a long-time professor at Syracuse University. This is a portion of Chapter 13 from their *Modern Newspaper Editing,* reprinted here by permission; The Glendessary Press, Inc. (now Boyd & Fraser Publishing Co.), San Francisco, copyright 1971.

Should the editor print the story?

This fiction brings into focus many of the most important pressures on an editor's ethics: the chance for a big headline and bigger sales. The right of Mr. Ragsdeal and Mrs. Hinslaw to be left alone. The rights of Mrs. Ragsdeal, and of any Ragsdeal and Hinslaw children, to be spared embarrassment. Advertising to be lost from the store and maybe the bank. A segment of the power structure unhappy about the publicizing of social scandal. And not least, the possible displeasure of the publisher himself.

Maybe the editor should forget the whole thing. But what will television do with it? And how will he settle his newsman's conscience, which tells him he lives to print the news, not suppress it?

The intelligent editor must think out a consistent ethical policy to guide him through such thickets. An editor with one policy will see the Ragsdeal piece as a sensational bonanza worth giving the titillating works to the limit of the libel laws. A more moralistic editor might give the story almost as much space and detail, but on an eye-for-an-eye theory that if Mr. Ragsdeal and Mrs. Hinslaw are going to cut capers, they must pay in public. If God made or let the accident happen, who is the editor to interfere with the world's knowing? Still another approach would be to print the news dead-pan, fairly and accurately, and let the reader make his own moral judgments.

One catch-phrase of ethical coverage is "All the news that's fit to print." The slogan was introduced into a front-page ear (upper corner) of the *New York Times* by Adolph S. Ochs, the publisher who brought the *Times* to greatness. It was 1897, when other New York City newspapers were vying in sensationalism, and Ochs used the phrase to emphasize the thoroughness and sobriety of ethical newspapering.

The cynic may say that the slogan should be "All the news that fits"—or that fits the editor's whims. Everyone knows that *all* the news can't be printed. But "all the news" implies a thoroughness which will not omit stories because of laziness or pressure. "Fit" implies that the editors will avoid sensationalism or pandering to low tastes. Yet they should find it fitting for the public to know what happens, however distasteful or terrifying, and regardless of pressures to leave out some events.

Some such principle would guide most good editors in the Ragsdeal accident. Newsmen of equal integrity might disagree about what to say about those whiskey bottles and how far to dig into the time and cause of Captain Hinslaw's death. But they would print a plain, factual account of the crash, the injuries, and the condition of the victim.

Freedom and responsibility. Some editors might say that what they print is their own business and not the province of philosophers. They would be right, in the sense that a free press is guaranteed by the Constitution, and that professional customs in the United States have evolved for handling these ethical questions. Mores probably control more stories than editorial ethics. Yet there are philosophical and even theological bases for the rights of newspapers to operate as they do, and publishers ignore these at their peril. Society has given newsmen wide latitude for their operations and decision, but what society grants, society can take away. The number of totalitarian countries in this century should be a reminder that press freedom is not automatic.

In the days of medieval kings, there would have been no argument of whether it was right or wrong to publish news of a scandal, even if there had been printing presses and editors. The monarch felt he had authority from God to make such decisions. A long trail of Star Chambers and jailed editors led from such dictatorship to a modern democratic system in which editors, within the framework of law, can print without license or censorship. Men at first argued, as in the Declaration of Independence, that they had such inalienable rights from God; more recently, it is claimed as an essential human right. The willingness of men to suffer and even die for this freedom is still the ultimate test of its survival.

John Milton provided the practical argument for press freedom. In the *Areopagitica* (1644) he argued for the "free marketplace of ideas." If all ideas were freely published, he said, the best ones would win out. It followed that men must have the right to know all the facts and arguments. So he rationalized the editor's freedom as one of the prerequisites for a working democracy. Thomas Jefferson argued for the citizen's right to the truth—being optimistic, like Milton, that a benevolent Providence allowed reasonable and moral men to run their own affairs. His idea of press freedom became one of the guarantees in the Bill of Rights.

But it is a truism that freedom implies responsibility. Those who get liberty must use it responsibly or risk losing it, whether in a developing nation or on a college campus. The grant of freedom to editors to purvey the news necessary to a democratic society carries the implied demand that they will print the news. When the press suppresses or distorts the news, it jeopardizes its claim to freedom. The unwritten expectation of American citizens is that the papers will give "all the news that's fit to print." This is the ethical imperative under which editors work.

Watchwords for ethics. Recognizing these obligations, publishers sometimes proclaim idealistic platforms or policies. At conventions they are especially prone to make the welkin ring with fine phrases. A major statement of high principle became the "Canons of Journalism," adopted by the American Society of Newspaper Editors when it organized in 1923. This code states that the "opportunities [of journalism] as a chronicler are indissolubly linked [to] its obligations as teacher and interpreter." The canons speak of "sincerity, truthfulness, accuracy," of "clear distinction between news reports and expressions of opinion" of "fair play." But they had no teeth and, while mentioned in journalism histories, are now almost forgotten. Few working newsmen could quote a single canon.

The difficulty is that, like democracy, freedom, and responsibility, principles of journalism must be stated as abstractions. Pessimists can readily dismiss pledges of *public interest* or *high trust* as pious hypocrisies. The problem is to relate high-sounding dictums to hard cases; and since no paper and no man is perfect, there are inevitably some tarnishes on the best papers, not to mention the corrosions of the worst.

Still, an effort must be made to set standards for the press. If such moral principles as love, compassion, and kindness are given lip service rather than devotion, they serve still as ideals or goals. Newspapermen need such abstractions to broaden their vision.

Truth is the word that summarizes many journalistic ideals. But what, philosophy has always asked, is truth? The working newspaperman knows well enough what truth means in his situation and doesn't worry too much about Truth. He checks the truth of small details but also the truth of the big picture, so far as he can discover and portray it.

One important facet of truth therefore is *accuracy*. Newsrooms rightly make a fetish of accuracy about names and addresses. But reporters must be at least as careful about accurate quotation, or about the accuracy of the impression which results from the way facts are put together.

Close to accuracy is *objectivity*. The reporter should keep himself out of the story, and the editors should see that he does. The conventional wisdom of the profession dictates that editorializing will be confined to editorial pages, yet editorializing barbs in stories are always slipping by copydesks. The authors know two or three reporters who produce "stories" that are really editorials, and their editors, with sloppy ethics, by-line them and print them in the news pages. The editor's job is to see that copy is accurate and free of editorial bias, whether it comes from a cub or a Washington or foreign correspondent of a famous press service.

The popular dichotomy of objectivity versus interpretation represents a misunderstanding of the journalist's problem with truth. The short dead-pan news account, the so-called objective story, the feature story, and the interpretive piece are all on one side of objectivity. Opposite them is the subjective story by the reporter who has, knowingly or unknowingly, distorted the news, whether of a minor accident or of international conflict. The sound interpretive story introduces the writer's evaluations (and these are admittedly subjective, with personal coloring), but as fairly and honestly—as objectively—as he can. The corrupt interpretation, by contrast, does not aim at truth but vents the writer's prejudices and slants. (Editorials and editorial-page interpretations are something else again, differing from news stories as oranges differ from apples.)

Intertwined with accuracy and the objective search for it is the concept of *fairness*. Human limitations may prevent a paper's being really accurate and really objective (the words are relative, no matter what grammarians may say), but readers know whether the editors try to be fair. They treat everybody alike. Ideally, they are as gentle with the poor unknown as with the big shot, with the hated political party or enemy nation as with their own faction or country. Per-

ceptive critics of the press see that it is the standard of fairness that is violated
when papers blandly print in their news columns accounts which refer to
"Huns," "Japs," "Commies," "Birchers," "peaceniks," and so on; the editor may protest that such highly connotative words communicate accurately in
some social moods—but are they ever fair?

Keeping the watchwords. Accuracy and fairness are often threatened by
pressures on the editor. Pressures from government he understands and can
combat. But many critics feel editors are less successful in combatting pressure
from advertisers. In an interpretive piece, the *Wall Street Journal* went so far as
to say that "many once-principled newsmen have been deeply demoralized by
their papers' surrender to advertisers' interest." The paper cited a study by
Prof. Timothy Hubbard of the University of Missouri revealing the ideas of 162
business and financial editors who responded to a questionnaire. More than
one-fifth of them said that "as a matter of routine they were compelled to puff
up or alter and downgrade business stories at the request of the advertisers."

The threat of unequal or unfair treatment is thus often seen as one of
special favors to advertisers or establishment figures; so publishers and editors
may underscore their pledge to print "without fear or favor" by publishing unfavorable news of themselves. The staff of one newspaper long told how a
divorce of the publisher's had been printed on the front page. The staff saw that
the standard of judgment was not simply the publisher's or editor's personal attitude toward the news but a standard of fair, full coverage. Similarly, the
former publisher of the *Pascagoula* (Miss.) *Chronicle* tells how he finally convinced detractors that his was "an honest newspaper printing the news without
favor":

> My son Maybin, 14, ran afoul of the law and was hailed into juvenile
> court. My practice had been to use the names of juveniles in police
> stories only if the youngsters were repeated offenders or if their crimes
> were heinous. My son's offense was minor, but his name appeared in
> a page-one story I wrote myself. He not only was named but was iden-
> tified as "son of Ira Harkey, *Chronicle* editor-publisher," so there
> could be no mistake.[1]

The ideals of accuracy, objectivity, and fairness are all contained in the
larger ideal of truth. But are these really phony ideals, used to delude, as hypo-
crites use flag and motherhood? Some hard-bitten cynics among newspaper editors would doubtless say "yes," and their shoddy papers reveal what happens
when principle crumbles. Yet even the most ethical editors tend to be pragmatic
about high journalistic principle. Pragmatism is an American philosophy that
holds that the best way is the way that works best. Americans are idealistic, but
they are also practical. So our editors do not usually mount white chargers.
They conform.

When the whole American society preaches that killing is wrong but sends
its youth abroad to kill and be killed, when it preaches brotherhood but remains

calloused about the hurt suffered by many Negro families, it is not remarkable that this society generates publishers and editors who preach the democratic canons but violate them in practice. They make practical compromises.

The realistic goal for the ethical newsman is to compromise as little as possible, for being pragmatic is not the same as being venal or cowardly. The best editors aim high and therefore hit higher than those who aim low.

Pluralistic foundations. Why is thorough news coverage better than slipshod, or an honest newspaper better than a dishonest one? The answer is self-evident to most of us only because it is woven well into the basic fabric of our philosophical and religious thinking. For there is no more general agreement in America on moral than on political issues. The intellectual problem of ethical journalism is rooted in the pluralistic nature of American society. Some Americans think, at least part of the time, as Christians, others as Jews, a few as Moslems or Hindus, while many eschew religion entirely. Of course some, including certain editors, worship only money or power. What is "right" by one standard is not necessarily right by another.

For example, some church people feel that newspapers should not mention gambling, yet others see nothing wrong if stories promote their bingo parties. One group of Christians wants thorough press discussion on liberalizing divorce or abortion laws; another group deplores it. But the clashes among our pluralistic segments are much more profound than suggested by these so-called moralistic issues. The deep differences among our world views condition the sharp variations in reactions on such questions as America's responsibility to peoples of the world, the proper response to Communism, the sacredness of human life, the relativity of moral values, and the ability of human beings to plan their own destiny. The role of the mass media is not the least of these major issues on which thoughtful Americans can have profoundly different views.

To understand and cope with these differences, we should understand two strands of American thought: first, the religious, or, more specifically, the Judeo-Christian; and second, the philosophical, particularly the pragmatic and utilitarian. We shall then turn to two strands of democratic thought: traditional concern for liberty and individual freedom and this century's growing emphasis on equality and social justice. Throughout, our purpose is to clarify our society's pre-suppositions so that editors may recognize the assumptions behind their practical decisions.

Christian backgrounds. The Puritan roots of American culture suggest Judeo-Christian ethics as an appropriate beginning in consideration of journalistic ethics. The approach can provide insight, even though there is little agreement on what the Judeo-Christian tradition would require. For example, journalistic morality in an Augustinian City of God would be one thing, in Mao's China another. The colonial New England theocracy did provide an official morality, but that church-led day vanished about 1700. The question is whether this strand in pluralistic thought leads to answers for the U.S. press today.

In this context "Christian" goodness may be considered as referring to kindness, generosity, compassion—in a word, love. It is the virtue extolled in the parable of the Good Samaritan and assumed in the Golden Rule. We saw in chapter 6 that editors cannot print the news with a philosophy of doing unto others as he would have done unto him. Much of the hard news in the paper deals with the wrong-doing or tragedy of people, and an editor cannot start leaving it out because he would shrink from seeing his own troubles in print.

An editor sometimes prints unpleasant news about someone by reasoning that he would print the item about himself because society deserves all the significant news. This rationale is close to that of the publishers who print unfavorable news about themselves or their families, in proof of fairness. But with this argument one is moving already from the Golden Rule of Christian love to the toughness of Christian justice.

The Golden Rule has bite because it is highly personal. The philosopher Immanuel Kant extended the Golden Rule to society: act so your actions can become a universal rule. His dictum incorporates both love and justice but diminishes personal involvement. It mediates Christian love to society and therefore helps the decision-making newsman.

Prof. Richard T. Baker of the Graduate School of Journalism, Columbia University, touches on the strand of justice in Christian thought by observing that "even the truth is not enough" for the journalist. Writing in *The Christian As a Journalist,* Professor Baker says:

> You should have extraordinary contributions to bring to your profession as an instrument for a more just society. You should know with precision when and how and where to throw the weight of your journal into the tactical struggles for fairness in human relations. You should not be cynical and defeated by the tragedies of injustice.[2]

The *Christian Science Monitor* takes this challenge seriously. This paper handles the news in a way consistent with its religiously optimistic point of view.

The utilitarian approach. Aside from Judeo-Christian principles, another widely held ethic promotes "the greatest good for the greatest number." As developed by Jeremy Bentham and John Stuart Mill, utilitarianism argues that good conduct is that which produces the greatest happiness for the most people. By dealing in quantities, utilitarianism appeals to the practical-minded. Another advantage of this concept of greatest-good is its democratic flavor. Milton and Jefferson argued for the freedom of the press as aid to the common reason; utilitarianism applies that freedom to the common good. While religious thought has proclaimed the sacredness of the individual personality, here is philosophy that rationalizes majorities and big circulations.

But for newspaper work this ethic, like the Golden Rule, has its difficulties. There is a practical problem in deciding what really is good for the most people. Can one be sure that the value to the public in printing the name of a rape victim is greater than the hurt to the girl—or vice versa? How, in fact, do you weigh such things? Yet an editor can feel "greatest good" does help him weigh.

This suggests a perhaps still greater problem: the tyranny of the majority.

Do the masses, just because they possess numbers, have an inalienable right to news whose publication will hurt a smaller group? Or, on the contrary, would a majority "vote" for suppression of news justify keeping the facts from a minority, simply because less good (arithmetically figured) appears to be involved?

Editors who print news of wrongdoing as well as progress, who publish a lot of comics and sports, and who perhaps circulate sensational accounts of sex and violence can rationalize that they are utilitarian. In fact, when they are criticized, the reflex of many editors is utilitarian; they say they are giving the public (presumably, the greatest number) what it wants. The very self-righteousness of such contentions, however, underscores the limitation of this philosophy: editors adhering to it too literally may slight the good of the cultured minority with higher taste than the masses, of the politically sophisticated minority jaded by the banalities of mass campaigns, and of the intellectual minority needing the free exchange of ideas and contributing to the real good of society.

To apply utilitarian theory most usefully, therefore, editors must consider the "greatest number of people" not as stupid, faceless masses but as groups of important, reasonable, individuals. Then the editor may justify overruling the restraints of religiously-motivated goodwill and print what he feels serves the greatest social good.

Rights and responsibilities. The Golden Rule and the rule of greatest-good do not exhaust the list which could be developed in a pluralistic society. Nor is balancing these two the only way to deal with the ethical problems of newspapering. If we approach the problem now from different theoretical vantage points, we get new slants on the tensions and balances ever present in editorial decisions.

The authors of *Four Theories of the Press* construct a framework important to any modern consideration of journalistic ethics.[3] The two most pertinent concepts for us are the libertarian theory and the social responsibility theory. (The other two theories are the authoritarian and the Communist, which bear only indirectly on our discussion of American journalism.)

Libertarian theory. Libertarian theory emphasizes the freedom of the newspaper editor. As we have said, this concept, developed by such men as Milton and Jefferson, opposes the autocrat's power to license and censor. It holds that editors should have liberty to print what they please (restrained only by such necessary laws as discussed in the chapter on press law). The assumption is that one journalist or another will dig out and print what the people ought to have.

The optimism of this theory may seem naive because of the horrible events of the last century and pessimistic intellectual trends since Darwin and Freud. Can men really discover through reason what is best? Many youth today, however, are starry-eyed about man's nature and here, curiously, go along with the assumptions of many of their elders. It is no doubt this tradition of hopefulness about men that most American editors embrace. They oppose government interference and control in the hope that common men will find the truth in what is printed.

This libertarian concept has its aspect of social good, a fact that is often overlooked. Selfishness is not part of the theory but part of the men who work under the theory. Editors—sinful, or at least as limited, as other men—have often abused this freedom; they have printed scurrilous political attacks, exaggerated and faked the news, scandalmongered, and pandered to the cheapest tastes. Before he died Jefferson himself was strongly impelled towards second thoughts about the virtue of editorial freedom. Yet according to the theory, out of the welter of what editors print will emerge the knowledge John Citizen needs for intelligent action. To work today, the theory requires reasonable printing costs and competition unrestricted by press monopolies. Then even those who are most hard-headedly realistic about the difficulties of opening the market-place to all ideas may still logically contend that the libertarian theory offers the brightest hope for society.

The theory of social responsibility. This social strength of libertarian theory is worthy of consideration because the rival theory of social responsibility, as its name suggests, tends to assume all claim to social good. Its advocates accuse newspapers of social irresponsibility and call for social instruments to see that the press fulfills its social responsibilities.

The authors of *Four Theories of the Press* trace the roots of this theory to the 1947 report of the Commission on Freedom of the Press, issued as the book *A Free and Responsible Press.* Known often as the Hutchins Commission—because it was chaired by Robert M. Hutchins, then chancellor of the University of Chicago—this group criticized press performance and listed several demands which society makes on the press. Among its suggestions was "establishment of a new and independent agency to appraise and report annually upon the performance of the press." [4]

Such suggestions and proposals have been increasing since World War II. In Britain royal commissions made blistering comments about the press, and since 1953 the British Press Council has monitored performance. On the ombudsman pattern, Sweden has a "court of honor" (*Pressens opinionsnamnd*) to adjudicate complaints against the papers. Harry S. Ashmore, executive committee chairman of the Fund for the Republic (and former editor of the *Arkansas Gazette*) has urged a similar body for this country. At a meeting of Sigma Delta Chi, Barry Bingham, Louisville publisher, urged that communities have citizens' groups to evaluate the efforts of their papers. But almost all American editors have shouted down suggestions like those of the Hutchins Commission as the worthless ideas of eggheads who "don't know anything about newspapers." [5]

Increased pressure to make newspapers more responsive to the needs of the people, however, was almost inevitable from the days of the New Deal, if not from the muckraking period early in the century. In the thirties social control moved from its previous domain of international trade (tariffs) and monopoly (trust laws) to wages and hours, unemployment and old-age benefits, and agricultural supports. Not the least of the intellectual pressures behind these moves were those religious and philosophical concepts of the Golden Rule and utilitarianism.

Conservatives dug in their heels, but greater government regulation has marched into such areas as health and medicine. Many corporation presidents and doctors have repeatedly warned that other businesses and professions would be next. Radio and television had faced regulation from their beginnings, and movement on to other areas of communication was theoretically inexorable. To some, religion or philosophy demand it. So far, the Constitution has protected the press. But basic laws can be modified or ignored. For a generation voters have endorsed numerous steps toward greater control in the name of the public welfare. A social-responsibility theory of the press would naturally garner wide support on similar grounds.

Pragmatic considerations. Pressure for the press to be socially responsible, in line with this theory, is real and recent. In a 1967 congressional poll reported by *Editor & Publisher* 91 out of 155 representatives and senators said they would favor a code of ethics for newsmen assigned to congressional galleries. The other 54, perhaps recalling that many congressmen want no code for themselves, were opposed or had no opinion. (One factor in the heavy vote was doubtless that 40 respondents said newspaper coverage was only fair or poor, and 15 said news coverage of Congress was "seldom" or "rarely" accurate!) In the *Harvard Law Review* of June, 1967, Jerome A Barron, an associate professor of law at George Washington University, contended that the First Amendment imposes on the press an affirmative responsibility to publish minority views. He argued that judicial remedy or legislation might guarantee the public limited access to press columns, as in the letters-to-the-editor section.

In one form the concept of social responsibility is familiar to all working newsmen. Chambers of Commerce, city officials, businessmen, and professionals may all argue to leave out, or at least "modify," some stories so they will not hurt the community. One graduate student came back from interning on a Midwest paper, for example, to say that it published *no* news which might be considered harmful to the community.

Advocates of social responsibility theory have several problems in explaining how it would operate. What kind of sanctions will restrict irresponsible newspapers? And if the teeth in controls are real, can the press still be called truly free? What watchdogs will watch the watchdog press? The journalistic battle of the young Ben Franklin against the ruling Mathers in colonial Boston is a bleak memory for the advocates of society's control, however highminded. Many liberals who are disturbed with press performance would be outraged if society were controlled, as is likely, by the industrial-military complex. Venal politicians, perhaps representing the least educated segments of the electorate, could be even worse. Would a cure by social control be worse than the disease of irresponsibility?

Editors nurtured on libertarian ideas tend to see all proposals for outside checks as revival of Star Chambers and censors. What is the practical difference, they argue, between a monarch like King George, a dictator like Hitler, a government agency, and a fancy social-control council? They all want to interfere with printing the truth. Prof. John C. Merrill of the University of Missouri is an authority on the foreign press who has argued that authoritarian regimes use the claim of public interest to censor their press.

> The only way a "theory" of social responsibility could have any significance in any country is for the government power elite to be the definer and enforcer of this type of press. Since in any country the organization of society—its social and political structure—determines to a large extent what responsibilities the press (and the citizen) owe society, every country's press quite naturally considers (or might logically consider) itself as being socially responsible.
>
> Assuming that a nation's socio-political philosophy determines its press system, and undoubtedly it does, then it follows that every nation's press system is socially responsible. For example, the Marxist or Communist press system considers itself socially responsible, and certainly it is responsible to its own social system. . . . The same thing might be said of the so-called "authoritarian" press system, exemplified in Spain.[6]

Society will want to move slowly in changing a system which has served American democracy for almost two centuries, however badly at times. If editors don't want this change, they relax in the hope that change will be glacially slow. A major part of their ethical and moral responsibility today is to develop instruments of self-control, whether codes or councils within the industry, to obviate the need for outside enforcement of social responsibility.

The libertarian theory is most popular among journalists and publishers, but all its advocates are not within the Fourth Estate. For example, from a perhaps unexpected source, Germany, Karl Jaspers, the famous existentialist philosopher, offers a view of the press quite similar to the views of Milton and Jefferson:

> What we call publicity today is more especially the world of speakers and writers, of newspapers and books, of radio and television. This publicity is not the proclaiming ground for a single truth, but *the battleground for all truth.*
> Writers are *the third force between the government and the people,* between the actions of politicians and the inarticulateness of the people. They create the communicating language. But this third force is significant *only if it is independent.* [Emphasis supplied][7]

In this decade libertarian press theory clearly has the edge from tradition, but the concept of social responsibility remains in conflict with it. The authors do not insist on a choice. Nor is America likely soon to make a clear decision between the theories, any more than it has chosen between those other similarly disputed abstractions "free enterprise" and "the welfare state." As the nation appears to be settling for a mix of "capitalism" and "socialism," it may settle too for a mixed theory of the press, with maximum liberty and responsibility for all. . . .

NOTES

[1] Ira B. Harkey, Jr., *The Smell of Burning Crosses* (Jacksonville, Ill.: Harris-Wolfe, 1967), p. 45.

[2] Richard T. Baker, *The Christian As a Journalist* (New York: Association Press, 1961), pp. 117–18.

[3] Fred S. Siebert, et al., *Four Theories of the Press* (Urbana: University of Illinois Press, 1963), chapters 2 and 3.

[4] For useful discussions of the report of the Commission on Freedom of the Press "twenty years after," see Edward Engbert's discussion in *The Center Magazine* (October–November, 1967), 22f., as well as the entire issue of the *Columbia Journalism Review* for Summer, 1967.

[5] For details on successful operations of press councils in Redwood City, California, and Bend, Oregon, see William B. Blankenburg, "Local Press Councils: an Informal Accounting," *Columbia Journalism Review* (Spring, 1969), 14–18.

[6] John C. Merrill, *The Press and Social Responsibility* (Freedom of Information Center Publication No. 001, University of Missouri, 1965), p. 2.

[7] Karl Jaspers, *Philosophy Is for Everyman* (New York: Harcort, Brace & World, 1965), p. 8.

Wilbur Schramm:

Quality in Mass Communications

THERE ARE only three great instruments which society may use to encourage or prod the mass media to responsible performance. These are government and its various regulatory bodies, national, state, and local; the media themselves, their individual personnel, and their formal and informal associations and administrative organizations; and the general public, with its formal and informal organizations and associations.

If we ask where, among these, responsibility lies for the kind of mass communication we have in this country, and for any change we want to bring about in mass communication, then quite clearly the answer is that responsibility is shared. Neither government, nor the media, nor the public can be counted on to do the job alone, and on the other hand, none of them is exempt from responsibility for doing it. What we are looking for . . . is a desirable balance of responsibility among them. . . .

Let us now consider the responsibility of the public.

The Commission on Freedom of the Press concluded that the more the media and the public are willing to do toward insuring a free and responsible communication system, the less the government will have to do; and that in general the "outside forces" of law and public opinion can check bad aspects of media performance, but only the media themselves can bring about good performance.

It is hard to disagree with these statements, but I depart somewhat from the Commission's emphasis. It seems to me quite clear that the media have the chief responsibility. If they do not assume it, if they do not voluntarily provide us with the public service on a high professional level which our society requires, then I do not see how our communication problem can be solved without to some extent going out of bounds, as we have defined the bounds of desirable action.

Dr. Schramm was the long-time director of the Institute for Communications Research at Stanford. He is presently Director of the Communications Institute at the East-West Center, Honolulu. This article is a reprint of "The Public" (pp. 249–252) in *Responsibility of Mass Communication,* Revised Edition, by William L. Rivers and Wilbur Schramm. Copyright © 1969 by National Council of Churches of Christ in the U.S.A. Copyright © 1957 by The Federal Council of the Churches of Christ in America. By permission of Harper & Row, Publishers.

What the media do not do for us they invite the government to step in and do or cause to be done. This, in our view, is a dangerous, an ominous kind of action. For that reason, I have urged that the government "keep its hands off" wherever it can, that it put down the temptation to step in and set things right, that it set strict limits on the kind of actions it will take with reference to mass communication, and that these actions should be chiefly facilitating, rather than restrictive ones.

I have therefore tended to put somewhat more responsibility on both the media and the public than did the Commission. Whereas the media must assume the central responsibility and do the job, I envisage the public as being prime movers in the communication dynamic. It is my firm belief that the public can come pretty close to having whatever kind of mass communication system it wants. Of course, this requires that it know what it wants and say what it wants. I do not accept the old idea that the mass-media public is a vegetable. I think that the "great audience" can be active rather than passive, that it can assay its needs and be articulate in getting them. Granted those assumptions, then it seems to me that the people hold the balance of power in determining the shape of their system and the service it gives them.

The listening, viewing, reading public underestimates its power. The media heads do not underestimate it. I have seen very few media men who look on the public as a mass to be molded and say, "This year we shall teach them to like thus and so." Rather, they are deeply concerned with what the public will be interested in, what the public wants and *will* like, and one of their greatest problems is trying to find out these things.

Anyone who looks at mass communication as a social institution cannot fail to note the tremendous push and pull of public interests and tastes on the institution. The program pattern of the networks vibrates like a windharp to the breeze from the monthly program ratings. New films go out to "sneak" previews, sample public reaction, and go back to the cutting room. One hundred letters to a network will often bring a review of policy; even fewer letters to a station will lead it to review a program or a program structure. One visit of a serious committee to a newspaper editor will make him think hard about what he is doing, even though he will be crusty about making promises. The motion picture industry has been in greater fear of boycotts than of censorship. Its code is spotted throughout with "special legislation" intended to appease this or that group and avoid boycott or public criticism.

In an earlier part of the book we mentioned how a comparatively slight outpouring of public indignation forced a network to take a well-known personality off the air because he had offended the friends of "Silent Night." Letters to the Federal Communications Commission get into station files, and they have a way of turning up embarrassingly in hearings. Listeners' councils have been able in many cases to exert a real and salutary influence on the kind of programs a local station carries. And underneath all this is the great groundswell of audience and attention, which none of the media can ignore. A newspaper publisher, who may resist what he considers a special interest group or special pleading, will pay attention if his circulation begins to fall off. A network or a station will perk up when the ratings begin to drop. A film studio is keenly aware what kind of business its pictures are doing. A magazine is compelled to worry when its newsstand sales fall off, or its readership studies indicate little interest in a certain part of its content.

Ultimately, therefore, the audience calls the tune. The people hold the trumps. And the only question is whether they will play their cards.

Is it realistic to hope that the public, the great audience, will seize this opportunity? This, of course, is the fundamental problem posed by the coming of bigness and fewness to the media. When media were many and audiences were small; when only a small percentage of the population could read, and only a small elite group formed the reading audience for most newspapers, magazines, and books; when the entertainment media were small and intimate—then there was a close connection between the men who made the media and their audience. There was a quick and vigorous feedback of demands and judgments. The audiences themselves felt the closeness of their relationship and took a lively interest in what the media were doing. The readers knew the editors. The performers knew some of their audiences. But now that audiences have grown so large that they include almost the whole population, when a great anonymity has settled over them, and they become known to the media only in terms of program ratings or percentages of readership or circulation figures—is there a realistic hope that some of this liveness and intimacy can be recaptured?

Of course, CBS or Metro-Goldwyn-Mayer or the *Reader's Digest* is unlikely ever to recapture the relationship which the *Dial* maintained with its audience when that influential magazine had 200 subscribers, most of them known personally to the editor, Margaret Fuller. It is certainly unrealistic to expect that situation to recur except in the case of a little magazine subsidized to serve a coterie. But between that situation and the far end of the scale, at which audiences are a kind of anonymous mass, I think it is clearly realistic and possible for the audience of mass communication to move a long way up the scale from anonymity toward personality. It seems to me clearly possible for the great audience to become a live, responsive, discriminating audience, to make its opinions and wishes known to the media, and in its own quiet way to enforce those opinions and wishes on the media. And if it should appear that in this audience there are a number of levels of taste and kinds of need, then I think it is clearly possible for the audience to insist that the media serve those different tastes and needs, instead of ladling up an insipid common denominator broth which appeals somewhat to each and satisfies none.

The basic responsibility of the public, therefore, is to make itself, as far as possible, an alert, discriminating audience. This may require a somewhat different habit of mind from the one we most commonly see on the part of many individuals who by virtue of position or education might be expected to be the leaders of and spokesmen for the public in their demands upon the media. This common attitude—"Oh, I never watch television except when there's something like a political convention on—it's just trash!"—is fundamentally an irresponsible attitude. It neglects the fact that television doesn't *have* to be all trash, if indeed, it is. Television is potentially one of our greatest windows on the world. It is one of the best ways in which we could expand our horizons, bring a sense of reality to faraway events, make a more informed judgment on public figures, share the lectures and demonstrations at our greatest universities, see the kind of opera, ballet, drama, museums, and concert artists formerly available only to a few fortunate people, most of them in great cities. If television isn't being used that way, what a great social waste it is! What a loss we are suffering! And whose fault is it? Basically, it is the fault of the people who don't watch it and don't do anything about improving it.

The greatest newsgathering services man has ever devised are connected to our home-town newspapers. Through wire services these newspapers are connected to every corner of the world where news is being made. A statement by Nasser in Egypt is perhaps twenty minutes away from each of our newspapers. An incident beside the Iron or the Bamboo Curtain is, at the most, thirty minutes away from our newsrooms. A full interpretation of Mr. Dulles' latest statement is available if a few persons in Washington or New York or on a university campus are given a few hours to think about it. In that situation, have we any right to say, as so many of us do: "I can't get any picture of what's happening in the world, from our paper; it carries only six or seven foreign news stories a day"? Or, "I can't understand what's really going on in national politics or this international situation. We never get any background." Have we any right to say that, if we never complain to the editor? He has the space to put in more world news, more background, if he thinks his audience wants it. He is putting that space into sports, or features, or society, or some other news. If he thought there was a serious demand for more world news or background, he would carry it.

The first requisite, therefore, is an alert, interested audience. This implies that we pay some attention to our media. We read, view, listen. We find out what is in the media. We don't wash our hands of the media in the supposition that they are being patterned for somebody else.

Then we try to make ourselves a discriminating audience. We give some thought to what the media *might* be giving us. We talk about the media with our friends. Perhaps we organize listeners' councils or readers' groups to talk about what we find in the media. We try to see that our schools give some attention to the question how to use the media intelligently; there are good textbooks now on such subjects as "How to read a newspaper," and many schools are helping their students to make best use of the mass media, just as they prepare them to make use of other parts of human experience. After all, these young people will be giving perhaps five hours a day, or nearly a third of their waking time, to mass media. This is too large a segment of life to use wastefully. And so we try to see that our young people have a systematic introduction to the media. We try to read newspaper or magazine criticism of the other mass media, just as we read book reviews. And in every way we try to build into ourselves some standards for judgment of what we see, hear, and read.

Another way in which we can develop discrimination is by controlling our attendance upon the media. If we don't want all movies to be made as though for children, we can keep our children away from *some* movies. If we don't want all television to be filtered out so as not to be above the sensibilities and sensitivities of *any* member of the family, then let us exercise some discrimination about what members of the family watch television at a given time. This is partly our responsibility. We can't expect the media to serve the interests of all kinds of people and displease or offend none unless we do something about getting the right kind of people to the media at the right time.

Then the next step in our responsibility is to make our views known to the media. One way to do this is simply by reflecting in our patronage our discrimination in what we subscribe to, what we attend, what we view or listen to. If enough of us do this, it will have an effect. But this method sometimes cuts off our nose to spite our face. For example, if we stop buying our home-town newspaper because it carries only seven foreign news stories a day, that will lose us *all* the local news. The big stick is not the best way. A better way is to tell our media what we do and don't like about them, and what would make us like them better.

This we can do through letters—to the editor, to the station, to the network, to the theater, or to the studio. The more individual these letters are, the better. The media tend to fill their wastebaskets with letters which are all written in about the same words and therefore reveal that they are inspired by some pressure group. But individual letters are read and valued. So are individual contacts, when those are possible. These help to tell media employees, and especially media heads, what you think of their product. If you feel seriously enough about it, you can call on the editor or the station manager or the theater owner. You can certainly take advantage of meetings or social events or casual contacts to talk to media people. They appreciate these little feedbacks, and over the course of weeks such contacts add up to a picture of what the public wants and thinks.

Things like this you can do informally and individually. Or you can organize and go about it more formally. We have occasionally in this book said unkind things about pressure groups, but there is nothing in our political philosophy to keep audiences from organizing whenever and however they wish, to communicate more effectively with the media. Listeners' councils, where they have been organized, have been very effective in this way. Organizations like the League of Women Voters or the Association of University Women have sometimes made the media their chief discussion topic and have sent delegations or resolutions to represent their opinions and needs to media heads. Sometimes community groups, or student groups, or church groups have arisen spontaneously because of dissatisfaction with some aspect of the media. Often these groups have asked newspapermen or broadcasters or theater operators, or magazine salesmen, to speak to their meetings, in order to get their side of the story and convey the feelings of the group.

There are already a number of well-organized groups active in the field, many of them with professional staffs watching the media, trying to keep out of them material offensive to the particular group. Such are, for example, the Legion of Decency, the Chamber of Commerce, the American Legion, et cetera. There is nothing wrong with this. Any group has a right to organize and tell the media what it thinks of them. But remember that our communication system is built on the theory of a free market place of ideas. It will not work right unless *all* viewpoints on a controversial question are freely presented.

Therefore, there is a kind of pressure-group activity which is as clearly out of bounds as is government interference with the media. I mean the kind of informal censorship which tries to remake the shape of the media in the image of one group's needs and sensitivities, at the cost of all other groups. The news about Christmas time, 1956, contained what may be an example of this kind of activity. Station WGN-TV, of Chicago, canceled the world première showing on television of the film *Martin Luther*. The station said the film was canceled because of the "emotional reaction" of the public to its plan to show the picture. This "emotional reaction," said the *Christian Century,* took the form of a telephone blitzkrieg "organized by Roman Catholics to keep WGN telephones humming with protests." The Chancellor of the Chicago archdiocese said that the Church had made no official representations to WGN-TV whatsoever, and that if any Catholics had protested it was an individual matter. It was claimed that the film was "down-right insulting" to Catholics.

Now I have neither investigated behind these facts nor seen the picture. It is a fact, however, that the film was shown in many theaters without any substantial opposition. If the facts are as suggested—an organized campaign by members of one religious sect to keep off the air a film about the founder of other religious sects—then this is a questionable kind of pressure-group activity. There could be no possible objection to one church exerting discipline over its own members and keeping them away from a theater or from watching a television program. But when such a group acts to deprive other groups of opportunitites they very much desire in the mass media, and which are not obscene or otherwise clearly censorable, then it would seem that this is restricting the free market place, and should be resisted both by the media and the public.

As I say, the Chicago incident may or may not be an example of this kind of action; I have not thoroughly investigated it. And the particular religious group mentioned is by no means the only group, religious or political, which has been accused of such activity. But whoever does it, it doesn't fit into our system.

Pressure groups, like government, are usually on less dangerous ground when their activity is facilitating, rather than restrictive. That is, they are more helpful when they try to represent the needs of the public than when they speak for the sensitivities of particular groups. But even here caution is needed. We can't expect mass communication to meet all our needs if we depend on a few well-organized groups, each with a special interest, to speak for us. These groups may keep the media free of material which disturbs, and encourage the media to present material which pleases, the Legion, the Chamber, the Roman Catholic Church, or some other organization; but they will not necessarily be concerned that the media carry what the rest of the public wants or needs. The remedy for this situation is not to complain about "pressure groups," but to organize groups to represent our own interests, if these are not being represented. And when the media heads see the full spectrum of public needs and wishes, they will be better able to plan their product.

A further responsibility of the public, it seems to us, is to encourage intelligent criticism of the media. This is not an attack on the media; it is rather a service to media and public alike. Book reviews, for many years, have served not only to sharpen the standards of taste on the part of writer, reader and editor, but also to call the attention of the public to new books of interest. It is amazing that so little criticism of broadcasting and newspapers has come into being. The influential daily critics of radio and television number less than a handful. No sustained regular criticism of newspapers has ever proved feasible. Yet criticism of this kind is surely a part of the professionalizing and general growing up of the media.

The Commission on Freedom of the Press recommended that "a new and independent agency" should be established to "appraise and report annually upon the performance of the press." By *press* the Commission meant all the mass media. This proposal was received with undisguised horror by the newspapers, and was equated with all sorts of dire threats to press freedom. Yet it is hard to see how such an agency, given a board of distinguished citizens and a competent staff, could really threaten freedom of the press. And it might do a great service, both in scrutinizing the media for the public and in representing to the media the dissatisfactions and unmet needs of the public. Such an agency would, of course, have no governmental connection and would represent the public in general rather than any segment of it. The Commission listed a long series of services such an agency might undertake, among which were the following:

Helping the media "define workable standards of performance";

"Pointing out the inadequacy" of media service in certain areas;

Investing areas and instances "where minority groups are excluded from reasonable access to the channels of communication";

Examining the "picture of American life" presented abroad by the media

Investigating charges of "press lying," with particular reference to the persistent misrepresentation of the data required for judging public issues

Appraising "governmental action affecting communications";

Appraising the "tendencies and characteristics of the various branches of the communications industry";

Encouraging the "establishment of centers of advanced study, research, and criticism in the field of communications at universities";

Encouraging projects which give hope of meeting the needs of special audiences;

Giving "the widest possible publicity and public discussion" to all its findings.

For any one agency, this might be an overambitious assignment. Yet the objective of all of it is simple enough—an agency to represent the interest of the public as a whole, as distinguished from the special interest of groups; to speak for the whole public in a way that the public could never speak as individuals; to observe the work of the media and think about it in terms of the needs and interests of the American public; and finally to report both ways to the media and to the public, and thus to serve as a valuable communication link between them. To choose the board and staff of such a public agency would be difficult. To outline and restrict its tasks to realistic goals and limits would take a great deal of thinking and some trial. But the result might be very salutary, might result in a much better mutual understanding between the media and their publics, and on the whole would be an excellent project on which a foundation might bet some money.

If such an agency of communication and observation is ever established, it is a responsibility of the public to do it. It should not be established by the government nor by the media, although it should counsel with both the media and government. It should represent public interest at the highest level. So far as the newspaper objection is concerned, it is a good guess that, after the first mechanical reaction of resistance, most of the newspapers and the other media would respect and welcome the new agency.

We said in the preceding chapter that it is a responsibility of the media to help in the establishment of adequate schools for prospective members of the profession, and also university research centers in mass communication. It is certainly a responsibility of the media to concern themselves with these problems and help with them, but the basic responsibility is the public's. The public has to found such organizations at universities, and send able young people to them. Over the next two or three decades the schools of journalism and their related training and research centers can make a profound difference in the level of media personnel. They can do so, that is, if they are used at their full potential which, as we tried to say in the last chapter, is not for vocational training, but for training of a breadth and depth which very few other occupations require.

Another way to say it is that journalism school and other mass communication curricula are not best used when they train students for the first six months of their employment; they should rather prepare their graduates for the years that follow the first six months: not in the skills which enable the young employee to do well at first, but rather in the understandings which enable him to do well throughout his career. There is no reason why he should not learn some skills, too; but, whenever there has to be a choice of time between learning the vocational skills and gaining the broad understanding of society and mass communication's place in it, the time should always be used for the broader and less immediately useful studies. The schools should aim for the long, not the short term; for on his job the new man can much more easily learn the skills of his job than he can learn to understand human beings, social organization, government, economics, and science.

Schools of journalism have been moving in this direction, but they are handicapped by a tradition which began in the land-grant colleges under the example of service to agriculture, and the early leadership of weekly newspapermen who wanted employees they would not have to train. Even now the schools of journalism are unlike other professional or quasi-professional schools in that *they* do not necessarily train the new members of the profession as do medical or law schools; their graduates have to compete on a level with graduates of every other curriculum in the university and with nongraduates of universities. Indeed, the fact that university graduates expect more salary gives an advantage to nongraduates on smaller papers and other media. Therefore, the school of journalism has felt some need to stress, by teaching journalistic techniques, its uniqueness in the university and its close relationship to the newspapers and the broadcasters. Even so, the best schools now build their curricula on a broad grounding of liberal studies in other departments, and this is a tendency which the public should certainly encourage.

Another healthy development is the establishment of research centers and programs in connection with a few schools of journalism and elsewhere in a few universities. This is a long step on the road to professionalization. Without strong research programs in connection with and feeding into schools of medicine, we should still be letting blood for various diseases and treating mental diseases with chains and dungeons. It should be pointed out that both the schools and the research centers in mass communication are essentially a public responsibility.

Another important way in which the public can demonstrate its discriminating concern with mass communication is in the encouragement of new ventures. It is increasingly hard to start anything new in mass communication because of the costs involved. Yet there is increasing need for new ventures, not only to provide a variety in viewpoint, but more important, to serve the needs of groups within the great audience who are not sufficiently served by "common denominator" media content. If the public, or segments of it, want these special services they must make their wants known, and be alert to support, or at least try out, new ventures when they come.

There could be more newspapers covering public affairs in somewhat the way *The New York Times* does, but in other parts of the country, if publishers thought people in sufficient numbers would buy them. There could be more and better community television stations, covering local public affairs and carrying the best in local entertainment and information, if audiences would give them a few dollars per viewer per year. The university radio and television stations would furnish a better service—indeed, they could give a very exciting service—if the public made known to administrations and legislatures that they wanted these activities adequately supported with budgets. There would be more theaters specializing in high-quality films, and more studios making such films for such theaters, if the public would patronize them. The possibility of endowed newspapers or broadcasting stations is a fascinating one, but it is not necessary to have financing from a foundation or a wealthy man in order to bring about superior communications. The thing most needed in order to have new ventures in mass communication is assurance that there is a discriminating public waiting for them, willing to support them.

In another way, too, the public has a peculiar responsibility in regard to mass communication. More nonprofessional members of the public must learn to use the media. There is no excuse for religious broadcasting being less skillful than entertainment broadcasting. There is no reason why the public should permit educational broadcasting to be any less skillful than entertainment broadcasting; yet the educational stations are starved for funds and are therefore unable to train and keep skilled performers. There is no reason why local broadcasting, radio or television, could not be more of a force than it is; for leaders in any community to acquire the basic skills of broadcasting would not be a great task. This implies also that more members of the nonprofessional public should come to understand the media—to learn what can be expected of the newspapers and the broadcasters especially, and how to work with them and make use of their media in the best way.

All this comes back to the question whether we can realistically expect to have a live, articulate, discriminating public concerning itself with mass communication. If so, great things are possible. If not, progress will be slow. For, as I have tried to indicate, responsibility in mass communication is a delicate balance between the media, the government, and the public. The chief responsibility for doing what needs to be done with mass communication is that of the media, but in a sense the basic obligation is with the public. The public's responsibility is to be an active, discriminating audience, to make its needs known to the media, to be helpful as the media try to meet these needs—in other words, to be full partner in the task of making the kind of communication society needs. To the extent that the public is less than a full partner, government and media will fill the gap, and we shall be less sure that we get what we want. For it is the public's own responsibility that is controlling in this case, and if we do not exercise it we deserve only what we get.

In a radio address to America in 1931, and in his usual salty, tongue-in-cheek manner, George Bernard Shaw startled some of his listeners with the following proposition: "Every person who owes his life to civilized society," he said, "and who has enjoyed since his childhood its very costly protections and advantages should appear at reasonable intervals before a properly qualified jury to justify his existence, which should be summarily and painlessly terminated if he fails to justify it."

I am not advocating such summary justice. But I should like to suggest that all of us who enjoy the protections and advantages of a free communication system do indeed have some obligation to justify our existence under it. I have been suggesting what that obligation consists of. And if we are not doing enough to justify such protections and advantages, then we certainly face the possibility in this fateful century of having our existence under them summarily but not painlessly terminated.

W. H. Ferry:

Masscomm as Guru

THE TOPIC of this paper is the social and cultural responsibilities of mass communications. My definitions are straightforward: "mass communications" means television, newspapers, mass-circulated paperbacks, radio, comic books, the great circulation magazines, and their accomplices and adjuncts: boards of directors, editors, public relations mechanics, advertisers, and writers. In including the last category I invoke the Nuremberg doctrine: great collective sins, as well as great collective achievements, are the products of individuals. Thus, the discussion must take in the scribblers and drudges of the trade as well as the Napoleons and Metternichs. "Responsibility" means the state of being responsible, that for which one is answerable—a duty or trust. "Social and cultural" signifies those areas of the common life apart from the political realm. I believe that the observations herein can be extended to the rest of the world, *mutatis mutandis,* even those portions as yet unexposed to the raptures of the TV soap opera, the gossip column, the dirty comic book.

Mr. Ferry, newspaperman and public relations practitioner, is a former vice-president of the Fund for the Republic. This article is reprinted by permission from an occasional paper ("Mass Communications") published by The Center for the Study of Democratic Institutions, Santa Monica, California, May, 1966.

At the outset I wish to stipulate that phrases like "notable exception" are salted through the following pages. I shall not attempt a weighing-up of mass communications, fair and balanced to the last gram. My thumb is firmly on one side of the scales. I shall be talking about macro-cause and macro-effect. I know about the occasional brilliant and illuminating broadcast, article, report, picture-essay, and I pay my respects to them herewith. They will be given no more attention in this paper. The acute sense of self-appreciation developed by mass communications tells us a great deal about them, for one thing. For another, it scarcely seems required to pay homage to an institution for doing what is expected of it.

I wish also to acknowledge that the common run of breaking news is probably as well reported these days as at any time. I am aware of the need of mass communications to make a living, its concern with "events," the impact of instantaneous electronic reporting. I know that mass communications are both cause and effect, acted upon by society as well as acting. There are titans in the field and I herewith salute them also. My comments are not directed at the conscientious and striving few but at the thoughtless and irresponsible many. I am not unsympathetic to the variety and intensity of the demands on mass communications, and I intend to add to them.

I shall use the word masscomm in the following pages, not because I like such ugly neologisms but to avoid the repetition of the equally dreary phrase mass communications.

A GOOD MANY THEORIES of the social and cultural responsibilities of masscomm have been elaborated over the years—by Walter Lippmann, Robert Hutchins, Father John Courtney Murray, the late Alexander Meiklejohn, by others. All of the theories are based chiefly on two grounds: the singular position accorded mass communications by the First Amendment, and the indispensability of criticism and guidance and fresh ideas to a democratic society.

The notion, of course, is that the people are sovereign, and need a clear stream of information and conflict of opinion to order the community. In 1947 a Commission on Freedom of the Press presented a Report which, in its five main requirements, provided a theory of responsibility. They are:

1. The press must give a truthful, comprehensive, and intelligent account of the day's events in a context which gives them meaning.

2. The press must provide a forum for the exchange of comment and criticism.

3. The press must project a representative picture of the constituent groups in the society.

4. The press must present and clarify the goals and values of the society.

5. The press must provide full access to the day's intelligence.

Though specifically addressed to newspapers, these requirements can readily be modified into a general theory applicable to the rest of mass communications. But that it is not commonly accepted is evidence by the reception of the Report by the press. It was vilified, misrepresented, and ignored. The Commission's mild recommendation that a group of private citizens be organized to appraise the doings of the press and make statements from time to time on its misadventures and accomplishments met with rockets of denunciation. There was a great deal of identifying of the press with what its proprietors wanted to do, which seemed to them identical with their responsibilities. The Commission's Report also provided the occasion for a campaign of unrelieved self-admiration. Today's counterpart is television's crankiness toward critics and its relentless glorification of what it is already doing when it is suggested that it might improve its output.

So much for a commonly accepted theory of responsibility. I suspect that there are deep historical reasons for masscomm's non-acceptance of well-defined obligations. But I think the main reason is that masscomm is preoccupied with another responsibility, that of making money. Masscomm argues that it cannot fulfill social and cultural responsibilities by going broke. Fair enough; no one expects the extreme sacrifice. This is not really the issue. The issue is whether masscomm has made the pre-condition of profits the entire reason for its existence, and its only basic responsibility. This is a different general theory, so to speak, and seems to me to be close to the cuticle. The matter may be stated otherwise. The United States, for better or worse, is a money-seeking culture; masscomm is a money-seeker like any other corporation. Thus, it argues, it ought to be measured by the amount of money it makes, not by archaic ideas about responsibility to the community.

I propose that masscomm begin to take itself more seriously. The balance of this paper suggests that masscomm bears social and cultural responsibilities of much greater weight than it has been willing to shoulder. Whether such responsibilities can be undertaken by masscomm while still remaining solvent is the question. Perhaps we could find out if masscomm were to seek not to make more each year than the year before but to concentrate instead on looking to its fundamental obligations. I know that it is not especially rewarding to exhort particular men to reform themselves, and so these remarks must be considered less a collection of remonstrances to those now running masscomm than a general prayer that masscomm as an institution may rouse itself somehow to the performance of duties long and dangerously neglected.

Few spokesmen in masscomm would assert a doctrine of social and cultural non-responsibility. Nor would many of them deny that in some way and to some degree masscomm has shaped American institutions. Scott Buchanan says that the First Amendment is the source of all of the duties, privileges, and immunities of education, though the word itself does not occur in the Amendment, or, for that matter, anywhere else in the Constitution. Perhaps masscomm recognizes, whether unconsciously or no, that its wide warrant is obtained in the same place and that its task is essentially education. This, it will be perceived, is a one-word summary of the five requirements of the Commission on Freedom of the Press.

My view is that masscomm's social and cultural responsibilities are those of the largest and probably most influential educational system any society has known. The relation is teacher and taught. I do not suggest that masscomm is like a university. The differences are evident. Nor can one suggest that everything would be fine if masscomm merely modeled itself on the university, which itself is having grave difficulties these days about its proper functions.

And it might well be maintained that education would itself take on the irresponsible aspects of masscomm if it in turn depended on paying customers, free to come and go, buy or not buy, look or not look. But this is a heavily debatable proposition, and in any case my topic is masscomm, and not the machines of formal learning for the young.

Aristotle provides the point: "Men by nature desire to know." They do not cease desiring to know at 16 or 21 or 25. Learning proceeds throughout life, willy nilly. The means of learning change and become informal. What is learned changes. For most people masscomm provides the means of their continuing education, for good or ill; and masscomm's choice of topics and emphasis decides, for most people, what is learned. It is in these respects that I confer on masscomm the accolade and obligations of educator.

I CANNOT THINK OF a nicer compliment than to call someone a teacher. But masscomm does not much care for the title. Perhaps that is because on every front it realizes that it must be given low marks as an educator. It does not fully inform, it mystifies as much as it clarifies, it seldom lifts up. The situation of American Negroes, for example, has been a disgrace from Reconstruction on, a running sore on the national body. It would be a festering canker to this day had the issue been left to masscomm. A few courageous Negroes and whites taught a public lesson in three years that was never in masscomm's curriculum, and the Negro now has at least a glimmering chance to break out of latter-day slavery. For generations two-thirds of our Negro population has lived in poverty or deprivation. Unemployment has been twice or more that of whites. Who knew these things?

It is commonly acknowledged now that the pot boiled over in Los Angeles in the summer of 1965 because of frustration and resentment and indignity stored up too long. How much were Californians told about the sputtering fuse? Even the best-intentioned of them were aware of little or nothing. Bishop Kennedy, the liberal and kindly Methodist leader of Southern California, apologized publicly for his ignorance after the Watts uproar. "I didn't know," he said, "that this was the way they lived."

Before Rosa Parks performed the momentous act of sitting in the wrong part of the Montgomery bus, what was the picture of the Negro nation presented to us by masscomm? Through its cloudy lens in the South we saw Negroes struggling patiently through courts to get their children into decent schools, indignant, perhaps even irritated, at the delays occasioned by the need to give the White South time to accommodate. Once in a while we picked up the odd bit of gossip in masscomm about the habitual injustice to Negroes in the criminal courts and their inability to vote in a good many places. According to masscomm, Southern Negroes were being treated well, in the Dixie version of that term, and were responding by forbearance and understanding. Mass communications portrayed a colored minority waking slowly to the possibility that it had some rights, even a few they had always known to be a white monopoly, and walking softly and patiently toward the Promised Land. Except for a troublemaking and querulous few, masscomm intimated, this minority was quite ready to forego voting, opportunity, schooling, dignity, until the white nation got used to the idea and became willing, piece by stubborn piece, to bestow these bounties.

The Northern portrait was even more illusory and vicious. Masscomm rejoiced that Jim Crow was not official doctrine in Detroit, Harlem, Chicago, Rochester, Philadelphia. Masscomm neglected to say it was standard practice. There was, to be sure, the occasional flare of trouble in these precincts, duly reported by masscomm and as duly attributed to Communists, Muslims, or chronic malcontents. Once again masscomm produced the wrong enemy. Inattentive authorities, greedy landlords, cybernation, bad education, all the complex causes of Negro misery that make up the real enemy, used to be mentioned by masscomm only once in a while. The favorite culprits of masscomm are, in the race situation as in all others, still Communists or agitators.

Masscomm assured us that Northern Negroes were aware of how much better off they were than their Dixie cousins. The white nation did not really need to be concerned about ghettoes, rats in bedrooms, the daily indignity of Negro life, because Negroes were used to them, grateful on the whole for the droppings from the white table. Above all, masscomm said, Negroes were accustomed to the thought that it would take generations of obeisance to white overlordship to win their way to equal justice and opportunity. If Northern Negroes were not entirely happy with their lot, they were not unhappy enough to say anything loud and impolite about it. The white nation needs a stereotype of the Negro, and masscomm was glad to provide the infamous caricature of him as gospel-hymning, crap-shooting, indolent, carefree, sex-powerful, and loving the squalor he lived in.

This, I think, is a not unfair outline of the general picture of the American Negro presented by mass communications in those pre-Parks, pre-SNCC, pre-roit years. It was not only a grossly unreal and ignorant picture—masscomm did not have Bishop Kennedy's excuse of not knowing—it betrayed irresponsibility toward millions of fellow citizens, and unconcern about a dirty condition by which the world would judge this country, even as South Africa is judged.

Masscomm felt free to ignore or misrepresent the real plight of the Negro North and South because it is white, rich, and privileged, because of sheer delinquency, and because masscomm believes its audience dislikes disagreeable realities. So, instead, it offered Potemkin villages and spun-sugar homilies about the success of the American Dream.

THESE ARE SIGNIFICANT and not isolated instances of the failure of masscomm in the first task of education, to inform and clarify. This sedulous nonconcern for the rights and dignity of Negroes may be contrasted to the roaring that goes up whenever a question is raised that seems to infringe on masscomm's rights and dignity. Freedom of the press was stridently invoked not long ago to justify masscomm's desire to underpay newspaper boys. Its role as conscience of the community is played with passion when masscomm's institutional interests are involved. The conscience slumbers when the interests are those of the unlucky or helpless.

Masscomm's role as defender of the strong against the weak is illustrated by the current concern with poverty. Americans found out about poverty when two or three angry young men pulled back a blanket of ignorance and neglect and uncovered 40 million or so Americans living in degradation. The invisible poor discovered by Michael Harrington were invisible because masscomm didn't care. Masscomm was busy elsewhere, counting profits, celebrating the status quo, selling rubbish. That masscomm even missed a bet with its constituency is evidenced by the current popularity of the war on poverty.

Masscomm's delight in the shoddy, the tasteless, the mind-dulling, the useless, is well-established. It is a direct consequence of masscomm's allegiance to organized rapacity. Ethical qualms about the effects of dishonest commercials disappear like morning mist in the glow of a comfortable advertising contract. Equally well-established is masscomm's tendency toward submerging significant issues in a sea of pointlessness. Thus an important public situation will somehow be related, in a cause-and-effect manner, to a participant's fondness for bowties or popcorn or beards.

These practices are said by some to be an inevitable concomitant of affluence and literacy, unimportant, and to be viewed merely as bubbly sidewaters to the strong central currents of American life. I do not agree. These practices amount to a policy of trivialization, and trivialization comes close to the heart of the indictment. For it is the human being, and his importance, that are finally trivialized. Masscomm is not interested in the human being as the subject of ultimate concern, but in consumers as the object of never-ending blandishments.

The general theory of responsibility stated earlier does not require that masscomm treat only important public matters, and that it ignore the immense carnival of contemporary life, its sideshows and heroes, achievements and banalities. Offerings for sale, and entertainment, and diversion are a part, but they are not all. The general theory requires only that fundamental duties not be obscured or neglected in favor of the carnival, that all be kept in context and balance. It is the context and balance that are destroyed by the policy of trivialization.

The pristine vision of the First Amendment is that of an untrammeled press, somehow standing apart from government and society, reining in excesses, raising standards, asking irreverent questions, cutting down villains and villainy, praising the virtuous. It is to be the master warts-and-all portraitist of the American scene.

But masscomm does not portray what is there. It does not stand apart. It has signed up with the Yankees, so to speak—with the rich and powerful, with the government, with the successful and prestigious. Signing-up means joining the team, contracting to safeguard its interests and to help win its games. It would not be easy any longer for masscomm to find its own ground, to achieve the separateness that seems to me its first requirement. Now this pledge of allegiance is a familiar enough count in the true bill against masscomm. But the supporting data are not merely those usually presented—the grotesqueries of advertising, the unwillingness to print the story about the wife of the department store owner, the unending concern with the Beatles and Dick and Liz.

The prime consequence of signing up is the stupefaction and brutalizing of the nation. All the dirty garbage in our social and cultural order cannot be dropped at masscomm's door, to be sure. Neither must its capacities, enhanced daily by new techniques, be under-estimated—the growing capacity to inform and clarify but also to assault, caress, fuddle, bloat, and deaden the human sensorium. Thus I agree with the Rt. Hon. W. F. Deedes, M.P., who recently said of television, "It has within its power to decide what kind of people we become. Nothing less." I would only make the statement retroactive and extend it to the rest of masscomm.

It seems to me beyond argument that masscomm is a chief contributor, though not the only one, to the social and cultural malaise lying on us all. This is so because masscomm is a major beneficiary. It can make more money not meeting its responsibilities than by doing so. American culture is marked by the compulsive consumption of trash, and by the ennobling of practices such as intentional obsolescence. Masscomm enthusiastically endorses such activities. Our environment turns into a visual junkyard, our rivers stink, and masscomm declares that it is all regrettable but commerce must be served. Strangers might conclude from masscomm that we are conducting a civilization virtually without blemish, full of grinning families playing games in marzipan neighborhoods, with no problems or future except those of assuring ourselves more grins and fun.

Nor is it happenstance—to move to another example—that violence, delinquency, and crime have mounted as this country has increased its reliance on the weapons of universal terror. We cannot really expect that counsels of reconciliation and reason will prevail in our domestic affairs when we resort to war abroad with all the lethal paraphernalia provided by technology. I do not intend to go into our national policy in Vietnam and elsewhere; I wish only to note masscomm's posture with respect to these policies and events and the effect of this posture on the ethical standards of the country. Americans are killing and maiming and burning and torturing in Vietnam. We may even get into a nuclear war, an eventuality that masscomm appears to believe may some time be necessary, though of course unfortunate. These present and potential activities display no fundamental moral issues, according to masscomm. They are acclaimed as a great patriotic exercise. Masscomm, putative bastion of our liberty, does not protest as we turn into a garrison state. Far from inquiring seriously into the demoralizing results on the nation of dependence on militarism, terror, and overwhelming might, masscomm applauds. "My country right or wrong" is the advice most often given to us, in these dangerous days, by editorial writers. Quite apart from the question of peace and coexistence, which must be our ultimate destiny if it is not to be that of a cinder, the issue is what happens to a civilization when its darkest instincts are constantly being stimulated. I think that what happens is that a civilization turns sour, and becomes insensitive, and sanctions murder and torture, and forgets its moral obligation.

LET US CONSIDER for a moment the instructive lesson in moral outlook of Germany twenty-five years ago, if one may do so without implying that the United States is tottering on the brink of Nazism. The worst thing that Hitler did to his country was to brutalize it. He ruined the national conscience. With the glad assistance of a signed-up mass communications system, he debauched the minds of two generations. Parading the spectre of communism up and down his country, he turned paranoia into patriotism. The people were being made ready for the great orgy, always with masscomm as the indispensable instrument.

In what ways are the situations alike, in what ways different? There is the same enemy, communism. There is the same concentration of industrial-military might. There are the same dreadful paradoxes dressed in newspeak, for example, calling acts of war acts of peace. The invasion of other countries is justified by appeals to national honor and security. Hitler had a final solution and used it on six million human beings. We have a final solution ready if all else fails, nuclear war. The difference in scale is impressive. It took Hitler many years, many people, many pits, gallows, and ovens to achieve his final solution. With far fewer helping hands and in one-thousandth the time we can exterminate fifty times as many people.

I do not suggest that it is the duty of masscomm to agree either with my analysis of where we stand in the race between genocide and humanity, or with my remedies. Its obligation is far greater: to remain disengaged from the apparatus, to criticize its aims and its claims, to keep ethical issues in clear view, to let the citizenry know what is happening to them as they lean more and more on muscle and less and less on mind; and, above all, to stay out of the cheering section. The press was guaranteed its freedom almost two hundred years ago so that it could keep an unwinking eye on government. The irony today is the degree to which it has become the apparatus's main support. Whatever sanity is entering U.S. policies in the Far East is coming via teach-ins and demonstrations, not via masscomm. I believe that our chance of becoming involved in nuclear war is directly proportionate to the shared warmth of the masscomm-in-dustrial-military-government axis. The heat is already intense.

Self-righteousness is a wonderfully effective emotion for brutalizing a nation, and there is no agent superior to masscomm for filling the reservoir of national self-righteousness. The apparatus, abetted by masscomm, needs to be able to call on two ingredients. First, great economic and military strength, preferably massive enough to be a source of embarrassment and guilt. These sensations cry out to be transmuted into something worthy, and masscomm obliges by making our overwhelming capacity for violence appear to be the gift of a far-seeing Providence. Thus we become the policeman of the world, with hosannas from masscomm for our manliness.

Second, we need an enemy—not just any old enemy, but one who is sinister, conspiring, terroristic, atheistic, power-hungry, monolithic, anti-human, and un-human. We possess this ingredient, too. How much this enemy is genuine historical development and how much a U.S. manufacture is something that history will have to decide. My view is that the enemy is in many respects a product of masscomm, especially in attributing to him those capabilities which make him seem so much smarter, stronger, and less human than Americans are. It seems to me an open question whether the apparatus and masscomm have gone to all the trouble of helping to fabricate such a terrible and terrifying enemy only to learn that somehow they have got hold of the wrong fellow. We are slowly beginning to see, despite masscomm, that nationalism and hunger are the true rascals. The chronic revolution that we shall all spend the rest of our lives enduring and trying to understand is no more a product of communism than a toothache is a product of the dentist's chair, or a neurosis the infliction of the psychoanalyst's couch.

But this is not what we learn from masscomm. Editors and publishers and broadcasters notoriously like uncomplicated views. Communism and the Communists are such satisfactory villain material too, stubborn, eccentric, close-mouthed, suspicious, that they can be used as excuses for any amount of immoral behavior. This is not to say that there are no genuine clashes of interest and principle, nor that Communists are particularly comfortable people to have around, either in the neighborhood or in the world. It is not to say either that masscomm in this country is alone guilty of enemy-fabricating, for we know its foreign counterparts are every bit as adept in the art. It is indeed one of the curiosities of our time that it is so hard to see much difference between controlled and uncontrolled masscomm in this respect. Both are vehicles—especially where the issues of war and peace are concerned—for ". . . all the smelly little orthodoxies now contending for our souls," as George Orwell pointed out.

We are here close to the crux of the matter. A signed-up system of masscomm is bound to present an unreal view of the world. This has consequences ranging from the merely mortifying to the possibly lethal. Thus we have, at the one side, got ourselves in the horrible box of identifying all "national liberation'' movements with communism, thus raising the status of Communists as incorrigible adventurers and military expansionists may lead us into the final big war.

HERE WE ENCOUNTER masscomm's first and last line of defense against irresponsibility: We give the customers what they want. We are, masscomm declares, stockbrokers of the national passions. Assuming as I do that masscomm's responsibility is primarily that of continuing liberal education, I do not take the defense seriously. Liberal education is education befitting a free man, and tending to make him more competent in the exercise of his responsibilities. Liberal education aims at improving the intelligence and sharpening perceptions of good and bad. There is no such thing as education, liberal or otherwise, based on the lowest common denominator, except the education of slaves and vassals.

Anyone acquainted with the literature of masscomm knows that the dispute about the validity of its appeal to democratic dogma is endless, the apologists for masscomm tirelessly intone the obligation to give the customer what he wants. The equating of audience ratings and circulation figures with political principles seems to me defective. But I do not propose to add much to this ancient rhubarb here, except to indicate a significant paradox. The democratic thesis is that of consent, participation, and improvement. Citizens agree to the basic structure and direction of the nation. They take part directly and indirectly in its governance, and have no choice except to do so. The commonwealth is supposed to move onward and upward as a result.

But if the customers decide what they want to see, hear, and read, and if the customers appear to want mainly piffle, what happens to their competence for self-government? What if the tendency of masscomm is to make difficult and in some cases impossible the conditions for self-government? In his book, *Not in the Public Interest,* David Williams says, ''An informed public opinion is the essential element in a country which claims to be democratic.'' But what is needed is not only information about yesterday's Congress and traffic accidents, but information about those crucial developments and those significant shadows on the horizon now seldom finding reflection in masscomm. I acknowledge that the country is somehow limping onward, despite the failures of masscomm and other great national institutions. But ''We're getting by'' is not a satisfactory answer either, for the ultimate questions are whether self-government is really working or is being turned over to elites and machines; and whether the criterion of consistent improvement is being met.

There is a variation in masscomm's answer about giving the customer what he wants. Masscomm says that it does not create social emptiness and cultural chaos, but merely reports what it finds. Masscomm portrays itself as the demotic conduit of social intelligence. ''Too bad,'' it says, ''that so much sludge passes through the conduit.'' Also, the answer continues, it is not the fault of masscomm that people prefer fantasy to fact and—this is always asserted with

great emphasis—it is not masscomm's problem but theirs if people prefer entertainment to clarification.

Masscomm's great delusion is self-delusion. It deludes itself that because
other institutions, the educational apparatus and the family among them, also
mould the community, masscomm does not really have any decisive effect on
social conditions and cultural development. This is why it can, in all in-
nocence, look under every bed but its own in a search for the explanation of
crime, vandalism, and race riots. This is why it accepts no institutional responsibility for the rape of rivers and forests, and for the bloodthirsty campaigns of
the right wing.

Another virulent species of self-delusion is masscomm's stated conviction
that it can meet the full range of its social and cultural responsibilities in spite
of its attachment to the highly favored sectors of the community. It is like trying to bunt toward third while standing on your head. Masscomm is, to repeat,
a fully paid-up member of the American palatinate, the confederation of the
powerful and privileged. Its loyalty and interest run to institutions, not to people. This signifies the bankruptcy of the educational function, where people are
the essence of the teacher-and-taught transaction. Self-delusion persuades masscomm that it is meeting its obligations when it is making money, and that its
critics are wrong in some sort of ratio to the margin of profit.

The best one can conclude, and also the worst, is that masscomm does not
know any better, and that it assumes it is doing as well as anyone has a right to
expect in functioning as the viaticum of privilege.

I WOULD MODERATE the severity of these remarks if some motion toward improvement could be discerned. I see little or none. After every social calamity—the race eruption, the escalation of crime, an American war against
Asians—acres of print and hours of network time are allotted to explanation
and analysis. For such performance, which becomes a little better as calamity
becomes more frequent, we owe brief thanks. But masscomm has not yet
learned the simple lesson that the time to deal with catastrophe is before it happens, and the companion lesson that in this respect it has very great responsibilities indeed.

In this anticipatory role its performance ranges from nil to silly. The upris-
ing of the California students was a masscomm scandal. But the problem at
Berkeley had been forming for years; President Clark Kerr described the causes
in a celebrated book months before the event. From the earliest flickerings of
trouble, masscomm misunderstood and misstated what was going on. Thus
must gratitude for the good post mortem be balanced with condemnation for
ante mortem bad performance.

It must be asked, therefore, where else one might look for the positive assumption of social and cultural responsibility, that is, for the shifting of taste
and sensibility and the general welfare to higher levels. One would hope first
that as more people are better educated, the result would be a general elevation.

The rising trade in concerts, good books and records, museums, and discussion groups is adduced as a fair wind already blowing from this quarter.

One would hope for the continuation of demonstrations, which by now are accepted as the "free press" of the movement to win justice for Negroes, to banish impersonality from the university and the corporation, and to spread the word that peace, not violence, is the only possible destiny for a nuclear-knowing world.

One would hope for the calling of a Constitutional Convention to get out into the open the great tangle of eighteenth century ideals and twentieth century conditions which produces the fundamental perplexities of our time. A Constitutional Convention would have to appraise masscomm and determine its fitness to continue under present immunities and privileges.

One would hope, without any good reason for doing so, that there might be a wholesale reform in the great Corporate Community, with priorities changed, in the words of the Administration, from "the quantity of our goods [to the] quality of our lives."

Perhaps no more utopian than these suggestions is the notion that the managers of masscomm might themselves, in the light of the enormous and increasing difficulties confronting the country, undertake a regeneration. They are after all not malevolent, or less patriotic and concerned about the fate of the commonwealth than anyone else. They are stuck in a system from which they could, given massive will, unstick themselves.

Yet these therapies are probably too unreal or drastic to be considered, and we shall have mainly to look to government, the resort when all else fails. Alexander Meiklejohn, one of this country's mightiest educators, was perhaps the most devoted friend that masscomm has ever had. Throughout his ninety-odd years he battled relentlessly for an absolute reading of the First Amendment. Precisely because he was an educator he saw in an unfettered system of mass communications the means of carrying out the social and cultural responsibilities available to no other institution. He saw mass communications as the necessary companion to his dream of lifelong liberal education. But just before he died a few months ago Mr. Meiklejohn perceived that the theory was failing, or had failed. So he proposed that his cherished First Amendment be revised by adding the words:

"In view of the intellectual and cultural responsibilities laid upon the citizens of a free society by the political institutions of self-government, the Congress, acting in cooperation with the several states and with non-governmental organizations serving the same general purpose, shall have power to provide for the intellectual and cultural education of all of the citizens of the United States."

The adoption of such a revision would express an official commitment to fill the holes left by masscomm in the continuing education of citizens. It would clear the way (if indeed the way needs to be cleared) for the establishment by government of a public network. Masscomm needs competition, contrast, example; the citizen needs alternatives and visions of better possibilities in his education as an adult.

But I have no idea whether affirmative government of the kind foreshadowed in such suggestions would work. What is significant to me in Mr. Meiklejohn's proposal is the inference that the private motors we have counted on to propel us constantly into a finer community are virtually out of gas.

IT WILL BE PROTESTED that I ask too much. The answer is that my demands are those made of liberal education wherever it is being conducted. It will be complained that all of the foregoing is a statement of personal predilections as to the proper course of society. I shall say that this is true, and grant further that I have a different opinion of Americans and their aspirations from masscomm's opinion of them. At the same time I assert that I have been expressing a general view.

I believe there is in this nation a rising awareness of the tendency toward demoralization of the common life; a growing appreciation that citizenship is more important than consumership; an increasing fear that the human being will be lost beneath the lumber of technology and bureaucracy; a quickening guilt about the friendless, the impoverished, the victims of wholesale injustice; a widening comprehension that getting richer is not synonymous with getting better; an impatience with half-truths and semi-realities. And I believe that I speak in some way for this forming consensus. If mass communications can catch a glimpse of this other yearning America, there is a chance, perhaps a very slight one, that they may yet share in the making of an active, moral democratic order, in the United States and the world.

Edward Jay Epstein:

The American Press: Some Truths About Truths

THE PROBLEM of journalism in America proceeds from a simple but inescapable bind: Journalists are rarely, if ever, in a position to establish the truth about an issue for themselves, and they are therefore almost entirely dependent on self-interested "sources" for the version of reality that they report. Walter Lippmann pointed to the root of the problem more than 50 years ago when he made a painful distinction between "news" and truth. "The function of news is to signalize an event, the function of truth is to bring to light the hidden facts, to set them into relation with each other, and make a picture of reality on which men can act."

Because news reporting and truth seeking have different ultimate purposes, Lippmann postulated that "news" could be expected to coincide with truth in only a few limited areas, such as the scores of baseball games or elections, where the results are definite and measurable. In the more complex and ambiguous recesses of political life, where the outcome is almost always in doubt or dispute, news reports could not be expected to exhaust, or perhaps even indicate, the truth of the matter.

This divergence between news and truth stemmed not from the inadequacies of newsmen but from the exigencies of the news business, which limited the time, space, and resources that could be allotted to any single story. Lippmann concluded pessimistically that if the public required a more truthful interpretation of the world they lived in, they would have to depend on institutions other than the press.

Pursuers of Truth

Contemporary journalists would have some difficulty accepting such a distinction between news and truth. Indeed, newsmen now almost invariably depict themselves not merely as reporters of the fragments of information that come their way, but as active pursuers of the truth.

Mr. Epstein is the author of *News From Nowhere,* a study of television news coverage. He is one of America's most perceptive press critics. This article is reprinted from *The National Observer* (*April 20, 1974*) where it was reprinted from *Commentary,* copyright 1974, The American Jewish Committee. Reprinted here by permission.

In the current rhetoric of journalism, "stenographic reporting," where the reporter simply but accurately repeats what he has been told, is a pejorative term used to describe inadequate journalism; "investigative reporting," on the other hand, where the reporter supposedly ferrets out a hidden truth, is an honorific enterprise to which all journalists are supposed to aspire. In the post-Watergate era, moreover, even critics of the press attribute to it powers of discovery that go well beyond reporting new developments.

Yet despite the energetic claims of the press, the limits of journalism described by Lippmann still persist in basically the same form. Individual journalists may be better educated and motivated today than they were 50 years ago, but newspapers still have strict deadlines, which limit the time that can be spent investigating a story; a restricted number of news "holes," which limit the space that can be devoted to elucidating the details of an event; and fixed budgets, which limit the resources that can be used on any single piece of reportage. Today, as when Lippmann wrote, "The final page is of a definite size [and] must be ready at a precise moment."

Under these conditions, it would be unreasonable to expect even the most resourceful journalist to produce anything more than a truncated version of reality. Beyond this, however, even if such restraints were somehow suspended, and journalists had unlimited time, space, and financial resources at their disposal, they would still lack the forensic means and authority to establish the truth about a matter in serious dispute.

Certified 'Bona Fides'

Grand juries, prosecutors, judges, and legislative committees can compel witnesses to testify before them—offering the inducement of immunity to reluctant witnesses and the threat of perjury and contempt actions to inconsistent witnesses; they can subpoena records and other evidence, and test it all through cross-examination and other rigorous processes. Similarly, scientists, doctors, and other experts can establish facts in a disputed area, especially when there is unanimous agreement on the results of a particular test or analysis, because their authority and technical expertise are accepted in their distinct spheres of competency. Such authority derives from the individual reputation of the expert, certification of his *bona fides* by a professional group which is presumed to have a virtual monopoly of knowledge over the field, and a clearly articulated factfinding procedure (such as was used, for instance, in establishing the erasures on the Nixon tapes).

Even in more problematic areas, like the social sciences, academic researchers can resolve disputed issues. Acceptance of such an academic verdict, however, will depend heavily on the qualifications of the researcher, the degree to which his sources are satisfactorily documented, and the process of review by other scholars in the field through which, presumably, objections to the thesis are articulated and errors corrected. In all cases, a necessary (though not sufficient) condition for establishing the truth is the use of an acceptable procedure for examining, testing, and evaluating evidence.

Reporters possess no such wherewithal for dealing with evidence. Unlike the judicial officer, journalists cannot compel a witness to furnish them an account of an event. Witnesses need only tell reporters what they deem is in their own self-interest, and then they can lie or fashion their story to fit a particular purpose without risking any legal penalty. Nor can a journalist test an account by hostile cross-examination without jeopardizing the future cooperation of the witness.

Indeed, given the voluntary nature of the relationship between a reporter and his source, a continued flow of information can only be assured if the journalist's stories promise to serve the interest of the witness (which precludes impeaching the latter's credibility).

In recent years, journalists have cogently argued that if they are forced to testify before grand juries about their sources, they will be cut off from further information. The same logic applies with equal force to criticizing harshly or casting doubts on the activities of these sources. The misreporting of a series of violent incidents involving the Black Panthers in 1969 is a case in point: The reporters closest to the Black Panthers could not dispute their public claim that an organized campaign of genocide was being waged against them without jeopardizing the special access they had to Panther spokesmen.

Moreover, since journalists generally lack the technical competence to evaluate evidence with any authority, they must also rely on the reports of authoritative institutions for their "facts." A reporter cannot establish the existence of an influenza epidemic, for instance, by conducting medical examinations himself; he must rely on the pronouncement of the Department of Health. (A journalist may of course become a doctor, but then his authority for reporting a fact rests on his scientific rather than journalistic credentials.)

Whenever a journalist attempts to establish a factual proposition on his own authority, his conclusion must be open to question.

For example, following the overthrow of the Allende government in Chile in 1973, *Newsweek* carried a dramatic report by a correspondent who claimed to have gained entrance to the Santiago morgue and personally examined the bodies of those killed after the coup. By inspecting the hands of the corpses, and the nature of their wounds, the correspondent concluded that these were workers with calloused hands who had been brutally executed.

When *The Wall Street Journal* challenged these findings (on the basis of inconsistencies in the description of the morgue), the reporter acknowledged that he personally had spent only two minutes on the scene, and *Newsweek* fell back on an earlier unpublished report of a United Nations observer who claimed to have witnessed something similar in the Santiago morgue at some different time. While the dispute remained unsettled, the burden of proof was shifted from *Newsweek's* own reporter to an outside "authority."

Identity of Sources

Finally, journalists cannot even claim the modicum of authority granted to academic researchers because they cannot fulfill the requirement of always identifying their sources, let alone documenting their claims. Protecting (and concealing) the identity of their informants is a real concern for journalists, and one on which their livelihood might well depend, but it also distinguishes the journalistic from the academic product. Without identifiable sources the account cannot be reviewed or corroborated by others with specialized knowledge of the subject. Even the most egregious errors may thus remain uncorrected.

For instance, in what purported to be an interview with John W. Dean III, the President's former counsel, *Newsweek* reported that Dean would reveal in his public testimony that some White House officials had planned to assassinate Panama's head of government, but that the plan was aborted at the last minute. This *Newsweek* "exclusive" was circulated to thousands of newspapers in an advance press release, and widely published. When it turned out that the story was untrue—Dean did not testify about any such assassination plot, and denied under oath that he had discussed any substantial aspects of his testimony with *Newsweek* reporters—*Newsweek* did not correct or explain the discrepancy. Presumably, Dean was not the source for the putative "Dean Interview," and the unidentified source had misled *Newsweek* on what Dean was planning to say in his public testimony. Since the error was that of an unidentified source, *Newsweek* did not feel obligated to correct it in future editions.

It is not necessary to belabor the point that gathering news is a very different enterprise from establishing truth, with different standards and objectives. Journalists readily admit that they are dependent on others for privileged information and the ascertainment of facts in a controversial issue (although some might argue that the sphere of measurable and noncontroversial issues is larger than I suggest).

Finding Sources

Indeed, many of the most eminent journalists in America submitted affidavits in the Pentagon Papers case attesting that "leaks" and confidential sources are indispensable elements in the reporting of national news. And despite the more heroic public claims of the news media, daily journalism is largely concerned with finding and retaining profitable sources of prepackaged stories (whether it be the Weather Bureau, the Dow Jones financial wire service, public-relations agencies, or a confidential source within the Government).

What is now called "investigative reporting" is merely the development of sources within the counterelite or other dissidents in the Government, while "stenographic reporting" refers to the development of sources among official spokesmen for the Government. There is no difference in the basic method of reporting.

Even in the case of Watergate, which has become synonymous with "investigative reporting," it was the investigative agencies of the Government and not the members of the press who assembled the evidence, which was then deliberately leaked to receptive reporters at the *Washington Post,* the *Los Angeles Times, Time,* and other journals.

Within a week after the burglars were caught in Watergate in June 1972, FBI agents had identified the leaders of the break-in as employes of the Committee to Re-elect the President (and former employes of the White House), traced the hundred-dollar bills found in their possession to funds contributed to President Nixon's re-election campaign, and interviewed one of the key conspirators, Alfred Baldwin, who in effect turned state's evidence, describing the wire-tapping operation in great detail and revealing that the transcripts had been delivered directly to CRP headquarters.

'Horror Stories'

This evidence, which was presented to the grand jury (and eventually in open court), was systematically leaked by investigative agents in the case. (Why members of the FBI and the Department of Justice had become dissidents is another question.) The crucial evidence which the FBI investigation did not turn up—such as the earlier burglary of Ellsberg's psychiatrist, the offers of executive clemency, the intervention with the Central Intelligence Agency, the suborning of perjury, the cash pay-offs made from campaign contributions, the "enemies list," and the 1970 subversion-control plan—came out not through "investigative reporting," but only when one of the burglars, John McCord, revealed his role in the cover-up to Judge John Sirica and when John Dean virtually defected to the U.S. prosecutor and disclosed the White House "horror stories."

Indeed, it was John Dean, not the enterprising reporters of the Washington press corps, who was the real author of most of the revelations that are at the heart of the present Federal conspiracy indictments and the impeachment inquest. (And it was Ralph Nader, another nonjournalist, who unearthed the contributions from the milk industry.)

To be sure, by serving as conduits for the interested parties who wanted to release information about Watergate and other White House abuses of power, journalists played an extremely important role in the political process—but not as investigators or establishers of the truth.

The reliance on "leaks" or "authoritative" sources might not be an insoluble problem for journalism if reporters had some means of evaluating them in advance, and publishing only those portions which did not distort reality, by being either untrue or out of context. Unfortunately, however, the inherent pressures of daily journalism severely reduce the possibility of verifying a leak or disclosure in advance of publication. Reporters can, of course, seek out more than one source on an issue, but there is no satisfactory way available, other than intuition, to choose among conflicting accounts. The democratic criterion of adding up, confirming, and disconfirming interviews, as if they were votes, produces no decisive result, as even total agreement might simply mean that a false account had been widely circulated, while total disagreement might mean that only the original source was privy to the truth about an event.

Evaluating Leaks

"Plausibility" is also an unsatisfactory criterion for evaluating leaks, since the liar is always capable of fashioning his account to fit the predispositions of the journalist to whom he is disclosing it, and thereby to make it appear plausible. Nor can a reporter simply give weight to the source that is most intimately involved with the issue, since those closest to a dispute might have the greatest interest in distorting or neglecting aspects of it, and might well be the least impartial.

In certain instances, leaks, if publication were delayed, could be tested by the direction of unfolding events—for example, the advance disclosure of John Dean's testimony could have been refuted if *Newsweek* had delayed its story until Dean actually testified—but such a procedure would undercut the far more basic journalistic value of signaling the probable direction of events before they fully unfold.

Given these circumstances, a journalist has little basis for choosing among conflicting sources. The *New York Times* thus carried two completely contradictory reports of the same insurrection in the Philippines in different sections of the same Sunday edition (Feb. 17, 1974). The News of the Week section placed the casualties at 10,000 dead or missing, while the general-news section refuted this higher figure and placed the total casualties at 276. Both accounts were based on sources within the Philippine government, and the editor of each section simply chose the account he preferred.

When journalists are presented with secret information about issues of great import, they become, in a very real sense, agents for the surreptitious source. Even if the disclosure is supported by authoritative documents, the journalist cannot know whether the information has been altered, edited, or selected out of context. Nor can he be certain what interest he is serving or what will be the eventual outcome of the leak.

Consider, for example, the disclosures by the columnist Jack Anderson of the minutes of a secret National Security Council meeting on the 1971 Indo-Pakistani War for which he was awarded the Pulitzer Prize for national reporting. Anderson claimed that the blunt orders by Dr. Henry Kissinger in these private meetings to "tilt" toward Pakistan contradicted Kissinger's public professions of neutrality; this claim received wide circulation, and sharply undermined Kissinger's credibility (although *The Wall Street Journal* demonstrated by printing the public statements to which Anderson referred that Kissinger was in fact consistent in both his private and public statements in expressing opposition to the Indian military incursion into East Pakistan).

Source of Leak

At the time it was generally presumed that the leak came from a dissident within the Administration who favored India, or, at least, opposed the Administration's policy in the subcontinent. Only two years afterward, as a by-product of the Watergate investigation, was some light cast on the source of the leak.

A White House investigation identified Charles E. Radford, a Navy yeoman, who was working at the time as a stenographer, as the proximate source of the National Security Council minutes supplied to Anderson. But the investigation further revealed that Yeoman Radford was also copying and transmitting to members of the Joint Chiefs of Staff highly classified documents in a "surreptitious operation" apparently designed to keep them aware of Kissinger's (and the President's) negotiations.

And Yeoman Radford has testified that he acted only on the express orders of the Joint Chiefs of Staff, and not on his own initiative, in passing documents. If this is indeed the case, it would appear that members of the Joint Chiefs of Staff authored the Anderson leak in order to undermine the authority of Henry Kissinger (who was involved in developing the *détente* with China and Russia at that time).

A Pawn in the Game

In this case, Anderson was used as an instrument in a power struggle he probably was unaware of—and which might have had nothing to do with the Indo-Pakistani War he was reporting on.

The important question is not whether journalists are deviously manipulated by their sources, but whether they can exert any real control over disclosures wrenched from contexts to which they do not have access or with which they are unfamiliar.

In most circumstances, the logic of daily journalism impels immediate publication which, though it might result in a prized "scoop," divorces the journalist from responsibility for the veracity or consequences of the disclosure. Jack Anderson was thus able to explain a blatantly false report he published about the arrest for drunken driving of Sen. Thomas Eagleton, then Vice Presidential nominee of the Democratic Party, by saying that if he had delayed publication to check the allegation he would have risked being scooped by competitors.

But even in rare cases in which newspapers allot time and manpower to study a leak, as the *New York Times* did in the case of the Pentagon Papers, the information still must be revised into a form and format which will maintain the interest of the readers (as well as the editors). Since the *Times* decided not to print the entire study of the Vietnam War—which ran to more than 7,000 pages and covered a 25-year period—or even substantial parts of the narrative, which was complex and academic, sections of the material had to be reorganized and rewritten along a theme that would be comprehensible to its audience.

Reader Interest

The theme chosen was duplicity: the difference between what the leaders of America said about the Vietnam War in private and in public. The Pentagon study, however, was not written in line with this theme. It was an official Department of Defense analysis of decision-making and, more precisely, of how policy preferences crystallized within the department.

To convert this bureaucratic study into a journalistic expose of duplicity required taking certain liberties with the original history: Outside material had to be added, and assertions from the actual study had to be omitted.

For example, to show that the Tonkin Gulf resolution (by which in effect Congress authorized the escalation of the war, and which was editorially endorsed at the time by most major newspapers, including the *New York Times* and the *Washington Post*) resulted from duplicity, the *Times* had to omit the conclusion of the Pentagon Papers that the Johnson Administration had tried to avoid the fatal clash in the Tonkin Gulf, and had to add evidence of possible American provocations in Laos, which were not actually referred to in the Pentagon Papers themselves.

Journalists, then, are caught in a dilemma. They can either serve as a faithful messenger for some subterranean interest, or they can recast the message into their own version of the story by adding, deleting, or altering material.

The first alternative assures that the message will be accurately relayed to the intended audience, although the message itself might be false or misleading.

The latter alternative, while lessening the source's control over the message, increases the risk of further distortion, since the journalist cannot be aware of the full context and circumstances surrounding the disclosure.

In neither case can journalists be certain of either the truth or the intended purpose of what they publish.

Tension of Dilemma

Such a dilemma cannot be remedied by superior newsmen or more intensive journalistic training. It arises not out of defects in the practice of journalism, but out of the source-reporter relationship which is part and parcel of the structure of modern journalism.

To some degree, the tension in the dilemma could be alleviated if journalists gave up the pretense of being establishers of truth, recognized themselves as agents for others who desired to disclose information, and clearly labeled the circumstances and interests behind the information they reported so that it could be intelligently evaluated.

By concealing the machinations and politics behind a leak, journalists suppress part of the truth surrounding the story. Thus the means by which the medical records of Sen. Thomas Eagleton were acquired and passed on to the Knight newspapers (which won the 1973 Pulitzer Prize for disclosing information contained in these records) seem no less important than the senator's medical history itself, especially since copies of the presumably illegally obtained records were later found in the White House safe of John Ehrlichman.

(In rifling through Larry O'Brien's personal files, the Watergate burglars were probably looking for material damaging to O'Brien and the Democrats; if they had succeeded, such material would no doubt have found its way into print by being leaked to "investigative journalists.")

The Unreported Part

Similarly, the motives and circumstances behind the well-timed leaks to the press by elements in the Nixon Administration which ultimately forced Justice Abe Fortas from the Supreme Court do not necessarily make a less important part of the story than any of the alleged improprieties committed by Fortas. And the leaks provided by senior executives in the FBI and other investigative agencies in an attempt to resist White House domination still remain the unreported part of the Watergate story.

Since journalists cannot expose these hidden aspects of a story without damaging the sources they are dependent on for information (and honors), they cannot realistically be expected to label the interest behind any disclosure.

(Indeed, it is a practice among journalists to mislead their readers by explicitly denying as occasion arises that they received information from their real source.)

Under these conditions, journalism can serve as an important institution for conveying and circulating information, and signaling changes in the direction of public policy and discourse, but it cannot serve as a credible investigator of the "hidden facts" or the elusive truths which determine them.

Donald McDonald:

Is Objectivity Possible?

> *Truth and politics are on rather bad terms with*
> *each other. No one, as far as I know, has ever*
> *counted truthfulness among the political virtues.*
> *. . . Seen from the viewpoint of politics, truth has a*
> *despotic character. It is therefore hated by tyrants,*
> *who rightly fear the competition of a coercive*
> *force they cannot monopolize, and it enjoys a*
> *rather precarious status in the eyes of governments*
> *that rest on consent and abhor coercion.*
> —HANNAH ARENDT

THE ANTIDOTE FOR political deviousness is journalistic integrity. Since truthfulness is not a political virtue, it has to be a journalistic virtue.

But perhaps integrity and truthfulness are terms that are too morally intense, too loaded with accusatory implications for an analysis aimed at discovering both the enabling and limiting elements in the practice of public-affairs journalism. Journalistic objectivity is a better term. Badly misunderstood and badly applied as it has been in the history of American journalism, objectivity subsumes all the mass-communication virtues—moral, artistic, and intellectual. It covers the individual journalist and the institution that employs him. And while it is a goal it is also a process, a kind of operational guideline, a demanding but not impossibly idealistic criterion of professional competence.

Objectivity (not to be confused with objectivism, a specialized and technical philosophical theory of knowledge) is here used to mean simply an essential correspondence between knowledge of a thing and the thing itself. The best translation of the term into its journalistic application may have been furnished by the Freedom of the Press Commission in 1947. The Commission said that, among other things, the press owes to society "a truthful, comprehensive, and intelligent account of the day's events in a context which gives them meaning."

Mr. McDonald is editor of *The Center Magazine* and former dean of the Marquette University College of Journalism. This article is reprinted from *The Center Magazine* (Center for the Study of Democratic Institutions, Santa Barbara, Calif.), Vol. IV, No. 5, Sept./Oct., 1971.

I suppose that no reporter or editor would take exception to such a definition of the journalist's responsibility. Not many reporters get up in the morning and say to themselves, "Today I am going to file a lying, incomplete, ignorant report of an event taken out of context." But then how account for the quality of public-affairs journalism in this country? Arthur R. Murphy, the former chairman of *McCall's* magazine, has said that in spite of our ten thousand newspapers, eight thousand magazines, and seven thousand radio and television stations, Americans suffer from an "understanding gap" and are "ill-informed and confused about major issues and events."

Objectivity is problematic in public-affairs journalism because elements and practices in the reporting process are taken for granted and perpetuated by journalists when they should be critically examined. The reporter, the reader-viewer, the conventions of American journalism, the forms and processes of the communications institutions, language, the investigative and interpretive functions of the reporter, all affect the objectivity of mass communication. A misunderstanding or malfunctioning of any of them is enough to defeat or at least seriously impair the efforts of even the most nobly motivated journalist.

LET US BEGIN with the reporter. From the myriad of details of an event or situation, the reporter selects those which seem to him most significant, investigates and asks questions to clarify the meaning of what he has perceived, and then organizes his knowledge in a report. What the reporter selects for attention, the weight he puts on the various elements, the kinds of questions he asks, are all influenced by the personal history he brings to his work.

Indeed, even what he initially preceives is conditioned by his history. Some years ago, Dr. Robert Livingston, then with the National Institute of Mental Health, on a visit to the Center, reported that experiments by neuro-surgeons and neurophysiologists indicate that man's entire nervous system, in its interpreting, sensing, and transmitting to the brain the information it receives, builds up through the years total-response patterns which, as they stabilize, thenceforth affect in a definite accept-reject manner the perceiving capacity of a person.

We are familiar with the classic psychological and sociological experiments testing the ability of students to perceive, recall, and report staged dramatic incidents they have witnessed. The wildly varying reports of the same incident reflect what Walter Lippmann has called the tricks of memory and the incessant creative quality of the imagination of the witness.

According to Lippmann, experience seems to show that the reporter brings something to the scene which later he takes away from it. A report is the joint product of the knower and the known, in which the role of the observer is always selective and usually creative. The facts we see depend on where we are placed and the habits of our eyes.

A few years ago, when Lillian Ross's book, *Reporting,* appeared, her publisher claimed that one never doubts that what she sees is the truth. But a reviewer in the *Times Literary Supplement* demurred. "One eyewitness," the reviewer said, "tells us what she has seen and heard and put together; it is not the truth about anything, but one person's selection from the chaos of facts, images, words, all the ingredients of experience she has witnessed from her single viewpoint. We might guess more about the truth or at least the heart of the matter, all the omissions and distortions, if we knew more about the reporter, her psychological blocks, and the limits of her experience, but it is a conceit of this school of reporting to pretend to omit the reporter. The reporter, however, is human and therefore limited, and if we have no knowledge of her limitations we are merely being deceived."

The reviewer went on to say that "James Agee was at the opposite extreme as a reporter. He wrote in perhaps the greatest work of reportage of this century, *Let Us Now Praise Famous Men,* about a tenant farmer: 'I know him only so far as I know him: and all of that depends as fully on who I am as on who he is.' Thus Agee accepted, as Miss Ross apparently does not, that any subject is sieved through a reporter's self and, therefore, Agee showed the interplay between himself and the people and places he was trying to describe."

Now, whether Miss Ross rejects what Mr. Agee accepted, and whether or how it would be feasible for every reporter to reveal within every report his "psychological blocks and the limits of his experience," and whether Miss Ross's reporting is "not the truth about anything" are all arguable. What is not deniable is the sieving process through which reality must pass in the reporter's work. The question is, how can reality emerge from this subjective process without being essentially diminished and distorted? I do not think the answer lies simply in the reporter's showing the interplay between himself and the things he is reporting. At best this permits the reader to discount the report for its acknowledged subjective elements, but it leaves him waiting for a more satisfying, more objective, less distorted account of public affairs.

When the reporter moves from relatively uncomplicated, concrete, even physical phenomena into the realm of the abstract and the complex—i.e., studies, conferences, programs, policies on urban affairs, race and ethnic relations, foreign and military affairs, economic and fiscal conditions, the administration of criminal justice, cultural ferment, youth unrest, population problems, environmental issues, politics, and government—the value judgments he must make at every critical stage in his investigation and interpretation of the facts must reflect the values he already holds. Again, these values flow from his personal history. They are the products of his education, his religious experience, his childhood, family life, social and economic background, friendships and associations, national ties and culture, as well as his emotional life and experiences, and his reason.

Take just one of the value-influences in the reporter's life: his national ties. Both individual reports of the Vietnam war and over-all coverage have differed markedly from nation to nation. This cannot be attributed altogether to external censorship. I. F. Stone once noted that an Associated Press dispatch on American military, political, and diplomatic activity in Vietnam, prepared for publication in the French newspaper, *Le Monde,* contained material far more critical of the United States than anything filed by the A.P. for consumption in American newspapers.

A book by Jay Epstein raised serious questions about the Warren Commission's investigation of the Kennedy assassination. Richard Rovere has said that Epstein is a scholar who had done what the American press should have done when the Warren Commission report was issued. "It should have cast a very cool eye on the report and sought to learn from those who prepared it how it was prepared, who did the heavy work, and what individual workers thought of the collective product. Mr. Epstein's scholarly tools happen to be those employed day in and day out by journalists. But the press left it to a single scholar to find the news."

Epstein suggested that a kind of national loyalty seems to have got in the way of the journalists and their reporting obligation. They produced a "version of the truth . . . to reassure the nation and protect the national interest."

George Orwell's classic essay, "Politics and the English Language," suggests not only that politics and language can be mutually degrading when in the hands of corrupt persons, but that all of us, including reporters, go along rather uncritically with the degrading process. A paragraph from Orwell's essay, written more than thirty years ago, is an uncomfortable reminder that little has changed in those three decades:

"In our time, political speech and writing are largely the defense of the indefensible. Things like the continuance of British rule in India, the Russian purges and deportations, the dropping of the atom bombs on Japan, can indeed be defended, but only by arguments which are too brutal for most people to face, and which do not square with the professed aims of political parties. Thus political language has to consist largely of euphemism, question-begging, and sheer cloudy vagueness. Defenseless villages are bombarded from the air, the inhabitants driven out into the countryside, the cattle machine-gunned, the huts set on fire with incendiary bullets: this is called *pacification.* Millions of peasants are robbed of their farms and sent trudging along the roads with no more than they can carry: this is called *transfer of population* or *rectification of frontiers.* People are imprisoned for years without trial, or shot in the back of the neck, or sent to die of scurvy in Arctic lumber camps: this is called *elimination of unreliable elements.* Such phraseology is needed if one wants to name things without calling up mental pictures of them. . . ."

No one can, or perhaps ever will, prevent politicians and political organizations from using language this way. The question is whether journalists can rise above natural allegiance to their nation and report the realities obscured by this kind of partisan euphemism.

ANOTHER ELEMENT in the reporting process affecting objectivity is the journalistic conventions, as distinguished from journalistic processes. The latter inhere in the very nature of the medium (newspaper, magazine, radio, television) and are to that extent inescapable, though sometimes they can be modified in the interest of objectivity. Journalistic conventions, however, were established to meet historical conditions. As such they can be sharply modified, or even discarded and new ones substituted when those historical conditions no longer exist, or when, again in the interest of objective reporting, the conventions are no longer useful or even obstructive. But conventions have a way of hanging on.

The most pernicious journalistic convention is the notion that a thing is not newsworthy until it becomes an event; that is, until something happens. Two things follow from this: first, significant phenomena that are not events (e.g., situations, trends, conditions) go largely unreported; second, often the context which can make even an event meaningful, is either not reported or reported inadequately.

It was not until Michael Harrington wrote his book on poverty in America (*The Other America*) that national consciousness was focused on a situation existing in the backyard of every metropolitan newspaper in the United States.

It was not until Richard Harris reported in *The New Yorker* on the unethical conditions in the ethical-drug industry that the American people were alerted to a situation that the wire services or even a metropolitan newspaper could have investigated and reported years before.

At the height of the Watts riots in 1965, a white Protestant churchman in Los Angeles shook his head and said, "I hadn't known such conditions [despair, unemployment, resentment among the blacks] existed in that area."

Even as sophisticated a newspaper as *The New York Times* has not always been able to free itself from the notion that "something has to happen" before you can publish. The May, 1966, issue of *Times Talk,* the house newsletter written by and for staff members of the *Times,* contains an article by Tom Wicker, of the *Times'* Washington bureau, on the circumstances surrounding the paper's publication that year of a series of articles on the Central Intelligence Agency. Six members of the *Times* had spent months interviewing, researching, writing, rewriting the material for those articles. At last they were ready for publication. But it seems they really were not ready.

"Turner Catledge [then executive editor of the *Times*]," Wicker said, "had insisted from the first on having an adequate news peg. Months now had passed since the 'Singapore incident' set the whole thing off. Weeks were to pass before the right time came to publish. Finally *Ramparts* magazine broke the Michigan State case, in which it was discovered that C.I.A. agents had been given cover in a big aid program the university operated for the Diem regime in South Vietnam."

Also in the news at that time was a slander suit in a Baltimore court involving a C.I.A. agent.

"Thus," Wicker continued, "with the C.I.A. in the news again, the time was ripe, public interest was awakened, and our editors thought we had the justification we needed for five articles, twenty-three thousand words in all, trying to answer the questions we had asked ourselves those long months ago. Hastily, over a weekend, we wrote the news-peg material into the pieces and gave the galley proofs a last close check for accuracy and for any updating needed."

Another convention of American journalism is that the reader interest can only be attracted by conflict, novelty, or recency. This leads the reporter to neglect that which can make his report meaningful, the context. The Los Angeles *Times,* ordinarily fastidious in its reporting of public affairs, lapsed a few years ago with some no-context reporting in its coverage of strikes by county social-welfare workers and hospital employees. The paper detailed the conflict elements in the strikes: the accusations and counteraccusations by strikers and county supervisors, the actions by pickets and nonstrikers, the threats and counterthreats. But aside from one vague reference to "working conditions" the reporters did not tell the readers the context of the strikes. The actual pay and working conditions of the workers, the level of their education, their compensation related to the nature of their work and cost of living, the history of salary increases, the comparison of pay scales with those of similar workers in other cities—none of this contextual material was furnished until a week or two later after letters had been sent to the editors pointing out the omission.

This convention—that reader interest can only be attracted and held by the bizarre, by conflict, novelty, recency—stemmed in part from the days when newspapers competed with each other for readers within the same community, when the educational level of the average American adult was low, and when the time and energy the American worker could give to informing himself on public affairs was sharply limited. Those conditions no longer exist.

There are other journalistic conventions that need reëxamination, perhaps discarding. James Reston has described, in *Foreign Affairs,* how the press associations invented the headline or all-purpose agency news story which could be published at length in the large city papers or cut in half for the middle towns or reduced to a paragraph for the very small papers. This solution to a technical problem had results nobody in the Associated Press or United Press International intended. "It tended to sharpen and inflate the news," Reston wrote. "It created a tradition of putting the most dramatic fact in the story first and then following it with paragraphs of decreasing importance. Thus it encouraged not a balanced but a startling presentation of the news, based on what one of my irreverent colleagues calls the 'Christ, how the wind blew!' lead. This was fine for the news of wrecks or murders, but was a limiting and distorting device as news of foreign policy became more and more complicated."

Reston is convinced that newspaper journalists must twist themselves around and "see these wider perspectives of the news, the causes as well as the effects. . . . Ideas are news, and are not covering the news of the mind as we should. This is where rebellion, revolution, and war start, but we minimize the conflict of ideas and emphasize the conflict in the streets, without relating the second to the first.''

I have often been struck by the way in which serious books—the "news of the mind''—are handled by the American press. When they are not ignored, they pop up in book pages, more often than not as notices rather than reviews. The idea that books such as Lewis Mumford's *The Myth of the Machine,* or Jean Gottmann's study of the metropolitan city, or Ivar Berg's *Education and Jobs: The Great Training Robbery* are important news events, or, better, serious treatments of public affairs worth reporting as such, does not occur in a climate of conventional journalistic values.

A THIRD ELEMENT in the reporting process is the thing reported. It is a commonplace that complexity is a characteristic of public affairs. Robert Lekachman, the economist, has criticized the mass media for not respecting the complexity of economic issues which, he says, almost always relate to other problems of civil rights, urbanization, transportation, education, space and science research. But with few exceptions these are reported, Lekachman says, as items of interest only to the business and financial community. Thus, a Presidential message on the budget and the economic condition of the nation— a matter of wide-ranging social, cultural, and political ramification—will be explained, if it is explained at all, in narrow terms and invariably in the business section of the newspaper.

Public-affairs issues are complex not only in their horizontal relationships with other issues but also vertically in their own historical antecedents. The meaning of American involvement in Vietnam is largely bound up with an historical sequence of events which started in the late nineteen-forties and which were themselves influenced by our obsession with communism (which had *its* antecedents), as well as with the history of Vietnam itself and that people's two-thousand-year relationship with China and its much briefer relationship with France.

Too, public-affairs issues are usually not neat, beginning-middle-and-end ''stories,'' but continually unfolding realities, and therein lies another dimension of their complexity. The reporter's accounts will be faithful to that fact if they are themselves open-ended, provisional, constantly revised as the issues play themselves out and as reactions follow actions.

The task of the objective reporter is to discover and communicate the coherence of a complex, unfolding reality. He can do it by his contextual reporting; by plainly showing the unavoidable but significant gaps in his information; by recapitulating and reviewing the reality in print when important new facts become available; by continuous surveying of the current literature which may illuminate shadowy areas; and by interviewing experts and scholars for further illumination.

Einar Ostgaard of the Peace Research Institute in Oslo and Jacques Ellul, the French social critic, are not the only ones to have commented on the discontinuities in the mass media's presentation of great public issues. But none have made the point more sharply.

Ostgaard traces the discontinuities to the way the media define newsworthiness. As long as news must have a certain simplicity, easy reader identification, closeness in either a physical or cultural sense, and excitement—as long as this kind of news barrier is in effect, there will be little or no continuity in the presentation of world events.

"Certain news media," Ostgaard writes, "will attempt to present a continuous report of what happens. But as long as a decision on whether or not to publish a story is also based on [the above] considerations, the result must be a certain degree of discontinuity. . . . A report from London may appear on a Monday, drop out of sight on Tuesday and Wednesday for lack of space (although the news agencies are still dutifully reporting), reappear on Thursday, but by now [there is] a mystery since what went on in the interim was never published."

The interim developments were omitted "because these happenings were no longer 'news.' Proximity in time is often a major prerequisite for a news story. Thus, the shorter the time it takes for an event 'to happen' the more likely it is to be reported fully, and conversely, the longer the time it takes, the larger the probabilities that only an incomplete picture of the event will be presented. This time factor is also probably related to the degree to which the event will appear to be exciting and this contributes to the 'sensationalism' factor."

Ostgaard quotes from Bernard Cohen's study of the matter: "In hopping from issue to issue, from crisis to crisis, the correspondent deals in political discontinuities" and gives a "grossly uneven, often misleading picture of the world and its political relationships and problems. . . . So far from reflecting difficult international realities as they confront the statesman [such reporting] has no politically relevant public-opinion uses. . . . If the reporting of developments in terms of conflict exacerbates conflict, then, *mutatis mutandis,* the simplification of foreign-affairs reporting exacerbates the dangers of simplification in the approach to complex issues."

Ellul noted in his book, *The Political Illusion,* that "man has discontinuous consciousness, and the first effect of news on him is not to make him more capable of being a citizen but to disperse his attention, to absorb it, and present to him an excessive amount of information that he will not be able to absorb, information too diverse to serve him in any way whatever. . . .

"As a result, a truly stupefying lack of continuity is created, for if one information item merely effaces the other on the same subject, it would not be so bad; but a continuous flow of information on a specific question, showing a problem's origin, growth, crisis, and denouement is very rare. Most frequently my attention, attracted today by Turkey, will be absorbed tomorrow by a financial crisis in New York and the day after tomorrow by parachutists in Sumatra. In the midst of all this, how can a man not specially trained perceive the slightest continuity, experience the slightest political continuity; how, finally, can he understand? He can literally only react to news.''

THE PROCESSES OF the communications media, as distinct from the conventions adopted by journalists, inhere in the nature of the media and in their forms— primarily the printed words and photographs of the newspaper and magazine, the broadcast language of radio, and the words and motion pictures of television. Obviously, inherent processes cannot be discarded and replaced. But if their distinctive effects are understood and their limitations recognized, they can be used more effectively in the interest of objective reporting; at the minimum, working journalists will be less likely to deceive themselves as to how ''truthful, comprehensive, and intelligent'' are their accounts of public affairs.

When the Army-McCarthy hearings were televised in the nineteen-fifties, it seemed that for the first time the essence of what had come to be called McCarthyism was communicated to the American people. Television sight and sound revealed something about Joseph McCarthy which print journalists had labored in vain to reveal in the preceding four or five years. Professional opinion poll-takers say that McCarthy's decline dates from those hearings.

Similarly, television documentaries on the working and living conditions of migratory farm workers, on life in the black ghettos, on the treatment given in homes for the aged and the mentally ill, on drug addiction, on conditions in prisons, have communicated those realities in a way that print journalists cannot hope to match through the written word.

And it was not until John F. Kennedy and Richard Nixon were simultaneously compared and contrasted in their televised Presidential campaign debates in 1960 that many American people formed a judgment as to the character and capabilities of the candidates.

We can go back to Cardinal Newman and all the way back to Aristotle for an explanation of what it is and why it is that televised communication has a more immediately powerful and gripping impact than print and why, at the same time, it is so severely limited in other respects.

Television simulates personal experience. While our understanding of a thing through experience may be far from complete, our assent to the existential judgment of the reality of that thing will be, in Newman's distinction, real as compared to notional. If one is told Britain is an island, Newman said, one makes a notional assent. If one actually sees that Britain is an island, sails all around it, one's assent to the truth becomes real.

But assent is not always equivalent to understanding. Experience, Aristotle said, is of individual things; understanding and wisdom are of causes and universals. ''We do not regard any of our senses as wisdom, yet surely these give the most authoritative knowledge of particulars. But they do not tell us the 'why' of anything.''

Although television is by its nature sense-oriented, engaging our sight and hearing, and therefore primarily concerned with particulars, it can explore the "why" of things when it also engages our reason. The more probing televised documentary films travel a respectable distance in that direction.

But it is the simulated personal experience, and all the moral and emotional content, the immediacy, and the self-involvement in personal experience that characterize television's effect. Undoubtedly we experience far more than we understand, and it is probably no less true that it is experience rather than understanding that most influences our behavior, even when the televised experience is not only simulated but manipulated, as Joe McGinnis showed us in his report, *The Selling of the President*. Certainly the contrived image of Richard Nixon and the rigorously controlled conditions under which he was presented to the viewers in 1968 resulted in many of them apparently acting on *that* experience of Mr. Nixon rather than on any genuine knowledge of the man.

The power of television to influence behavior is not diminished because politicians, and the television journalists themselves, can falsify the reality they are broadcasting. Indeed, the effectiveness of the deception underscores the power of the television medium as such.

But for an understanding of complex public-affairs issues and a grasp of the "why" of an event, we need more than the sight and the sound provided by television, more than the uncontrived experience of what the camera and microphone in the hands of truthful and competent broadcast journalists can convey to us, more than the moral conviction and emotional involvement aroused by such an experience. We need the opportunity for recurrent study and reflection on these issues. In short we need to make room for the work of reason. And for that, the printed word is indispensable.

It is the special temptation of television newsmen to believe that visibility and meaning are synonymous. But one television journalist, Walter Cronkite, resists the temptation. He has said that electronic journalism will never replace the written word in the communication of the meaning of public affairs. In the interest of objectivity, television reporters can, in the very act of reporting, make clear to their viewers what aspects of an issue or situation their medium must leave either unreported or only partially reported, and the reasons why.

The time and space allotted for reporting significantly affect the objectivity of the journalist's work. It can be argued that speed is a convention rather than an inherent process of mass communication. I think it is more accurate to say that the daily rhythm and tempo of mass communication correspond to the rhythm and tempo of human life itself. But it must also be said that a mutual, or reciprocating, action occurs: i.e., the rhythm and tempo of human action, the affairs of mankind, can be adjusted to meet the requirements of the communications media. When a President times an outburst of indignation so that it will be seen on the television screen in the evening or be read in the Sunday morning metropolitan papers of the nation, obviously public affairs have been adjusted to the rhythm of the media. (The Presidential display, at its inception, may be what Daniel Boorstin has described as a "pseudo-event," but once it occurs it is an authentic public affair, more or less rich, more or less significant, but a public affair nonetheless.)

Objectivity is affected not so much by mutual adjustments in rhythm and tempo between the media and the actors in the drama of public affairs as it is by the easy—often lazy—assumption adopted by some journalists that their breathless journalism is adequate to the communication of public affairs. It is the indiscriminate application of speed and the forcing of all public affairs, no matter how complex, obscure, and developmental they may be, into the mold of instant journalism that threatens objectivity.

Obviously many human affairs have their regular diurnal aspect. Sporting contests, stock-market activities, educational programs—these have their clock-like patterns, they are predictable, they mesh with the mass media communication timetables. But it is axiomatic that the more serious and consequential the public affairs, the untidier they will be and the more unmanageable they will be by any of the metronomic standards set by the print and electronic media.

Those metronomic imperatives sometimes exert a fascinating effect on editors and a bizarre, distorting effect on their journalism. Douglass Cater in his book, *The Fourth Branch of Government,* tells about one Washington wire-service editor who, in a running story, in order to have ''something of interest'' for editors of both morning and afternoon papers, ''creates'' stories by baiting public officials with ''conflict queries.''

ALTHOUGH LANGUAGE is the indispensable tool of the journalist, one need not read very widely on the subject nor think about it at any great length to realize that language demands the ultimate in craftsmanship, moral sensitivity, and intelligence. How language is used is crucial to the possibility of objective journalism. Herewith, some testimony to the difficulties in making language serve the cause of objectivity:

> Much self-control and great disinterestedness are needed by those who would realize the ideal of never misusing language. A man who habitually speaks and writes correctly is one who has cured himself, not merely of conscious and deliberate lying, but also (and the task is much more difficult and at least as important) of unconscious mendacity.
>
> —ALDOUS HUXLEY

> Nothing is more common than for men to think that because they are familiar with words they understand the ideas they stand for.
>
> —CARDINAL NEWMAN

> [The Thomists] showed that language and meaning depend on the past experiences of men; that different words can mean different things

to different men; that neither language nor knowledge is identical with reality. The Scholastic maxim—"never deny; rarely affirm; always distinguish"—is a medieval way, if you wish, of warning against the dangers of over-generalization.

—MARGARET GORMAN

If there is one thing certain, the truth will not be caught once and for all in a net of words alone.

—WELLER EMBLER

The spoken word and the reading of its written equivalent are both of them fundamentally the exercise of choice at every step—choosing not only the right sounds and combinations of sounds but also the right words and combinations of words to fit the continually emerging patterns both of language and of life.

—JOSHUA WHATMOUGH

The fact remains that, imperfect as words are as symbols of our ideas and as expressions of our thoughts, the journalist cannot dispense with them. Words may not be sufficient, but they are necessary. Even Marshall McLuhan's envisioned electric future in which experience will be communicated visually and configurationally rather than in the sequential, linear form of the printed word is a communication impossibility without the use of language.

Let us stipulate, then, that language alone is an imperfect medium for the expression of truth. Words can be inexact when precision is needed; ambiguous when univocal meaning is required; connotative when definition and denotation are demanded; allusive when identity is sought.

But it would be too easy and certainly misleading to conclude that the infelicities of language are indefeasible. After due allowances are made for the irreducible element of imperfection in words as signs of things and thoughts, it seems obvious that the task of communicating through language is primarily intellectual. Clear expression begins with clear thinking.

The task is also one of artistry. The craftsmanship of putting clear thoughts into clear language is complicated, but not defeated, by the ambiguity of words. Here the emphasis on speed in mass communication can be a crippling condition imposed on the public-affairs journalist. No matter how much the responsible journalist respects words and the intellectual and craft demands which their usage imposes, it is virtually impossible for him to develop the requisite intellectual and artistic habits if his editors enforce their deadlines inflexibly and indiscriminately, no matter how complex, subtle, and historically embedded may be the thing he is reporting.

ORDINARILY PUBLIC AFFAIRS do not happen or exist with their explanatory context already built into them. They must be investigated, not simply looked at. And then the materials must be interpreted.

American editors and publishers old enough to remember the era of personal journalism which existed well into the twentieth century are still wary of any effort to interpret the news. They identify interpretation with opinion, prejudice, slanting, distortion, surmise, speculation, and advocacy. And all of these qualities were indeed distinguishing features of old-time personal journalism. It sought to move and persuade rather than enlighten readers.

Reacting against this, publishers developed what they thought was a splendid alternative, an objectivity so narrowly defined that what was eliminated was not only opinionated editorializing in the news columns but also any opportunity for the reporter to put what he was reporting into a context which would make it meaningful. This was thought to be the objectivity of the scientist in his laboratory, meticulously recording what his senses perceived, impersonal, unprejudiced, and, above all, humble before the demonstrable fact. Actually the scientist was doing much more than this: his investigations led him to look for causes and relationships, and his intuitive and creative faculties were never idle.

But this only partly understood scientific model on which journalistic objectivity was patterned is ill-adapted to the work of the public-affairs reporter. The truths of public affairs are not encompassed by their appearances, or by what can be perceived only by the senses. As Eric Sevareid pointed out some years ago, when journalists confined their coverage of the late Senator Joseph McCarthy simply to what the senator said and did, far from producing objective journalism they were producing "the big lie." For the truth, or the meaning, of McCarthy could never be discerned from any particular statement he made or act he performed. It could only be discerned by relating the particular action to previous, possibly contradictory, actions; to the web of current and contemporary history in which the actions took place; and to known realities which the senator had ignored or misstated but which were relevant if readers were to be able to understand the senator and to form a judgment about his responsibility.

Of course, publishers and editors are not so naïve as to think that flat, one-dimensional, surface reporting is adequate to the needs of readers. But the solution some of them propose—a division of labor, with the reporter furnishing the facts in the news columns and editorial writers supplying the interpretation and analysis on the editorial page or in specially designated columns labeled "interpretive report"—is practically ineffectual and, I suspect, even theoretically untenable. It assumes that fact-gathering and interpreting are separable reporting functions. I think a convincing case can be made that fact-gathering, investigation, and interpretation are integral aspects and, for the purpose of the objective report itself, they are indivisible.

Certainly interpretive reporting contains subjective elements. But it will be an essentially objective act to the extent that the interpretation is grounded in the realities of an event or situation and to the extent that these grounds are clearly shown and evaluated by the reporter within his report. There is no reporting—even the "scientifically" objective, bare-facts reporting—which is free from subjective influence; the reporter does have to be subjective in selecting which of the bare facts he will include in his report. But the reporter's subjective judgment cannot be described as manipulative and distorting when it is oriented to the objective realities of the thing he is reporting.

The interpretive reporter and the editorialist both make judgments. The reporter's judgments are aimed at clarifying the meaning of public-affairs issues and problems. The editorial writer's judgments are aimed at persuading the reader about the rightness or wrongness of policies, programs, ideas; and at moving him to take a position on them. The distinction here is between clarification and rhetoric.

The most useful analysis of how the public-affairs reporter must work in investigating and interpreting his materials is in a book that was not written for journalists. In *The Modern Researcher,* Henry Graff and Jacques Barzun, two Columbia University historians, take up the problems of the working historian which happen in most respects to be the problems of the working public-affairs journalist: finding the facts; verifying the facts; handling ideas; truth, and the causation of and conditions surrounding events; discernible patterns in public affairs; and the sources and correctives of bias.

WHEN DOUGLASS CATER wrote his book on journalism in Washington, D.C., in 1959, he noted that there were more than three thousand public-information officers working for the federal government compared to twelve hundred newspaper and broadcast reporters in the capital. I doubt whether that ratio has altered significantly since 1959. And if you add to government public-information officers all the public-relations men working in Washington for private and special-interst lobbies and organizations, one can begin to perceive the magnitude of the journalist's task as he seeks to write objectively about what is happening.

The relationship of the reporter to his source is complicated not only by the sheer numbers of governmental and private public-relations men who stand between their clients and the public as shields and interpreters. It is also complicated by the special power of some of the highest government officials to reward or punish journalists by giving or withholding information according to how ''coöperative'' the journalists are; by the present Justice Department's unprecedented harrassment of reporters (requests for identification of their sources, attempts to subpoena the notes on which they have based their stories and broadcasts, grand-jury investigations of reporters who publish classified government documents); and often by the journalists' own inability, or unwillingness, to develop investigative techniques to counter the manipulative and intimidating tactics of government officials.

It must also be admitted that laziness and lack of enterprise in the use of alternative sources of information are not unknown vices of journalists. T.R.B., the Washington columnist for *The New Republic,* once attended a hearing by the Senate Judiciary Subcommittee on Anti-Trust and Monopoly. He discovered that "the one hundred largest manufacturing monsters in the United States increased their share of net capital assets of all U.S. manufacturing from 45.8 per cent to 56.9 per cent in the years from 1947 to 1962. . . . Textron has acquired sixty-nine manufacturing enterprises; Martin-Marietta picked up two hundred and forty-six million dollars worth of mergers. . . . Three big oil companies recently—Continental, Socony, and Gulf—each absorbed a fertilizer company; only one major independent fertilizer company remains. . . . Only three reporters were at the hearing when we looked in."

But even the most enterprising and intelligent of the Washington journalists are victims of that peculiar capital infirmity known as the "background briefing," that device by which government officials float trial balloons, attack their critics, and gild their programs on a not-for-attribution basis. The inviolable ground rule is that, while reporters may use anything they wish from these briefings, they must not identify the government official who gives them the information. The reporter who disobeys the rule is banned from background briefings, loses out on stories that his competitors are filing, and may lose his assignment if not his job.

Ben Bradlee, executive editor of the Washington *Post,* has complained bitterly about the background briefing: "We shudder righteously at the thought of withholding the name of a bank robber, a party giver, a campaign contributor. Why do we go along so complacently withholding the identity of public officials? By doing so we shamelessly do other people's bidding. We knowingly let ourselves be used for obvious trial balloons and for personal attacks. In short, we demean our profession."

Bradlee suggests that the more flagrant abuses of the background briefing might be eliminated if the press sharply limited and persuaded government officials to limit the amount of unattributed information; insisted on at least agency attribution ("White House sources," "State Department experts" instead of "high government officials" or "government sources"); and refused to let a background briefer indulge in personal attack without being identified.

Presidents as news sources use the immense authority of their office and have developed over the years a variety of wiles to keep reporters in line and to minimize the possibility of the searching and informed questions ever arising at news conferences. James Reston has recalled how Lyndon Johnson tamed the reporters: "He knew that the Washington press corps was full of specialists, some of whom had devoted most of their careers to the study of foreign affairs, or the federal judiciary, or science or military affairs, and therefore not only knew their subjects, but probably knew more about them than he did. If he announced his news conferences in advance, they would come running with their well-informed and awkward inquiries. So he simply did not announce his news conferences. He called them when only the White House correspondents were around, and then usually on the weekends when only a few of them were on duty. He held them in his own executive office, where he was not on display before the cameras, but talking intimately with the reporters who travel with him all the time and are not only familiar to him but subject to his system of punishments and rewards, which can be embarrassing to a reporter on a highly competitive beat.''

The objective public-affairs reporter, whether he is working in the super-heated atmosphere of Washington or covering City Hall in Milwaukee, has to walk a narrow line. He must develop a relationship with his source that is intimate enough to generate confidence and yield information but detached enough to enable him to be truthful in his writing even when the truth may not flatter the source of his information. The goal of government officials and the goal of journalists are one—the common good. But it does not follow that the journalist serves the common good by joining hands with and following the bidding of the officials. He serves it by maintaining that amount of distance which is required for cool, detached objectivity.

IT IS POSSIBLE for most, if not all, reporters for a newspaper, news service, television station or network to be objective in the performance of their individual tasks, or to aspire to objectivity, but for the institution which employs them to be profoundly nonobjective. How the institution uses its reporters, the working conditions it has set up for them, the news policies it has established, the extent to which the commercial and profit interests influence its communication performance all determine in the end whether the journalism produced will be objective.

Out of the thousands of events, situations, and conditions that might be reported each day, only a relatively few are printed or broadcast. Despite its slogan, *The New York Times* does not really publish all the news that is fit to print. It selects some news and it rejects other, even though both may be fit to print. The *Times* receives two and a half million words a day; it selects 185,000 (less than one per cent) for publication.

The question is, what is the basis and what are the principles which guide newspaper editors and television news directors both in their selection and in their handling of news? Historically, the answer to that question has been diverse, as all the foregoing might have suggested by now.

There is a sense in which a communications medium can be said to be objective if all of its individual reports, no matter how trivial the subjects, are true accounts. A newspaper like the *Daily News* in New York, assuming its various sensational items are accurately reported, can be said to be just as objective as *The New York Times*. But in a much deeper sense, the picture of the world as found in the *Times* is far truer, more objective, more bona fide than that in the *News*. This is partly because there is between all newspapers and their readers an implicit contract, a promise that they will furnish readers with the information they need if they are to function as responsible citizens in our society.

I do not think the problem of objectivity—whether in the individual reporter or in the institution—can be separated from the question of the over-all significance of the final product. Just as the objectivity of the individual reporter depends on his perception, selection, and ordering of the essential rather than the accidental elements of the event or situation he is reporting, so the objectivity of the newspaper or television station or network depends on the consistent selection of the most important aspects of contemporary life that will be assigned to the reporters for their investigation and interpretation.

It is not enough for the institution to be occasionally significant in many areas of public affairs, or to be consistently significant in one or two areas. If it falls short of over-all significance it presents a distorted picture of the world to its clientele.

What is required for a journalism of significance in any communications institution is a wise, experienced person with sufficient authority to make and enforce news policy for his paper, wire service, television station or network, and with sufficient resources (able reporters and editors, adequate time and space) to carry out that policy. Each of these elements—wisdom, experience, authority, enforcement, resources—is indispensable. One still hears of newspaper situations, which must be astounding to laymen, in which the wire editor (the real gatekeeper who selects the non-local stories that will pass through the news barrier and into the paper) is virtually sovereign and, in actual effect, determines news policy which may or may not be the policy the publisher or editor-in-chief would adopt if they were at that gate.

The wise director of news policy knows: (a) what constitutes "the good life," humanly speaking; (b) the present human condition; and (c) the contemporary events, developments, and forces which most directly and profoundly affect the human condition and the prospect for the good life.

Theoretically the commercial profit-making nature of mass communications need not compromise the efforts to produce a journalism of integrity. In practice, the theory often fails to stand up, or, more accurately, it is allowed to collapse.

It is true that newspaper editors no longer suppress stories that offend their advertisers. But I do not recall that the television industry, when it was heavily supported by tobacco advertising, came even remotely close to the newspapers and magazines in the number of news stories it aired about the relationship between cigarette smoking and lung cancer. And I cannot recall any television documentaries on this disease which national health officials say is of epidemic magnitude; if there have been documentaries, they cannot begin to compare in number or depth with those done by the television industry on the problem of, say, drug abuse. The commercial influence is always present in the media. The evidence suggests that the opportunity, desire, and ability to make enormous profits in the communications media sometimes results in shabby reporting of public affairs. Network officials say that they have corporate responsibilities to their stockholders and must show an improved profit picture each year.

When Fred Friendly, then a top news executive with the Columbia Broadcasting System, wanted to broadcast Senate Foreign Relations Committee hearings five years ago, the network overruled him and scheduled a rerun of an "I

Love Lucy'' show. Friendly resigned and later pointed out that he had not asked C.B.S. to suffer a net loss but only to take a very mild reduction in the gigantic profits they were making.

When Kenneth A. Cox was a member of the Federal Communications Commission, he criticized the F.C.C. and the radio industry for a situation in which the commission could renew, as they did on one occasion, the licenses of twenty-one stations without bothering to inquire into the adequacy of their service, as required by law, in the areas of public affairs, agriculture, instruction, and religion. The stations had proposed devoting less than five per cent of their time to those areas.

Mr. Cox noted that radio is now about fifty years old and that "surely it should strive to be—with due allowance for the admitted need for a viable economic base—something more than a jukebox, a ball park, and a news ticker." He said it was ridiculous to argue that the broadcaster who devotes twenty-three hours of each day to commercially sponsored programming is being subjected to an impairment of his freedom to speak if he is asked by the F.C.C. whether it would not better serve the public interest if more than twenty-five or thirty minutes of the remaining hour in the day could be devoted to public affairs.

I once took part in a seminar with newspaper, radio, and television news officials on the question of what the media can contribute to intergroup understanding and harmony in the community. One of the radio officials rather proudly reported that his station had often presented public-service programs on community problems, and he stated—also very proudly—that some of these "programs" ran as long as five minutes. It was obvious that, by his standards, five minutes of air time represented a considerable amount of money. But, of course, it bore little relationship to the magnitude and gravity of the problems in his community.

It is common knowledge that salaries paid to business, management, and advertising staff members of newspapers are substantially higher than those paid to reporters. Salary is not the only measurement of the regard which publishers have for the quality of public-affairs reporting, but it is a major measurement and, in the minds of most reporters, the decisive measurement.

Competent, highly motivated public-affairs reporters have been migrating for a generation from the newspapers and wire services to para-journalistic work (e.g., administrative and legislative work for congressmen). In one recent year, only twenty per cent of students graduating from journalism colleges chose to go into news reporting.

THE READER OF THE newspaper account or the viewer of a television news broadcast or documentary brings to it his own personal history. And if the reporter is subject to "tricks of memory" and the "incessant creative quality of his imagination," the reader is no less susceptible. If he distorts or misreads a report it may be his fault, the reporter's fault, or just due to the ambiguity of words. Barzun and Graff say:

"The reader brings something with him to every act of reading. He brings his own experience of life and a variable amount of knowledge gathered from previous reading. The result is that unless the vocabulary of a new piece of reading matter is visibly technical and strange to him, he will almost always think he understands it. This will happen even when what is said is badly put, repeatedly misleading, or adroitly tendentious. The whole power of propaganda lies in this human propensity to catch the drift, to make out a meaning, to believe what is in print, with no thought of resistance by analysis and criticism."

It may be assumed that if reporters will write with precision, make distinctions not fussily but with an exactness necessary to an understanding of the material, in short, if reporters will display in their work intellectual and critical power, their readers will develop a comparable virtue. The possibility will then be enhanced that what the reporter has understood and put into words (or, for television, into words and motion photography) the reader will understand. In that event, objective communication will have been accomplished.

BUT IS OBJECTIVITY in the over-all reporting of public affairs generally and consistently possible in American journalism? I think it is, not in the sense of objectivity as the total truth about anything (something which historians have never succeeded in capturing), and not in the sense of objectivity as meaning the absence of all subjective elements. But objectivity as meaning a substantially truthful account of contemporary public affairs is well within the possibility of the mass-communications media despite many practical difficulties.

These are some of the things that must be done to overcome the difficulties (other suggestions have been made in the course of this article):

Recognition of the existence of the reporter's personal history and experience and their effect on his work, with constant effort made to broaden and objectify that experience, and hence his values.

More professional education and training in the art of investigative reporting, both in professionally-oriented journalism schools or university departments (preferably following a liberal arts undergraduate education) and on the job with newspapers and television stations.

Insistence that reporters and editors bring to their work a broad educational experience so that they can interrelate the economic, political, social, and cultural elements of public affairs and provide the context which will illuminate what they are reporting.

A proper balance of specialization and rotation of reporters' assignments to avoid superficiality on the one hand and the boredom, laziness, and uncritical, routinized approach often associated with the unvarying assignment on the other.

Vigilance from the editor's desk (spot comparisons, for example, of the reporters' dispatches with those of other American reporters and, in the case of international assignments, with the reports of foreign writers).

Careful fitting of reporters to the kinds of assignments on which they could probably be more consistently objective, and a constant review of that fit.

Providing the working conditions (sufficient space, time, and professional understanding) to enable reporters to do careful work.

A continuing communications commission to monitor the performance of the press and television and to make public its evaluations.

Extension and refinement of the ombudsman-like idea initiated by a few newspapers to give readers a critical voice that will be heard in the operation of the papers.

Subordination of the profit-making of a newspaper or broadcasting station to the service of its communication function.

Better use made of the wire services by subscribing papers and, where the wire services are inadequate, more rigorous demands by the individual editors.

It is possible for the citizen with a great deal of time and a considerable expenditure of money to keep himself adequately informed on the public affairs of the day by reading several newspapers and a half-dozen or more journals and magazines, watching the televised documentaries, and picking up the best of the books on contemporary issues.

But it should be equally possible for citizens, without making such an extraordinary investment of their time and money, to subscribe to their hometown newspaper, watch the television news and public-affairs programs, and perhaps subscribe to one magazine or journal and be confident that their opinions and actions on public affairs are based on an understanding of the issues. I do not think this is now the case. But I do think it is possible.

Paul H. Weaver:

The New Journalism and the Old

THE "FOURTH ESTATE" of the realm—that was Burke's way of summing up the role of the press in his time, and when one has discounted the medieval terminology, his phrase is no less apt today. It reminds us that the press, as the coequal of other "estates," is a political institution in its own right, intimately bound up with all the institutions of government. It affects them and is affected by them in turn, and together they determine the nature of the regime and the quality of public life. Governmental institutions have political effects through their exercise of legislative, executive, or judicial powers; the press achieves its impact through the way it influences the entry of ideas and information into the "public space" in which political life takes place. So the basic question to be asked about the press is: What is its relation to other political institutions, and how does it consequently manage the "public space"?

The aftermath of Watergate provides a suitable occasion for rethinking this question—though not because the press was in any way at fault in this episode. The Watergate scandals emerge solely from the Nixon Administration's abuse of its Presidential powers in matters ranging from campaign finance and civil liberties to national security. By covering the emerging scandals as it did, the press was acting in accord with a venerable journalistic tradition that dates back to *The New York Times'* exposé of the corrupt Tweed Ring in 1871.

Yet Watergate was more than a series of criminal and corrupt actions; it also has raised basic Constitutional questions concerning the interrelationship among all our political institutions, including of course the press. One of these issues was the freedom of the press. Many of the abuses symbolized by Watergate—the Plumbers, unjustified investigations and wiretaps, and so forth—were in fact directed at the press as part of the Administration's campaign to make the news media less critical. If these efforts had been successful, they would have reduced press freedom and altered the balance between government and the press in favor of the former. For the time being at least, that danger has been averted.

Dr. Weaver, formerly Associate Editor of *The Public Interest* and on the Political Science faculty at Harvard, is now Associate Editor of *Fortune*. This article is reprinted by permission from *The Public Interest* (No. 35, Spring, 1974), 67–88. Copyright © 1974 by National Affairs, Inc.

So the press emerges from Watergate as free, self-confident, and enterprising as at any other time in its history. But it also emerges a bit different from what it was before. For the press today is an institution in limbo—an institution in that distinctive kind of trouble which derives from not having a settled idea of its role and purpose. It is in limbo because it now occupies an ambiguous middle ground between its longstanding tradition of "objective" journalism and a new movement for an "adversary" journalism—no longer massively committed to the one but not yet certain, let alone unanimous, about the other. To the extent that it is committed to the new movement, it is committed to a journalistic idea that is not easily compatible with American institutions in their current form, nor easily reconciled with some of its most valuable traditions. And to the extent that the press embraces this movement, its political role will remain in flux until some new practical adaptation to adversary journalism is worked out by government, public opinion, and the press itself. Watergate did not create this problem—it has been growing for a decade now—but it did intensify it. And this is the problem which confronts American journalism after Watergate.

Two Kinds of Journalism

To put the matter briefly: Traditionally, American journalism has been very close to, dependent upon, and cooperative with, official sources. This has been one of its problems, but it has also been its greatest strength and virtue. For in various ways this arrangement has maximized both the openness and flexibility of American government and the amount of information available to the citizenry. Over the past ten years, however, a small but significant and still-growing segment of the journalistic community has begun to revise this relationship by assuming a posture of greater independence and less cooperativeness. They see this change as a modest reform which will render American journalism purer, better, and truer to its traditional aspirations. In fact, it represents a radical change. In the long run it could make the press "freer" but also less informative and possibly more partisan; and this in turn could make the political system more closed, less flexible, and less competent.

To appreciate the meaning of what has happened, we may begin with the simple fact that journalism is the enterprise of publishing a current account of events.[1] As such, it cannot proceed until three prior questions have been settled. First, there is the question of how, where, and on what basis to find and validate information. Second, there is the question of the point of view from which events are to be surveyed and characterized. And third, there is the question of the audience to be addressed and the basis on which it is to be aggregated. Abstractly, one can imagine any number of possible resolutions of these issues, but in practice things work out more simply. For wherever one looks in the modern world, daily journalism seems to assume one of two general forms: the partisan and the liberal.

Partisan journalism, which prevails in many European countries, and which has traditionally been represented in the United States by the "journal of opinion" rather than the newspaper, begins with an explicitly political point of view. It is ideological journalism. It aims at assembling an audience that shares its point of view; its object is to interpret public affairs from within that point of view; and it gathers information for the purpose of illuminating and particularizing such interpretation. Such a journalism is less concerned with information as such than with the maintenance and elaboration of its point of view. To it, events are more interesting for the light they cast on its "position" than for what they are, or seem, on their face.

Liberal journalism, by contrast, which prevails in the English-speaking world, is characterized by a preoccupation with facts and events as such, and by an indifference to—indeed, a systematic effort to avoid—an explicitly ideological point of view. It aims instead at appealing to a universal audience on the basis of its non-political, "objective" point of view and its commitment to finding and reporting only "facts" as distinct from "opinion." Liberal journalism strives to be a kind of *tabula rasa* upon which unfolding events and emerging information inscribe themselves. Its principal concern is to find as many events and as much information as it can, and it does this by going to "sources"—persons and organizations directly involved in the events, upon whom it relies both for information and for the validation of this information.

Throughout the 20th century, American journalism has been solidly in the liberal camp. It has sought a universal audience rather than a factional one; its central objective has been to find and publish as much information about as many events as quickly as possible; and it has striven to do this on the basis of a non-partisan, non-political, "facts-only" point of view. Or at least these have been its ideals; the extent of their actual realization has been subject, not only to the vicissitudes of human judgment, but also to two tensions inherent in the very idea of a liberal journalism.

The first of these is the tension between access and autonomy, between the effort of the press to get as much unambiguously true information about as many events as possible—which requires a maximum of access to the actors in these events, which in turn entails a maximum of dependency on these actors— and its effort to preserve its capacity for independent judgment. The second tension arises out of the desire of liberal journalists to avoid taking a political point of view, which conflicts with the inevitability that, in the course of describing events, some sort of point of view will be assumed (observation and writing cannot proceed in the absence of one), and that no point of view will ever be totally devoid of political implications.

Access and Independence

To these complex problems, the established liberal tradition of American journalism provides a suitably complex resolution. As between access and autonomy, the tradition opts massively and with a clear conscience for access. This choice is reflected not only in the way newsmen go about their work, but in almost every other feature of American journalism as well, from the form of the news story to the role of the newspaper owner. By opting for access, the American press has given priority and reality to its ideals of acting as a *tabula rasa* and maximizing the amount of raw information it provides to the electorate. This same emphasis on access also goes a long way toward settling, if only unintentionally, the problem of point of view. A *tabula rasa* that is written on primarily by persons involved in events inevitably reflects their slant on the world.

In practice, then, this emphasis on access means the following:

First, virtually all the information published by the press is derived from (and is validated by) "high-level sources," i.e., persons, officials, and organizations actively involved in the events in question.

Second, what newsmen know about the events and issues they cover, and about the general context in which these occur, they acquire almost exclusively from the persons involved rather than from external professional, academic, or ideological sources and authorities.

Third, the point of view from which newsmen write is largely determined by the views, concerns, vocabularies, and situations of those actually involved in public affairs. The viewpoint of the American press is thus a practical rather than ideological or theoretical one.

And fourth, as a result of this emphasis on access, newsmen are routinely aware of—or can easily gather—a truly immense amount of information. They are authentic ringside observers of men and events. They can never publish more than a small fraction of what they know (or have reason to believe), and what they do publish is backed up by a large, if often unarticulated, familiarity with the persons, institutions, and issues involved.

Yet if the "objective" tradition defines American journalism as a primarily derivative and dependent enterprise, it also provides the newsman with a limited but still quite important sphere of independence. Partly this independence has existed by virtue of the sheer volume of events and information which are routinely available to the working newsman. He therefore is confronted with the daily and hourly necessity of choosing, and to choose is to exercise a measure of independent power. This power is enhanced by the fragmentation and indiscipline of American government. Not only do they increase the number of points of access for the newsmen seeking a given bit of information, but they also create for him the opportunity—often exploited in practice—to follow the maxim *divide et impera,* an approach whose utility is made much greater by the almost insatiable appetite of most officials for the two political resources which the newsman possesses automatically: publicity and information. The traditional journalist, then, is not utterly at the mercy of his sources.

Just as important as the fact of the newsman's power is the independent way in which the liberal tradition of American journalism has encouraged him to use that power. To begin with, the tradition demands that the newsman maintain a strict formal independence of his sources: There are to be no financial conflicts of interest, and excessively close personal or ideological relationships are frowned upon. Second, each of the newsman's uses of his selective power is subject to a process of review by his journalistic peers and superiors; not only is the newsman supposed to be free of obligations to his sources, but also he is held answerable before the court of journalistic opinion. Third and most important, there is the traditional norm of "independent" judgment. The newsman is not to have a single, comprehensive, ideological point of view, but the liberal tradition of American journalism does encourage him to have an occsional *ad hoc* opinion and to bring such views to bear in his reporting—provided they pass muster with his journalistic colleagues and superiors, and provided also that there aren't many such opinions and that they manifest themselves only infrequently. (James Reston is an exemplar of this ethos, a man of judgment rather than a man of partisan ideology.) And as vehicles for the expression of these modest and occasional opinions, the liberal tradition sanctions, in addition to "objective" reporting, the devices of muckraking and the "crusade" against a particular instance of inequity. These latter are not often used, but they do remain in the newsman's arsenal to define alternative modes of dealing with institutions and events—and to give the newsman further room for exercising independent judgment.

The Liberal Tradition

In the liberal tradition, then, the relationship between newsman and source, between press and government, is one of structured interdependence and bartering within an atmophere of amiable suspiciousness. Each side knows its role. The job of government is to give access and information—*and to do so to a far greater extent than would or could be required by law*. This last point is worth emphasizing, since in this respect American government differs markedly from European (even British) governments. All European journalists are immediately struck by this difference. The American reporter not only has access to official announcements and press releases; he also has the opportunity of becoming the confidant of the official and of enjoying limited but regular access to his personal thoughts, official secrets, internal departmental gossip, and the like.

Of course, there is a price tag on such extraordinary access. The reporter is expected to be generally sympathetic to the public official and his government and to cooperate with them as far as his sense of professionalism permits. Beyond that, the press is expected to have no strong and comprehensive ideas about the general shape of public affairs; it is officialdom which is collectively entitled to define the topography and limits of public discussion and the news—and each individual official is to have the further opportunity of attempting to shape the content of news to suit his own preferences or purposes.

But the press also has its role and rights. Its main job is to exploit its access and, one way or another, to get as much information as it can into public circulation. It has the right to select freely among the often widely divergent ideas and information circulating within officialdom and to expose corruption and foulups. In exchange, it is expected to see to it that the impression being made on the public is not radically at odds with the reality of affairs as newsmen and officials, from their ''inside'' perspective, know it to be.

At the level of day-to-day individual interaction, of course, the relationship between press and government in the ''objective'' tradition is ill-defined and highly variable. There are a few rules of thumb that all parties are expected to observe. Officials are not supposed to lie—at least, hardly ever, and then for some good public reason. They are also supposed to keep their efforts to deceive newsmen and the public to modest proportions. And they are not ever to use the powers of government to harrass or coerce newsmen. Newsmen, for their part, are expected not to ''editorialize'' in their news stories and are supposed to give persons accused or disputed in a story an opportunity to tell their own side of the matter. And newsmen are also expected not to publish certain kinds of information without permission: official secrets, information about the seamy side of officials' private lives, and ''inside dope'' of no particular relevance to public policy. But within these limits, more or less anything goes. There is much uncertainty and much room for maneuver, manipulation, and enterprise on both sides—and for all their mutuality and cooperation, there is also endless conflict between government and press. But in this general scramble there are limits that both of the parties respect.

The great virtue of the liberal tradition of American journalism is that it enables the press to find and print a great deal of information—much more of it, and more quickly, than partisan newspapers can. For the newsman, it has the further advantage of affording him an opportunity to become truly learned and sophisticated about public affairs through an informal process of close personal observation. And for the citizen it has the virtue that it produces news which is generally intelligible. One can know that the content of news is a more or less faithful reflection of affairs as they are understood by the persons engaged in them, or at least as officialdom as a whole sees them. What is more, the general perspective on events is a practical one. News presented in this way, is sensitive to the practitioner's questions of ''What next?'' and ''How to?'' and ''Who are my friends and enemies?''—and this in turn increases the possibilities that public opinion, reacting to the news, will have significant impact on the day-to-day conduct of government.

Of course, the established tradition has its shortcomings as well, and some of them are quite severe. It is a kind of journalism that is very easily (and very often) manipulated, especially by government but also by newsmen themselves. In any particular instance, the reader can never be absolutely sure that the impression being conveyed to him is a reasonably accurate reflection of the reality of affairs. And beyond that, traditional liberal journalism is perhaps excessively controlled by the ethos and conventional wisdom prevailing among ''insiders'' and shared by newsmen. In short, the "objective" tradition has the vices and virtues inherent in the idea of acting as a *tabula rasa*. But the virtues are substantial ones too, and the vices, serious though they are, are to no small extent inherent in the very mission of journalism as defined by the liberal tradition: publishing a current account of current events for "the general reader," i.e., the ordinary citizen.

The Origins of "Adversary" Journalism

What I have just described is the operational reality of the liberal tradition of American journalism. The image which that journalism has of itself is not exactly congruent with the reality. Some elements of this image, to be sure, are accurate enough. For instance, newsmen correctly believe that they perform three quite different public functions: For the most part, they act as neutral finders and conveyors of information; to some extent they are the "watchdogs" of government; and on rare occasions they advocate the reform of observable inequities. But in other respects, and especially as it depicts the relationship between press and government, the image ia a romantic fiction. To listen to traditional newsmen, one would think that the press is completely independent of government in its quest for news, that it routinely searches out vast amounts of hidden, jealously guarded information, that it is constantly defying persons in high office, and that it is the day-in, day-out adversary of "the Establishment" and the equally faithful defender of "the People."

Now this myth of the autonomous, investigative, adversary press does serve a useful purpose. One of the greatest problems of traditional journalism is its proneness to cooptation by its sources. To the extent that newsmen believe and act on their romantic notion of who they are and what they do, the likelihood of their becoming mere uncritical puppets in the hands of their sources is diminished. Moreover, their morale would be lower, their energy smaller, and their self-respect weaker if they subscribed to a truly realistic conception of daily journalism. The romantic image of the "adversary press," then, is a myth: "functional" for certain purposes, but wholly inaccurate as a model of what newsmen actually do or can hope to achieve.

The movement for a new, genuinely adversary journalism which has gained such ground over the past decade arises out of this romantic myth; it is to the liberal tradition of our press what, in a religious context, heresy is to orthodoxy. It is the nature of a heresy to isolate a part of a tradition or doctrine and to treat the part as if it were the whole. The current "heretical" movement in American journalism is defined by the fact that it takes the mythical part of the "orthodox" tradition—the fiction of the autonomous, investigative, adversary press—for the whole of that tradition. It presents itself as an effort to make our press live up to what it always said it was: a journalism that is autonomous instead of interdependent, original instead of derivative, and in an adversary instead of cooperative relationship with government and officialdom. Like religious heresies, the movement *appears* to be a ''reformation''—an effort to recover the core of a partially but not irrecoverably corrupted tradition. But such appearances are misleading. For, because heresies are simplificatory, what they profess to be ''recovering'' is actually something that never was and that was never intended to be. What they really advocate, therefore, is the creation of something quite new and different under a smokescreen of rhetoric about restoring what is old and familiar.

Although this movement for a newly purified journalism did not attain real strength until the late 1960's, its origins lay somewhat farther in the past. Within the journalistic community, three events were critical in fomenting dissatisfaction with the existing press-government relationship: McCarthyism, the U-2 incident, and the Bay of Pigs. Each cast discredit upon the Cold War itself or the spirit in which government conducted it, and together they caused newsmen to revise their opinion of American institutions and their own relationship to them.

In a way, McCarthyism was the most important. It was a powerful, nationwide movement, and no demagogue can create such a movement without a sounding board in the press. By uncritically repeating and dramatically displaying the sensational charges made by a Senator—in keeping with the usages of objective journalism—the press provided Joe McCarthy with just such a sounding board. In the aftermath of the McCarthy era, newsmen increasingly agreed that they had permitted themselves to be used irresponsibly. A member of government had abused the power that the objective tradition gave him over the press. The answer, it was generally agreed, was that the press should become more vigilant and critical, and should exercise much more discretion about what it printed in connection with known demagogues, even those in high public office.

Then came the U-2 incident and the Bay of Pigs. In the former case, it may be recalled, various government agencies first said that the flight was for weather research and not espionage (the plane had presumably strayed off course), then said that it was for espionage but that President Eisenhower had not known about it, whereupon Eisenhower came forward and publicly declared that he had known and approved of the program. In the latter case, President Kennedy persuaded *The New York Times,* on grounds of national security, not to print a story on preparations for the Bay of Pigs invasion. After the invasion flopped he publicly stated that the *Times* should have printed the story because he would then have been forced to cancel the invasion, sparing the United States one of the worst foreign policy fiascos in its history. It was not merely that government had lied and suppressed news, and been caught at it. Nor was it only that the press had been used, used easily and with cavalier disrespect, and used wrongly. It was rather that two *Presidents* had publicly admitted lying and suppressing news, and that one of them said the press shouldn't have listened to him. Clearly the problem which the press had identified in the aftermath of McCarthyism was not confined to an occasional demagogue in Congress; it extended to the highest and most respected officials in the land. If one couldn't trust them, evidently one couldn't trust anyone.

The Experience of the 1960's

These events marked the beginning of both the "credibility gap" theme in public affairs reporting and a growing truculence among newsmen. By 1966 Clifton Daniel, then managing editor of *The New York Times,* could give a speech saying that the *Times* had been wrong not to print the Bay of Pigs story and would not make such a mistake again. The *Times* is of course our preeminent journalistic institution; it had previously been cooperative with government about national security matters; and it does not make admissions of error lightly, if at all. The speech was a watershed in modern journalistic history, and it served notice that an important article in the informal covenant between press and government was being renegotiated, if not unilaterally repudiated.

This issue might have been resolved satisfactorily had not four further developments supervened. One of these was the steep decline, during the 1960's, in the competitiveness of the "prestige" newsmarkets, especially New York, which quietly but effectively shifted the balance of power between newsmen and sources. When *The New York Times* had been actively in competition with the *Herald-Tribune,* their newsmen felt constrained to maintain friendly relationships with sources so that their opposite numbers would not get "exclusives"—and sources, as a consequence, could "whipsaw" newsmen to keep them in line. When the *Times,* the Washington *Post,* and other leading newspapers no longer had any true local competitors, their newsmen became less beholden, and sources became relatively weaker. Since these newsmen worked for newspapers which were widely respected and emulated by lesser publications, and since in any event they produced a large portion of the national news coverage published in the country, this shift had effects out of all proportion to the number of newspapers immediately involved. (Significantly, the only truly competitive comprehensive national news services—AP and UPI—have been little effected by the emergence of the movement for an "adversary" journalism.)

A second important development was the growth in the visibility, self-consciousness, and self-confidence of the journalistic profession, and especially of the Washington press corps. Traditionally, reporting had been a low-prestige occupation; some studies reported it to rank *between* the blue-collar and white-collar occupations. In the 1960's this began to change. President Kennedy showed a special fondness for newsmen; the inauguration in 1963 of the national half-hour television news programs gave the press a new vehicle of unprecedented power and created, overnight, a batch of journalistic celebrities; officials became ever more attentive to the press, and their efforts to manipulate the news grew in scale and sophistication; books and articles about the press began to proliferate; and by the beginning of the 1970's scale salaries at leading newspapers approached (and, in TV, exceeded) those of Assistant Secretaries. Whatever the cause, newsmen had a growing sense of their importance and a corresponding unwillingness to accept the dependency and subordination which, as it seemed, had been characteristic of the position of the press in earlier decades.

Third, there was the extraordinary political and cultural ferment of the 1960's, involving a dramatic expansion and intensification of political conflict and the emergence of countercultural, anti-establishment, and other oppositional movements. The spirit of the age had its impact on the journalistic community, especially on its younger, newly-recruited members. The psychological distance between press and government and the frequency of stories critical of established policy grew.

More important than this direct form of cultural influence, however, was the indirect influence of the spirit of the 1960's upon journalism. As we have noted, the traditional mode of American journalism was dependent and derivative; the press largely reflected the ideas and balance of power in official circles. As the 1960's wore on, an even larger segment of officialdom itself became sympathetic to the oppositional fashions of the decade. Not only "the kids" and other people "out there," but also Senators, committee chairmen, Washington lawyers, and Assistant Secretaries began to articulate the spirit of "confrontation" and "alienation." Thus, as ideological movements of opinion became stronger, traditional journalism found itself having to choose from among a variety of perspectives, all of which could claim some official standing. Merely by continuing to report public affairs in the traditional way, the press gave increasing exposure to the ideas and symbols of the oppositional movements.

The White House vs. the Press

This led in turn to the fourth development which fostered the current movement for a "new journalism": the intensification of opposition to the movements of the 1960's, both in public opinion at large and within specific institutions and political circles. One of the ways in which such "backlash" sentiment expressed itself was by attacking the press for giving exposure to those movements, and one of the most prominent sources of such attacks was the White House, beginning with Lyndon Johnson. For a variety of reasons— good, bad, and indifferent—both Johnson and his successor chose to resist the growing truculence of the press and the exposure it gave to the growing anti-war and other oppositional movements in the country as a whole. As in Vietnam, so on the homefront: With each escalation of the President's campaign against the press, the press seemed to counter with an added measure of defiance and a little more coverage of oppositional politics.

At first the belligerents fought their battles with the conventional weapons of legitimate political warfare. LBJ used the personal approach (flattering and punishing reporters, making telephone calls to network executives, etc.) and the traditional devices of political public relations (emphasizing good news and deemphasizing the bad, manipulating the appearance of events, wheeling out various "experts" and "authorities" to defend his positions, and the like). The Nixon Administration, in its early months, added to these devices the long-range artillery of Agnewian rhetoric and an elaborately centralized system of "public information." These tactics not only didn't work, they seemed only to confirm the press in its new determination to be independent, which in context meant critical.

As feelings on both sides grew more embittered, their tactics became more unconventional and the struggle more total: It was an omen of the Watergate era to come. The Administration—which in this escalation was clearly the aggressor—launched FBI investigations of newsmen it felt to be hostile; deprived the press of traditional forms of access, such as the press conference, the casual telephone conversation, and the cocktail party; threatened television stations with loss of their licenses; in the first case of prior censorship in American history, brought suit to enjoin the publication of the Pentagon papers; and set up the Plumbers to stop unauthorized leaks. The press countered with heavy coverage of anti-Nixon political elements, publication of secret government documents (the Pentagon and Anderson papers) which they would not have dreamed of making public ten years earlier, and a growing pattern of refusing to accept the legality of subpoenas issued by courts in the course of due legal processes. There was also a certain tendency to begin ignoring traditional journalistic standards of fairness and truth. When the Supreme Court issued its "Caldwell" decision in 1972, which at most only upheld the existing rules defining the testimonial obligations of newsmen, the press interpreted this as a *change* in Constitutional law that reduced freedom of the press. A year before, in "The Selling of the Pentagon," CBS-TV editors falsified the continuity of a filmed interview with a Pentagon official. And when the actions of any newsman were challenged or criticized, increasingly the journalistic community as a whole drew together in defense of its own, right or wrong. Jack Anderson was given the Pulitzer prize for publishing a National Security Council minute concerning the American position in a current, explosive diplomatic situation, and "The Selling of the Pentagon," despite its dubious editing, was cited for excellence in the television documentary category.

The New Mood

The upshot of these developments was that the liberal press particularly—and to an increasing extent other parts of the journalistic community as well—found itself ever more committed to a stance of truculent independence from government and officialdom. Increasingly it felt that its proper role was not to cooperate with government but to be independent of it, or even opposed to it. Increasingly newsmen began to say that their job was to be an autonomous, investigative adversary of government and to constitute a counter-vailing force against the great authority of all established institutions. And increasingly they began to see as illegitimate the few traditional formal constraints upon the press: libel law, "fair trial" restrictions on news coverage, testimonial obligations upon all citizens to give their evidence under subpoena, and the laws defining and protecting government secrets. These sentiments, and the actions which in modest but growing number gave concrete expression to them, define the movement for a "new journalism" which exists today and which poses the central question which the press will have to cope with after Watergate.

It is impossible to state with any precision or sense of certainty just how widespread and securely entrenched this movement is. Its only clearly identifiable location seems to be generational: It is young reporters, in their twenties and early thirties, who seem most to share the attitudes that define the movement. In general, though, it is more a mood than a settled, behavioral pattern; a thing more of the spirit than of the flesh; a tendency or yearning more than an established and institutionalized accomplishment. And yet it is a fact. If it is not so widespread or influential as current conservative critics of the media insist, it is also more substantial than defenders of the movement admit. It exists; it really is unlike that which has prevailed in our journalism for decades; it could yet become dominant; and it makes a difference.

The Blasi Findings

A recent study by Professor Vince Blasi of the Michigan Law School suggests something of the extent to which the attitudes of this movement have gained ground in the journalistic community. As a means of measuring the need for and effects of "shield" legislation, Blasi in 1972 asked a non-random sample of almost 1,000 newsmen to respond to the following hypothetical situation:

> You have a continuing source relationship with a group of political radicals. They have given you much information in confidence and this has enabled you to write several byline stories describing and assessing in general terms the activities and moods of the group. During the course of this relationship, you are present at a closed meeting with ten of these radicals at which the group vigorously debates whether to bomb a number of targets, including the local police station. The consensus is against such bombing, but two members of the group argue very heatedly in favor of bombing and are deeply upset when the others refuse to go along. These two then threaten to act on their own. The discussion then turns to another topic. Two weeks later the local police station is in fact bombed. One officer is killed by the blast and two others are seriously injured.

The first question Blasi posed with this: "In these circumstances, would you on your own initiative volunteer the information you learned at the meeting *right after the meeting* (i.e., before a bombing took place)?" Of these who responded, 26.2 per cent answered "yes," 55.5 per cent "no," and the rest gave no answer.

Question #2: "Would you volunteer the information on your own initiative to law enforcement authorities *after the bombing* (but before you were contacted by the police or subpoenaed by a grand jury)?" Answer: 37.6 per cent yes, 36.0 per cent no, 26.4 per cent no answer.

Question #3: "Assume that you were subpoenaed by a grand jury investigating the bombing but that an absolute legal privilege were established so that you could not be compelled to answer questions against your will. Would you voluntarily answer if the grand jury asked you whether this group of radicals had ever discussed the possibility of bombing the police station?" Answer: 45.5 per cent yes, 36.0 per cent no, 18.5 per cent no answer.

Question #4: "If the grand jury asked you to name the members of the group who had advocated bombing?" Answer: 36.9 per cent yes, 44.1 per cent no, 19.0 per cent no answer.

Question #5: "Assume that one of the members of the group who had argued vigorously *against* the bombing was indicted for the crime and that you believed, on the basis of the meeting, that it is highly unlikely that this particular member was the bomber. Would you on your own initiative volunteer this information to the prosecutor?" Answer: 60 per cent yes, 22.2 per cent no, 17.8 per cent no answer.

Question #6: "If this member's defense lawyer subpoenaed you at the trial would you testify about the meeting you had witnessed (including giving the names of those who did advocate the bombing) even if you were protected by an absolute privilege so that you couldn't be compelled to testify?" Answer: 43.2 per cent yes, 36.4 per cent no, 20.4 per cent no answer.

In the liberal tradition of "objective" journalism, newsmen cooperated with government and especially with law enforcement officials in serious felonies like bombing and murder. One may safely assume that, at some point, a traditional reporter would have given his information to the authorities and defense lawyers—albeit with a guilty conscience over having broken his pledge of confidentiality.[2] Blasi's newsmen show the opposite inclination. Even in a case of bombing, death, and serious injury, only one fourth said they would warn authorities of the possibility of a bombing beforehand; only two fifths said they would volunteer their information after the bombing; less than half were sure they would tell a grand jury that the group had discussed the possibility of bombing; and only two fifths were willing to name the persons who had advocated the bombing. And most startling of all, *almost three fifths of this sample of 1,000 reporters were unwilling to say that they would go to court to testify in defense of persons on trial for murder even if they had information tending to show the defendants to be innocent and others to be guilty.*

Issues of Confidentiality

Of course, these are only attitudes; it is quite possible—even likely—that, in the crunch, no more than a handful of newsmen would actually withhold their evidence in such circumstances. But in a way that is beside the point. What is to the point is that these attitudes are widely perceived to exist among newsmen, and that a few newsmen have begun to act on the basis of them. Together these developments have raised two large and disagreeable issues which our political and legal processes are now forced to grapple with.

One of these is the problem posed by the unauthorized publication of secret or confidential government documents, ranging from White House memoranda and secret depositions before grand juries to Jack Anderson's National Security Council minute or William Beecher's summary of the U.S. fallback position in the SALT-I negotiations. In large part, to be sure, the issue here should focus more on the persons responsible for leaking documents than on the press, which merely publishes them; surely the proper initial defendant, in a legal test of this process, is not *The New York Times* but Daniel Ellsberg, not Jack Anderson but his sources (apparently in the Pentagon). Yet it is also an issue that concerns the press itself because, until recently, the press, out of regard for national security or fear of the consequences, would not have published the Pentagon papers (though it might well have written *about* them, in a veiled and guarded way). Today, obviously, it will publish them, and the result is that we are confronted squarely with a new issue that we would be better off not having to deal with.

It is an impossible issue. However it is resolved, or even if it is not resolved, we will be worse off than we were before it was raised. It involves a conflict among three valuable traditions—press freedom, confidentiality in government, and the relatively open or amorphous quality of American government. Conflicts among these traditions have heretofore been resolved on an informal, *ad hoc* basis. To attempt to resolve them systematically and formally is to lose much and to gain little, if anything. One does need secrecy and confidentiality in government: to protect national security from enemy powers, to ensure that persons in government will feel free to write down on paper their best individual judgments on issues of fact and policy, and perhaps most of all to preserve the ability of officials (especially the President) to be flexible and to take initiatives. (Premature leaks are the tried-and-true device for forestalling Presidential initiatives in policy and administration, or for rendering them ineffective once taken.) On the other hand, one does not want Congress to make any law abridging the freedom of the press in order to preserve this confidentiality. Nor does one want to take the path of enacting an official secrets act that provides severe penalties for any civil servant who leaks information without formal approval from the highest authorities. This last measure would sharply reduce the amount and range of perfectly harmless and also useful information that would be made—is now made—available to the press, usually to the benefit of us all; it would also reduce the ability of Congress to oversee the Executive, since it would know less about what was going on. Thus, by retreating from its old cooperative notion of public responsibility, the press has created an issue which cannot be resolved without changing the American system as a whole in some fundamental—and unattractive—way.

More or less the same is true of the second issue raised by the current movement for a new journalism: the question of the testimonial obligations of newsmen. In the past several years, journalists have begun to insist with increasing frequency and vehemence that they should not be compelled by grand juries or courts to disclose information they have gathered from sources on a confidential basis. To do so, they say, will cause sources to give less information to the press, which in turn will reduce the amount of information citizens can glean from newspapers. Previously, newsmen had generally cooperated with the law enforcement establishment. Now, partly because of the increasingly adversarial stance of newsmen towards government, and partly also because more newsmen have begun to cover the activities of radical, violent, or criminal groups, this has changed. A number of newsmen have chosen to go to jail rather than reveal the identity of confidential informants or the substance of what they learned from them. And in defense of this choice they have offered the further argument that the press is now subjected to so many subpoenas—over a four-year period beginning in 1968, for instance, the Chicago *Tribune* received more than 400—that its operations are truly disrupted and its freedom, as a practical matter, is reduced.

Should we then enact shield legislation exempting newsmen from their testimonial obligations? Perhaps, but to do so it not without its costs. With certain minor and traditional exceptions, all citizens are now obligated to give their evidence before courts of law. It is hard to see why newsmen should be made a class apart in this respect; and it is likely that such an exemption would render our system of criminal justice less effective. The price of immunity for journalists would be less justice for everyone else. Here, too, we have a dilemma that is created by the newsman's increasing withdrawal of his consent from the traditional covenant of cooperative suspiciousness between the press and government. To resolve the issue is to change the American system in fundamental—and, again, unattractive—ways.

A Retreat from the Liberal Ideal

The deeper problem with this movement for a new journalism, however, is that it represents an incipient retreat, not merely from an intelligible idea of the public interest and of the responsibility of the press to serve it, but also from the entire liberal tradition of American journalism and the system of liberal democracy which it has fostered and served. The problem of the press publishing a few government secrets or withholding the names of an occasional criminal may be serious in principle but it is usually negligible in practice. But there is a larger practical question raised by "adversary" journalism that is not at all negligible: the question of the persistence of the open, fragmented, liberal system of American democracy as we have known it and benefited from it for the past many decades.

Our instinct is to assume that this system is virtually indestructible, rooted as it is in the pragmatic temper of the American people, the Constitutional system of division of powers, and other such factors apparently beyond the influence of what we do or think. This is a reasonable assumption within limits, but it isn't entirely true. The system also depends on many institutions and attitudes which are indeed changeable, and one of the most important—if least acknowledged—of these is the kind of press we have. Its capacity to find and publish vast amounts of information about politics and government, and its success in reaching universal audiences without regard to ideology or political affiliations, have contributed in an important way to the openness and flexibility of American government and to the ability of public opinion to influence the conduct of public affairs and to attain consensus. As the press has become wealthier in recent decades, its ability to gather and print information has increased; as political party organizations have declined, the need and willingness of officials to give newsmen access have also grown; so even while the complexity of government and the amount of "classified" information have increased, the capacity of the press to help the American system realize its ideals has at least kept pace.

The new movement abroad in the journalistic community threatens all this. For the press can make its contribution to the system only by maintaining close access—a closer access, as I have said, than can ever be provided by law. The price of such access is some degree of cooperation and sympathy for government—*not* a slavish adulation, as is sometimes said, but a decent respect for authority, a willingness to see government and persons in government given the opportunity to do their job, and at least a slight sense of responsibility for and commitment to the goals inherent in those jobs. When these are not present, access diminished. And when newsmen begin to assert they are positively the adversaries of government, access diminished drastically, and with it not only the contribution journalism can make but also the openness and flexibility of government itself. Politicians and officials are no more than human; they have their needs and interests; above all they intend to survive. If they feel themselves to be threatened or harmed, they will eventually take steps to insulate themselves as best they can from the danger.

The history of the Nixon Administration shows some of the ways in which this can occur. At one extreme there is Watergate itself—that is, the Plumbers, wiretaps and investigations of newsmen, harrassment of news organizations, and the like. This is an irrational and pathological response which is as unnecessary as it is intolerable, and we are not likely to see a recurrence in the discernible future. But the Nixon Administration used other methods as well, and these we can expect to see more of, regardless of who is in the White House, if the movement continues to gain ground. There is "jawboning": making speeches criticizing press coverage in hopes of reducing the press' credibility and increasing its cooperativeness. More important, there is the technique of organizing and formalizing all press-government contacts through the instrument of the Public Affairs/Public Information office and the centralized public relations operation, such as the one inaugurated by Herb Klein. And most powerful of all, there is the simple device of self-isolation, on the theory that it is better to have less of a bad press than more of a good press, especially in light of the fact that the effort to seek the latter can so easily end up earning one more of the former. Such a "low-profile" strategy—with infrequent and irregular press conferences, sharply limited informal contact between officials and reporters, even reliance on a praetorian staff lacking extensive ties outside the official family—is one of Richard Nixon's original contributions to the American political tradition. It is clearly an undesirable contribution, especially in its Nixonesque form, and yet it represents a logical adaptation to the perceived existence of an adversary press; the chances are we will see more of it insofar as the new movement gains ground. By the end of his campaign, even George McGovern seemed to be changing his mind about the desirability of having an "open" staff in constant informal contact with the press. The result, as he not unreasonably perceived it, was a bad press which emphasized the confusion and in-fighting within his official family and which thus suggested that McGovern was not a competent executive. It is hard to imagine that if he had won in 1972 he would have continued his policy of openness. The price is simply too high for any rational man to want to pay, and the benefits, if any, are too few and too small.

And as government adapts to the situation created by the current movement for a new journalism, so will the entire profession of journalism—and in ways that it does not now envision. As has been pointed out, the traditional form of the news story, the news organization's pattern of recruiting and training newsmen, even the format of the modern newspaper are all geared to the liberal, orthodox mode of journalism, with its preoccupation with facts and events, its relative unconcern for the problem of point of view, and its intention of appealing to a universal audience. In order to work, such a journalism needs reporters to have access to government, and when they no longer have it the capacity of newspapers to maintain the other features of the existing form is weakened, as is the whole idea of and justification for those features. Journalism will change—and the logical direction of change is toward the partisan form of journalism, with its ideological basis, politically based relationship to the government in power, and fractionated audiences. It is possible, of course, that an adversary journalism could persist indefinitely, but this seems unlikely. A stance of "pure" opposition—opposition as an end in itself, rather than as an expression of some larger, positive political commitment—is self-contradictory in theory and likely to be short-lived in practice. The probability is that an adversary press would eventually ally itself with a political faction and so become partisan—an ideologically divisive factor rather than a politically unifying force. The consequences could be enormous.

Two Scenarios for the Future

Now the partisan mode of journalism has its virtues. It does not evade the problem of "point of view" as liberal journalism does, and in this sense it has an appealing honesty. It also has the capacity to create and sustain coherent bodies of political opinion; at a time when political opinion in this country so often contradictory and inchoate, that is a very important trait. This is why "journals of opinion," existing on the margins of American journalism, have been so important and desirable.

But if, over the long run, American journalism were ever to turn massively to the partisan mode, the consequences of this development would extend to nearly every aspect of our political system. Partisan journalism would not increase the openness of the system, it would sharply decrease it. It would not reduce the scope of political conflict, but enlarge it. It would not increase the capacity of American government to act effectively and flexibly in meeting emergent needs, but would tend to paralyze it. It would not empower public opinion as a whole, but would transform it into a congeries of rigid ideological factions eternally at war with one another and subject to the leadership of small coteries of ideologues and manipulators. Indeed, it would tend to transform the entire nature of American politics: From having been a popular government based on a flexible consensus, it would become Europeanized into a popular government based on an equilibrium of hostile parties and unchanging ideologies.

The alternative to such a "Europeanization" of journalism and politics, it should be emphasized, does not have to be a massive and uncritical reversion to the way things were during the 1950's and early 1960's. Even if this were possible—which it isn't—it would clearly be undesirable. Both officialdom and the press were then busily abusing the "objective" tradition, officialdom by treating the media as an institution to be deliberately "managed" for its own expediential purposes, and the press by encouraging and acquiescing in these efforts out of inertia and a generalized avidity to print "big news" as often and as easily as possible.

There are ways to curb these abuses while still preserving the benefits of the liberal tradition of our press which the "adversary" approach would squander. Government can increase the amount of information which is formally made available on the public record. It can scale down its "public relations" operations to the point where they cannot easily operate as instruments of press management and are content instead merely to disseminate information. As Joseph Lee Auspitz and Clifford W. Brown, Jr., have suggested, the "strategic" cast of mind giving rise to, among other things, the habit of "managing" the press for purposes of personal power can be discouraged by strengthening the political party, which embeds individual actors in an institutional context, channels and restrains their ambition, and promotes a "representative" as against a "strategic" ethos. And the press, for its own part, can help to recover the objective tradition by abandoning its flirtation with the "oppositional" posture and by ceasing to exploit public affairs for their sensation value (since the desire to exploit public affairs in this way is the main incentive leading the press to acquiesce in the manipulations of "strategically"-minded officials). The result, I believe, will be a journalism that provides more, and more useful, information to the citizenry, and a political system that, in consequence, comes a bit closer than in the past to realizing its historic ideals.

NOTES

[1] I should point out that I am using the terms "journalism" and the "press" in these pages to refer to *daily* journalism only—that is, to daily newspapers and broadcast news programs. There are other forms of journalism, of course: weekly, monthly, quarterly, general purpose, special purpose, and so on. These other forms are important and interesting, and they perform crucial functions vis-à-vis government and the daily press itself. Unfortunately, space prevents me from considering them in this essay.

[2] Writing in the January 15, 1973 issue of *New York,* Richard Reeves described a classic instance of the traditional relationship. "I remember . . . my first big story with *The New York Times* in the summer of 1966 . . . a homicide case against a young man named Ernest Gallashaw, accused in the shooting of a ten-year-old boy during racial rioting in the East New York section of Brooklyn. . . . In ten days or so . . . I came back with notebooks full of interviews and evidence that made it clear . . . that New York City authorities were playing fast and loose with Gallashaw's life and freedom. . . . I wrote a three-column story, but just before deadline . . . I was told that it would not be published immediately and that I was to turn over our evidence to the Brooklyn District Attorney's office.

". . . Clifton Daniel, then the managing editor . . . explained . . . that homicide investigations were government business. . . . The *Times* ran the complete story a day later, beginning on page 1 with a lead saying the District Attorney was investigating new evidence in the case."

Michael Novak:

Why the Working Man Hates the Media

OFTEN AT MY DESK high up on the forty-second floor of the *Time-Life* building, I look out at the blue and silver skyscrapers of mid-Manhattan and imagine all the other managers, assistants, lawyers, trustees, officers and publicists who fly on the same planes with me and read the same magazines. *Here,* I think, is the culture of the national news. It is not the most populous culture in America. It has little emotional and symbolic connection with the other Americas. Now that brisk winds have blown euphoria away, the rise of Gerald Ford may reveal how isolated this culture is, how resentful millions have become of it.

Nonliberal politicians these days disguise their distance from the interests of working people by a simple tactic: they attack the national media. Such a temptation will soon haunt the sleep of Gerald Ford; his pardon of Richard Nixon made him seem to millions foolish or corrupt. To defend himself, Ford will remember what all nonliberals know, that cynicism about the culture of the national media flourishes in the neighborhoods and small towns. Only a few Americans—national journalists among them—fly on airplanes, have expense accounts, are photographed with the glamorous and the powerful, bask in the corrupting glow of well-publicized success. National journalists do not seem to be wage earners, representatives of neighborhood people. Nonliberal politicians exploit this wedge. They try to show that *they* are more like people in the neighborhoods than is the press. Neighborhood people, looking at government and at the media, are apt to cry, "A plague on both your houses!"

In Pennsylvania, recently, a long-time voter for Democratic candidates told me in a voice of certainty: "You know who did it? The media—they did it. They'd have never got him if they hadn't drummed away at it, day after day."

Usually, this man doesn't talk that way. So I pressed.

"They lie," he insisted. "Walter Cronkite lies. John Chancellor never tells the truth. They all lie."

I could hardly believe the certainty in his voice. He wasn't angry; he was exhibiting "the new cynicism."

Mr. Novak is a prolific writer on the mass media and their problems. This essay is reprinted from *(MORE)*, Oct., 1974, by permission of *(MORE)*, 750 Third Ave., New York, N.Y. 10017, copyright Rosebud Associates, Inc., 1974.

I had been reading some of David Riesman's early articles, from the 1950s, about the precarious position of intellectuals in American life and the need for a critical public. It struck me that, emotionally, the tables have been turned. Many ordinary citizens feel that the intellectuals—and, of course, they include newsmen—have now gained enormous powers they themselves do not possess: power to expose their ideas, power to set the cultural tone and style, power to reveal or to hide what they will. In a huge and complicated continental nation, those who guard the gates of the national media determine what will be perceived by millions, from what angle, for how long: power over reality itself. What does not get "out" in the national media might just as well—it sometimes seems—not exist. The new cynicism, then, is a defense against enormous power. Those in the national media who hoped to develop a public more critical about its government, its merchants and its corporations have also made the people cynical about the press.

For some years now, psychologist Robert Coles has been trying to alert us to the dangerous hostility toward the media growing in every section of the country—in Mississippi, in New Mexico, in Massachusetts. I saw it happen in 1970 in more than two dozen states in congressional elections: attacks upon the media had become almost a mandatory ritual, even for left-of-center politicians. Representatives of the people still have to put some distance between themselves and the culture of the national news. When citizens begin to look at "us" and "them," a political leader doesn't want to be among "them."

WHAT DISCONNECTS the national news culture from the local cultures in which most citizens live? It is a mistake to describe the disconnection in terms of political doctrines or ideologies, for it is, rather, a disconnection of cultures—even, perhaps, of social classes.

David Halberstam took a shot at defining the disconnection in *Esquire* last April; practically every journalist is trying to understand this disconcerting cynicism he can almost taste. The cynicism, to Halberstam's ear, runs like this: Richard Nixon is a victim "of an Eastern-bred, Eastern-educated elite working for Eastern newspapers and the great networks. They do not like him and never have; they will never give him a fair chance. They are against him because of his ideas . . . because he is too American, too representative of American culture . . . His vision of America was more accurate than theirs. For that, for being more right about the country, they can never forgive him."

In reply, Halberstam argues that the press is not "liberal" in any simple sense; most national reporters, like other Americans, have rather complicated political and social views. Moreover, he notes, most national news reporters are not in fact Easterners. (The same issue of *Esquire* carries a long portrait of Dan Rather of Houston.) Chet Huntley, David Brinkley, Harry Reasoner, Walter Cronkite, Eric Sevareid, Jim Hartz, Tom Wicker and many other stars of the news were born, bred and educated in the heart of the country. "Eastern," indeed, is an odd term. To be born in Queens or Newark, in Dorchester or Lackawanna, or North Pittsburgh, is not exactly to be "Eastern" in the sense intended.

Halberstam goes wrong, however, in arguing that what makes national reporters special is their critical faculty. They are "more skeptical and less reverent than their fellow Americans," he says. But truck drivers and construction workers are quite capable of irreverence; farmers in Iowa and ranchers in Wyoming have been known to be skeptical; some people of Missouri say "show me." It is not that they are Eastern, Halberstam then writes of reporters; they are "a product of something more complex, an educational system that is largely Eastern (but often not: Oberlin, Stanford, Tulane, Northwestern, Reed), where the *critical facility* [sic] is appreciated, developed and honed. The ability to sit outside, think and analyze is appreciated." Here the Harvard-educated Halberstam gives away his own outrageous bias: "Most American universities do not develop the critical faculty; they mass-produce education . . ." If Halberstam would check the school roster from which our national journalists come—Willie Morris, Bill Moyers, James Naughton, Bill Kovach, R. W. Apple, Max Frankel, Frank Mankiewicz, and all the others—the distribution seems quite representative of small colleges, sprawling state universities, Catholic schools, subway campuses—all the varieties of American schools.

National reporters are not any more cynical or skeptical or critical than ordinary American farmers, workers or other taxpayers. But a university education does change their class status. Reporters tend to identify with different objects of reverence, to exhibit a different cognitive style and to nourish a different vision of the nation's past, present reality and future. Their class interests are different from those of many of their fellow citizens.

Nonetheless, journalists do have a preponderant role in shaping the public universe of discourse. *Their* vision becomes a public fact, in the papers and on the television. Other Americans must cling to their own private vision, defending it against media bombardment. National reporters have a monopoly on national attention; citizens who see things differently are—so far as public communication goes—in a position of virtual helplessness.

The media create a public symbolic reality, a main line mythical world more real than any private world. It is a world in which status is ascribed, narrative position is assigned ("forward-looking," "old-fashioned," "timely") and values are lavishly or faintly praised (the "new" morality, the "old" morality). However realistic and correct a private person may judge his or her own attitudes to be, when these attitudes are not confirmed in the public media they cannot help seeming rather sectarian, narrow, even "uninformed." It is assumed that the media represent some public norm, or at least a mainstream reality—and that those not in tune with it are quaint, out of touch, not "with it," not where "it's at." (What is this "it" that we should be "with"? The action, the front edge, that which makes "news." "It" makes news and news discerns "it.")

Many professors and intellectuals do not identify with what is represented as reality in the supercultural seven: *The New York Times, The Washington Post, Time, Newsweek,* ABC, CBS, and NBC. Many other citizens also do not identify reality with the reports of the supercultural seven. But the supercultural seven *do* create a reality with which all citizens have to deal. In September, 1967, I recall vividly an argument at a conference of academics on the Eastern seaboard. I had been teaching at Stanford for two years and came fresh from observation of the Student Left and the then unnamed "counterculture" of the Bay Area. The Easterners present were drily skeptical about my anticipation of a coming era of radicalism and mysticism; in their environment, it had too little reality. Then *Time* discovered "the new generation" and "the flower children." In 1968, "Clean for Gene" and Columbia and then the Chicago convention "radicalized" many; Martin Luther King's death, the rioting, and the assassination of Robert Kennedy added to the mood.

In that year, step by step, the national media "legitimized" perceptions previously shared by tiny minorities. The swiftness of the process of "radicalization" was breathtaking. Friendships of long standing were ruptured, marriages dissolved, lives were dramatically altered. Through vicarious experiences gained through the media, many "changed their life-style." This power of the media to alter convictions of a lifetime was impressive. Could an exuberant right-wing radicalism, expressed freely and dramatically, with a certain awe-inducing sincerity, also sway many people suddenly?

The mood of the 1960s—evanescent but made intimate by television and the vivid "new journalism"—obliged many journalists to declare themselves. Sickened by the sights of the Chicago convention, one reporter wrote in pain: "They are beating our children." The young policemen and guardsmen were also, however, to another social class, "our kids." Events portrayed as a war between the generations might equally have been portrayed as a war between social classes. The highest level of support for George Wallace came from those between 21–29 years of age.

The point is that, whatever was in fact taking place in 1968, the media had to select what to report, how to report it and how to interpret it. And these decisions gave the media enormous power over the public perception of reality—in a sense, over reality itself. "And that's the way it is," Walter Cronkite ends his show. But what if it isn't that way? The justification given at awards banquets is that the media "enlighten." But one man's enlightenment is another man's bullshit. In shaping the public perception of social life, the media enforce a version of reality.

Suppose, for example, the media had chosen *not* to report the civil rights struggle of 1963 and 1964; never to give space or time to militants like Rap Brown or Stokely Carmichael; not to cover local struggles over integration; never to air confrontations or riots; then, the civil rights "movement" might not have been a movement at all. It surely would have lost its single most potent political weapon: public awareness, outrage and support. Without the media, minorities are reduced to isolation. In the balance of powers in the

United States, the media are an absolutely crucial fulcrum. A leader who knows how to use the media achieves sudden eminence, prestige—and, concomitantly, power and resources. That the media are accessible to disadvantaged minorities is a great credit to them; but in giving one group such social power, journalists will in fact be taking sides. There are wise and unwise ways of doing that.

NATIONAL JOURNALISTS are not different from Sicilian longshoremen, as Halberstam would have it, because they possess more native cynicism. They are different because they have more power—more social power and more personal power. Halberstam describes journalists as a "product" of "something more complex, an educational system"; they have the ability to "sit outside." That they have the luxury "to sit outside" is mainly the function of a high class position. Who can forget CBS George Herman questioning Senator George McGovern during the California primary of 1972 about the Senator's one-thousand-dollar "demogrants"? What will the impact of these grants be, Herman asked incredulously, on people with ordinary incomes, well, like myself? Let us suppose for simplicity's sake that Herman's income was $25,000 per year. That placed him in the top 5 per cent of all Americans. He seemed oblivious to the distance between him and others. Hardly a quarter of American families have an income over $15,000 per year; and the vast majority of families find their income is fixed for the rest of their lives by age 35. National journalists tend to lose touch with the daily economic hardships of a majority of the American people.

National journalists participate in the culture of the upper classes—in the mobile, fluid, national superculture of America's higher circles. Most do not rank as high on scales of status as the landed rich or university professors; they are subject to snubs and slights, too. But from the point of view of those who travel less and earn less and meet no celebrities, national journalists live in the world of glamour, wealth, status, and power. They are no longer representatives of ordinary people. A national journalist like Tom Wicker, say, outranks most U.S. congressmen, and even a great many U.S. senators, in most social contexts—is better known, has a greater public power, has a certain power *over* "men of power" (just as Washington reporter Rich Morgan has in Wicker's novel, *Facing the Lions*).

The national press represents a far greater social power in a post-industrial society than it used to represent in an agricultural society; for so much of today's marketing and sudden obsolescence depend upon images projected by the media. Not only private careers, even whole industries, depend upon image making. The makers and creators of images are today stronger than local realities, because outside of the public information systems there are weaker social ties than ever before. What the public networks say is true is less and less balanced by effective and organized private networks. Sen. Hugh Scott is known to the citizens of Pennsylvania through the media, not through personal contacts. He is what he *appears* to be. Few public figures are so well known to their constituencies apart from the media that they are invulnerable to fluctuations in media approval.

What people resent in the media, therefore, is not the irreverence of outsiders, not the sharp skeptical minds of innocent, powerless reporters. Quite the opposite. What people resent is the new economic power of the media, the myth-making which erects great new realities. They also resent the arrogance that tells people every day: "We're smarter, better-informed, more critical, more skeptical than you. You've been mass-produced; we've been specially produced, custom-made." They also resent the fact that *they* are so often excluded. The news so seldom reflects their point of view, their values, *their* skepticism.

In the massive publicity about social reforms in the 1960s, for example, national reporters seemed to be the true believers, the enthusiasts, even the missionaries. It was ordinary people who were at times (while providing huge voting majorities) more skeptical; and for that they were sometimes chided for being reactionary, stupid and mean. Concerning school busing, it was again millions of ordinary people, white and black, who were skeptical and cynical; national reporters tended—and still tend in 1974, although with noticeable wavering—to believe that some great ideal would be realized through so fallible and flawed an instrument. For ordinary people understand the realities of class, pluralism and institutional racism in America, their key life decisions about where to live are made with these realities in mind. The children of a Ukrainian auto worker, none of whose family has ever yet gone to college, will if bused to a school in a black neighborhood experience no class gain. His children will not be going to a better school than the one they are in. Why should people who believe in the possibility of upward mobility surrender to enforced downward mobility? Such people are liable to be more skeptical than David Halberstam and his colleagues—and reasonably resentful of the palpable moralistic innuendoes they are made to suffer because they cannot make their stubborn realism go away.

OUR POLITICS is complicated by the fact that each person belongs to more than one group, and that each group is involved in more than one coalition with other groups. Few Americans try to be doctrinally pure. Most try to be realistic about their own interests, as they perceive them. National newsmen, too, have interests—interests, for example, in a supercultural rather than subcultural point of view, and in the patrician high civil religion of their employers. Both conservative and liberal journalists on the national level have such interests. Indeed, many Americans do not make sharp distinctions between liberal and conservative newsmen so much as between national and local newsmen. Not very many Americans actually live in "superculture"; almost all live in some subculture or other. For this reason, the national newsmen, speaking to superculture, are nearly always out of focus in the eyes of the many who live in other cultures.

National news reporters fail to make connection with many people because of a structural flaw in the concept of "national news." In order to take a national point of view, and to report on events from a national perspective, a more or less national language, style and point of view have been constructed. While there are some millions of Americans who *do* live in this national superculture, there are many millions who do not, who identify rather with their own cultural or regional or local history. Most Americans have never been on an airplane. Even a great many colleges and universities tend to reflect local, cultural or regional perspectives rather than national perspectives; are agencies rather of local subculture than of national superculture. Moreover, the national superculture is not, precisely, cosmopolitan, except in flavor. It is true that persons from many subcultures enter into it. But, once there, tendencies they encounter are not so much directed toward gaining insight into and sympathy for the many subcultures of America as toward imagining the vast surrounding set of subcultures as some sort of inferior and homogeneous "middle America." That expression, "middle America," reveals an indifference to diversity that is not truly cosmopolitan.

There is a related structural flaw in the national news. Reporters are commonly sent into subcultures to "report on" what is happening there *from the perspective of* and *with the tastes of* representatives of the national superculture. Seldom does it happen that reporters go into communities in order *to express the perspective, the way of life,* and *the attitudes of* the members of that community. A vivid example of this difference occurred in the television reports on the riot at Attica. All three contending parties—the prisoners, the townspeople and the families of the prisoners—felt that their own stories had been distorted. How could this be? Reporters, apparently, did not try to tell the three separate sorts of stories, in a full and sympathetic way, but rather to tell a single story. They simplified the story from their own point of view. They did not show it as a conflict among (at least) three separate cultures. Many stories are cut to procrustean shape in this way.

IT WOULD HELP national reporting if reporters were given to freer rein to do what some of them already do splendidly: to report *from* various American subcultures to the larger world, rather than to report *on* such subcultures from the perspective of the national culture. What I have in mind are people in towns and neighborhoods all across the United States which I visited in the political campaigns of 1970 and 1972: I recall faces in Jeannette and Central City, Pennsylvania; the Irish quarter of Manchester, New Hampshire; a school yard in Youngstown, Ohio; a motel in Laramie, Wyoming; a Spanish-surname festival in Albuquerque, New Mexico; a lodge in Sioux Falls, South Dakota. Seldom does one see these people again, ever, on television, or hear again their accents and their surprisingly complicated views. They are not smooth and slick like the actors on TV, or reduced to a slogan or a single sentiment in a sidewalk "opinion sample." One wonders, indeed, whose world *is* represented on television? It is no one's world. It is a fantasy. A report on no place.

CBS' Charles Kuralt, it is true, keeps a "journal" on the unusual character, the colorful angle of vision, the extraordinary person. And this is a help, like drops of water in a desert. But a larger strategy is needed. News programs, as "reports on America," should confirm in image what is true in reality: the diversity and concrete complexity of this land. The medium, one would think, would prosper from attention to nuance and concrete difference. It would gain in novelty and variety. Above all, it would gain in credibility—not that credibility which comes from "not telling untruths" (almost abstract) but that credibility which comes from reflecting back the actual concrete texture of American diversity.

National reporters would have to be allowed to present themselves in rather new postures. Tom Wicker, for example, reflects in his novel on the complicated vision of self and world that is the heritage of the born Southerner; yet somehow, in his reporting, one gains the impression of a Southerner trying to prove to his readers that he is at least as liberal as they. One does not often gain the impression that the distinctive experience of the South, whether liberal or conservative, has truth and wisdom to it that need no apology. Willie Morris describes well the pressures of New York: the national culture makes Uncle Toms of local boys. It ought, instead, to recognize that those who can put into words a distinctive local culture are an invaluable resource. Reporters now must prove their aptitude for grasping the national point of view. The new criterion would be whether they can represent local points of view so accurately that local people say: "That's how I feel."

Imagine taking a film crew into five different neighborhoods in Toledo, Ohio, in order to film five different families' response to death. Or filming the kitchens in five different homes, showing in how many different ways a kitchen functions in different cultures. Or filming five weddings, or births, or graduations. Such ritual occasions exemplify quite different conceptions of life.

Similarly on occasion of social conflict. A high proportion of political conflict in the United States is group conflict, and arises not only out of conflicting material interests—income, jobs, neighborhoods, scholarships, etc.— but also out of conflicting cultural perceptions. Matters would be simpler if what was at stake were simply a straightforward competition over the distribution of goods. Instead, perceptions are almost always in conflict, too. Imagine an Italian-American neighborhood in Brooklyn, whose families have lived there with remarkable stability ever since their first arrival in America about 1910. When their neighborhood school is obliged to admit black students from nearby areas, what are the real economic interests of this community and what are its actual perceptions? It is not likely that the neighborhood views the in-migration of blacks as a signal of improved services and long-range stability, or as a portent of upward mobility for their own children. What that is good will probably now happen to their community? On their arrival in the United States, Italian-Americans were being paid *less* than black workers doing comparable work. They were not responsible for, and do not feel guilty for, the three centuries of slavery suffered by blacks; indeed, they themselves have been free from the institutions of serfdom in Sicily about the same number of decades as blacks. They tend to be cynical about the superior morality affected by leaders of the New York City establishment, who speak so eloquently about civil rights, equality, and opportunity; for the *price* for the mistreatment of blacks is usually not exacted from the establishment that benefited from it. Who pays the price? The newer immigrants. And yet the community has many resources for coping with black in-migration. Its preference for staying put is one such resource. Its self-reliance upon family networks is another. Its shops, cafes, stores, and special character are a third. Its hardheaded realism and distrust of moralism is a fourth.

There is, in short, a way of reporting on such a community locked in such a struggle that gives the viewer a sense of the very real tentacles and loose ends of the story. Who are the blacks who are moving in? Are they successful, reasonably affluent blacks looking for a stable, integrated neighborhood? Or poorer blacks, less well off than the Italian-Americans? What have their family trajectories been like these past three or four generations? In what ways are their values and life-styles similar, or dissimilar, to those of the community they are entering? What are their perceptions, aspirations, fears? Do they perceive their future neighbors as "Whites" or as "Italian-Americans"? Are their perceptions of Italian-Americans accurate, and have the Italian-Americans an accurate perception of them?

The point is that it is not enough for a national newsman to sample opinion from two or three citizens. The cultural ecology of our cities must be explained, and the secrets of communal living brought to the surface. Integration can and does proceed under certain circumstances. What are they? How can integration be rewarded, so that communities desire it? Why should a community be punished for it by a decline in services, as at present? Integration is one of the greatest and most complex dramas of American history; it is occurring in every major city of the land, and television has yet to explore its cultural ecology. Where it has not simplified, the television news has appeared merely to moralize. As at Attica, so almost everywhere both black and white workers feel that their point of view has never yet been aired on the news, in the full context of their own experience.

WHAT I HAVE HERE tried to suggest about one neighborhood might be said of virtually every neighborhood in every American city. The newspapers and the broadcast journalists seldom render the realities of a city's neighborhoods. The major metropolitan organs proceed as if they were reporting on a more or less homogenized melting pot, with a "citywide" perspective. But a majority of the citizens in any neighborhood almost certainly do not maintain a citywide perspective in their daily lives. This is why so many Americans feel that the media leave them out, forget them, do not notice them. When they do appear in a news item, it is ordinarily in the grossest of cliches: a "tight-knit ethnic neighborhood, with row after row of neat homes, where men and women work hard to make ends meet . . .''

Clearly, the national news is geared to too high and general a focus. It assumes that there is a national homogeneous point of view. It does not adequately focus on America's real diversity of soul—a profound diversity of perception and point of view. The problem is not so much the assumption that there is a common national culture; in a certain sense there is. The problem is, rather, the choice of one part of that culture—those who live on a national wavelength, attuned to a national perspective, a kind of overclass—as the vehicle through which all others will be understood. This is where the distortion arises, and where it must be overcome.

John C. Merrill:

The "Apollonysian" Journalist

THE JOURNALIST SHOULD recognize the imperative of freedom, but he should incorporate into his journalistic philosophy the two other emphases of tremendous importance: rationality and commitment. At the same time he must—and *will* with these philosophical dimensions—become a kind of journalistic scientist-artist, part Apollo and part Dionysus, a person who merges the perspectives of objective reason and existential subjectivity.

Such a synthesis will produce a journalist who may well be called the "Apollonysian"; a person who thinks *and* feels, who is both rational *and* sensitive, who is both concerned with facts *and* with feelings, who is dedicated to the objective world "out there" *and* to his subjective world "in here." He is, in essence, the rational synthesizer—the journalist who is able to *intentionally* develop a journalistic philosophy which merges the strains (or stances) of freedom, rationality and duty. As has been stated earlier, "responsibility" (noticeably missing in the above lists) is considered implicit in each of these orientations: the free journalist who tempers his journalism with reason, sensitivity and commitment *is a responsible journalist*.

Dr. Merrill is professor of journalism at the University of Missouri—Columbia. This chapter is reprinted here by permission from his *The Imperative of Freedom: A Philosophy of Journalistic Autonomy* (New York: Hastings House, Publishers, 1974).

Freedom, Rationality and Commitment

In a very real sense these three terms form the philosophical framework of this entire book; they certainly converge to describe the proposed journalistic philosophy. In them are found the strains of existentialism, rational humanism and Kantianism which flow throughout these pages; implicit in these terms, also, are found the orientations—the *intellectual* (rational) and the *mystical* (emotional)—designated by Nietzsche as "Apollonian" and "Dionysian." Let us look briefly at the three strains of freedom, rationality and commitment before considering each of them in more detail.

First, *freedom*. As the French writer and journalist, Albert Camus, has said: "When the press is free it may be good and bad—but certainly without freedom it can never be anything but bad. . . . For the press, as for man, freedom is the opportunity to become better: servitude is the certainty of becoming worse." [1] The whole idea of ethics depends on personal freedom—freedom to make choices. Ethics is, as Hazel Barnes says, "an inner control which the individual exercises over himself," [2] and certainly freedom to exercise this control is basic to any moral concept. Existentialism puts supreme value on freedom, contending that if "one accepts freedom as a fact, then no act is ethical which acts as if men were not free." [3] Not only Existentialists, but rationalists and Kantians place great importance on freedom.

Second, *rationality*. This is one of the cornerstones, along with freedom, of a journalistic philosophy. Objectivists such as Ayn Rand and humanists such as Erich Fromm pay homage to it. Even the Existentialists agree that it is important, although they would certainly accord the emotions and the senses equal status. What the Existentialists want to do is to reunite the "irrational parts of the psyche" with the rational parts. It is a shift of emphasis only, a shift to the thinker who has the idea and away from the idea itself. Existentialism accepts as valid and important man's thought—but goes further and stresses the validity of other aspects of man: his body, blood, bones, his frailty, contingency and fallibility. [4]

Hazel Barnes stresses the importance placed on rationality by the Existentialist:

> An ethics must introduce rationality as one of its criteria even though it may at the same time insist that its goal is happiness or satisfaction or some other state which is closer to emotion than to reason. Fidelity to the truth of man and the Universe is essential. . . . Rationality involves more than intellectual honesty. It requires as one of its corollary values a respect for consistency. [5]

Any philosophy which does not admit rationality to the field of ethics would, undoubtedly, be cooperating with anarchistic or autocratic forces which would tend to regulate man's affairs or would inject chaos into them. [6] If there is not a large dose of reason in one's ethical determinations, there can really be little or no consistency and predictability to ethical actions. And, of course, one of the main purposes of ethics is to serve as a reliable and helpful guide to right actions. Such a guide cannot be provided simply by whim or instinct; otherwise we could talk of dogs and cats as being ethically motivated.

Now, lastly, *commitment* or *duty*. The existential commitment is very similar to Kantian duty; both actually imply a rational choice and a determination to be loyal to that choice. The concept of "either/or" is important to the Existentialist; one should commit himself either to this or to that. A choice is forced upon him. Karl Jaspers says that when, in any matter, a man is truly himself he will recognize that there are alternatives and that his action will not be a compromise. "He will want to force a decision between the alternatives he has recognized," Jaspers writes.[7] This choosing between alternatives is actually the basis of ethics; in choice there is a rational commitment. Kant, too, insists on personal commitment; for each man must rationally come up with his own standards and values, and he must *obey* them. Ethics, to Kant, is as personal as it is to the Existentialists. It is actually one's duty to obey the laws of logic, of reason, and to have very high (and strict) personal standards of conduct—not to be rationalized away by thoughts of consequences.

Acting morally, for Kant, is acting on the basis of duty or on principle itself and not on any outcome (supposed or otherwise) of the action. Thus the principle is *a priori*—prior to the action—and when we take a principle as an inner rule for ourselves, it is a maxim which we have a commitment to. For example, in journalism, if a newspaper accepts the maxim that villainy ought to be exposed, then it has a *duty* to that principle; it should not consider consequences or try to rationalize it in any way—it should simply proceed to expose villainy. The British journalist, Arnold Goodman, makes this specific point in the *New Statesman,* when he writes:

> A great newspaper—if it believes that villainy ought to be exposed—
> should expose it without hesitation and without regard to the law of
> libel. If the editor, his reporters and his advisers are men of judgment
> and sense, they are unlikely to go wrong; but if they do go wrong the
> principle to publish and be damned is a valiant and sensible one for the
> newspaper and it should bear the responsibility.[8]

The authentic journalist—the truly moral one—would not act to please somebody or to gain some advantage or to secure some reward. If he acted on the basis of consequences, his journalism would fall to the level of expediency. The act should be done because the journalist is convinced that it is right. The Kantian journalist, like the Existential journalist, is not one who looks around for reasons to justify his action; he is unimpressed with the consequences of his journalism (honor, self-preservation, comfort, status, love, happiness for self or others, etc.). The basis of duty, according to Kant, is conformity to principle, and principle is a rule that can apply to all men; thus man makes his actions moral by bringing them up to the level of universality.

Now, a word on the synthesis of these three strains. Connected with the strain of *freedom* (with its existential emphasis) is the journalistic orientation which has been referred to earlier as "Dionysian." And, connected with the philosophical strains of *rational humanism* and Kantian *obligationism* is the orientation which has been called "Apollonian." These strains merge to result in a journalistic philosophy which I am calling "Apollonysian"—an orientation which makes for a kind of rationalistic commitment to humanistic existentialism. It is this philosophy that the *Apollonysian* journalist embraces. His main dedication is to *freedom;* but he recognizes that freedom is empty unless merged with commitment, rationality, and other residual concepts stemming from Kantianism and Objectivistic Humanism. Let us now look more closely at these three strains.

Freedom: The Existentialist Strain

What a journalist does in specific cases does not matter as much as the fact that he *does* something. The supreme virtue for the Existentialist is probably the most old-fashioned of all: *integrity*. And a person cannot have integrity unless he utilizes his capacity to choose, to act, to make decisions. Basic to man is this act of choosing; the Existentialist sees man's very nature consisting of choosing. And this choosing is an outgrowth of freedom; or, said another way, it can have real meaning only in an atmosphere of freedom. To the question, "What good is life?" comes the answer: Life in the abstract is worthless. As a person lives his life, its value can be judged by what he puts into it. Values are a projection of man's personal freedom. For the Existentialist, man *is* freedom; he does not *possess* freedom. Freedom, for the Existentialist, comes as close as possible to constituting man's very essence. Man's most basic desire is for independent, free choice.

The Existentialist sees responsibility as freedom's anchorage. Man is responsible for himself, of course, but also for each act, and for the consequences of each act. Nobody else can be responsible for what a person is; each person must act freely and accept the responsibility for his action. And to choose for oneself is to choose for others. What would others do in my place? Strangely, perhaps, Existentialists view this universalized personal choice in much the same way as the coldly formal Kant did: You must never will what you cannot consistently will should be willed by other rational (i.e., free and responsible) beings. This heavy sense of personal responsibility the Existentialists call "anguish." Sartre has said that man is "condemned" to be free, and Kierkegaard wrote of the necessity to choose only "in fear and trembling." But choose we must—for ourselves and for all others, with no final assurance that our choice is the "right" one.[9]

Naturally we attempt to escape the implications of this existential situation. Often we try to deny that we are responsible for our actions by denying that we are free. The journalist, for example, may often say that *he* would not have written the story in such a way—or would not have written it at all—but that he "had to do it" because he was told to by his editor. He is thereby denying his freedom and refusing to accept personal responsibility for his actions. In practical terms, this embrace of "determinism" in various of its forms, amounts to denying that we are to blame for our actions—or for our morality. Existentialists, enthroning freedom, have no sympathy for these deterministic philosophies. And people who accept them, who try to escape from the human condition of freedom and personal responsibility, are seen as cowards. The Existentialist realizes that man must accept unquestioned responsibility for his ethical choices and actions. Man is an individualist: he is the end-all and be-all of values.

Self-deception, for the Existentialist, is the greatest vice, for it robs man of his personhood, his integrity; it deludes him into thinking that he is nothing more than a robot having an essence pushed upon him by *outside* forces. Man *makes himself*, says the Existentialist, or defines what he is in the course of choosing, acting and existing.

The philosophical strain of freedom is basic to a sound and authentic journalistic orientation. Existentialism stresses this strain; so does Kant, but there is a difference. Sartre agrees with Kant in conceiving of freedom as desiring "both itself and the freedom of others." But, Sartre notes, Kant believes that "the formal and universal are enough to constitute an ethics"; Existentialists, on the other hand, "think that principles which are too abstract run aground in trying to decide action." [10] Sartre emphasizes personal responsibility—absolute responsibility for actions taken in specific cases and considering specific circumstances. So we see that the Existentialist, though prizing freedom, is basically a situationist while Kant is a universalist.

Action implies freedom. Since Existentialists advocate action, they would, of course, place freedom near to the heart of their philosophy. They have a passion for freedom; this is true of all varieties of Existentialists. Freedom for the Existentialist (as for Kant) is a basic postulate for action; it is already present as a condition for human existence. Freedom, of course, is dangerous; it even tends to contain in itself the seed of its own destruction. Nikolai Berdyaev, an Existentialist who has written articulately on the subject of freedom, puts it thusly: "The tragedy of the world process is that of freedom; it is born of the inner dynamic of freedom, of its capacity of changing into its opposite." [11] In striking this note, Berdyaev is consistent with many of his fellow Existentialists. Plato, of course, in his classic "Paradox of Freedom," had pre-dated the Existentialists in pointing out this danger centuries earlier when he noted that free men could freely decide to become enslaved.

Freedom may indeed be dangerous. And for many it is uncomfortable; they constantly try to "escape" from it. Nevertheless, freedom is absolutely necessary to an open society, to a democracy, to a libertarian people—and certainly to a pluralistic and diversified journalism. And, as Existentialists contend, there is no human dignity without freedom—and "the risk of increasing freedom must constantly be taken,'' as John Macquarrie puts it.[12] Existentialists generally link freedom with creativity. Without freedom *from* restraints, man cannot have freedom *for* creative activity. Berdyaev and other Existentialists reveal a certain elitist or aristocratic tendency: the masses, they say, do not really value freedom and are satisfied with the routine daily existence. For this reason the masses ''are peculiarly exposed to the dangers of dictatorship, founded on demagogy.'' [13] This is perhaps true, for it is the rebel against the tyrannizing and conformizing influences of the masses who cherishes freedom; it is he who protests against every attempt to diminish freedom. It is he who realizes, as did Albert Camus, that ''freedom preserves the power to protest and guarantees human communication.'' [14]

The freedom-loving journalist can find perhaps his greatest support from the Existentialists, for here is a philosophy which rebels against any social control system which tends to enslave the individual human being and to lead to his depersonalization. Frederick Patka writes that Existentialists ''protest against this total subjection of the individual by the organized many'' and that they ''demand a bold revolt against this state of affairs with a view to the emancipation and autonomy of the individual person.'' [15] Existentialists, however, often draw attention to the danger inherent in mass communication. The following words reflect existentialist thought on this subject:

> The existentialists rightly point out that mass-communication, or systematic manipulation of human beings, does not and can not achieve the goal of self-transcendence. On the contrary, it becomes the responsible cause of the complete depersonalization, disintegration, and self-estrangement of the individual human being. This situation imposes the need to reject the assumptions of mass-conditioning and to bring human communication back and up to the personal form of an ''I-Thou'' relationship, which will eventually lead to the satisfaction of man's higher aspirations for the immaterial, cultural, moral, and religious ideals of existence.[16]

The modern journalist, within whom the strain of existentialist freedom is strong, will recognize the potential danger of manipulating and enslaving others. If he desires freedom for himself, he will desire freedom for others and he will cherish their authenticity and autonomy as he cherishes his own. The real freedom-lover, in other words, will defend freedom for others as well as for himself. He knows full well that when only *some* have freedom, they are tyrants and autocrats—or at least they have the potential within them. When *all* have freedom, at least everyone has the power to counteract tyranny and autocracy—or to escape from it through his own freedom. The existential journalist is certainly free to exercise his freedom in ways considered irresponsible to others, but the rationalist, the humanist and the Kantian in him will temper his activities with moderation, concern and reason and will keep him from falling into the abyss of nihilism.

The existential strain is especially important for the journalist for it provides the fundamental foundation of freedom. It gives him the spirit of creativity, of action, of commitment, the desire to launch out into new journalistic regions and the willingness to take the consequences for his actions. What he *does* makes him authentic, real, human. How he reacts to his world through his journalism defines him as a journalist. *"Respondeo, ergo sum."* [17]

Journalists must respond to their environment—to their own journalistic situation. They are more than neutral observers; if they are not, say the Existentialists, then they are *nothing*. The true Existentialist in journalism gets *into* the story, becomes part of the story. His sensitiveness to the stimuli of the story infiltrates the story; in short, the existential journalist is part of the story and the story is part of him. This, of course, affects the journalistic Self and disrupts any demeanor of "objective neutrality"; it brings subjectivity to bear on the Event-Reporter-Report nexus, and it is what largely injects journalism with Dionysian ingredients of artistry, sensitivity, emotionalism, personalism, mysticism and opinionism.

Reason: The Objectivist-Humanist Strain

The importance of reason is not to be denied in any kind of viable system, journalistic or otherwise. It is really the link that connects Existentialism, with its freedom, and Kantianism, with its duty. Reason is especially strong in the Objectivist-Humanist strain. This is true even among such diverse thinkers as Erich Fromm, Ayn Rand, Aldous Huxley, Ortega y Gasset, Eric Hoffer and Max Eastman—all of whom embrace some form of objectivism or rational humanism. These are, in general, the thinkers who reject the subjectivist notion that value judgments have no objective validity; Fromm and his philosophical kin believe that some values are better than others and that not all opinions, notions or people are equal—that there are objective differences.

Ayn Rand, expressing her "objectivist" philosophy, places special importance on reason. Her "New Intellectual" is a person "who lives up to the exact meaning of his title: a man who is guided by his *intellect*—not a zombie guided by feelings, instincts, urges, wishes, whims or revelations. . . . an *integrated* man, that is: a thinker who is a man of action." [18] And, like the Existentialist, Rand sees the strong connection between reasons and freedom. She writes:

> Reason requires freedom, self-confidence and self-esteem. It requires the right to think and to act on the guidance of one's thinking—the right to live by one's own independent judgment. *Intellectual* freedom cannot exist without *political* freedom; political freedom cannot exist without *economic* freedom.[19]

Objectivists and rational humanists also make much of self-esteem, and Ayn Rand, of course, has built a whole philosophy on rational self-interest. Erich Fromm points out that there is nothing wrong with selfishness, and that the self must be affirmed; in fact, he says that if a person "can only 'love' others, he cannot love at all." [20] Eric Hoffer stresses the importance of self-esteem and self-confidence throughout his writings; he even sees a lack of self-esteem as a chief cause for persons willingly submitting to "holy causes" and other forms of collectivism where they lose themselves in "spectacular doings of a leader or some collective body—be it a nation, a congregation, a party, or a mass movement." [21] And Bertrand Russell maintains that rational men always consider their own self-interest of great importance. "If all men acted from enlightened self-interest the world would be a paradise in comparison with what it is," he writes, and goes on to stress the "enlightened" aspect of this self-interest, saying that it is "very rarely to a man's interest to do anything which is very harmful to others." [22]

Rationality, for Ayn Rand, is man's basic virtue and the fountain of all his other virtues. This virtue means, she says, "the recognition and acceptance of reason as one's only source of knowledge, one's only judge of values and one's guide to action." [23] The emphasis here is on the "focused" mind, a person's "full, conscious awareness" and a "commitment to the fullest perception of reality within one's power." [24]

Such a position on selfishness is not inconsistent with humanism, although it may seem so at first glance, Ayn Rand's thought is quite humanistic and also shows a great affinity with that of Kant when she insists that the basic *social* principle of her Objectivist ethics is that *life is an end in itself.* She maintains that "every living human being is an end in himself, not the means to the ends or the welfare of others—and therefore, that man must live for his own sake, nether sacrificing himself to others nor sacrificing others to himself." [25] So we can see that in such a philosophy as has been sketched above, rationality is connected with freedom, with consideration of others, and also with man's self-esteem and self-interest.

Intertwined in such a philosophy is the existential emphasis of commitment and personal responsibility. Hazel Barnes writes that Randian Objectivists and also Existentialists "argue that every person is responsible for what he has made of his life" and goes on to relate humanism to this aspect of Objectivism and Existentialism: "In so far as they claim that man himself is his own end and purpose, both may properly be called humanistic." [26] One also hears in these words the reverberations, again, of Kant.

All people have the power to respond to reason and truth, says Aldous Huxley, but so, unfortunately, do they have the tendency to respond to "unreason and falsehood." [27] It seems that our minds generally are filled only with bits and pieces of information and we have not been really educated to *think*— to use Reason, to use our minds creatively. Erich Fromm lays much of the blame for this state of affairs at the door of our educational system, and proceeds to describe ways education discourages thinking. [28] One barrier to thinking is the emphasis placed by education on knowledge as facts—or as information. Fromm maintains that the superstition persists that by knowing more and more facts one arrives at a knowledge of reality. (It is amazing how prevalent this idea is in journalism.) Another way thinking is discouraged, says Fromm, is a practice of regarding all truth as relative. "Truth is declared to be an entirely subjective matter almost a matter of taste," declares Fromm.[29] Fromm, of course, disagrees with this contention.

A person is also discouraged in his thinking by the general assumption that problems are too complicated for the average person to understand. The journalist, for example, is often led to feel that a particular event or subject is too complex for adequate explication or discussion; this feeling of inadequacy leads to the journalistic technique of "simply giving the facts" without any reportorial judgment or perspective being included. It is Fromm's belief that many of the basic individual and social issues are really very simple and can be communicated so that everyone can understand them. Another way, according to Fromm, of paralyzing critical thought is the "destruction of any kind of structuralized picture of the world." He blames the mass media largely for this— pointing to the fact that "the announcement of the bombing of a city and the death of hundreds of people is shamelessly followed or interrupted by an advertisement for soap or wine." [30]

Fromm believes that newspapers too often "tell us the trite thoughts or breakfast habits of a debutante with the same space and seriousness they use for reporting events of scientific or artistic importance." And what is the result? We cease to be related to what we read or hear; we cease to be excited—and says Fromm, eventually "our attitude to what is going on in the world assumes a quality of flatness and indifference." Life loses all structure, he insists, and is "composed of many little pieces, each separate from the other and lacking any sense as a whole." [31]

A respect for Reason, a determination to mentally "focus" on journalistic problems will bring new form to the reality-linguistic problem, will eliminate much of the fuzziness in journalism, and will develop in the journalist a preciseness based on rationality. The worst thing that can happen to a journalist is for him to get to the point where he loses faith in Reason. Socrates warned against what happens to a person when he becomes a *misologist*—one who has lost respect for human reason: he is, in a very real sense, dead.

Journalists, like everyone else, generally pay lip service to Reason, but in the daily routine of their work it is very easy for them to perform their tasks and make their decisions with little mental focusing; it becomes ever easier to simply turn loose and float on the smooth waters of instinct and intuition. Mental focusing is difficult; seriously thinking about alternatives is hard work. It is easy to become a misologist almost without realizing it, as we increasingly do routine tasks, take orders and directions on more and more things, and give in to our "feelings in more instances. We are all threatened by our irrational and emotional tendencies, although we may not ever become complete misologists. The worst thing that can happen to any man is to cease to think. And the worst thing that can happen to a journalist is to give up his autonomy, his authenticity; for then he becomes nothing more than a puppet, a robot which moves and has his being as forces or persons beyond himself dictate. Reason is undoubtedly the key philosophical *force* in authentic journalism, and, operating in conjunction with personal freedom, it provides a motivating power source for the development of a meaningful, self-satisfying journalistic philosophy.

Duty: The Kantian Strain

A commitment to reason and a duty to follow basic principles rationally adopted: this is the gist of Kant's moral philosophy. Kant is close to the objectivistic humanists in his respect for reason—and for freedom. In fact, Kant contended that "morality makes sense only if men are free; freedom is just the ability to act from reasons; thus morality will make sense only if it is grounded on rationality." [32] A person, then, for Kant has a duty to rationality and to freedom. At first glance Kantian "duty" seems very similar to the Marxist-Leninist concept; but there is a big difference. For Marx, duty was the "moral necessity or obligation to subordinate one's individual interests and conduct to the interests and demands of the social units." [33] It was always social in nature. For Kant, duty was to one's *own* principles, freely determined. Moral law, to which a person has a duty, is derived from reason and results in universal or "ultimate principles" which Kant considered "the metaphysics of morals."

A *good will,* for Kant, is indispensable and basic; actually his oft-quoted remark is the key to his ethics: "It is impossible to conceive of anything in the world, or indeed out of it, which can be called good without qualification save only a good will." [34] The term "good" takes on meaning not as one considers a consequence (for Kant was a consummate foe of utilitarianism), but as one takes up what Kant thought to be the definitive characteristic of moral consciousness—*duty.* A will which acts for the sake of duty is a good will.

This may be clearer if "for the sake of duty" is contrasted with "in accordance with duty." The latter could include honest reporting in journalism because it is prudent; it would be hypothetical and not binding. Certainly, it would not be universal (since *dis*honesty in journalism is viewed by some as the best, i.e., most prudent, policy). But "duty," according to Kant, "is the necessity of acting out of reverence for the law." [35] And the law he refers to is a standard or test in terms of which worldly decisions must be made if they are to be of moral (i.e., nonutilitarian) value: "I am never to act according to any maxim which I would not want to be a universal law." It will be noted that this negatively paraphrased version of Kant's famous Categorical Imperative is absolutely binding on everyone, everywhere, forever.

Kant's Categorical Imperative also includes the concept that people should always be treated as ends and never merely as means; the result of following such a principle is very similar to the Existentialist's "authenticity." Sartre, for example, saw the authentic man as one who related to others as individuals ("persons as ends")—persons who were not to be used, or changed, but to be related to as autonomous persons with every right to be themselves and not mirror-images of others.[36] Another implication of Kant's Categorical Imperative is that any concept of the "end justifying the means" is basically immoral; from the purely moral viewpoint, Kant would say, not even the loftiest end can justify evil or harmful means; evil remains evil, whatever its purpose or result.

Kant's emphasis is on acting out of duty and duty alone. Consequences are not to be considered. A good act done to please somebody or to gain an advantage or to secure a reward would cease to be good; it would fall to the level of expediency. An act should be done because the actor sees for himself that it is right, that it is his duty to perform it. The moral imperative is here categorical, not hypothetical—in other words, it is unconditional obedience.[37] Actually Kant contends that morality is not contingent on changing institutions or varying situations; his is really an *a priori,* prescriptive ethics. We do not get these "guides" to morality from social sanctions or from "feelings" as to rightness or wrongness of actions, but from reason alone. This reason is regulative; when we accept a principle by reason, it then regulates our activities.

Acting ethically for Kant would mean acting on the basis of duty—or acting for the sake of some principle. Thus the justification of an action is not in the action itself but in something outside it. The moral value of an action, likewise, must not be in the consequences of the action, but rather in the *principle* of the action. Since the principle is prior to the action, it is *a priori,* and when we internalize a principle or make it our own private rule, then it becomes a maxim. Conformity to principle is the core of the Kantian concept of duty. An ethical action means that I act in such a way that it is possible for me to will that the maxim of my action become law for everyone at all times. The journalist of Kantian persuasion would make the journalistic decision that he would like to see all journalists make. He would not tell the truth because he sees a good reason for telling it, some benefit accruing to him or to others if he does it. He would not consider the consequences; he would do it simply because he felt duty-bound to do it. He would let his journalistic act be an end in itself.

The Kantian journalist, for example, might well feel a duty to reveal the sources of his information, to let his audience know who provided the particular facts. He would not provide the source because it might prove useful to do so or for any specific reason; he would provide it simply because he felt it was his *duty* to give it. His dedication would be to the rationally derived *a priori* principle (or maxim) of providing the reader with important related information necessary for validating the story and appraising the reliability of the attributed information. The reporter's rationalization that he will sometimes *withhold* the source's name so as not to "dry up" that source in the future is a utilitarian concern and one which the Kantian would not consider; it would be beside the point of true morality. Providing the reader the news source is an end in itself; it is ethical *in principle,* and that is all there is to it. The Kantian journalist feels he has an obligation to act in a certain way (e.g. to present as much of the "truth" of the story as he has); he does not "rationalize" his action *a pos-teriori;* rather he rationally accepts the principle (that exists prior to the act) which he then feels duty-bound to follow.

Bertrand Russell points out that the only moralists who have seriously attempted to "be consistent in regarding virtue as an end in itself are the Stoics and Kant." [38] Russell proceeds to summarize the spirit of Kant's ethics (as he sees it) of non-utilitarianism in these words:

> Kant was never tired of pouring scorn on the view that the good consists of pleasure, or of anything else except virtue. And virtue consists in acting as the moral law enjoins, *because* that is what the moral law enjoins. A right action done from any other motive cannot count as virtuous. If you are kind to your brother because you are fond of him, you have no merit; but if you can hardly stand him and are nevertheless kind to him because the moral laws says you should be, then you are the sort of person Kant thinks you ought to be. [39]

Russell, of course, is being somewhat subtly critical of the Kantian position in this passage. He is pointing out one of the oft-mentioned weaknesses (or suspected weaknesses) of Kant's morality of duty: that it is a very mechanical—and perhaps weak—rationale for ethical action. This criticism of Kantian ethics is often combined with another: that Kant's universalizing of an ethical maxim is nothing more than a person projecting his *subjective* opinion on everyone. A contemporary philosopher, R. M. Hare, has argued that Kant's notion (implied in his Categorical Imperative) is "really quite radically subjective in character" and that "no matter how evil or unworkable the state of affairs, if the agent is willing that he and everyone else labour under it, then the judgment is moral." [40]

Kant, of course, would consider such arguments as nonsense. He would say that *merely subjective ends* have no place in determining the nature of rational morality; he would point out that *objective* ends are those which a rational being *must,* in so far as he is rational, desire or promote. "Kant assumes that there is only one such end and thinks it quite obvious what this end is—*rational nature* itself." [41] Kant appears to believe that the rational person will insure that he is attempting to reach his own ends (whatever they may be), and he is quite willing to let every other rational being have the *freedom* to pursue his own ends. This stance points up the *personalism* in Kant, the respect for the individual's autonomy, and the faith in the rational process itself. In other words, Kant trusts others as ends in themselves, not because he thinks it is a good policy, but because they *are* ends in themselves. Kant is really saying: "I treat other rational beings as ends in themselves by respecting in them that same value which I find and seek to defend in myself—freedom." [42]

This concept is very important to the rational and free journalist. If he really respects libertarianism, for example, he will respect it (have a duty to it) in *principle* and will defend it everywhere, in all persons, at all times, If he really respects libertarianism, for example, he is going to respect the *freedom* with which other journalists perform their acts even though he might not respect their *acts*. He is really concerned only with his own actions; regardless of what others use as their ethical guides, he wills to act in a way which he would like to see become a universal journalistic principle. As Jeffrie Murphy has put it: "The essence of morality is revealed in maxims which respect the value as an end in itself of each rational being, i.e. maxims which would, if acted on, leave each rational being free to pursue his own ends in acting." [43] It would be difficult to find a better statement of the stance of a libertarian journalist.

Kant would see the rational man adopting his Categorical Imperative; [44] only when we are not fully rational would we feel an inclination to adopt a contrary morality of subjective situationism or utilitarianism. This is why, according to Kant, the will must be commanded to a considerable extent. "Journalists shall not lie" is better than "It is wrong for a journalist to lie." The first is an imperative which demands allegiance; the second is stated as a value judgment which a journalist might feel inclined to ignore or to depart from. If the journalist accepts a principle such as "I will tell the truth in my journalism," then he will not lie. He will not simply refrain from lying in *certain circumstances;* he will refrain from lying in all circumstances. If he always tells the truth, he will not even have to worry about when he will lie and when he will not. Regardless of the surface "narrowness" of such a position, Kant maintains that it is necessary for true morality. A journalist—or any person—cannot be ethical if he applies certain rules of morality only when he feels inclined to apply them.

The concept of duty to principle, then, is the third strain of the journalistic philosophy advocated in this chapter. It anchors freedom and fulfills rationality. It keeps the journalist from being blown back and forth by the winds of social pressure and personal expediency. It protects him against the morality of utilitarianism. The journalist pursues truth because he would will that all journalists pursue truth; he has an obligation to pursue and present truth, not out of some conviction that "truth will make for better government" or out of some other hoped-for benefit, but simply because he has a duty to the maxim that *journalists must present the truth*. This non-utilitarian emphasis of morality provided by Kant is very important in giving the journalist philosophical stability which is largely lacking in other strains of ethical theory.

The Kantian strain, along with Existentialism and Rational Humanism, contributes ingredients of freedom, personal responsibility and rationalism to the "Apollonysian" synthesis being proposed in this chapter. But it stresses the aspect of *duty* which is considered peripheral in the other strains that merge into the Apollonysian stance. Kantianism also joins in with Rational Humanism in providing an objectivist or rational (Apollonian) side of the synthesis. It is the Existential strain that contributes a strong dose of Dionysian sensitivity and subjectivism into the scientist-artist synthesis.

The Existential strain also emphasizes the main concept of this book—*freedom,* along with its natural corollaries of commitment and personal responsibility. All three of these strains which have been discussed are important; all have valuable contributions to make to the "Apollonysian" journalist. Certainly duty and reason and freedom are all extremely important to this kind of meaningful, authentic journalistic philosophy. But the most important of these is *freedom* since it is the very ground of being for the other two; for without freedom there is really no authentic (human) sense of duty, nor is there a rationale for the creative use of reason.

NOTES

[1] Lee Hills, *Don Mellett's Unfinished Story* (booklet containing the 31st Mellett lecture at the University of Oklahoma, March 29, 1960), p. 15.

[2] Hazel Barnes, *An Existentialist Ethics* (New York: Random House Vintage Books, 1971), p. 8.

[3] *Ibid.*, p. 26.

[4] Gordon E. Bigelow, "A Primer of Existentialism," *College English* (Dec. 1961), p. 173.

[5] Barnes, *op. cit.*, p. 26.

[6] For a detailed treatise on the importance of rationality in ethics, see Stephen Toulmin, *Reason in Ethics* (Cambridge: Cambridge University Press, 1968).

[7] Karl Jaspers, *Man in the Modern Age* (New York: Doubleday Anchor Books, 1957), p. 81.

[8] "As it is Writ," *New Statesman* (March 31, 1972), p. 426.

[9] Abraham Kaplan, *The New World of Philosophy* (New York: Vintage Books, 1961), pp. 97–128.

[10] Jean-Paul Sartre, *Existentialism and Human Emotions* (New York: Philosophical Library—The Wisdom Library, 1957), p. 47.

[11] John Macquarrie, *Existentialism* (Baltimore: Penguin Books, 1973), p. 140.

[12] *Ibid.*, p. 141.

[13] *Ibid.*

[14] Albert Camus, *The Rebel* (New York: Alfred Knopf, Inc. and Random House—Vintage Books, 1954), p. 291.

[15] Frederick Patka in F. Patka (ed.), *Existentialist Thinkers and Thought* (New York: The Citadel Press, 1966), pp. 42–43.

[16] *Ibid.*, pp. 57–58.

[17] See Ch. 12 ("Respondeo ergo Sum") in F. H. Heinermann, *Existentialism and the Modern Predicament* (New York: Harper Torchbooks, 1958), pp. 190–204.

[18] Ayn Rand, *For the New Intellectual* (New York: New American Library Signet Book, 1961), p. 51. Rand also thinks true happiness is derived from using reason. A. N. Whitehead agrees, saying that "the function of Reason is to promote the art of life." *The Function of Reason* (Boston: Beacon Press, 1958), p. 4.

[19] Rand, *For the New Intellectual*, p. 25.

[20] Erich Fromm, *Escape from Freedom* (New York: Avon Books, Discus ed., 1968), p. 136.

[21] Eric Hoffer, *The Ordeal of Change* (New York: Harper Colophon Books, 1964), p. 9.

[22] Bertrand Russell, *The Will to Doubt* (New York: Philosophical Library, 1958), pp. 15–16.

[23] Ayn Rand, *The Virtue of Selfishness* (New York: New American Library Signet Books, 1964), p. 25.

[24] *Ibid.*

[25] *Ibid.*, p. 27.

[26] Barnes, *An Existentialist Ethics*, p. 125.

[27] Aldous Huxley, *Brave New World Revisited* (New York: Harper & Row—Perennial Library, 1965), p. 33.

[28] Fromm, *Escape from Freedom,* pp. 247–77. Compare with very similar comments of Ayn Rand about education in *The New Left: The Anti-Industrial Revolution* (New York: New American Library Signet Books, 1971), pp. 152–204.

[29] Fromm, *Escape from Freedom,* p. 274.

[30] *Ibid.,* p. 276.

[31] *Ibid.,* p. 277.

[32] Jeffrie G. Murphy, *Kant: The Philosophy of Right* (New York: St. Martin's Press, 1970), p. 42.

[33] Richard T. DeGeorge, *Soviet Ethics and Morality* (Ann Arbor: University of Michigan Press—Ann Arbor Paperbacks, 1969), p. 74.

[34] T. K. Abbott (trans.), *Kant's Critique of Practical Reason and Other Works on the Theory of Ethics* (London, 1909, 6th ed.), p. 9.

[35] *Ibid.,* p. 16.

[36] Anthony Manser, *Sartre: A Philosophical Study* (New York: Oxford University Press. 1967), p. 158.

[37] E. L. Allen, *From Plato to Nietzsche* (Greenwich, Conn.: Fawcett Publications, Inc.—a Premier Book, 1964), p. 126.

[38] Bertrand Russell, *Human Society in Ethics and Politics* (New York: New American Library—Mentor Books, 1962), p. 39.

[39] *Ibid.*

[40] Murphy, *op. cit.,* p. 66.

[41] *Ibid.,* p. 73.

[42] *Ibid.,* pp. 74–75.

[43] *Ibid.,* p. 87.

[44] See H. J. Paton, *The Categorical Imperative: A Study in Kant's Moral Philosophy* (New York: Harper Torchbooks, 1967) for a detailed discussion of the implications of Kantian ethics.

Part Two

Ethical

Problems

THE TERM "ETHICS" seldom occurs in the following writings, but the concept permeates the commentaries. Only one writer approaches specifically, if obliquely, a definition (J. K. Hvistendahl says if it is "right," it is "ethical"). Lee Hills, on the other hand, in "The Reader: Journalism's Forgotten Man," sets up a number of audience-oriented criteria for newspaper credibility (perhaps even media credibility, generally), which might well provide a touchstone for discussions of ethics, particularly in the context of Hvistendahl's social rightness.

In the first article, "Truth and Error," J. Edward Gerald touches a sensitive nerve as he describes sets of conditions under which the ethical is least likely to occur, and, indeed, focuses on what might be detected throughout the volume as a major deterrent to ethics in communications. He describes mass media utterances as the product of commentators who observe the great and small conflicts between Truth and Error. However, by necessity, the commentator sees only a very narrow segment of the broad field on which the continuing battle is fought. This suggests the ludicrous example of a sports reporter commenting on a basketball game, though his vision is confined to the strip of playing floor several feet each side of the center line.

Perhaps a natural product of the inevitable self-deceit resulting from the unending series of narrow observances is the arrogance the late Chet Huntley noted in the second article, "A Disturbing Arrogance in the Press." Arrogance might not be so destructive, he felt, except as it contributes to faulty "advocacy." It is advocacy, he speculated, to which the press, particularly the print media, may feel it has been driven. If the press has indeed been driven to the "judgment kind of journalism," he declared "it has not yet figured out how to handle it."

It is judgment of another sort that concerns *Wall Street Journal* writers in their "Unethical Newspaper Practices" which follows. They see a dependence on advertising leading media decision-makers into judgments that introduce distortions into the way institutions and events are viewed. In particular, sins of omission, and the creation of "unpersons" are discussed.

The "narrow view" thesis described by Gerald gains increasing support from Jacques Ellul, in "With a View Toward Assessing the Facts," and Hvistendahl as they contemplate some problems of reportage. Ellul sees this as causing difficulties for political leaders concerned with long-term decision making. In such instances, he notes, there is necessarily a gap between the political leaders' judgments and the impressions of the average citizen.

Hvistendahl's "An Ethical Dilemma," on another tack, introduces the concepts of micro- and macro-ethics as philosophical explanations of behavior in the mass media. The micro-ethical position calls for publication of material without fear or favor (a plunge-ahead view), while the macro-ethicist seeks, in Hvistendahl's terms, to assay the potential consequences of discussion—leading to his conclusion that ethical can also be read as "right."

It is not depth, but breadth of perception that concerns Eugene Pulliam in his essay on the reporter's responsibility to be certain he has covered alternative viewpoints, instead of merely spotlighting the sensational.

Lee Hills and Peter Clark bring ethical considerations in a democracy into sharper focus by pointing out the crucial component of a mass communicator's life that may often be ignored: the reader (or viewer). Hills warns that, no matter what direction the press goes, "audience groups are beginning to make their own rules—arriving at their own view of the world and selecting their facts accordingly."

In the same vein, Clark, in "Newspaper Credibility: What Needs to be Done?," points to problems of keeping mass media material relevant to audiences, suggesting the media tend to answer questions the audiences are not asking, but ignore "questions about events they do ask."

Robert K. Baker, in a provocative report to the National Commission on the Causes and Prevention of Violence, "Functions and Credibility," outlines a number of ways in which the press is limited in its influence and effect, and provides an informal tabulation of the social cost of a press that has lost its credibility.

In "No Business Like News Business," a satirical essay on the comparative social roles of journalism and other institutions in the United States, Zoltan Sarfathy suggests a number of unique areas in which journalists should be defended, though he points out the journalist is particularly unsuited for defending himself.

In the next two articles, Clive Irving and Eugene Methvin discuss, from different vantages, some considerations of pseudo events that make news. Irving's "All The News That's Fit to Film" deplores the restraining influence of television on the news process. He sees television not only as a medium that does not produce news "scoops," but that televised news conferences reinforce passivity in both reporters and audience. Methvin recalls in "Objectivity and the Tactics of Terrorists" historical events that have lead to a "little extra sense of heavy responsibility" among southern newsmen working in a biracial context.

The two following articles provide an exploration in contrasts. J. F. ter-Horst discusses "What the Press Must Do" from his vantage points as former press secretary to President Ford and as a Washington newsman. He outlines the mandate he feels the press has in coverage of the president and, by extension, the government. Simon Head, on the other hand, discusses "The Super-Journalist" in Washington and speculates on forces that may keep him quiescent.

An imbalancing force as the journalist walks the ethical tightrope is a bias which Thomas Griffiths suggests, in "A Few Frank Words About Bias," is inevitable and inherent, while Barry Goldwater, in his article, "The Networks and the News," accuses newsmen of specific acts of blatant bias.

However, in "Ethics in Television Journalism" television newsmen Gabe Pressman and Robert Schulman defend, before critic Robert Lewis Shayon, their own "taste" in news coverage—and, in a notable instance, the taste of the industry to demonstrate that coverage policies have pragmatic bases.

Extent of news coverage and commentary is the topic for Nat Hentoff's "How 'Fair' Should TV Be?" as he questions whether the Fairness Doctrine of the Federal Communications Commission helps them avoid responsibilities or is a Sword of Damocles forcing them to accept the responsibilities of full discussion of public, or controversial, affairs. Roy Danish extends the discussion in "Broadcast Freedom: It It Still There?" to include other aspects, such as the anti-commercial challenges, of Fairness Doctrine implications.

Turning to advertising, the late Aldous Huxley defined some differences between a propagandist and an advertiser, detailing in "The Arts of Selling" his views on the critical differences between their loyalties, and the consequent effect of these loyalties on the society they both work to influence. In a milder frame, George Gordon offers a view of the role of advertising, pointing out that the "showmanship (of advertising persuasion) . . . almost invariably requires certain measures of hyperbole and deception." However, his "Making of a Consumer" warns, all mass communications are the result of the same commercial forces that created advertising.

Focusing on television advertising, Daniel Henninger describes one educational experiment in preparing youngsters to analyze and evaluate commercial messages in "No Fooling . . . Youngsters Analyze TV Commercials."

Returning to the press in general, Richard Strout ("The Capitol Gallery Case") and William Blankenburg and Richard Allen ("The Journalism Contest

Thicket'') discuss two contemporary continuing ethical problems, conflict of interest and professional contests. Both articles again confirm the controversy over location of dividing lines between the ethical and the unethical in mass communications.

And, in the closing article, "The Ways of Corrupters," Ralph Barney points to two types of corrupters of the journalist and his ethics, discussing a few of the reasons why corruption can be a painless process.

J. Edward Gerald:

Truth and Error—
Journalism's Tournament of Reason

OUR PROFESSION, to judge by the trade press, feels that it is in the public's doghouse, that it is being criticized too much and does not enjoy public confidence.

From my quiet seat in the stands this phenomenon appears to deserve a different interpretation. My generation of journalists did not expect to be loved. We merely hoped to be respected. Today's generation, particularly that part of it on television cameras, apparently wants to move through political conventions like an evangelistic army, making critical decisions normally reserved to the delegates, and still be loved.

The present season of criticism is merely a tribute to the power of the press. This engine of word, picture and print—of information and propaganda—has succeeded in raising a political splinter group made up of vital young men and women to a position of temporary importance comparable to that enjoyed, on a long-term basis, by union labor in the Roosevelt years. If the student riots at Columbia University resembled anything it was the General Motors sit-in strikes when the industrial unions first demonstrated their raw power.

Dr. Gerald is professor emeritus, School of Journalism, University of Minnesota. This is an excerpt from a speech he made in 1969 at a Region 8 Sigma Delta Chi Conference in Lubbock. Texas. Reprinted from *The Quill* (July 1969) by permission.

By its definition of news, the press enabled this splinter group and its senior political advisers—some of them from Minnesota—to drive a President of the United States from office and utterly confuse the most important political issues of our times—that is, the issues of racial equality, equal justice, and fair economic opportunity for all.

Let us look at our professional theory of reporting, writing, and presenting the day's news, for this is the 40th anniversary of what we call interpretative reporting. This style actually came into wide use during the Great Depression, the onset of which was indicated by the stock market crash of 1928–29.

We journalists like to explain our role in terms of a model called the Tournament of Reason, after John Milton, or the Market Place of Thought, after Justice Holmes. We all know the catchwords that identify the model: "Let Truth and Error grapple. Who ever knew Truth to be put to flight in a free and open encounter?"

Acting out our role, we sit in the press box and watch these two knights on horseback, Truth and Error, fly at each other with all the force at their command. Dipping into our knapsack of cliches, we label them the *White Knight* and the *Black Knight*. The playing field is rather large and we report only that part of the action which we can see. We dislike the limitations of our field of observation, but we rationalize it by saying that the game continues from day to day and we will be able to report new facts as the tourney goes on. If the public is patient, we will be able to piece out a more complete story.

The antagonists are elaborately suited out and their helmets keep us from seeing their faces. We know little about them and must depend on releases to the press by their managers to write our stories.

The Black Knight, on the standard color scale, may be more purple than black and the White Knight may be, in several senses of the word, dirty. He also may be a mercenary soldier from hell, but because of his choice of colors and his self-deprecation we won't become suspicious of his motives.

Moreover, it could be that the antagonists are not properly chosen to represent either Truth or Error. Truth, instead of being in the tournament, may be bound and gagged in a rice paddy down the road. Error may really be only 20 proof, far less than the Kentucky bourbon standard, and our journalistic conventions don't always permit us to point this out. After all, to most of us, he looks all black. In fact, if he says he is 100 proof we let it go at that.

WHEN SPECTATORS read or listen to our account of the match, and criticize it, our defense has been that we report only what we see, that editorial comment is not consonant with our wish to be fair and objective. Please note that word *objective*. We will dwell on it.

I am a graduate of the University of Missouri, class of 1928. To my knowledge the dean of the School of Journalism, Walter Williams, and his contemporaries never subjected this tournament model to critical analysis. It was many years later that I read Milton's phrase carefully enough to note that the words "free and open encounter" set up some significant conditions that require careful definition. Until then, when the thought came to me that I was an objective disseminator of *Truth,* I just glowed with pleasure and never questioned the quality or substance of what I wrote.

Beginning with the stock market crash, however, some of us began to doubt the adequacy of this model. After all, we had believed, and we had taught the public, that prosperity was a permanent fixture of our national heritage. A long dialog between journalists ensued during which we failed to settle upon a definition of objectivity. The serious thinker among us suggested that the concept of objectivity, as the obverse of bias, is faulty because bias is associated with frame of reference—that is, bias is built into our lives, journalists and readers alike, and even the best language skills cannot sort out all the conflicting positive and negative factors in communication.

Our several critics keep comparing actual events with our description of them and we are made uneasy by the evidence in our frame of reference problem. Some of us have found objectivity an impossible dream and now boldly proclaim either that we have no standard of truth outside of ourselves or that we aspire to be fair and accurate and no more. The test being substituted for objectivity is how the reporter "feels" about the accuracy of the story rather than how the object, that is, the news source, "feels." As a consequence of this switch in values much news today, particularly that from Washington and other world capitals, mystifies the reader and viewer. The consumer cannot tell how much of the story is fact and how much is reporter's feelings.

THE SUBSTITUTION of a subjective for an objective test brings to our attention another great word in our journalistic theory—responsibility. Many of us define it differently. My generation defined it as "answerable to or accountable to." . . . "having a capacity for moral decisions and therefore accountable." As I hear the word defined by some of my "involved" students and fellow journalists now, responsibility means "in charge of" or "in a position to influence or control." The two definitions represent precisely opposed professional positions which may be likened to democratic and authoritarian governments. In one the official and the journalist, although they have clear roles to play, are responsive to the people and can be rewarded or punished by them. In the other, particularly in this age of mass communication, the people are responsive to the journalist and he will lead them according to that gutsy feeling he has about men and issues. The only way the people can correct or change the gutsy journalist is by revolution—the alteration or destruction of the privately-owned mass communication system.

The disabilities of the consumer of information have been increased by television. This medium takes ordinary journalists, pedestrians and drivers all, off the news desk, dresses them reasonably well and sends them breathlessly and repeatedly across the world. They are then presented personally on our home television screens as men of unusual wisdom, understanding and perceptivity. There is a sort of national veneration of them as the last word in authority. I am told that some of them receive more invitations to speak than the President. I assume that, as modified by the conditions under which they work, they deserve all of these things. But every time I see a Roper survey saying that the public trusts them, as a source of news, more than it does the print media journalists, I think the public should see both sets of newsmen rip copy off the same press association teletype before processing it, one by print, the other by voice, for the consuming public. Such knowledge would, I think, help nonjournalists look beyond personality for a test of reliability somewhat more substantial.

Let me summarize as to the frames of reference problem by saying that reliability in news is to be judged by the news sources—the sources of information as well as bias—and not by the way a reporter feels. The journalist has a right to feel successful only if his news sources feel adequately reported.

In addition to frame of reference, other problems arise when the journalist is called upon to comprehend a subject matter built up by scholars and professional persons. Economic theory would be one example. As I said, we are about to celebrate an important anniversary. The Depression brought with it the interventionist state and rejection of the economic and social principles of laissez faire prevalent to that time. I must digress to report, ruefully, that one of the laissez faire conventions that declined at this time held that newspaper editors are more important than advertising managers. But that is not a necessary part of this story.

At the time of the market crash I was a junior staff member of United Press Association's bureau in Denver, Colo. The office was staffed by competent senior men because it was the chief relay point between New York City, Chicago, and the Pacific Coast. The staff had to summarize, edit and rewrite the output of several wires because only one-third of the copy received from the east could be relayed to San Francisco and Portland.

I remember our bureau manager at his typewriter during a bad day on Wall Street searching his mind for the meaning of the events he was reporting. Like nearly everybody else, he could do no more than apply his skill as a sports writer to explain what turned out to be one of the great events of American history. He wrote that the number of shares offered set a new record. The ticker was far behind. Brokers were demanding more margin, and the customers, some of them near panic, were losing their shirts. Stock Exchange officials were conferring on how to catch up with their backlog of work. The cause of the crash was speculation, everybody said, but that word wasn't defined, either. There was not much information about the relationship of the stock market to the economy and no one could make clear the basic implications of the day's events.

For me, these implications were not long in showing up. In a few weeks the bureau had to retrench. The senior men were mostly transferred and I kept my job, I was told, only because I was a university graduate. Other men, it was made clear, were more competent than I, and were laid off only because they lacked the growth potential supposedly inherent in a college education.

At the time, I was not aware of any specific benefits of education. I knew only that I had finished school because my mother nagged me into it. I did not realize, until much later, that a university education could be utilized to think with—that is, to analyze events, great and small, and to derive from such analysis some sense of perspective and direction.

As I watched senior journalists over the country try to interpret the Great Depression, it seemed to me that Dean Williams, back at the University of Missouri, had overlooked several points important to my education:

First, how do you recognize an economic depression when all you can see is a stock market crash?

Second, in looking for news sources, how can we distinguish between economists and bankers?

Third, assuming one is fortunate enough to locate a genuine economist who is not selling anything, how do you determine the degree of authority with which he writes or speaks?

Fourth, assuming that a competent scholar has been found, what is the state of his art, that is, how competent and reliable are the tools of analysis used by the profession to which he belongs?

Unless these questions can be carefully answered, interpretative reporting is the work of a blind man leading the blind. For that reason, we must ask a final question: How does a journalist exercise due care in such matters and how does he become and remain competent?

I HAVE RAISED questions of bias, of frame of reference. I have said that the only remedy I know for bias is information—lots of it—obtained as a discipline, not as a hurried hobby. My reference to economic insight is solely by way of example and time does not permit attention to other areas of public affairs in which we needed then, and now, to become expert. Even so, I want to acknowledge the particular debt of journalism to the Supreme Court of the United States. This debt has accumulated over 40 years and we do not readily recognize it because so few of us are trained in law to the point where we can report it understandingly. Judging by some of our papers and commentators, we seem to feel that the Bill of Rights, for example, is our property and the Supreme Court is trespassing on our territory and often misinterprets it.

Nevertheless, the press has benefitted from a long series of court decisions that define, clarify, extend, and reinforce individual freedom and freedom of the press. In much of the world, including France, one of the cultural centers of the West, the mass media have suffered setbacks and repressions. But in the United States even the ancient tyranny of the civil and criminal libel laws has been modified to promote criticism and discussion of self-government. Supreme Court justices, who have always taken an oath to administer justice for rich and poor alike, have finally put this oath to work through a series of badly-needed decisions to reform the administration of the criminal law.

One small part of that reform has been a courteous and deferential request to the mass media to reduce the extent to which newspapers and television try defendants in advance of the court. In spite of almost 40 years of uninterrupted gains in freedom of the press, some important press leaders persist in believing that the press is still locked in combat with government and must withhold its co-operation even from the courts. Some of our leaders have portrayed voluntary press-bar-bench councils as limiting the freedom of the press. It might contribute perspective with which to judge the press-bar-council idea if it is realized that the *Sheppard, Miranda v. Arizona,* and *Miranda*-related decisions of the Supreme Court provide all the authority individual judges in criminal cases need to safeguard defendants against prejudicial news reports. In fact, the American Bar Association Reardon Report was held up before release and revised to conform to the *Sheppard* decision. This opinion spelled out the authority of trial judges to protect defendants, witnesses and jurors and to curb gabby, publicity-seeking police and prosecutors. *Miranda* and *Escobedo* guaranteed every man the right to silence under custodial interrogation by police and, if wanted, a lawyer to help him get a fair trial. Rich men have always had that right. Poor men got it only as a result of the *Gideon, Escobedo,* and *Miranda* decisions.

A great deal of news and editorial comment in the media represented these fair trial decisions as interference with the police and as court subversion of justice. It was said, in spite of the New York *Times* libel decision, that the watchdog role of the press was impaired. The truth seems to be to the contrary, for it is as much the obligation of the press as of the court to assure criminal defendants a fair trial. Now that every court and every lawyer in the country have been given explicit instructions on how this shall be done, the press need no longer exercise its watchdog role on a lonely and occasional or sporadic basis. It can now operate under court protection at all times. Journalists should become adept at detecting illegal coercion of and cruelty to persons accused of crime, and help the courts apply the guarantees of the Fourth, Fifth, and Sixth Amendments. We should recognize that the Court which approved the *Sheppard* and *Miranda* decisions also was the architect of a steady 40-year expansion of the First Amendment. We have the freest press in the world. The persons tried under our system of criminal justice should have fair trials under that same Constitution.

HAVE WE produced journalists who can now understand economists and judges better than in 1928–29? I think we have but for the most part these men are working for two or three very large newspapers or for the syndicates. When editors of most large daily newspapers demand the kind of men who could hold jobs on university faculties we will solve our frame of reference problem, insofar as solutions are available under the present state of knowledge.

The only way I know whereby our observers at the Tournament of Reason will understand what they see and interpret it reliably is to keep on raising the educational level of the journalists who have the most difficult and critical assignments in public affairs reporting. The education that saved my job in Denver in 1928 is certainly not enough for serious interpretive reporting today. No man can recognize Truth and Error on sight. Only scholarship, which is the product of hard labor while confined in that concentration camp, the modern university, and experience in that tough laboratory, public affairs reporting, can provide the critical faculties needed. Even then, Truth may elude us, but the degree of journalistic knowledge is increased and the quality of the information improved enormously when interpretative reporters operate on the level of the scholar rather than what Dean Williams called the recorder.

Journalism needs competent interpretative reporters trained in law and in all the major natural and social sciences, political science, economics, education, chemistry, physics, medicine, public health, social welfare, and urban studies. In my opinion, no young journalist should limit his professional preparation on the basis of contrary signals he may get from employers today. The concept editors and publishers have of the training needed for tomorrow's journalism is based on today's journalism and on what they think they can pay for without undue anguish. I recognize the importance of the generalist. There will always be a place for him, particularly if he is paid what he is worth. The same conditions apply to journalism as to medicine. If you want family doctors you have to pay them as well as specialists—not less.

Today's journalism, as we all know, is changing rapidly and the men making decisions now will not be long with us. If they insist that they cannot pay for better-trained men, if they point out that already there is a heavy turnover rate in journalism because salaries outside are higher than inside, and if a journalist's interests, nevertheless, run to interpretative reporting, he should not be deterred.

The proprietors of the mass media have no alternative other than to pay the market price for good men. They must recruit high quality minds to carry on the business or there will be no business.

Our national security requires that the press reach and inform us all. Information is near the top of the list of national necessities. Our society always has provided what is essential to self-government.

Chet Huntley:

A Disturbing Arrogance in the Press

I WANT TO MAKE AN off-the-cuff remark on the "to whom it may concern" basis. An old friend of mine, Lou Mayor of New York, has an incredible sense of humor. Not long ago, he had an excruciating prostate problem. The operation was terrible and extended, and there was the waiting period to determine if it had been successful. Lou was accepting this in good spirits, but finally the day of truth came when the last examination had been made and the doctor said, "Lou Mayor, my friend, you are a whole man. You are well. You are restored. Everything is fine. After a short recuperation, you can pick up your life and go back to work. Everything is normal, fine and wonderful."

Lou said, "That's great." Then he reflected for a moment and said, "There is one question that occurs to me. What about my private life? You know what I'm talking about."

The doctor said, "Lou, I told you—everything is fine, wonderful and beautiful. Pick up your normal routine."

Lou said, "For my wife, Trudy, put it in writing. On second thought, make it 'to whom it may concern.' "

I do want to talk to you seriously about the state of journalism. In this third year of a new decade—as we approach the 200th anniversary of this nation—I am sure it has occurred to you that it is important to consider the status of this institution and reflect on it, because it is the only instrument there is to keep the people of this country informed and to let us know what is going on. There are no alternative devices or institutions for the dissemination of information. It's the press and that's it.

I hear a genuine feud is going on between much of the press and this administration—a feud that goes somewhat beyond the normal, traditional, healthy coolness that always has characterized relations between the national press and the government.

Actually, I suppose we might be somewhat more concerned if the truth at

This article comprises excerpts from a speech by Mr. Huntley at the Montana Press Association convention in August, 1973, at Big Sky, Montana. Mr. Huntley, former NBC News announcer and commentator, died March 19, 1974. Reprinted by permission from *Montana Journalism Review*, No. 17, 1974.

this moment were that the national press and the administration were in bed together and were engaging in a total show of harmony. Some conflict and some mutual suspicion are just right, and we want to keep it that way. But it has gotten a bit out of control, in my opinion. So we ask, where did this begin? What is the origin of this suspicion and this climate between the national press and this President of the United States?

I have a guess. I have known the President since the first time he ran for Congress in 1946. At that moment and from that time on, this man and the press never got along very well. He did not enjoy being with newsmen, and they did not enjoy being with him. There was always this coolness. And, being very candid, I might say that there is a lack of style, a lack of great flourishing prose so far as this President is concerned. He doesn't coin the great ringing words and phrases that came from other Presidents, and so there was always this business about Nixon being unable to excite the press. Newsmen didn't particularly care for him, and he didn't particularly care for them. So the coolness started, in my opinion, as early as 1946.

There is a story that might cast some light on this issue. I was on the Truman train going through California in 1948. I got aboard at Berkeley to ride to Los Angeles, and—I think it was at Fresno—Truman held a press conference on the train. Nixon was running for reelection to a second term in Congress, and he had lambasted Truman and the Democrats in a speech in the state. During the press conference, a California reporter asked, "Mr. President, are you aware of what Congressman Nixon said about you and the Democrats this morning?"

Mr. Truman said, "Yes, I saw that. And by the way, in his remarks Mr. Nixon used a very mild four-letter word that was not all that bad. I have one observation to make about Congressman Nixon: It seems to me that he doesn't even know how to swear or cuss. He's got the words but the melody ain't right."

At first I could only quarrel with Vice President Agnew, in his now famous remarks about the American press (and I include both print and electronic media in the word "press"), on the grounds that some of his charges were ill informed and ill founded. I can find no monopoly of news distribution as Mr. Agnew charged. In broadcasting, for example, the networks are responsible for a very modest percentage of the total news output of all the television and radio stations in the nation. I think we would be hard put today to prove that there is a monopoly of the American print media. But to whatever extent Mr. Agnew was attacking the new journalism—the journalism of advocacy and involvement, personalized and subjective journalism—then I am on his side. In my opinion, there is an arrogance, a haughty smugness, a conceit running through too damned much of our journalism today.

It is not too difficult to figure out how this developed and what happened. I remember going to conferences and conventions of press associations, publishers associations and network-affiliate associations 10 or 15 years ago. And it was conceded, more or less, 10 or 15 years ago that because broadcasting had taken over the hard news and spot news, there hadn't been a newspaper extra on the streets of our principal cities for a long time.

Coping with a New Role

The publishers realized that broadcasting had taken over the spot news, the instant news, the hard news, the frontpage banner news and, therefore, the print medium would have to do something else. Of course, the only alternative left was to go into the judgment kind of journalism—analysis, comment or whatever you choose to call it. I think possibly we are still in that transformation period. But I do believe that several of our colleagues in the print business still haven't quite figured out how to handle this new assignment, this new role, this new kind of journalism, particularly when it appears on the front page.

This arrogance by too many newsmen has disturbed me for several years. That a reporter on the *New York Times* or the *Washington Post* or whatever can write a respectable sentence in English, or perhaps even in a foreign language, or that he once interviewed General De Gaulle doesn't impress me at all. And as far as journalism being the Fourth Estate, an altogether noble calling, I would be much more tempted to subscribe to all of that if someone other than newsmen thought so.

So it was proper, it seems to me, that all of us should have noted Mr. Agnew's criticism and applied it to whatever degree was justified. In my opinion, it had enough merit that it simply couldn't be rejected out of hand, and I don't think it has been rejected out of hand. It has been there bedeviling us and annoying us since it was delivered.

A press that dutifully believes that it is privileged and dutybound to criticize government cannot object too strongly when government decides to respond in kind.

But since Mr. Agnew's critique some disquieting developments suggest that the government was rather eager to go beyond the healthy exchange of criticism and started tampering and fumbling with the First Amendment. And now we have offered to the Congress several propositions on how to restrain these dangerous newsmen, and we have the courts on the new tack of throwing these reporters in jail because they refuse to reveal their sources of information.

I believe there is a dilemma concerning the problem of jailing reporters for failure to reveal sources. I certainly would subscribe heartily to the notion that the reporter is not a privileged person. He is no better than anyone else. But the flow of free and unrestricted information is highly privileged and is, indeed, sacred.

If government is all that eager to apprehend the wrongdoer, the crook and the cheat—and it says that is what this exercise is all about—then doesn't it occur to you that government has powers far beyond the humble powers of any poor benighted reporter? Government has the power of subpoena, investigation-making policies, search and seizure, inquiry, wiretapping and eavesdropping—

my God, does it have that! The grand jury can examine income-tax returns and, in some cases, other private documents. So my reaction to all this is to let government do its own sleuthing and policing. Newsmen have no desire to work for the government and should not be required to do so. They should not even be asked to do so.

If it comes down to Congress passing a shield law for newsmen and reporters, I must say I have rather mixed emotions about that. I would rather rely on the court's interpretation of the fine old First Amendment, which has done us very well over these past 200 years. But if it becomes necessary and if exceptions to the First Amendment are about to be made by the courts, then I would say yes—I suppose we must be provided with a shield. This disturbs me. But if a shield is to be provided by the Congress, it had better be one with no exceptions. It had better be a blanket one, because the minute you start making exceptions to a proposed shield law, the Congress always can provide more exceptions in future years. Furthermore, what Congress gives us today it can very well repeal next year.

There is in the American press one other general characteristic that remains somewhat inexplicable to me. In all sincerity, I believe there exists in our journalism today a fundamental antipathy toward business and industry. I think business and industry—more than any other sector of our society—find it difficult to get their stories told accurately and fairly. Labor does fairly well in getting its point across to the public. Government, for all that it is frequently criticized in our press, certainly has no trouble getting its share of space and time and telling its story. Education, religion, the arts, the professions all seem to do comparatively well in this respect. But too frequently the American businessman, in my opinion, is justifiably appalled at how his story appears in the newspaper or on television or radio.

Why should this be so? Well, once in a while the American businessman chooses to speak to the public through his public-relations counsel. Business would be well advised, particularly in critical situations, to speak to the American press more directly. There exists among journalists a traditional and, I believe, healthy and certainly cultivated antipathy toward the professional hired spokesman.

There may be another reason. We have seen it happen time and again in situations involving an industry. Labor comes into the meeting or final confrontation or conference well prepared, well rehearsed, speaking with one voice. Government is equally well prepared, speaking with one voice. But repeatedly, business and industry, revealing no exchange of information or ideas beforehand, will speak with as many different voices as they have representatives at the meeting. This is not too difficult to figure out. Naturally, the Justice Department is there, and the charges of collusion are there, and the Sherman Antitrust Act is there. So business and industry are very careful and sensitive about phoning each other or meeting in advance to decide what they will say or what their case will be or what their policy will be as they go into a meeting of this kind.

There is one other possible explanation. The press—radio, television and print—does not hire enough reporters with training or background in economics. Everyone wants to be a political reporter. Every cub reporter wants to be a Walter Lippmann within six months. And there is no way. Some of these fellows should be put on the economic beat, the business, industrial or corporate beat, the police beat. Or they should cover education or medicine and science or whatever. But it is the political area that is the great zenith of every young reporter. And there is just not that much room for them.

A Romantic Mythology

Also, there floats around too many editorial rooms a romantic mythology about the virtue of brotherhood in the American labor movement. Nonsense.

I have seen old hard-bitten, cynical reporters, particularly in New York, grow positively lachrymose, with the aid of a couple belts of Scotch, about the poor benighted, beaten-up guys on the picket line. There is a tendency constantly to equate George Meany with Samuel Gompers.

Finally, I suspect that once in a while an American businessman does himself—and all of us—great damage by marshaling an argument in something less than a rational or convincing way. Once in a while, we hear an old troglodyte in American business or industry asserting that the sole reason of American business or industry is to turn a profit. Well, he should be read out of the society, because it is erroneous from the start and it is dangerous. He might be reminded that the free-enterprise, capitalist or profit system is not part of the Constitution. And even if it were, it could be amended or discarded. We might remember that it is a privilege to do business in this country. It is a franchise, and the American people are going to award that franchise or privilege to the system or the practice that best serves their needs and their desires and their wants. Thus far, our profit system has been rather well accepted, and its performance without doubt has been the best on this planet. But it has worked not because profit was the sole objective but because profit always has been a kind of incentive plan or fringe benefit, a bonus, a windfall, if you please.

The businessman who will stand up and say that profit is the sole payment for what he does, and who practices it, is creating whole battalions of Ralph Naders and is getting the entire American economic situation into serious trouble. Consumerism can destroy business in this country unless we realize that satisfaction of the consumer, and not profit, is the sole purpose and function of business. The consumer does not begrudge a business profit if the performance is satisfactory. This means we must stop regarding marketing as a way of looking at the world from a seller's point of view. The consumers who look at the world from a buyer's point of view have the businessmen outnumbered in this country several hundred to one. Furthermore, the businessman or industrialist who declares that profit is all there is, is indeed asking for a very bad press.

I have come to some tentative conclusions about journalists, now that I am a safe distance from where the action allegedly occurs—mainly New York City—and after being able to look at the forest instead of the trees. We may be captives of a false orthodoxy. American journalism, I believe, has its roots and its beginning in the classic liberalism of the 18th and 19th Centuries—that kind of liberalism that produced the Declaration of Independence and the Constitution, the great state papers or doctrines of Abraham Lincoln, and all the rest of our great state papers and institutions. I wonder to what extent we journalists of 1973 may have adopted this new liberalism, or whatever it is, more out of habit than anything else, for we have not yet had time to think through what this new liberalism is today.

In my conversations with men and women of the White House and Congressional leaders and other principals in the government, sooner or later, after much dancing and prancing around, we get down to the final and ultimate question: "Now wouldn't you agree that if I backed you up against the wall and twisted your arm sufficiently, wouldn't you agree that most of you guys are Democrats or liberals?" And I think I would have to say, in that situation, "yes." I would have to guess that most of my colleagues in this trade are liberals and that most of them vote the Democratic ticket.

Why should this be so? It is just a guess of mine that we have been voting for liberal or Democratic candidates out of blind faith because that is what the doctrine and the doctrinaires tell us liberalism is all about. In my opinion, liberalism—as we use the term today and as the profession or the orthodoxy is being pursued and practiced in this country—has no particular relationship with the classic liberalism of the 18th and 19th Centuries.

It would be my guess again that the majority of journalists in this country today accept, rather on blind faith, the Keynesian theory of economics. They accept without too many questions the practice and the theory of big government, of centralized government. They accept without too many questions the practice and presence of big and rather uncontrolled labor. They accept without too many questions the whole philosophy of a little bit of antibusiness attitude, a little bit of suspicion or hostility toward the profit system and a very healthy contempt for state and local government. All accept it as a bit of the articles of faith of what is called the new liberalism.

I would recommend to all journalists of 1973 that if we could ever get a week off—if we could ever get away from our eternal, everlasting deadlines—it might do us all good to come out here in an area of quiet and serenity and do some thinking about what is going on in our trade and in our lovely, beautiful and highly important profession.

New Ideas Needed

Our press begs for improvement, for some rethinking, new ideas and new practices. But politicians and government are not the people or the institution to do the improving, and I will fight those people to the bitter end. Whatever improving and whatever change comes about must come from readers and listeners and journalists. Criticism, yes. That is very healthy. But let us go very cautiously about reinterpreting and rewriting the First and Fourth Amendments of the Constitution.

Wall Street Journal:

Unethical Newspaper Practices

IN BOSTON AND CHICAGO, newspaper investigations into suspected hanky-panky suddenly are aborted. In one case, a subject of inquiry turns out to be a stockholder of the paper and a friend of the publisher. In the other, the investigation threatens to embarrass a politician who could help the paper in a building project.

In California, a batch of small newspapers run editorials endorsing the Detroit position on auto safety. All are worded similarly. An incredible coincidence, this identity not only of opinion but of phrasing? Hardly, for all the articles are drawn from a single "canned" editorial emanating from an advertising agency in San Francisco.

In Denver, the advertising staff of a big daily wrestles with an arithmetic problem. A big advertiser has been promised news stories and pictures amounting to 25% of the ad space it buys; the paper already has run hundreds of column inches of glowing prose but is still not close to the promised allotment of "news" and now is running out of nice things to say.

All this hardly enhances the image of objectivity and fierce independence the U.S. press tries so hard to project. Yet talks with scores of reporters, editors, publishers, public relations men and others reveal that practices endangering—and often subverting—newspaper integrity are more common than the man on the street might dream. Result: The buyer who expects a dime's worth of truth every time he picks up his paper often is short-changed.

All newspapers, including this one, must cope with the blandishments and pressures of special interests who seek distortion or omission of the truth. And no newspaper, again including this one, can ever be positive that every one of its staff always resists these blandishments and pressures. But on some papers, the trouble starts at the top; it is the publisher himself who lays down news policies designed to aid one group or attack another.

Those publishers who do strive to report the news fully and impartially—and their number appears to be growing—have been taking several steps in recent years to make unethical or questionable behavior less likely on the part of their newsmen.

They have boosted editorial salaries sharply, thus making staffers less susceptible to bribes and favors offered by outsiders and reducing their dependence on outside work—which can, and sometimes does, result in conflict of interest. And more papers are laying down rules that forbid or discourage practices they consider unhealthy.

All in all, there is considerable evidence that "the ethics of the American press are probably at the highest level now in the history of the press anywhere," as claimed by Russell E. Hurst, executive officer of Sigma Delta Chi, the professional journalism society. But this is not the same thing as saying they are uniformly high; the press may have come a long way in recent years, but interviews disclose it has a long, hard climb to go before reaching any summit of ethical purity.

Ideally, a newspaper is supposed to pluck out the truth from the daily maelstrom of events, make independent and objective judgments as to its importance to readers, and print it without fear or favor. Resistance to outside pressures, including those applied by advertisers, is considered a must.

[It is plain, however, that a sizable minority of newspapers still are putty in the hands of their advertisers, that they allow personal as well as business considerations to flavor the news to a marked degree, that their salaries are low and that they tolerate staff practices hardly conducive to editorial independence and objectivity.]

The discerning reader sometimes can tell when a newspaper is "puffing" a favored advertiser or other outsider, but it is much harder to detect the sins of omission—the legitimate story suppressed, the investigation scotched for fear of offending someone. Readers of the *Chicago Tribune*, for example, probably never realized why one crusade against a truck licensing scandal faded from that paper this year.

The reporter in this case was Pulitzer prize winner George Bliss, who last year revealed that trucks engaging solely in intrastate commerce within Illinois were using cheap out-of-state licenses in order to avoid paying the relatively high fees required for Illinois plates.

The *Tribune*, proud of the exposes, boasted: "Illegal out-of-state truck licenses were costing Illinois millions in lost taxes. . . . until the *Chicago Tribune* exposed the racket." Or so read a front-cover ad in the July 23, 1966, issue of *Editor & Publisher*. The *Tribune's* attitude changed markedly, however, after McCormick Place burned down in January of this year.

The lakefront exhibition and convention hall was a mammoth monument to the memory of the late Col. Robert McCormick, who for so long guided the destiny of the *Tribune*. The paper naturally was eager to gather the financial and political support necessary to have the hall rebuilt and expanded, and after the fire Tribune Editor W. D. Maxwell met with exhibition hall officials to see what could be done. Also at the meeting was Paul Powell, Secretary of State of Illinois.

Mr. Powell is said to have great influence with some members of the state legislature, which subsequently voted state funds to help finance the hall's rebuilding (two such bills are before the governor now). Also, Mr. Powell's office had jurisdiction over truck licensing. Reporter Bliss already had disclosed that Mr. Powell's chief investigator had a criminal record, a story resulting in the immediate resignation of the investigator and the claim by Mr. Powell that he didn't know about his aide's background. At the time of the fire, Mr. Bliss was working on leads to another story that might have proved embarrassing to Mr. Powell's department—but shortly after the fire and the subsequent meeting, Mr. Bliss was told to lay off.

Was a deal made, the *Tribune* agreeing to stifle its investigation in exchange for whatever help Mr. Powell could give in gathering support for the rebuilding of McCormick Place? Though he refuses to talk to *The Wall Street Journal,* it is known that reporter Bliss was enraged by the order to halt his inquiry and flatly declared there was a deal between the two. Other sources say there was, too. Another possibility: That there was no definite quid pro quo, only a decision by the *Tribune* to avoid offending a politician whose help might prove valuable.

Editor Maxwell says he made no deal with Mr. Powell and scoffs at the idea that the official has enough political pull to make such an agreement worthwhile.

Such blackouts of news involving newspapers are quite common; hardly a working journalist could deny that one of the gravest weaknesses in coverage exhibited by the American press is its coverage of itself. This became apparent in Philadelphia recently when Harry Karafin, a prize-winning investigative reporter for the *Inquirer* and a staffer for nearly 30 years, was arrested on charges of blackmail and extortion. *Philadelphia* magazine, not a local newspaper, printed the first blast at Karafin in its April issue.

From then until the reporter's arrest earlier this month, the rival *Philadelphia Bulletin* carried not a word on the case—even though the *Inquirer* itself (which claims it had repeatedly pursued tips about Mr. Karafin's activities but could not prove anything) fired him shortly before the magazine expose and carried the whole story afterward.

More often newspapers try to cover up when unfavorable news breaks about their own operations. A few years ago the *Clarion-Ledger* and *Daily News,* jointly owned papers in Jackson, Miss., were hauled into court by U.S. officials on charges dealing with violations of Federal laws governing overtime pay. The court action resulted in a permanent injunction barring the papers from continuing the offending practices. Not a word of all this appeared in the Jackson papers; staffers were even ordered to stay away from the court, and they did.

News blackouts aren't always limited to a paper's problems. Sometimes they make unpersons out of individuals who somehow have come into bad odor with the paper. On the *Philadelphia Inquirer,* for example, a blacklist of names not to appear in print is believed to have long existed. News executives at the paper say there hasn't been any such list, to their knowledge, but many Quaker City newsmen find that hard to believe.

So might Gaylord P. Harnwell, president of the University of Pennsylvania. Though a newsmaker by the very virtue of his position, his name regularly was expunged from the *Inquirer* and its sister publication, the *Philadelphia Daily News,* roughly from December 1963 into March 1964. All the while, his name was appearing in stories printed by the rival *Bulletin.* On one occasion, when Mr. Harnwell called for an extensive survey of athletics at Penn in a letter to an annual alumni banquet, the *Inquirer* attributed the letter to "a high university official."

This went on until a *Philadelphia* magazine, which broke the Karafin story, drew attention to the blackout. The reason for it is still a mystery; *Inquirer* officials blandly deny a blackout was ordered and Mr. Harnwell's office won't discuss the matter.

Discovery that a staffer is "on the take" is, of course, ground for immediate dismissal at any paper with the least respect for honesty. By their very nature, though, such arrangements between reporters and outsiders are clandestine and hard for a paper to uncover.

In the vast majority of instances, however, the reporter is honestly employed by outside interests with the knowledge of his newspaper bosses (but not the public who reads his articles). Often the reason is low pay on the paper; a reporter for the Jackson, Miss., papers says: "Almost everybody here does some kind of outside work. With the salaries they pay, you have to." Pay scales at the *Clarion-Ledger* and *Daily News* are guarded like atomic secrets, but staffers put the range at roughly $65 to $150 a week for reporters. In the past employes have labored at such sidelines as making slogan-bearing license plates and running photography studios.

There's little chance of conflict of interest in jobs like these. But there are numerous examples of outside work by newsmen that clearly could prejudice their coverage of certain stories.

On some papers, courthouse reporters have been appointed by courts as estate appraisers. Are they in a position to write critically of the courts if the facts dictate it, considering they might be risking the loss of their outside income? For the same reason, how much objectivity in rail strike coverage could have been expected from the labor reporter of a sizable East Coast daily—who until recently had an outside publicity job with a major railroad?

Some highly respected veteran reporters are in the same position. In January, for example, Bob Considine wrote a column brushing off Detroit's auto safety critics and championing the position of the embattled manufacturers. What of it, considering Mr. Considine has every right to his own opinion? Nothing, except that he also was being paid for appearing in and narrating a Ford Motor Co. movie on its auto safety research and engineering. There's no secret about Mr. Considine's work for Ford—it was publicized—but it was not mentioned in the column.

Junketing also is widely viewed as a threat to objectivity, but is widely practiced nonetheless. Junkets are trips by reporters whose travel and other expenses are paid by the news source, not the newspaper. The source often stages some "event" or shows off some facility of marginal interest, to give the reporters some excuse for going, but the real intent in many cases is to maintain good relations with the press as well as to garner some publicity in the process.

These junkets sometimes are little more than bacchanals for attending newsmen. Reporters still recall with relish a Caribbean trip staged by one big company a few years ago; the firm bankrolled everything, including the services of a bevy of prostitutes. On one stopover during the return trip, some of the more rambunctious journalists were jailed by the police, and company attorneys used their good offices to get them sprung ("These are very important editors from New York. . . .").

The "news" stories that emerge from such affairs are almost always complimentary, if not gushing, and almost always have little or no intrinsic worth. Some editors frankly admit this, and say they use junkets mainly as a way to give deserving staffers expense-paid vacations.

Such measures, however, actually do little to correct another grave fault of a good many papers: Favoritism toward business in general and advertisers in particular. Indeed, it seems apparent that a double standard exists at many papers; reporters and editors are expected to eschew practices that might compromise the paper's integrity, while the paper itself, by actual policy or common practice, distorts the news to suit advertisers or literally hands over news space to them.

At the *Herald-News,* an 80,000-circulation daily in Passaic-Clifton, N.J. outside jobs that might constitute conflict of interest are frowned on; the paper once ordered a staffer to give up a $50-a-month job writing news releases for the Clifton Red Cross. Yet once a week the paper carries a "weekly business review" page comprised of ads and a "news story" about an advertiser—a story contracted for by the advertiser when he buys his ad space. The stories are uniformly complimentary. "Everybody's the greatest," says Managing Editor Arthur G. McMahon.

The *Dallas Times Herald* does much the same thing, printing each Monday from 2½ to 3 pages of "commercial, industrial news of Dallas." The "news" coverage of each company depends on how much ad space it buys; an eight-inch ad run weekly for a year, for example, qualifies for eight pictures and eight stories throughout that year, whether there is anything significant to report or not.

Jack Padgett Sr., who produces the page for the paper (he is not a staffer but an independent contractor), claims, however, that his product is one of the most successful of its kind in the country "because we try to make every story as newsy as possible."

The general interests of the business community, rather than those of a specific advertiser, also affect news content. To the *Sacramento Bee,* for example, the weather never is hot, even when you can fry an egg on the pavement. The most the paper will concede is that it is "unseasonably warm." Anything stronger might scare off prospective new business and industry, it's felt.

Some time ago Boston papers also fudged on the weather reports; when a deluge was on the way, the papers would tell readers there was a "possibility of showers." Heavy rains, of course, are bad for the retail trade.

There is evidence that many once-principled newsmen have been deeply demoralized by their papers' surrender to advertisers' interests. A recent survey of 162 business and financial editors, for example, revealed that 22.6% of them "indicated that as a matter of routine they were compelled to puff up or alter and downgrade business stories at the request of the advertisers." The survey found that "such pressure is most effective when it is brought to bear through the publication's own advertising department."

Prof. Timothy Hubbard of the University of Missouri, who conducted the survey, says many editors object strenuously to such attempts at distortion but often lack backing from higher management. "As a result," he says, "some seem curiously resigned to trimming their editorial sails to the edicts of the ad department, particularly on smaller dailies."

—A WALL STREET JOURNAL NEWS ROUNDUP
1967

Jacques Ellul:

With a View Toward Assessing the Facts

THE PHENOMENAL DEVELOPMENT of the mass media has revolutionized politics. Not simply because propaganda and biased news can be so simply and

Mr. Ellul is a French sociologist and political commentator. This article is reprinted from the *New York Times,* July 1, 1973. © 1973 by the New York Times Company. Reprinted by permission.

widely disseminated, but by the very fact of the availability of so much information. Every day, via radio, TV and print the citizen is flooded with thousands of messages. (We will not complicate the argument by trying to figure out the differences in the ways the three media affect us.) Thus, we have to realize that the individual retains only a small proportion of these messages. European analysts have found that the average newspaper reader retains about 10 per cent of the political news he reads. That is probably fortunate; if he remembered it all, he would go mad.

This, of course, raises questions: If the reader retains 10 per cent of the political news, what is political news? What is the filtering system by which he retains certain parts of the news? Why does he remember this rather than that?

This is not a serious problem for the average citizen. He remembers what touches him closely: local news will interest him more than international news; news that directly relates to his job, for example, the imposition of new tariffs, interests him more than a discussion of general economic policy based on remote decisions made long ago.

In addition, we know that the more distant and general the issue is, so much more will the average citizen's viewpoint and opinions be based on vague ideas, feelings, and impressions rather than on facts and hard information. Indeed, precise information only nourishes and confirms his prejudgments. In general, the citizen possesses adequate information about matters that touch his interests and concern him personally. He judges and evaluates other issues by criteria that have nothing to do with information. His choices and, therefore, his retention of certain news items rest totally on irrational ideas and feelings.

In each of us, then, these two mindsets operate on entirely different patterns. (I am hypothesizing the best of cases, namely, that the newspaper performs its function well and really furnishes the reader honest information without biased commentary.) This condition is not very serious in the case of the ordinary citizen who exerts little influence over political decision-making.

But there is another consideration that is very important. In a democracy a politician must put himself on the voter's wave length. Otherwise, he will not be re-elected. If we stick with the traditional definition of politics—the conquest and use of power—without considering values, aims and ideal objectives, we have to realize that the politician's first questions about information are: How has the citizen been informed? What does he remember? Which, among all the thousands of economic, social, and international events, has he understood and interpreted correctly? How can I put myself into his point of view? How can I put myself on his level, both in order to get elected and in order to express his desires and will in political action?

If the politician is brave, he may try to use power for change, bringing the mass of citizens with him. In this case, he becomes a model for the collectivity. He changes its opinions and orientation. But this raises the problem of how rigorously we interpret democracy. Do we always operate democratically? What about a government that, instead of following and expressing the will of the majority, seeks to change public opinion and persuade the majority to follow it? How could it be otherwise, with such volumes of information available? We don't even have to discuss secret information that the politician may possess. Such information is generally much less important than is imagined. A good newspaper provides all the information needed for correct political reflection and decision-making. The difficulty lies elsewhere.

I believe we must distinguish three levels of events about which political decisions are made. The most superficial are day-to-day events—the accidents which spark interest precisely because they have just happened. On a deeper level there are long-range trends—economic facts, the structures and phenomena of power and administrative growth. On the deepest level, there is the course of major, worldwide developments—demography, for example.

One responds to each of these with a different kind of opinion. On the deepest level we find the ideologues, utopians, the theoreticians. Public opinion, formed (and deformed) by the stimulus of the latest thing, operates on the most superficial level. But the politician normally must position himself between the two. He must formulate policy designed to last for an extended period, whose content must be open to thorough examination. It must fit action to the structures of society and not waver in the face of accidental developments. This presents him with two problems: first, he is not going to be on the level of his constituents' public opinion; second, he must continually evaluate the information he receives and distinguish between what has decisive political significance and what will be forgotten tomorrow.

The hardest problem is exactly that these day-to-day events tend to overwhelm us. The journalist has a duty to catalogue and transmit the greatest possible number of them. But this leads to psychological and intellectual difficulties. Because we are constantly observing what is going on here and now, we become more and more convinced that it is important; it is increasingly difficult to detach ourselves and reflect on the more enduring and decisive problems. When we succeed in doing so, we may feel that we have retreated from reality, whereas we are trying to see it from a more profound vantage. We also may miss a piece of important news. Nevertheless, it is my constant observation that a correct frame of reference is a better basis for accurate interpretation of reality than merely following events day by day.

Let us take two specific examples. During the cold war, while all Europe was quaking with fear of being invaded by the U.S.S.R., a few individuals calmly affirmed that this was absolutely out of the question on the basis of careful analysis of Stalin's thinking and of his policies since 1934. (The Soviet-German pact, on the other hand, would have been predictable on the basis of similar analysis.)

France in 1968 furnishes a second example. While almost everyone was declaring that the "Revolution of 1968" had changed everything, and that nothing would ever again be the same, a few observers, not limiting themselves to the daily events or the daily pronouncements of politicians and revolutionary leaders, predicted (correctly, as it has turned out) that nothing would change. Their judgment was based on analysis of two realities: first, the direction in which the French Communist party and the Confédération Générale du Travail [the largest French labor organization, led by Communists] had been evolving over the previous ten years; and second, the drive toward centralization and executive control that is characteristic of the French State. These could only be accelerated, not reversed, by what took place in 1968. This is how it has turned out. But to understand it one had to be detached from what was working everybody up and see what was going on its real context as part of a logical sequence of events.

In short, undigested-up-to-the-minute information is not enough. We have to know what to do with it and how to utilize it. Above all, one must avoid the passion and enthusiasm aroused by passing events.

Here we must be very demanding of our politicians. We must choose those who can rise above the everyday, who do not react without reflecting, who can judge and interpret events against the background of a broad range of knowledge. They must be strong enough to resist the immediate pressures of public opinion, which may very well change in a month when another sensation comes along. Failure to recognize this can be tragic, because public opinion considers what is most spectacular to be most important, and views what has just happened as fundamental, forgetting what happened a year, or ten years, ago.

The very mechanism of the dissemination of news leads necessarily to a gap between the political leader's judgment and the impressions of the average citizen and, by the same token, between the whole political apparatus and the body of the nation.

Here we are in the presence of the most serious problem that faces a democracy. It cannot be resolved by institutions but only by a new pedagogy.

Eugene C. Pulliam:

The Newspaper in a Changing Society

THIS IS ONE of the happiest days of my newspaper career . . . to come back home to my native state of Kansas—home, where I was born, where my son was born, and where I began my newspaper work—to meet so many of my newspaper friends and to be reminded of so many friends who came out of K. U. to become nationally-known newspapermen. Oscar Stauffer and Roy Roberts were among my fellow reporters when I was breaking in on the *Kansas City Star*—Marin Creager, Courtney Riley Cooper, George Longden, John Lovett, Jerome Beatty, and so many other great ones.

We all had tremendous respect—almost an awe—of William Rockhill Nelson, then publisher of the *Kansas City Star*. He was one of the three or four greatest newspapermen of his time and we all knew it.

But even then it was William Allen White who was really the great inspiration of us who aspired to greatness. Most of us had the privilege to know him personally, for he was never too busy nor too bored to have a chat—to offer a word of advice or a paragraph of encouragement to his still-unknown young colleagues.

More than any other man, William Allen White embodied the tradition and the spirit of independence for which Kansas was renowned; more than any other man he encouraged and expanded that spirit across the country. More than any other man of his generation he inspired newspapermen—of all ages— to strive for steadfast adherence to the highest ideals of journalism. In our hearts we revered and cherished him. He was the reporter, the editor, the newspaperman we most wanted to be like.

The annual award of the William Allen White Foundation gives continuing recognition to the great man himself and this is as it should be—for no American more truly embodied the noblest ideals of American journalism in his life and in his work. It's now more than a quarter of a century since he left the scene, but the "words of his mouth and the meditations of his heart" are still an undiminished inspiration to all newspapermen who want to become great newspapermen.

This paper was delivered as the 21st Annual William Allen White Memorial Lecture at the William Allen White School of Journalism of the University of Kansas on February 10, 1970. Reprinted by permission of the author. Mr. Pulliam, who died in June, 1975, was publisher of the *Indianapolis Star, Indianapolis News,* the *Arizona Republic* and the *Phoenix Gazette*.

And so you can surely understand why this is a sentimental journey for me—to come back to the University of Kansas to be recognized by my own colleagues in the field of journalism . . . and you must know I am honored and humbled to accept the William Allen White Award for Journalistic Merit.

And now—today—how can we best express our love and esteem for William Allen White? How can we translate it into practical service? What must we do to reaffirm and strengthen the determination of American newspapermen to protect and perpetuate, as a basic right of the free press, the inviolable right to know and to print the truth? Let us examine our situation.

We have crossed the threshold and have stepped into the 70s. Once again the American press faces a great challenge. We commence this new decade as the strongest, freest, most compassionate and humane nation on earth; yet from all sides we daily hear intemperate criticism and ridicule of our way of life, of our cherished values, or our inspired traditions and of our national character. And millions of us, in what President Nixon has called the "silent majority," are silent, doing nothing to challenge and to disprove these criticisms.

For more than ten years a hodgepodge of downgraders of America has tried to convince us that everything we believe in, everything we have done in the past and everything we plan to do in the future, is wrong. Their violent actions on college campuses, their desecration of public buildings, their despoilation in our cities—mostly unhindered and unchecked—are paraded before us in newspapers and magazines and on TV as though these people actually were the destroyers of both our necessary public institutions and our private property.

We are bombarded by these downgraders of America with their claim that our system is oppressive of freedom. Can they name any country that really permits more personal freedom? That willingly extends more private charity— over six billion dollars of it per year? That guarantees more civil rights, has more democratic institutions, more freedom of speech, more freedom to travel—in short, more of everything that makes life promising and good and rewarding?

To be sure I am shocked and ashamed and often angered by some of the things these people have said and by most of the things they have done. But they have a right to say what they believe. No good will come from silencing them. We have to listen—and, in fact, we need to listen. But we do not have to follow—nor do we have to stand by in silence and inaction.

Let us look ourselves straight in the face. As newspaper people—who always have insisted on objectivity and still do—we have got to ask ourselves whether we honestly have been objective in our coverage of the violent words and actions of the dissenters. Have we really printed both sides—or have we succumbed to the lure of printing essentially the sensational? What have we done to awaken Mr. Nixon's silent majority? What have we done to make it a vocal majority—with a voice powerful enough to be heard at least as clearly as the voice of the dissenters?

In this troubled era, have we given all the facts—or have we allowed the self-appointed leaders, the noisy publicity seekers, the quasi-righters-of-all-wrongs to make the news by over-coverage of their criticisms and condemnations? In short, have we honestly served our country and our consciences by reminding our readers again and still again that in spite of our weaknesses, and they are plenty, there is, nevertheless, much that is right with America?—and that this and this and this is what it is?

More than a hundred years ago Abraham Lincoln cautioned us thus—"never to violate the laws of the country and never to tolerate their violence by others" . . . to "let reverence for the law . . . be taught in the schools, seminaries and colleges, let it be written in primers, spelling books and almanacs, let it be preached from the pulpit and proclaimed in the legislative halls, and enforced in the courts of justice" . . . in short, to "let it become the political religion of the nation."

That was Lincoln's reaction to the murder of Elijah Lovejoy. But long before that he had recognized the danger of unrestrained and unpunished violence. He was castigated far more bitterly then than any of us who, today, insist that there must be respect for the law or the country is doomed.

If we object to the law, let us amend it or modify it or repeal it. But while it is the law, let us obey it. Violence in expressing opposition to the law has become a way of life with far too many among us today. The health—and in fact the survival—of this country demands that this be stopped; and as the freest voice on earth, the American press must face the hard fact that this job is squarely on our shoulders. It is on our shoulders because we elected to become newspapermen. As newspapermen, we rely upon constitutional guaranties of our right to know—and to tell—the truth; and we are charged with the responsibility to arouse the people of this country to the danger of their silence and their inaction; for they, in turn, must arouse their elected officials, including the Congress of the United States, to the fact that the American people demand action; that they will no longer stand silent, lulled by the affluence of this era or spoiled by the permissiveness and indulgence which seem typical of the century.

Now about Mr. Agnew and his blunt criticisms of the network newscasters and commentators and of those newspapers which follow a policy of sensational instant-presentation of the news and their interpretations of it.

If this were a one-time shot, a one-time complaint, we wouldn't need to be too disturbed about what the Vice President said. All of us know that much of what he said is true. Despite all the disclaimers to the contrary, however, there was at least an implied threat of a crackdown on network licenses in the Vice President's remarks. The public, more wide awake than usual I think, felt he was sounding a warning to the networks to behave—or else. And we have been told and told again that the Vice President spoke with the President's advice and consent.

If Mr. Agnew's remarks had gone unchallenged it is quite possible that the Federal Communications Commission would—before long—have taken some restrictive or even punitive action against the networks; if not now, then at some later date when some other government official lashes out at TV and the press.

Of course government officials have a right to complain, as often and as loudly as they wish, about how bad they think the press and TV are. But if newspapers and TV did not answer these complaints with the truth, and with a reaffirmation of their right to know the truth and to give free expression to it, it wouldn't be long until network news would be regulated outright. After that, there would most certainly be an all-out effort by the federal bureaucracy to license and regulate the press.

Right here I want to emphasize the compelling responsibility which newspapers have to defend the networks and TV in their program of covering the news. We may not agree with everything they say and we may not agree with how or when they say it. Granted they have hardly over-exerted themselves to defend the nawspapers when we instead of they have been under attack, nevertheless the fact remains—their fight is our fight, just as ours is theirs.

We must remember that when the First Amendment to the Constitution was adopted there were no such things as radio and TV. From their beginnings, radio and TV were obliged to get their license to live from the federal government . . . and they still are even today, when radio is more than forty years old and TV has come of age. Even today, neither is permitted to run its own affairs without having the federal government looking over its shoulder and so, at best, radio and TV remain only half-free, subject to the caprice of the federal government.

I would remind you that in January of this year the task force of Dr. Milton Eisenhower's Commission on Crime and Violence dared to suggest, in all seriousness, that the government set up a review commission to pass upon the performance of TV and newspapers. It was a definite and direct call for positive censorship of the press. It was done in the guise of trying to show the press how it could solve all the problems of violence on the campus, in the streets, et cetera et cetera, for which Dr. Eisenhower's task force charged that TV and newspapers are largely responsible. That charge, of course, is ignorant and mischievous nonsense.

Newspapers are a unique sort of institution. They have been set apart for the protection and the promotion of the public welfare. They have been set apart as the guardians of the peoples' freedom, individually and as a people. They have a continuing and constant responsibility to present not only both sides but all rational viewpoints.

One of the most interesting and significant things in the history of the free press in America—far too often overlooked—is that almost without exception every great leader in American history has spoken out emphatically in support of freedom of the press. In 1786 Thomas Jefferson, who often criticized the press, said: "Our liberty depends on the freedom of the press—and that cannot be limited without being lost."

Recall a few more of our own great men and those in other parts of the world who agreed with Jefferson. Immediately, of course, we think of George Washington and Abraham Lincoln; of Madison and Adams; of Emerson and Dickens and Henry Ward Beecher; we think of Disraeli and Churchill and Justice Hand; of Joseph Pulitzer; of Senator Borah and Justices Brandeis and Frankfurter . . . it is a long and an illustrious list.

These men were not theorists. They were men in positions of great responsibility and their experience told them that only with a free press could any government endure. In the knowledge of such overwhelming support and appreciation of a free press by so many great world leaders, we can reassure ourselves that it is ridiculous and irresponsible for Dr. Eisenhower's committee—or any other—to charge that newspapers and TV are to blame for the crime and violence in this country and that the government should establish a commission to review their performance.

Today, on this occasion of again recalling the greatness of William Allen White, I want to come very close to home now—and call to mind the American Society of Newspaper Editors, of which I have long been a member. I am shocked and nearly incredulous that any member of that Society should be influenced by demands such as those made by the Dr. Eisenhower task force. I am appalled that a handful of the members of that Society have seriously proposed the establishment of a so-called "grievance committee" of the Society to review the performance of its members. Whether it is by the government, by the American Society of Newspaper Editors or by any other group—no matter who it is—I say with all the strength at my command that if any organization is ever set up for the purpose of censoring the press of this country—and succeeds in doing so—it will be the greatest disaster which could possibly befall the American people. I have sufficient respect for the membership of the American Society of Newspaper Editors to predict that any real attempt to establish a "grievance committee" to review the performance of its members would be overwhelmingly defeated. Let me recall once again the words of Jefferson which I quoted earlier in this speech; "Our liberty depends on the freedom of the press, and that cannot be limited without being lost."

William Allen White and all his peers in the roster of great American newspapermen committed themselves to a lifelong fight against censorship. They committed themselves to the proposition that the American press has the right to know the truth and freely to report it to the American people. Any curtailment of that right by any committee or bureau or official of the government is undisguised censorship; and, as of today, thank God, our Constitution forbids it.

The world has changed dramatically since William Allen White lived in it, but the things he believed in are timeless and unchanging. And so I have spoken today, as he so often did, with emphasis on the preservation of freedom of the press and, through it, the protection and perpetuation of the peoples' right to know.

Without a free press, who can truly speak for man? Who can present to him the truths he must have in order to develop enduring solutions to the agonizing problems which plague the world today—the problem of finding the means for stopping war; for ending real poverty and ignorance and racial stress with their concomitants of crime and violence and disregard of the law; the problem of rescuing man's environment from further corrosion before our air and water and food sources are permanently poisoned and our invaluable treasury of wildlife totally wiped out.

These are only a part of the problems which man faces. But make no mistake about it, without a free press he faces these and all others practically without a prayer. Only the newspapers have the peculiar resources to arouse the American people to the part they can and must play in demanding the solutions to their problems—and to back them up in their demands until they have been met.

I urge all who are newspapermen and all who would be to face up to the awesome challenge of today. Unless we do, we are not fit to be newspapermen and our newspapers are not deserving of the singular safeguards given us by the First Amendment.

In closing, I want to salute the William Allen White Foundation, the University of Kansas and its great school of journalism. It is an admirable service to America to have accorded this continuing recognition of the splendid contribution William Allen White made to freedom of speech and of the press during his lifetime. We can be everlastingly grateful that his example continues to be the inspiration of America's greatest reporters and editors and publishers; that his goal is their goal.

Lee Hills:

The Reader: Journalism's Forgotten Man

MUCH HAS changed since I left the University of Missouri at Columbia a few years ago with Walter Williams' dictums and edicts still ringing in my ears.

Lee Hills was editor of the *Detroit Free Press* when he delivered these remarks at the Journalism Week banquet of the University of Missouri on May 9, 1969. They appeared in *The Quill* (July, 1969), published by The Society of Professional Journalists, Sigma Delta Chi, with whose permission they are reprinted here.

Our profession has moved far from the days of the yellow press and the alcoholic city room. Some good newspapers have become great ones and a few less competent have died by their own hands. Our journalists are better educated and better paid, better equipped and far more dedicated than ever before. We know much more today about our world and our society and how they operate. We dissect and analyze and define and categorize with a precision and certainty that would dumbfound the journalists of a generation ago.

And yet, despite this great progress and new knowledge and greater dedication, I believe we are in danger of losing our most important asset: The friendship of our readers.

Evidence is not difficult to find that an important element is disappearing from the relationship between this country's newspapers and the 62 million Americans who buy a newspaper every day. The issue of credibility is everywhere. But for us the larger and more important question is: Why? What happened? Where did we lose touch? What must we do now to re-build these critical friendships?

I think several things have happened which deserve our attention. I will be brief, perhaps even brutal in my judgment.

The mass audience is, by and large, a silent one. Its needs and desires are largely unspoken and we have—too quickly and often too arbitrarily—arrived at our own definitions of what people ought to have in their newspapers.

Arthur Christiansen of the London *Express* warned of this fallacy years ago. He told his staff:

> "I journeyed from Rhyl to Prestatyn on Sunday, past lines of boarding houses, caravans, wooden huts, shacks, tents and heaven knows what. In every one of them there were newspaper readers. Happy citizens, worthy, fine people, but not in the least like the reader Fleet Street seems to be writing for.
>
> "These people are not interested in Blyndebourne or vintage claret or opera or the Sitwells, or dry-as-dust economics, or tough politics.
>
> "It is our job to interest them in everything. It requires the highest degree of skill and ingenuity."

The problem is that we have considered that there was a consensus at work out there, a broad simple set of common denominators that determined what it was that interested the greatest number of people.

That consensus, if it ever really existed, now seems to me to be coming apart. Our audience is breaking up into smaller, self-selected groups that make their own rules and arrive at their own philosophical and moral views of the world, choosing their facts accordingly. That process of fragmentation probably started developing sometime in the 1950s, under the stress of urbanization, racial conflict and the explosion of technology. But whenever it was, I think we missed most of it. We were writing about *society* while the people were think-ing about their *individual selves*. We weren't communicating—one-to-one, newspaper-to-reader.

And if we didn't recognize it then, we should have learned about audience fragmentation last summer in Chicago. There we were—the most powerful gathering of journalistic talent in the country—reporting that Chicago was an armed camp, that police were attacking newsmen and otherwise peaceful dem-onstrators without cause, that quasi-military rule prevailed on the floor of a na-tional political convention. And look at the response:

Overwhelming numbers of people told us either that we were wrong, or that they didn't care. Hundreds of thousands watched on television and saw for themselves police attacking the crowd outside the Conrad Hilton and the great majority of that audience made it clear that they thought this was fine.

There was a momentary adult consensus, all right, one that we didn't ex-pect and knew little about. We had not prepared two full generations of Ameri-cans over 30 to deal with hippies and yippies and the phenomenon of the New Left in anything but the shallowest, knee-jerk fashion.

Those "over 30" didn't understand it and we must take some responsi-bility for their failure to comprehend the conflict of the forces that came together in Chicago.

My point is this: We run the risk of forgetting whom we're talking to and writing for and who our friends really are. We were not wrong to report the truth of what happened in Chicago; we WERE wrong in the years before if we neglected to pay attention to the people to whom our newspapers properly belong.

I'm sure many of us consider that we have been paying attention to our readers all along. After all, we go to all the city council meetings; we print government handouts and support our local charity drives; we regularly record the day's traffic toll and when our congressman comes to town, we interview him. Isn't that paying attention?

In and of itself, I suggest that it is not. The more important question and the essential foundation of all credibility is simply this: How honestly *relevant* is the newspaper to the lives of its readers? How meaningful—how helpful—is it in terms of their day-to-day lives? What direct and immediate use can the readers make of the information the newspaper provides?

I am afraid that—even today—our newspapers are too often serving up a sea of words—all of them true but all too few of them relevant to the great ma-jority. Paying attention to the readers means doing something *for* them, giving them information they can put to use immediately; in short, providing them the instant opportunity to improve the quality of their daily lives.

More and more, I believe the reader's most pressing concerns revolve around his growing sense of impotence in dealing with forces that shape his physical and social environment.

He feels he simply cannot cope with large problems such as racial conflict, pollution and high taxes, or direct personal problems such as walking safely on the streets or what kind of education his kids are getting.

The tremendous success of good Action Line columns shows the need for the kind of person-to-person journalism that helps people solve their individual problems.

In dozens of ways, newspapers perhaps can help people with their problems better than anyone else. But are we doing it?

One common denominator of our readers is their shared role as consumers.

It is accepted truth that competitive newspaper advertising—from the little classified ad that talks person-to-person right up to the fanciest full-color display—has played an indispensable role in developing our affluent American economy.

But have we as editors done an equally good job of helping our reader-consumer walk confidently through that market place?

Some newspapers, including mine, have made a start. But what are we doing to help this reader-consumer make wise decisions? Are we telling him enough about new products and what they can do for him? Are we teaching him to be the most knowledgeable buyer in the world?

By and large, I don't think we are—and we should be.

Let's consider still another problem area: Our event-centered news report.

Our definition of news is pathetically simple: An overt act takes place at a particular point in time and we assess the act's significance. If it measures up, it's news. But someone has got to *do something*—fight a war, hold a press conference, punch a policeman—before we'll accept it as news.

Meantime, our readers are thinking thoughts, forming attitudes, expressing opinions, voicing concerns—all of which are much more important to THEM than someone else's acts are.

Do we report our reader's attitudes—bring their thoughts out into the market place for others to consider, provide the thinkers themselves some notion of how many other people feel the same way—and provide news that relates directly to these concerns?

The answer again is no; in large measure, we do not.

Does racism exist only when there is a riot? Did the taxpayer rebellion begin at the instant the phrase was coined on Capitol Hill?

Are those who sit quietly at home, abiding by the law, therefore unconcerned or disinterested in the problems and direction of our society? Certainly not—yet they go largely unreported in the public press.

In the past decade, we have acquired the machinery to report the changing public mind.

We have improved to near-perfection our polling techniques, and the tools of survey research can now be mated with computer tabulation to produce an instant index of the reader mind. We can provide accurate answers to many questions that concern what our taxpayers, black voters, or our teenagers, are thinking.

In Detroit, for instance, we surveyed the black community immediately after the 1967 riot to get a breakdown on specific complaints, then polled them again a year later to see how attitudes had changed.

In Miami, we did the same thing just before and just after the assassination of Martin Luther King.

These sophisticated surveys were not cheap. But they provided a new dimension of information that our communities must have.

The important point—the thread that runs through all these examples—is that we must pay attention to people's *real* needs, *real* interests and *real* attitudes. Our definition of news, and of newspaper responsibility, must broaden to include ever more information that is relevant to the daily lives of our readers.

Every human relationship depends on a set of implied promises. They exist between husband and wife, parents and children, friends and honest foes. Where the press is concerned, our promise is clear: We belong to the public. There is no other argument that will justify the constitutional protection which we enjoy. Consider the implications of that promise:

—Every goal that we set for ourselves must be measured in reader terms. Is it in the best interests of the reader? Is it helpful? Do we serve his cause? These are the tests.

—The validity of what we do is decided by what the readers do with what we do. It is not sufficient that we—and I quote—''just print the news.'' It is imperative that the news which we print be read, be absorbed and be believed. We are *obligated* to be interesting and exciting and attractive.

All this, in the most complete sense of the word, is a dependent relationship between newspaper and reader. It is the only one on which we ought to rely—and we ought to rely on it completely.

We are no separate institution. Our newspapers are run by one set of people to serve another, large group of other people. While we are dissecting and analyzing, grouping people together in *this* sub-set and *that* category, we ought to remember that we started with individuals. It is time for us to sit down in a collective bunch of backyards and chat quietly with our friends. We might have a good deal to say to each other—once we've met.

Only then—when that conversation is candid and complete—only then, and only together, can we reach for the stars.

Peter B. Clark:

Newspaper Credibility:
What Needs to be Done?

DURING THE LAST DECADE, newspapers ran into so many problems that a slight loss of credibility should not surprise us.

Some occasional errors of fact or interpretation were made.

Critics, mostly of the political left, loudly criticized the newspaper industry for too much "sensationalism," for too little "sensitivity," or for having too few owners.

Critics, mostly of the political right, boisterously criticized newspapers for interjecting a leftward bias into some news coverage.

Critics of all persuasions solemnly chastised newspapers for failing to solve many tormenting public policy problems.

Many tormenting public policy problems arose, and newspapers did not solve them. As the bearers of continuing, exceptionally bad tidings, newspapers were resented. Perhaps for this reason they were distrusted more than in calmer times.

Television network news made its mark. Millions of TV viewers—many of whom had in the past paid little attention to news of any sort—intently watched network television pictures, took them to constitute reality, and judged both events and newspapers by those pictures. Newspapers were not bright enough to turn the tables and show people how to judge television and events by newspaper standards.

"Advocacy journalism" made its self-conscious appearances. Whatever may be the truth to the argument that journalists have always been advocates, the 1960's took that argument to the public. Except for a handful of philosophical sophisticates, the argument made the public even more skeptical of journalists.

This list of troubles helps us understand why newspaper credibility may have declined somewhat. But there is a broader yet simpler explanation. It not

---

Mr. Clark is chairman of the board and president of The Evening News Association, publishers of *The Detroit News*. This article reprinted by permission from the *Michigan Business Review* (January, 1973), published by the Graduate School of Business Administration, The University of Michigan.

only helps to explain the newspaper credibility problem, but it also helps to explain the origins of the other troubles listed above, for it accounts for many of the troubling American phenomena of the 1960's.

My explanation is simply this: the American people are becoming increasingly divided about the way they see the world. Most newspapermen, and some others, who, taken all together, constitute a minority of the population, tend to see things one way. Many of our readers, the largest part of the population, tend to see things another way.

The basic proposition is this: we, in newspaper journalism, tend to *see* events differently than many of our readers see them. Hence we *describe* events differently than they see them. We answer questions about events that they do not ask. We do not answer questions about events that they do ask. Thus many of them come to doubt us—especially during a time of intense social strain and disagreement.

When I say that we see things differently than many of our readers, I do not mean merely that we perceive the same specific facts differently. This, too, sometimes happens. But we approach the events we report with a different set of expectations, hopes, fears, likes, and dislikes than a very large number of our readers.

Put more formally, we approach the events we report with different implicit social theories (to explain how people have behaved or will behave) and different philosophies (to express how people *should* behave) than a very large number of readers.

Consider some illustrating news-making events of the past decade. I shall give a kind of summary caricature of how the influential newspapers and news services treated those events and then characterize the reactions of large numbers of readers to those same events.

These two sets of reactions to events (obviously simplified and exaggerated for argument) express two quite different kinds of concerns.

The journalist attached a lot of importance to politics and to what people said about things. The reader, in the past decade, attached a lot of importance to violations of the criminal law and of other traditional standards of behavior.

For the reader, philosophy was more important than social theory. That is, he expressed strong moral judgments of approval or disapproval. He was less interested in *explanations* of why people behaved as they did than in whether they *should* or *should not* have behaved as they did.

The journalist appeared to be very interested in explaining behavior. But a second look suggests that he made moral judgments, too. These were merely more artfully concealed. The questions he asked implied sympathy for some causes, groups, and individuals, and distaste for others. The small edge of the journalist's philosophy which he exposed often differed from the reader's.

The journalist's social theory tended to seek the "causes" of behavior in "environmental" factors—perhaps material factors. He seldom seemed to look for the "causes" in *ideas*. In contrast, when someone behaved in an unconventional or bizarre manner, the reader often instinctively reacted with the naively canny question: "Wherever did he get that idea?"

At least one embryonic social theory shows up in reader reactions to events. That is what might be called the "power elite" or "social conspiracy" theory. It postulates that somewhere a group exists which possesses the vast power to affect vital social, economic, and political circumstances. But "they," the reader has sometimes ruefully concluded, "have generally failed to help us during the past ten years."

A large number of people seem unable to believe that the actions of Congress, for example, are as random as they actually are; that the economy is influenced by so many independent (and uncontrollable) forces; or that American affairs are not conducted according to a master plan drawn up in some single hidden Washington office.

The purpose in reviewing these two sets of somewhat contrived but indicative reactions is to suggest three things: (1) a newspaperman's social theory and philosophy somehow influence the kinds of questions he asks about events, (2) the kinds of questions he asks will strongly influence the kinds of stories he writes, how he writes them, and how they are played, and (3) these stories are not congruent with many readers' perceptions because they answer different questions than many readers are asking.

At this point, newspapermen may say, "Of course, we answer different questions than the readers ask. That's our job. We know a hell of a lot more than they do."

But it is at *this* point that the matter becomes interesting. For what, exactly, is it that we newspapermen know a hell of a lot more about than our readers?

LOGICIANS SAY there are two quite different classes of propositions: (1) Those we *can demonstrate* to be true or false by using our knowledge, formal education, research, experience, and good, hard legwork to gather empirical evidence; and (2) Those we *cannot demonstrate* to be true or false (and no one else can either) because they are matters of preference, faith, taste, or some other subjective value.

In the first class of cases, the things we know a lot about are absolutely essential. We can help our readers, perhaps, by demonstrating that certain economic or social theories that they believe are true, or that they are false, incorrect, or misleading. A good example of the latter is the popular belief in a "they" who conspire to control our destinies. In most important matters, good, hard digging will probably demonstrate that this particular theory of American society is just not true. If our stories explain this, we shall help our readers better to understand the life with which they most cope.

But in the second class of cases, all we can do is help our readers understand the preferences, faiths, tastes, or other subjective values among which *they must choose*. We have no right to impose our own preferred social theories

Differing perceptions of news.

Event	Journalistic Reaction	Popular Reaction
1) The Southern civil rights demonstrations, 1961–1964.	What obstacles lie in the path of the Black struggle for equality?	Why can all these people get away with that law-breaking? What will it lead to?
2) The assassinations of President John Kennedy, Senator Robert Kennedy, Reverend Martin King and the attempt on George Wallace's life.	Who perpetrated these crimes? What will be their *political* consequences?	These cases look like some kind of conspiracies. How come the other conspirators were never discovered and published?
3) The rioting at colleges and universities, 1964–1970.	Precisely what *objectives* are the students seeking to achieve through their demands and demonstrations?	Why do they let those college kids get away with this? Who is behind it?
4) The Vietnam War, 1961–1972.	How and why did we get into the war? Should we fight it?	(In the early stages) It will not be very big or take very long. The President will do what needs to be done to win. (In the later stages) We won World War II against two powerful countries. How come we have fought 10 years against this little farming country and still have not beaten them? If we need to fight a war, why don't we really fight it?
5) The peace demonstrations, 1965–1972.	How much—or how little—effect are they having? How much attention is the government paying to them?	Why do they let these kids get away with it?
6) The urban riots and continuing urban crime, 1964–1972.	What are their underlying causes?	Why don't they do something to stop this? Why don't the police get tough? Why don't they tell us who is really behind it all?
7) The "Pentagon Papers" publication, 1971.	How and why did we get into the war? Will the government succeed in inhibiting freedom of the press?	These just show us that we have not been told everything. We knew that. Also, it is breaking the law to steal and publish secret documents. How can they get away with it?
8) The inflation, 1968–1972.	What political infighting is going on among the people and agencies involved in the effort to control inflation?	How come they don't do something about it?
9) The changing and increasingly permissive standards of personal behavior, literature, entertainment, etc.	What are the underlying social causes of these changes? What risks to civil rights would arise in attempts to limit them?	Why do they let this go on? Why are the people who live decently so often ignored while the wrongdoers are sometimes even rewarded?

upon them, if those social theories have not been—or, in their nature, cannot be—demonstrated to be correct. Even more surely we have no right to impose our philosophies upon our readers. We cannot demonstrate, for example, that college anti-war activists are better (or worse) than college-age servicemen. We should not appear to try. Philosophies cannot be demonstrated to be true or false. We especially have no right to impose them upon our readers in a masked form, concealed among the questions we ask and answer in our stories, and among the questions we do not ask and which are thus never answered.

I BELIEVE THAT, today, the largest number of Americans share viewpoints which I shall label, for convenience, "realistic." But a great many newspaper-men—especially the younger ones and those working for some of the most influential papers—can be described as "idealists."

This is a very old distinction and a vague one. But it usefully evokes some important ideas which help to explain the strains and doubts that sometimes arise between citizens and newspapermen. My generalization is a sweeping one. But it results from reading public opinion polls and lots of reader mail.

"Idealists" can be distinguished from "realists" on many basic topics of social theory and philosophy. They can be distinguished even if their views are not as sharply or clearly opposed as those I shall state to illustrate my point. See if you agree with me that the distinction somehow roughly corresponds to real differences in attitudes you have encountered.

TOPIC 1. The view of human nature.

(a) Idealist view. Mankind is inherently good and is perfectible. Evil institutions are the causes of evil behavior; for example, specific social systems produce and maintain selfishness in individuals; if the social system were to be properly changed, selfishness would disappear.

(b) Realist view. Mankind cannot be judged to be inherently good. Human perfectibility is limited. Some form of self-interest is inherent in mankind. Thus, social, economic, and governmental institutions should be arranged—not to seek perfection—but to minimize the mutual damage men can cause to other men.

TOPIC 2. The view of social change.

(a) Idealist view. Social change is both inevitable and good. Change is good because progress is good and no progress can occur without change. Social change should be encouraged because it unleashes positive forces for human improvement.

(b) Realist view. Social change is sometimes damaging in its consequences, disruptive of men's values, works, institutions, and peace. There is no necessary relationship between social change and what sometimes comes to be labeled as progress. History records long periods in which social change produced retrogression, when judged by most civilized values. Social change should not be valued for itself. (Those with leftward inclinations who believe that social change is inevitably good sometimes omit cases such as the rise of Nazism.)

TOPIC 3. The view of social conflict.

(a) Idealist view. The natural state of mankind is harmony and peace. Only evil, imperfect social systems and institutions lead to conflict among men. If these systems and institutions can be changed, conflict can be eliminated.

(b) Realist view. Conflict is highly probable. The wise course of action is to accept the probability of conflict and evolve social systems or institutions to minimize it, confine it, or at worst, to cope with it successfully. Even the efforts to overcome or to eliminate conflict through massive education or propaganda have themselves sometimes produced more conflict.

TOPIC 4. The view of the causes of behavior.

(a) Idealist view (which is, at this time in history, almost a total reversal of the classical "idealist" conception. Today, many "idealists" are often in fact "materialists.") Environmental circumstances, especially material circumstances, condition and ultimately determine behavior. Attitudes are a by-product of this process. The independent influence of ideas is minimized.

(b) Realist view. Many factors influence behavior. Besides material factors, they include ideas, attitudes, and moods. These latter factors have an independent force. They affect behavior as much as material conditions do and often they affect it independently of material conditions. Indeed, over time, changed attitudes may *produce* changed material conditions.

TOPIC 5. The view of authority.

(a) Idealist view. All systems of authority are repressive, inhibiting, and inherently evil. Authority negates the opportunity for each individual to participate in the decisions affecting himself.

(b) Realist view. Some system of authority is inherently necessary in all societies and in each part of them. Anarchy is a consequence of the absence of authority and anarchy will not long be tolerated. The problem is not to eliminate authority but to achieve the best possible system of authority which produces the least injury to other values.

THERE ARE, of course, many other vital topics but these may suffice to outline my point. A very large number of newspaper readers tend to take what I call the realist views for granted. The realist views are, I submit, their instinctive bases for their considerations of important events. But many newspapermen are overt or covert idealists.

"Idealistic" writers serving "realistic" readers set up interesting strains. The writers seek to "uplift" readers, improve their morality, and induce them to do good and practice benevolence. This puzzles many readers. Some of them think the stories it produces are simply beside the practical point. Because they are skeptical (a characteristic which often accompanies the "realistic" view) a significant number of readers believe that writers are trying to manipulate them. Readers believe that newspapers (and others) are trying to change their opinions.

The strain, in America, between realistic readers and idealistic newspaper writers probably did not always exist. During this century, up to the 1930's, most newspapermen were recruited from the philosophical center of the country. They stayed there, no matter how far they traveled. They largely shared the native realism in which they had been raised. Little in their newspapering experience changed their viewpoints except, perhaps, to increase their skepticism.

There has occurred, however, a gradual change in newspapermen's attitude over the past forty years—largely unnoticed. Nor was the change intended by anyone. It was caused by too many very complex factors to discuss here. Not the least important was the fact that the newspaperman went to college. And the college was different than it once had been. College, as we can learn from our own children, does not merely teach facts, relationships, and skills. It changes attitudes. It changes social theories and philosophies—if only temporarily.

Because of substantial differences from one newspaper to another in staff attitudes, the credibility problem is much less severe for some papers than for others. Similarly, it is sometimes unfortunately true that a newspaper which is highly credible to one audience appears absurd to another audience.

This is my diagnosis of our credibility problem. The diagnosis implies the cure.

If our readers have attitudes different than ours, if they are now more realistic than we are, if they prefer different social theories and philosophies than we do, and if we cannot demonstrate that our preferences are better than theirs—if we really wish them to believe what we report to them, and if we do not just write to please ourselves, then we should work much harder to find out how *they* see things.

We should try even harder to answer questions which follow from *their* hopes and fears, from their expectations, from their values, even from their prejudices. We should spend less time answering the questions which result from our style of life and the values it has encouraged.

I am not really suggesting that we write a kind of Archie Bunker journalism. But is it possible that we could actually learn something from the Bunker phenomenon? Perhaps we could learn something about our readers from the fact that Archie Bunker has become so popular, despite the fact that he is always portrayed as a loser and as an object of ridicule. How much more popular would he have been if, every Saturday night, a sympathetically treated Archie Bunker, a winning Archie Bunker, were projected in millions of homes? Maybe we could learn something about ourselves if we ask why Bunker is ridiculed so unmercifully? As a social science Ph.D., I am free to hint that, for example, social science Ph.D.'s taken as a group are at least as deserving of ridicule as the people of whom Archie Bunker is an unsatisfactory parody.

Is it even possible that we should write more stories which reflect Bunker's values but our I.Q.'s, and fewer which express our values, and Bunker's I.Q.? In our instinctive answers to this question may lie the seeds of a better understanding of our problems.

IN MY OPINION, the cure for the newspaper credibility problem requires that newspapers take very conscious account of the wide range of attitudes and values which today exist in America. We should avoid the slightest appearance that we have allowed ourselves to become a profession which shares, and writes from, only a single viewpoint.

If newspaper journalism is to be believed, indeed if it is to survive, it must do *something that people want done* better than anyone else can do it. We must offer a distinctive competence. Our distinctive competence is accurately to answer the question that citizens want answered, to help them understand the probable meaning of those answers, and in general to help them cope with their increasingly complex lives.

We must never offer a distinctive point of view or social theory or philosophy, instead of a distinctive competence.

It does not require that we become social scientists or philosophers in order to increase our awareness of how other Americans see things. Quite the contrary. There is much to be said for insulating ourselves from such people. It does require that we reflect very carefully upon the possible effects upon our perceptions of our own formal educations and lives. It does require that, when we are on the job, we always struggle to see the world in the complex, and not always pleasant, variety of ways in which our readers see it.

These requirements lead us back to the primary instruction of philosophy: Know thyself.

Robert K. Baker:

Functions and Credibility

*Those who make peaceful revolution impossible
will make violent revolution inevitable.*
—JOHN F. KENNEDY

All social progress is laid to discontent.
—ABRAHAM LINCOLN

CONFLICT IS PART OF the crucible of change. It may yield progress or repression. But conflict is not a state of social equilibrium. Whether conflict is resolved by violence or cooperation will depend in part upon the actors' perceptions of the world about them. Providing an accurate perception of that world is the media's most important responsibility. Conflict may be resolved by force, but, in every conflict, there is a point short of the use of force that would be to the mutual advantage of the participants and society. Violence takes its toll on the victor, the vanquished, and the nation.

Conflict cannot be resolved rationally unless each participant has an accurate perception of the intentions and goals of others. Mutual trust must exist. Confidence must exist in the desire of each person to reach a nonviolent and mutually satisfactory accommodation of divergent interests. And a rough equivalency must exist in the conflicting groups' perceptions of reality. The media cannot make the unwilling seek mutual accommodation, but they can make an extremist of the moderate. Regardless of their performance, the media will never be able to assure the non-violent resolution of conflict, but they can assure the violent resolution of conflict.

In our increasingly complex and urban society, interdependence has increased greatly and the need for cooperation between various groups has grown in direct proportion. The rate of change has grown geometrically and the requirement for information about this changing environment has expanded in a

Mr. Baker was Co-Director of the Task Force on Mass Media and Violence which made a report in 1969. This selection is reprinted from *Mass Media and Violence,* a Report to the National Commission on the Causes and Prevention of Violence (Washington, D.C.: U.S. Government Printing Office, November, 1969).

similar progression. At the same time, the individual's capacity to acquire knowledge through personal experience has increased only marginally, if at all. Similarly, his ability to communicate with others informally has increased only slightly, and is totally inadequate. Rational and non-violent readjustment to a changing society requires accurate information about our shifting environment.

The news media are the central institutions in the process of intergroup communication in this country. While face-to-face communication has an important role in intergroup communication and may serve a mediating role in the process of persuasion, to the extent that the news media are regarded as credible, they are the primary source of information.

Never before have the American news media been so defensive while being so successful. Today, more information is disseminated faster and more accurately than ever before. The standards of reporting and the sense of responsibility have improved measurably since the beginning of this century. But the changes in American society have been more than measurable; they have been radical. The issues, more numerous and complex, require greater sophistication and time to report adequately. The need for more and different kinds of information has mushroomed. The broadening of the political base and the growth of direct citizen participation in politics and institutional decision-making require not so much a larger flow of words as a more sophisticated treatment of information.

An apparent unwillingness by the journalism profession to analyze its utility in a rapidly evolving democratic society has resulted in a sometimes blind adherence to values developed in the latter half of the 19th century. Old practices have been abandoned only when the most contorted rationalizations have been unable to provide any support. Energy has been wasted on mischievous attempts to justify practices of the past and to explain why they are serviceable for the present. Little attention has been given to what will be needed in the next two decades.

When the layman inquires about today's practices, he is frequently told that "news is what I say it is and journalism is best left to journalists." This kind of arrogance does not lead to understanding between the public and the news media. If the media cannot communicate their own problems to the American people, there is little hope that they can function as a medium of communication among the several groups in society.

Have the media failed to achieve perfection or to perform the impossible? Walter Lippmann has written:

> As social truth is organized today, the press is not constituted to furnish from one edition to the next the amount of knowledge which the democratic theory of public opinion demands. . . . When we expect it to supply such a body of truth, we employ a misleading standard of judgment. We misunderstand the limited nature of news, the illimitable complexity of society; we over-estimate our own endurance, public

spirit, and all-round competence. We suppose an appetite for uninteresting truths which is not discovered by any honest analysis of our
own tastes. . . . Unconsciously the theory sets up the single reader as
theoretically incompetent, and puts upon the press the burden of ac-
complishing whatever representative government, industrial organization, and diplomacy have failed to accomplish. Acting upon everybody for thirty minutes in twenty-four hours, the press is asked to
create a mystical force called "public opinion" that will take up the
slack in public institutions.[1]

To suggest that the media cannot compensate for the defects of other institutions is quite different from urging that all is well.

The journalists do not have principal roles in making the news and have
only limited power to determine what will be read, watched, or believed. But
they do have the power to determine the relative availability, and non-
availability, of millions of daily transactions, their mode of presentation, and
the context in which they will be cast. While this view suggests that the responsibility for disaffection with the media should not be placed entirely on the profession and their employers, it also suggests that they stand in the best position
to do something about it.

The inadequacy of traditional journalistic values is clearest in the case of
television. It has not yet defined its role in the news communication system. A
desire to be first with the news, linked with the logistical problems of providing
pictures and action, plus an inherited show-business ethic, have imposed
serious limitations on the medium. The heavy reliance of a majority of Americans for their news on a medium that is unwilling or unequipped to provide no
more information than the front page of a newspaper has resulted in additional
stress. The limited number of channels, television's relatively greater impact,
and a preoccupation with pictures substantially increase the burdens of the medium. Finally, the requirement that television serve a truly mass audience and
that it be licensed and subject to regulation by a Congressional agency has
made it both more timid and more responsible than other media.

Although the development and growth of radio and television news have
generated some thought among the print media about their changing role,
reorientation has been painful and slow.

As a result of changes in technology, financial and political organization,
the educational level of the public and its shifting information needs, the forces
of dislocation continue to operate on the news media. Technological developments could, within the next two decades, radically reconstitute the media.

The news media have vigorously urged the government to recognize the
people's right to know. Harold Cross, a newspaper attorney, has summed up
the argument:

Public business is the public's business. The people have a right to
know. Freedom of information is their just heritage. Without that the
citizens of a democracy have but changed their Kings.[2]

Lately, a similar argument has been used to meet a perceived threat of government intervention. Said Walter Cronkite:

> When we fight for freedom of the press, we're not fighting for our rights to do something, we're fighting for the people's right to know. That's what freedom of the press is. It's not license to the press. It's freedom of the people to know. How do they think they're going to know? By putting television news or newspapers or any other news source under government control? [3]

The press vigorously asserts its rights to the access to the government information and defends the first amendment on the ground that the people have a right to know. Rightly so. But if the people have a right to know, somebody has the obligation to inform them: an obligation to provide the accurate information necessary to rational decision-making and a rational response to a changing environment. That obligation devolves upon the news media.

A. Functions of the News Media

Again Walter Lippmann has said it best:

> If the country is to be governed with the consent of the governed, then the government must arrive at opinions about what their governors want them to consent to. How do they do this? They do it by hearing the radio and reading in the newspapers what the corps of correspondents tell them is going on in Washington and in the country at large and in the world. Here we perform an essential service . . . we do what every sovereign citizen is supposed to do, but has not the time or the interest to do for himself. This is our job. It is no mean calling, and we have a right to be proud of it and to be glad that it is our work. [4]

The purpose of communicating news should be to reduce uncertainty and to increase the probability that the audience will respond to conflict and change in a rational manner.

Harold D. Lasswell suggested the media have three functions:

> (1) *Surveillance* of the environment, disclosing threats and opportunities affecting the value position of the community and the component parts within it; (2) *correlation* of the components of society in making a response to the environment; and (3) *transmission* of the social inheritance. [5]

These are primary functions of the news media today.

Surveillance of the environment describes the collection and distribution of information about events both inside and outside a particular society. Roughly, it corresponds to what is popularly called "news." *Correlation* of the components of society to respond to the environment includes news analysis, news interpretation and editorials, and prescriptions for collective response to changing events in the environment. *Transmission* of culture includes messages designed to communicate the attitudes, norms, and values of the past and the information which is an integral part of these traditions. This third category is the educational function of the media.

In 1947, the Commission for a Free and Responsible Press set forth five goals for the press so it could discharge its obligation to provide the information the public has the right to know:

1. A truthful, comprehensive, and intelligent account of the day's events in a context which gives them meaning.
2. A forum for the exchange of comment and criticism.
3. A means of projecting the opinions and attitudes of the groups in the society to one another.
4. A method of presenting and clarifying the goals and values of society.
5. Full access to the day's intelligence.[6]

Although most of these suggestions drew on recommendations or ideas generated by editors and publishers, the media greeted the Commission's report with hostility and it received a rather general denunciation in columns and editorials and at professional meetings.

Perhaps most important to the non-violent resolution of social conflict are two much more specific objectives: 1) The news media should accurately communicate information between various conflicting groups within society and the circumstances surrounding the conflict; and 2) they must make the "marketplace of ideas," a fundamental rationale for the first amendment, a reality.

The news media cannot perform their important functions unless they have the public's confidence. Any decline in the credibility of formal channels of communication will invariably result in the development of informal channels of communication. Under conditions of mild stress, such channels may serve moderately well to provide accurate intelligence on the surrounding environment, but it is impossible for such informal channels to serve the needs of the people in a democratic society as effectively as a free and responsible news media. Moreover, during periods of great stress, complete reliance on informal channels of communication can result, and has resulted, in a completed breakdown of social norms, and has produced irrational responses. The credibility of the media is a function of the perceptions of its audience, not "truthfulness" in some abstract, Olympian sense. The basic issue of media credibility today is whether the media are presenting a biased or distorted picture of the world through selective reporting, rather than a concern for fabrication of facts. Nevertheless, if the audience does not believe that the media are providing all relevant facts, it will rely on informal channels of communication and its own imagination to supply the perceived omissions, creating a substantial potential for distortion.

It therefore matters little whether the news media have favored one particular point of view over another. What does matter is the effect of media practices and values on the public's perception of the media's credibility, on the public's perception of reality, and the manner in which these practices and values might be changed to facilitate more effective communication of the information the public has a right to know. In some instances, an allegation of bias will be the result of deviation from some abstract concept of "truth"; as frequently, however, it will be the result of the media's failure to tell its audience what it would like to hear.

B. Credibility of the News Media

A crisis in confidence exists today between the American people and their news media. The magnitude of the problem is open to debate; its existence is not. Concern ranges from a high-level official at the *New York Times,* who believes that readers see the editorial policy of the *Times* controlling the content of news, to a western newspaper editor, committed to improving race relations, who believes his paper's standing and credibility in the white community have declined as a result of his commitment. It extends from the network news commentators, who hypothesize the public chose not to believe the scenes of disorder broadcast during the 1968 Democratic National Convention in Chicago, to the general manager of a midwestern metropolitan television station who has run over one hundred five-minute spots dealing with race relations and speculates that his station has alienated a significant part of its white audience.

The concern is not totally unfounded. In a recent issue of the *International Press Institute Bulletin* it was reported:

> In the United States, where journalists have long enjoyed a special position compared with colleagues elsewhere, a disquieting development has been noted. . . . Newspapers, it appeared in surveys, were no longer trusted by their readers, who felt that they lie, manufacture news and sensationalize what they do report. . . . For the press of America and elsewhere, its own communication problem of reestablishing the trust of the readers may prove harder to solve than the technical and economic problems which beset it.[7]

There is evidence that the news media have been developing a credibility problem, at least since the early 1960's. One study of a medium-sized California city found that respondents discounted, on the average, a third of what they read in the newspapers and a fifth of what they saw on television.[8] A 1963 study—two years before the Watts riots—showed that, among Los Angeles Negroes, only 32 percent felt the metropolitan dailies would give a black candidate coverage equal to that given a white opponent; only 25 percent felt Negro churches and organizations had a chance equal to that of white organizations of getting publicity in the daily press; and 54 percent felt the daily press was not fair in treatment of race relations issues.[9]

Yet there is little hard evidence of any widespread public belief that the facts provided by the media are false. The primary objection seems to be that the news media either omit imporatnt facts or slant the presentation of the facts they do report. In Chicago, for example, the evidence suggests that the objection was to the media's failure to provide adequate coverage of the provocations by the demonstrators toward the police, and some objection to network personnel who were perceived as critical of the police.[10]

For example, a survey in a large midwestern city conducted while the events of Chicago were still fresh in the public conscience found that among viewers interested in civil disorders: "Foremost, viewers desire more 'honest' coverage." Approximately 49 percent of the Negroes and 41 percent of the whites believed that television stations are hiding the "truth" in their coverage of rioting;

> they desire that the coverage of rioting be more candid and the "truth" be told. In terms of specifics, one-half (52 percent) of the whites and one-third (36 percent) of Negroes request more "balanced" or "fair" news coverage. . . . In addition, some viewers maintain that stations are unfair in their coverage of riot situations because they focus solely on the sensational rather than balance it with the mundane. Thus, both Negroes and whites believe that stations should de-emphasize the sensational aspects of riot coverage or, in some cases, eliminate it entirely.[11]

C. The Importance of Being Credible

When the public does not believe the information they receive from the news media or thinks the media are omitting important facts, there will be increased reliance on less formal sources for information. Ordinarily, this means they ask their friends and neighbors, or worse, they supply the information from their own imaginations. The consequences of such a breakdown of formal channels of communication can be very serious.

Shortly after the bombing of Pearl Harbor, for example, the credibility of the media was seriously questioned by a large number of Americans, because, in part, they did not trust the source of much of the pertinent information—the Roosevelt administration—and because, in part, of the adoption of wartime censorship.

In their pioneer study of rumor, Allport and Postman analyzed more than 1,000 rumors from all parts of the country during World War II. Of these, almost 67 percent were categorized as "hostility (wedge-driving) rumors." These included such "news" as the Jews were evading the draft in massive numbers, American minority groups were impairing the war effort, and Negro servicemen were saving ice picks in preparation for revolt against the white community after their return home. Another 25 percent of the rumors were classified as "fear (bogy) rumors," e.g., the government is not telling the truth about the destruction of our fleet at Pearl Harbor or, in another instance, a collier was accidentally sunk near Cape Cod Canal and New Englanders believed that an American ship filled with Army nurses had been torpedoed, killing thousands of nurses.[12]

Similarly, almost any after-action report on the recent civil disorders will confirm that rumors run rampant during periods of great stress and almost invariably involve gross exaggerations. The direction of the exaggeration depends upon the community in which the rumors circulate. In the black community, for instance, rumors prevail about extreme police brutality or about camps like the concentration camps in Germany during World War II. In the white community, it is not uncommon to hear that Negroes are arming themselves to invade the white section of town.

The direction of distortion of information received through informal communication is almost invariably toward the group's preconceptions. In one series of experiments reported by Allport and Postman, they first showed one of twenty subjects a picture of people in a subway car. One person in the group was black and the rest were white. There appeared to be some dispute among them. A white man held a razor in his hand. The subject of the experiment viewed the picture and was asked to describe it to the next person; the second, to repeat the description to the third, and so on. In over half the experiments using white subjects, the final version had the Negro (instead of the white man) brandishing the razor. Among the possible explanations for this distortion, all were related to the subject's preconceptions about blacks:

> Whether this ominous distortion reflects hatred and fear of Negroes we cannot definitely say. In some cases, these deeper emotions may be the assimilative factor at work. And yet the distortion may occur even in subjects who have no anti-Negro bias. It is an unthinking cultural stereotype that the Negro is hot tempered and addicted to the use of razors as weapons. The rumor, though mischievous, may reflect chiefly an assimilation of the story to verbal-clichés and conventional expectation.[13]

A review of the literature on rumor indicates that at least two conditions are prerequisite to their circulation: an event that generates anxiety—an event about which people feel some need to know—and a state of ambiguity concerning the facts surrounding that event.[14] The extreme case for these two conditions is a major event, such as the assassination of a prominent public figure, and non-coverage by any of the news media. These conditions can also exist where the event is reported and anxiety aroused but the message is characterized by a high degree of uncertainty. Such uncertainty can result either from the omission of significant facts or the lack of credibility of the communicating me-

dium. Under these circumstances, the message recipient has considerable latitude to supply the missing information from his own imagination or adopt the
speculations of others he receives through informal channels of communication.
Such informal communications are popularly referred to as rumor.

At the very least, rumors tend to reinforce present positions, and in most
cases the recipient will move further toward one of the attitudinal extremes than
if he had received the kind of full and fair account of significant facts a skilled
journalist can provide.

In an era that demands the subjugation of our emotional attitudes about
race, either a decline in credibility of the media or the failure of the media to
meet the demand for information on issues of race relations will solidify rather
than dissolve prejudice. The same is true in varying degrees on other issues,
depending upon the strength of audience predispositions.

A full and credible presentation of the news also serves the interests of the
news organization. The eventual impact of increasing polarization will reduce
the media's ability to hold a mass audience. Through the process of selective
exposure, people will tend to listen to those voices that agree with their special
point of view.[15] Where the society is highly polarized, it will become increasingly difficult for the media to communicate effectively except by tailoring their
presentation to the predisposition of particular audiences. What will develop is
a series of media, each appealing to a small section on the continuum with
strongly held and relatively homogeneous views. Under such circumstances, intergroup communication substantially decreases.

D. Credibility and Audience Bias

Accusations that the news media are biased are frequently the result of
strong political, attitudinal, or behavioral convictions. Many of the same
charges of bias, for example, are raised against the media from both extremes
of the political spectrum. The charges made by the conservatives at the 1964
Republican convention, for instance, remind many observers of those made by
liberal Democrats throughout the years.[16]

A 1960 study showed a much greater perception of political bias in the
Dallas News among Catholic priests than among Baptist ministers. More significant, it found that, among *all* clergy, the perception of political bias increased
if the individual thought the paper unfair to his religious group.[17] If the reader
gives the newspaper low marks for accuracy or fairness on one subject, he is
likely to apply it to others.[18]

Further, experimental studies on attitude change also suggest this situation
is general. Hovland and Sherif reported that respondents tended to distort the
location of other points of view as a function of their own position on the continuum. Thus, those at either extreme tend to shift the midpoint toward themselves, thereby exaggerating the extremity of other positions as well as putting
the objective neutral position "on the other side." [19] A member of the John

Birch society, for example, may perceive former Chief Justice Earl Warren as a Communist, while students on the far left may regard Hubert Humphrey as an arch-conservative at best and a Fascist at worst. Clearly, strongly committed persons at either end of the spectrum will regard a newspaper that follows an objective and neutral course as biased and lacking in credibility.

The news media are inevitably bound by this paradox. Traditionally, they have attempted to extricate themselves by distinguishing between "news" and "editorial comment." More recently, a third category, "news analysis," has been added. Newsmen are increasingly recognizing that some degree of interpretation inheres in the very act of reporting, regardless of the medium. At a minimum, interpretation results from individual differences in physical perception and social and cultural background.

The news media will not be able to meet the communications needs of the country in the coming decades until they acknowledge—at least to themselves—that the old distinction between "news" and "editorial comment" is inadequate.

NOTES

[1] Quoted by Robert E. Park, "The National History of the Newspaper," in *Mass Communications,* Wilbur Schramm, Ed. (Urbana: University of Illinois Press, 1960), p. 13.

[2] Harold Cross, *The People's Right to Know* (New York: Columbia University Press, 1956), p. xiii.

[3] Walter Cronkite, *"The Whole World Is Watching,"* Public Broadcast Laboratory. Broadcast Dec. 22, 1968, script p. 56.

[4] Walter Lippmann, "The Job of the Washington Correspondent," *Atlantic,* January, 1960 p. 49.

[5] Harold D. Lasswell, "The Structure and Function of Communication in Society," in Schramm, *op. cit.,* footnote 1, p. 130.

[6] Robert M. Hutchins, Chairman, *A Free and Responsible Press,* Commission on Freedom of the Press (Chicago: University of Chicago Press, 1947), pp. 20–21.

[7] *International Press Institute Bulletin,* January, 1969, p. 4. See also Norman Isaacs, "The New Credibility Gap—Readers vs. The Press," *American Society of Newspaper Editors Bulletin,* February, 1969, p. 1.

[8] *Jack Lyle, The News in Megalopolis* (San Francisco: Chandler, 1967), pp. 39–42.

[9] *Ibid.,* p. 171.

[10] Thomas Whiteside, "Corridor of Mirrors: The Television Editorial Process, Chicago," *Columbia Journalism Review* (Winter, 1968/69), pp. 35–54.

Commenting on his involvement in the events in Chicago, Walter Cronkite said, "I am ashamed of having become emotionally involved, if we are talking about on-air involvement, when our own man was beat up before our eyes on the floor of the convention. I became indignant, said there were a bunch of thugs out there I think on the floor. I shouldn't have. I think that's wrong." Broadcast Dec. 22, 1968, 8:30 p.m. EDT, by the Public Broadcast Laboratory, script p. 43.

[11] The Survey was commissioned by WFBM-TV at the direction of Eldon Campbell shortly after the assassination of Senator Kennedy and was performed by Frank. N. Magid Associates. We appreciate the generosity and cooperation of Messrs. Campbell and Magid in making it available to us

and discussing it with us. Unfortunately it was not completed in time for us to make more extensive use if it. pp. 130–31.

[12] Gordon Allport and Leo Postman, *The Psychology of Rumor* (New York: Holt, Rinehart & Winston, 1947).

[13] Gordon Allport and Leo Postman, "The Basic Psychology of Rumor," in *The Process and Effects of Mass Communication,* Wilbur Schramm, Ed. (Urbana: University of Illinois Press, 1955), p. 153.

[14] Tamotsu Shibutani, *Improvised News: A Sociological Study of Rumor* (Indianapolis: Bobbs-Merrill, 1966).

[15] Lazarsfeld, Berelson, Gaudet, *The People's Choice* (New York: Columbia University Press, 1948); Cartwright, "Some Principles of Mass Persuasion: Selected Findings of Research on the Sale of United States War Bonds," *Human Relations, II (1949), pp. 253–*67; Starr & Hughes, "Report on an Educational Campaign: The Cincinnati Plan for the United Nations," *American Journal of Sociology* (1950), pp. 389–400; Cannel & MacDonald, "The Impact of Health News on Attitudes and Behavior," *Journalism Quarterly* (1956), pp. 315–23.

[16] Lyle, *op. cit.,* footnote 8, p. 171.

[17] *Ibid.,* pp. 44–45.

[18] James E. Brinton, *et al., The Newspaper and Its Public* (Stanford University, Institute for Communications Research, undated).

[19] Carl Hovland and Muzafer Sherif, *Social Judgment* (New Haven: Yale University Press, 1961).

J. K. Hvistendahl:

An Ethical Dilemma:
Responsibility for 'Self-Generating' News

DURING THE MCCARTHY ERA when an unusual amount of official and unofficial bigotry was in the air, the news director of a large Iowa radio station faced a problem in news ethics which is still unresolved. Are the news media responsible for the *effects* of what they publish, or just for getting the information from the source or the event to readers or listeners fairly and accurately?

In this instance, a swastika was painted on a Jewish synagogue. The fact was routinely reported by the station. A second swastika was painted on another synagogue in another city. The event was again reported. Four more similar desecrations occurred, after which the news director told his staff:

Dr. Hvistendahl is professor of journalism and mass communication at Iowa State University. This article is reprinted by permission from *Grassroots Editor* (Sept.–Oct., 1973).

It is apparent that our reporting of these events is actually encouraging them to happen. Therefore, our policy as of now is to report no more stories about swastikas being painted on synagogues unless some entirely new angle develops.

The reporting of the swastika-paintings stopped and so did the painting of the swastikas.

The other option of the news director was to continue reporting the paintings until they lost news value or, more likely in Iowa, the swastika-painters had run out of synagogues. But he did what he thought was the "right" thing (read "ethical") despite the fact that the events still had news value.

Because he himself was not sure he had made the correct ethical decision, he reported the situation to a meeting of radio newsmen in the state.

"The effect on two-thirds of them," he says now, "was somewhat like arguing legalized abortion before the College of Cardinals. The other third seemed to agree that what I had done was right, but they may have just been trying to be polite."

This example is of only passing importance in the grander scale of press ethics but it serves to illuminate a basic philosophic difference among newsmen as to the responsibility of the press. The difference is seldom articulated as a philosophical problem, but newsmen almost always recognize the issue when it confronts them, and vehemently line up on one side or the other.

In the fall of 1972, the *New Yorker Magazine* in the "Talk of the Town" agonized over the "self-generating effect" of news which was apparent in the killing of the Kennedys and Martin Luther King, the shooting of George Wallace, and the possibility of the effect again manifesting itself in the letter-bomb assassinations of Israeli diplomats. Said the *New Yorker:*

"NEW TYPE OF BOMB USED IN MAILING," says the paper in front of us, which then quotes "London sources" on the general procedure for making such a device and on the considerable destructive power of the explosive. This is freedom of the press, we think, which has its own ethics and its own logic, but it is also a means of providing information, and the information is provided in full knowledge of a now nearly universal propensity for madness, for wild, murderous faddism, which in recent years has all too amply shown the world—the world of newspaper editors as well as readers—its own deathly logic . . . Is it enough to say that everybody has been doing his job—the reporter, the editor, the publisher? At this moment, we doubt it. A better way must be found, we think, of dealing with "news" of this sort, which is both "news" and something else.

Those who condemned the Iowa news director for refusing to report more swastika paintings probably would also condemn the *New Yorker* for suggesting that there is a serious ethical problem involved in "self generating" news.

Many reporters and editors would reject the *New Yorker's* conclusion that what is needed is:

> . . . some kind of coherent, responsible, nontrivial agreement among news organizations that they will play this kind of news down rather than up, and that whenever someone discovers, say, a new device for killing people, they will report the discovery with non-dramatic coolness, and certainly not furnish us with how-to-do-it details of its construction. We (by which we mean those of us who are in the press and who care about the press) have to stop saying we are just doing our jobs, are fulfilling our functions, are being professional. No amount of professionalism can recover lives lost in a contagion of violence.

Those newsmen who disagree with both the *New Yorker* and the radio news director believe their function is to provide their readers with an uninterrupted flow of news based on the values of interest, significance, and importance. Any interruption of the flow of news, except for the exigencies of time and space, is unethical.

They believe their ethical compact is to quote the source correctly and describe the event accurately without the intrusion of their personal feelings or judgments. Beyond that, they disavow responsibility for the effect of what they write on readers and listeners, either temporary or cumulative. Their ethical responsibility is oriented more toward the source than the reader.

Those who subscribe to this philosophy of the press might be said to be practicing *"micro-ethics."*

The aphorisms of the profession attest that this philosophical position is real and broadly accepted. "We don't make the news, we just print it." "Give the people the facts, and they'll make the right decisions." "What God in His wisdom has permitted to happen, I'm not too proud to print."

The philosophy of *micro-ethics* has worked well in reducing the influence of self-seeking pressure groups, advertisers, and politicians on the press. The key belief of *micro-ethics* is that in the long run humanity will benefit because the truth will be told without fear or favor; the guilty will be punished, exposed or at least identified, and the innocent will benefit. Full disclosure of the news is ethical because it is in the best interest of readers and listeners to know what is going on.

But what is the ethical situation when the unwanted *effects of a news article far overbalance the beneficial effects of the "right to know?" What if that which the reader learns benefits him little or not at all while the "self generating" effect triggers violent and destructive acts which make the reader or listener's world predictably worse rather than better?*

It is at this point that those who practice *macro-ethics* depart from those who practice *micro-ethics*. The *macro-ethicists* follow the basic principles of the teleological philosophers, who claim that an act must be judged ethical or unethical by its consequences. If the effects of an act are more negative than positive for humanity as a whole, the act is considered unethical.

The *micro-ethicist* believes that the consequences of what he writes are outside of his responsibility. He believes that in supplying readers and listeners with all the information that could possibly interest, amuse, or inform them he is being both ethical and professional.

Those who take the *macro-ethics* view believe that the mass distribution of news to millions of people, rather than to thousands, demands a new journalistic ethic. The newsman, if he is to make a claim to being a professional, must begin to take more of the responsibility for the unwanted effects of his stories.

Whether he is guided by *macro-* or *micro-ethics,* no newsman can hold himself responsible for miscellaneous and irrational effects which may result from even a routine news story. He cannot, for example, be expected to suffer pangs of conscience when, after he has written a story about the Dow-Jones averages dropping 36 points, one of his readers goes out of the window.

But the *macro-ethicist,* when he sees that publishing a certain article will be of only minor importance to many readers, but the consequences of publishing may have predictably bad results, believes it is his ethical duty to "cool," delay, or withhold parts of the story.

The micro-ethicist *will argue, with considerable justification that he indeed is being professional and serving a democratic society by* not specifying what *is in the interest of society. In a true democracy, no person or group, including reporters and editors, has the right to dictate what is in the best interests of others. The newsman who is the most professional is he who delivers the news "straight," holding nothing back, and presenting no point of view.*

He will argue that "consequences" are sufficiently ambiguous and unwieldy so as to make them a totally inadequate test of rightness or wrongness— only the reader or listener can determine that. Further the newsman is required not only to determine in advance what consequences are likely to accrue from what he writes, but he is forced to make the moral judgment as to whether the consequences are likely to be good or bad.

The *micro-ethicist* claims that his job is to hold a mirror up to society and reflect what is there. The *macro-ethicist* agrees, but points out that the mirror is raised *selectively.* Only a small fraction of the world's events reach print or the airwaves. The minute the mirror comes up, the possibility exists that the nature of the event will be changed, especially for the millions who get the reflection from a distance and second hand. The mirror has become part of the event as it is perceived by the readers.

In most instances, the effect of the mirror is unimportant and leads to no serious consequences. But in other instances—like the swastika paintings—the mirror touches off a series of events that would not otherwise occur.

The macro-ethicist *claims that when it can be predicted with reasonable accuracy that the very process of raising the mirror will change the nature of the event, by intensifying it, glamorizing it, or causing it to be repeated, cau-*

tion is in order. How, for example, does it serve the public interest to give the details of the construction of a letter bomb?

Ethics are always easier to apply in the abstract than in the concrete. In the swastika episode, the ethical decision based on ethics seems clear: The public had already become generally aware that swastikas were being painted. The news director was acting ethically in refusing to broadcast further stories once he was convinced the events were self generating, and perhaps media induced.

The letter bombings could hardly have been ignored under almost any ethical framework, but it seems unnecessary and contrary to the best interests of readers and listeners to show society's eccentrics how the bombs are made. Further, except in the New York and Washington, D.C. areas, where knowledge of the letter bombs might serve as a warning for diplomats and others, why was it necessary to run the story under a banner headline on page 1 as far away from the event as the West Coast?

How would the philosophy of *macro-ethics* square with the decision of the *New York Times* to publish the Pentagon Papers? The case is a classical moral dilemma—the people's right and need to know on one hand against the government executive's privilege to withhold and classify information—which he also considers in the public interest.

The *Times* deliberated—indeed agonized—and came to the conclusion that greater good would result for the American people through publishing the papers than in respecting the government's right to classify and withhold. The *Times* did its best to minimize the danger to the government by itself withholding some of the information and by going so far as to retain a cryptographic expert on the question of the possibility of compromising government codes. But the *Times* published.

Macro-ethicists would agree that it is good to uphold the law. But when the law clashes with other considerations, the final ethical decision must be made on the same basis: what are the probable consequences, which choice is ultimately better for the people? If Socrates had been publisher of the *New York Times* rather than Arthur Ochs Sulzberger, the Pentagon Papers probably wouldn't have been published. Socrates believed that law was of a higher order than individual moral considerations. If the state says you take the hemlock, it's "bottoms up." Greater harm to society results from eroding the law than in eliminating an aged philosopher, no matter how unjustly. (But Socrates was an old man; he might have made a different decision, as he himself admitted, if he had been a youth.)

The *Times* editors also made a *"macro"* decision when they decided not to tell the public all of what they knew about the impending Bay of Pigs invasion during the Kennedy administration. In this case, they thought it in the best interest of the public to withhold the information, rather than publish it.

In retrospect, the Times *appears to have been wrong on this one. But when a newspaper accepts the responsibility of evaluating the news on the basis of probable effects, the probabilities are that once in awhile they are going to be wrong. The* micro *approach is much simpler: if it's legal and accurate, let the fallout drift where it may.*

No newspaper is likely to follow consistently either the *micro* or the *macro* pattern. *The Wall Street Journal,* which usually takes a *macro* approach to the news, went down the *micro* route in October of 1972 when a reporter was sent into North Carolina to interview low income and welfare recipients who were participating in a University of Wisconsin study on the effects of guaranteed annual wage. The published interviews, plus the additional publicity, could have destroyed the scientific validity of the research.

No question of legality was involved, but a dedicated *macro-ethicist* might ask what the public had to gain from the premature disclosure of research compared to the damage done to a research project which might answer some of the most vexing questions of public welfare.

The *macro* approach not only demands that a newspaper, magazine, radio or television station be responsible for the short term effects of its output, but that it also be responsible for the cumulative, long term effect. Richard Tobin, writing in the November 9, 1968 *Saturday Review,* quotes Psychologist Herbert Otto as saying, ''The widely prevalent concept of what constitutes news is a narrow, destructive concept—a sick concept, destructive to society as a whole.'' When news is defined almost entirely in terms of catastrophe, disaster, crime, and cupidity, and when it is gathered from the four corners of the earth, the cumulative effect on the reader and listener is at best one-sided, and at worst psychologically disturbing.

The micro-ethicist *may insist that a controversial story be reasonably balanced, with both sides being given a square shake, but he is likely to deny that it is his responsibility to give a reasonably balanced picture of the world.*

The approach of macro-ethics *is that the communication media are a functioning part of the social system. The function of the media is not merely to mirror the rest of the social system but to participate actively in it, generating news as well as reporting it. The* macro *approach is centered more on the perceived needs of people, rather than in events in which people wittingly or unwittingly become involved.*

The full acceptance of *macro-ethics* would signal a new press in America: less strident, more willingness to accept responsibility for effects, a better balance of the ''right'' things in life with the wrong, less reporting of what officials say and more reporting of the effects of political institutions on people, more emphasis on news originating with people, less hysteria over the hysterical acts of others, less emphasis on recency and more emphasis on importance.

But the great attraction of the *macro* approach—accountability for predictable effects—could also be its greatest weakness. To what extent and to whom is the press to be accountable? If the press is accountable to government, we have an Agnew-Nixon press theory in which the press, out of patriotism, supports the president even when it appears to some newsmen that he may be lying or that he is totally wrong. If the press is accountable to business, labor unions, religious leaders,the rich, university professors, or others with vested viewpoints, it has sold its soul; the press is no longer accountable to the individual readers and listeners to whom it owes its strongest allegiance. Accountability in either approach, if it is to be consistent with the idea of an open, pluralistic society, must be to the individual, not to interest groups or government.

There may be less reason to fear the effects of self-generating news than a philosophy of news that says there are some things that the people ought not to be told. Yet, a more sophisticated press, with more insight into its effects and with more concern for readers and listeners, might be able to take the "cooler" *macro* approach without selling its soul to the devil. We may have reached a point in time where it is at least worth a try.

Zoltan Sarfathy:

No Business Like News Business

NEWS, A BUSINESS, has constantly been harassed by the Administration, a government. Those who speak Administration, a language, say that people in the News business are no different from anybody else. But that is clearly wrong, because no other business has constantly been harassed by the Administration.

News answers badly. People in News have certain remarkable ineptitudes; notably, answering the Administration. News quotes the First Amendment to the United States Constitution, not, as it has been successfully used, to protect the rights of highway billboard owners to a piece of highway or the rights of dirty movie makers to make and show dirty movies, but to protect the rights of people who read or watch news to read or watch news of which the government is not co-author. It says the First Amendment establishes rights not for people in News but for people who consume News.

This is very dumb.

These days no one is very convincing fighting for somebody else's rights.

Or very efficient. If people in News want to fight for anybody's rights, they should fight for their own rights. No one will believe them otherwise. Especially the Administration. They should say the First Amendment gives us rights, we News, we ourselves. If they don't believe that, they should say so anyway. If they say we are fighting for somebody else's rights, everybody will think they are dishonest. If they say we are fighting for our own rights, everybody will think they are Pragmatic.

Being Pragmatic is something the Administration respects.

They will earn the respect even of Conservatives.

Conservatives do a special job for the Administration in its role as a government. All governments act against some people and for some people. There are people who get rich and people who get fired, people who get subsidies and people who are lectured about self-reliance. After such actions are taken, it is the job of Conservatives to help the Administration by expressing these actions as Ideas.

People in News must understand these relationships and stop relying on the Constitution and the Courts. They should use the Constitution and the Courts skillfully the way other businesses do, which is quite different from relying on them. The problem of people in News is like the problems of people who lay pipelines and build roads and pack meat and lay keels. The Administration, which says it wants more competition in the News business, has not said it wants more competition in these businesses. The Administration thinks the News business is different.

How is it different?

It is different because it is inept, and those other businesses are very ept indeed. They are eptest at getting what they want from the Administration and fighting for what they want until they get it. The most important way they fight for what they want is to hire someone else, someone who knows how, to do the fighting. You do not see oil field boomers testifying for the Alaska pipeline or ditch-diggers making speeches for the pristine integrity of the Highway Trust Fund. They have lawyers, lobbyists, and communications experts do their fighting for them. People in the News business, who are called journalists, think they can do this work themselves, and they are very wrong.

No journalist is a communications expert. Any journalist who could or bothered to become a communications expert would stop being a journalist. It is the job of a communications expert to know what effect an event or a report about an event will have on most people, what it will make them do. The best communications experts know what they want the public to do and put out those reports which will bring this about, and no others. Journalists are very bad at this and tend to report everything they know. It is inconceivable that they could fight their own fight successfully.

Not long after Vice President Agnew said in Des Moines that the Administration was moving against the News business, some other government officials ruled that the price of milk must not be raised. Since then the price of milk has been raised but the Administration continued to harass the News business until Watergate entered upon the scene. The difference is that the people who sell milk knew what to do about their problem.

They hired somebody to give a lot of money to the political fund the Administration was collecting. Although it was indeed a very large sum of money, the price of milk went up several hundred times that amount. So every seller of milk who contributed to this donation got his contribution back very fast, and now keeps getting it back over and over. People in News could do that. It's not hard.

First, every person in the News business would be assessed one-tenth of one percent of his income from News. This would amount to about two million dollars a year if you leave out publishers. This would rent an office and hire a lobbyist with a secretary and an expense account. (Police, court, and legislative reporters could contribute half of their Christmas booze to keep the expense account down.) It would also put a major law firm on retainer, and still leave enough for a substantial contribution to the right political campaign fund which would be contributed not when a political campaign is about to start but when the News business needs some help. The word will get around that the News business is a possible source of political contributions and News will have a new stature.

As for the First Amendment, it should not be forgotten. It has a ring to it. The Conservatives could use it to transform into an Idea whatever it was the campaign contribution bought. The retained lawyers could use it in a most effective way. On those frosted glass double doors which lawyers like, with the names of the partners on the left-hand door, the right-hand door could say: "Committee for the Preservation of the First Amendment."

If it is a go-getter sort of law firm it will profit from this new approach, and in time, things being as they are, the right-hand door would also say:

"Committee for the Preservation of the Second Amendment."

"Committee for the Preservation of the Third Amendment."

"Committee for the Preservation of the Fourth Amendment. . . ."

Clive Irving:

All the News That's Fit to Film

GOD KNOWS WHAT IT COST the ego of Ron Ziegler, the man with the asbestos mouth, to apologise to the *Washington Post*. But when the full flush of a vindicated press has died away, you know that the old hostilities will resume. The *Post* deserves its glory, but Watergate makes that collective entity known as the media smell better than it really is. The bandwagon of a great scandal gives courage to many who were once derelict. If the normal pattern is followed, this will mean a later political backlash alleging that the media are an organised conspiracy and altogether too powerful. So this is not a bad time to assert that the truth is less sinister and more risible: the process of news gathering is random, grossly inefficient and beset by a number of unedifying constraints like budgets, technical fallibility and human frailty.

The fallibility of news gathering has remained very largely a trade secret of journalism. The mystique of the media, and especially of television, has heightened the deception. As the novelty of television journalism wears off it is possible to examine it with a little less of the customary awe. A good start in this direction has just been made by Edward Jay Epstein in a book called *News From Nowhere—Television and The News*.

Epstein, who made his name with *Inquest,* a critique of the Warren Commission's methods, spent three years looking into how the three American national television networks put together their newscasts. Amongst other things, he has destroyed the Agnew media-plot theory. He shows that the nightly newscasts, seen by an audience of 51 million, are shaped primarily by the capacities of elaborate and ponderous equipment, and by the restraints of fearsome costs. To maintain one camera crew for a year costs $100,000; a foot of broadcast film costs $20, or $720 a minute. But if the disciplines of accountancy set the limits of coverage—behind every reporter, after all, there is not only an editor but a budget—what happens within this framework is disturbing not because of political motivation but because of other endemic distortions. Epstein quotes Reuven Frank, a former president of NBC News:

> Every news story should, without any sacrifice of probity or responsibility, display the attributes of fiction, or drama. It should have struc-

This article reprinted by permission of *New Statesman* (May 18, 1973).

ture and conflict, problem and denouement, rising action and falling
action, a beginning, a middle and an end.

British broadcasters might disown such a naked dictum, but it describes a fairly
universal attitude in a medium where the line between content and form has
moved well away from the conventions of printed journalism, and where the
temptations of technical manipulation are far greater. TV news has created its
own language, where the emphasis is on pace and visual dramatics. According
to its own 'news value', a strongly visual story, especially one rich in action or
violence, rates more time and prominence than one which cannot sustain these
dynamics.

There is an inherent illogicality in such a value system: most spontaneous
events do not occur within the range of television cameras. This has had two
effects: the development of techniques to re-create an event which the cameras
have missed, and the 'staging' of news for the convenience of the cameras.
Each of these has had a profound influence on the quality of the information
available from television.

The most familiar way of re-creating an event is the eye-witness interview,
even if it means taking the witnesses back to the scene for filming. By this convention 'background' is an inert but essential element in a drama. If eye-wit-
nesses are lacking, the reporter resorts to the often bathetic device of putting
himself on camera at the spot to narrate what could have been told in a studio.

Such pseudo-actuality is costly. It involves a cameraman, a 'grip', a sound
man, often a lighting crew and their supporting equipment, then film processing
and editing. The same story in the studio could be delivered 'straight to camera' at a fraction of the expense, and yet the cliché—outside a court, in Parlia-
ment Square, in the street where a bank has been robbed—remains sacred.

The staging of news by press conference, demonstration or interview is
now so widespread a practice because television news could not exist without
it. Over the years politics has been transformed by the roles introduced by
staged news, and the kind of personalities that prosper by it. These contrived
occasions have corrupted the news gathering system in a very real way. Their
purpose is to satisfy curiosity under conditions which are carefully controlled,
in which an etiquette has evolved to ensure that reporters are prescribed in their
questions and 'authority' shall not be seen to lose its composure. For television
news, this satisfies the requirement at the most superficial visual level. Like
much television, it also helps to create an illusion, in this case that of conveying the feeling that society's transactions are being conducted in public.

These are the areas of real conflict, as opposed to the fake conflict sought
by Reuven Frank. When resolved, and even when not, these real conflicts are
carefully laundered by the involved parties before they are allowed to pass into
the arena of staged news. We know that the conciliatory euphemisms of the
news conference are often papering over what may be quite severe divisions
but, even if we only suspect as much, the convention of televised news tends to

deflect our suspicions. It is opacity by consent: television reinforces the passivity of reporters and audience.

Television news seldom produces a scoop. The complex logistics involved, the dependence on predictable events for visual content, and the institutional conservatism are all pressures which discourage the pursuit of the exclusive story. Newspapers allow a reporter to conceal his sources and they encourage, by specialisation, the cultivation of those sources. These methods are inimical to television. Apart from a handful of specialists, most television reporters are generalists who can be in Vietnam one week and Ulster the next. They are too itinerant ever to be able to develop a private intelligence service.

Passive as a partner in the staging of news, and timid in the pursuit of hunches, television news becomes assertive in determining the format of both individual stories and the bulletins as a whole. A common fallacy about television, subscribed to by both programme makers and critics, is the 'mirror' theory. When television is accused of magnifying aberrations of behaviour by devoting too much coverage to them, the answer is that television is merely holding a mirror to society in order that it may behold itself. Epstein's book challenges this analogy. He argues that television manipulates reality, by technical virtuosity, to conform to a set of stereotypes which have roles to play according to a predetermined scenario. Since the television camera deals effectively only in small-scale action, the people and issues it selects as its stereotypes are promoted to a wider significance by alleging that they are 'symptoms' or 'microcosms'—two favourite video-words—of national or universal experience.

Epstein laments that investigative reporting has been neglected by television, but in this he expects more than the medium can deliver. In America and Britain the regulatory restraints have emasculated all serious attempts at muckraking. Then consider the technical problems. Most investigative reporting makes a cumulative effect: fact piled upon fact, often with a complex plot line. The camera cannot assemble a case in this way; as it moves it discards, leaving imperfect memory. Granada's Poulson report, castrated politically by the IBA, was finally frustrated by the impossibility of digesting so much detail. Watergate leaves television similarly stricken with indigestion.

The basic differences of organisations and dependency between television news in America and Britain do not invalidate the Epstein thesis here. The techniques of over-simplification and the fondness for stereotypes are similar. There is only one marked exception: in America the newscasters have been inflated by a star system into quasi-statesmen—Walter Cronkite, for example, was at one point seriously considered as the vice-presidential running mate of George McGovern. The latitude allowed these men for editorialising, in the guise of 'analysis', would be unthinkable at the BBC or ITN, and rightly. If you mix opinion with such a flawed news gathering system the result is superficial to the point of irresponsibility.

This has been demonstrated by another American report, an analysis of the network coverage of the 1972 Democratic primaries. By dissecting every story on the campaign broadcast from November 1971 until July 1972 the researchers discovered a remarkably consistent metaphor in the reporting. They call it the 'horse-race theme'. In this race, Muskie began as the favourite, supposedly with a clear lead. In New Hampshire, according to the rules of the tipsters, Muskie needed a plurality of more than 50 per cent to be secure. He got 'only' 48 per cent and McGovern, tipped for 25 per cent, got 37 per cent. From this point Muskie was said to be flagging under pressure from the 'dark horse', McGovern. Mixing the metaphor a bit, the denouement came in California with the contest between McGovern and the 'desperate underdog', Hubert Humphrey.

Once these themes were established, emphasising personality over issues, they became unshakeable. And where issues were inescapable they were simplified in an ominous way, as in the metamorphosis by television of George Wallace. Wallace shrewdly changed his role from that of a one-issue, racist candidate to that of an anti-establishment populist, picking up the network's sense of a strong current of reaction against big government and big business. This view was typified in a commentary by Eric Sevareid, the silver-haired mandarin of news-analysts, on CBS News:

> At bottom, the Wallace phenomenon is a reaction against, not so much the failures of liberal government, but against the inevitable tensions released by its successes in producing more freedom and more equality. What this political year will teach us is how deep and how wide this resentment has been . . .

When this horse fell by gunfire it was rapidly gaining a position which could have transformed the outcome. The 'analysis' was self-fulfilling, and acceptable to the networks because it personalised an otherwise rather abstract issue.

British election campaigns don't afford such a long-running melodrama, but television has encouraged the same dominance of personality over issues. The candidates themselves become preoccupied with their performance on the box to the exclusion of all else. I was inside 10 Downing Street the morning after the 1970 election, waiting to get Harold Wilson's 'concession' interview with David Frost. It seems richly ironic now, but when Wilson was asked why he thought he had snatched defeat from the jaws of victory he replied: "Potatoes have been very dear. It's very difficult to argue them out of the price of the potatoes they are buying. But these potato prices should go down."

Preparing for that campaign, Wilson had read *The Selling of The President*, but not the public mood. No wonder that in retrospect the Sixties resemble one extended television commercial, populated with manufactured personalities and extravagant claims, and producing a devalued political ethic which found its ultimate expression in Nixon's Watergate speech. By exhausting his audience's credulity television will destroy its own creatures. Meanwhile, for television journalism, the limitations should at last be clear if we no longer confuse ubiquity with influence.

Eugene H. Methvin:

Objectivity and the Tactics of Terrorists

IN 1906 ATLANTA had a race riot that offers an unsettling lesson to those contemporary journalists who assert that they must "cover the news even if it is unpleasant and unattractive."

In 1906 Georgia experienced a bruising gubernatorial contest, the bitterest in over a century. Race and political and economic measures against the state's black populace were the chief issues. And in April 1906, the Atlanta *Georgian* was founded, giving the city three evening newspapers competing against each other and the morning *Constitution*. The Atlanta *News* was only four years old and not solidly grounded. It attempted to capture circulation from the *Georgian* and the *Journal* with a vicious brand of racism the likes of which you could find today only in the Black Panther Party's newspaper. The *News* began to play up lurid assaults by Negro men on white women. It openly suggested and commended lynching. Its two evening competitors not to be outdone, joined the game in only slightly less lurid tones.

After several weeks of heavy racist political campaigning and newspaper sensationalism, Atlanta's psychological climate was explosive. On Thursday, September 20, 1906, the Governor had to order out the military to convoy a Negro suspected of assaulting a white woman safely to jail. On Friday, the trial of a suspect in an earlier assault almost erupted into violence.

Then on Saturday September 22 the Atlanta *News* bannered four alleged assaults by Negroes on white women. It put out *five* extras, with double banner headlines five inches high that proclaimed simply, "TWO ASSAULTS," "THIRD ASSAULT," and so on. And the *Journal* and the *Georgian* were not far behind in either extra editions or lurid headlines.

As it turned out, two of the cases may have been attempts at assaults, but

Mr. Methvin, a senior editor of the *Reader's Digest,* delivered this speech at the National Newspaper Association convention in Atlanta, Georgia, October 31, 1970. Printed by permission.

two were palpably nothing more than hysteria on the part of white women. In one instance, a woman going to close her blinds in the evening saw a Negro man on the sidewalk outside and screamed in fright. Police were called, but before they could respond the woman phoned back to tell them to ignore it.

Regardless, the newsboys went screaming out the story all over town—"EXTRA—FOURTH ASSAULT!" By sundown, downtown near Five Points in the gin mill and pawn shop area a crowd of 2000 gathered, mostly teenagers and young men. They were led and keynoted by a few well-known hellraisers and troublemakers. The police, as is almost always the case in early phases of major riots, conspicuously did nothing. The mob started chasing every Negro in sight, stopping streetcars and invading the railroad station. The savagery would turn your stomach. The fire department hosed down the crowds, and after midnight the militia deployed to restore order. Before it was all over, at least a dozen people had been slaughtered, some most horribly, and more than sixty had been badly mauled by the mobs.

On Sunday Atlanta's civic leaders met and demanded a suppression of the newspaper extras. Later a grand jury investigation "severely condemned" the evening newspapers, citing the Atlanta *News* by name, for their editorials and extras. The whole episode provoked great soul-searching among the journalists of Atlanta, and Georgia and the South generally. The morning *Constitution* spoke a common theme. It declared in an editorial response to the grand jury that it did not pretend to have had an attitude "materially different from its afternoon contemporaries." It declared that "all Southern newspapers have erred," and wondered out loud whether it was not time to start treating such reports in "a safe, sane and sensible manner." The Atlanta *News* went into bankruptcy within four months, and the two surviving pm's were vastly sobered by the experience.

It would be hard to overestimate the influence of this sordid lesson in the journalistic tradition of Georgia and the South. I heard the story as a lad growing up, from my father who had worked there years afterward. Still later as a teenage cub reporter riding the police beat here in Atlanta for the *Constitution,* I heard it again from others. The story lived in the oral tradition around the city's news desks for three full generations. Literally hundreds of top-flite journalists came through Atlanta and all imbibed the story. It always left a sense of shock, and not a little malaise over the power in the hands of the journalist—power to call up the gorgon, to loose the lion in the streets.

As a result of this and other such experiences the Southern journalist always carried a little extra sense of heavy responsibility, a feeling that he had a special role as a keeper of the community's state of mind and mental repose. He learned that to play with words is to play with fire if one is not careful. He learned the ancient lesson of history—that the mass killings result from holy wars of self-righteous hate in behalf of *The Word*. To him this lesson was not merely a curiosity to be found in dusty books: He had to deal constantly with the phenomena of mass psychological epidemics, race riots and lynchings, which were endemic threats. He had to deal daily with the problem of race, and the perpetual necessity for controlling the community cleavages and the virulent extremisms latent in the bi-racial society. Just to make that society work at all was a major concern. Southern editors were instinctively aware that somehow, functioning as they did at the nerve centers of the community's communications media, they were keeping the keys that locked in the savage beast. Somehow they had to control it, to prevent violence, to maintain peace, to help reason prevail, to foster brotherhood and due process of law and ordered liberty. This consciousness was sometimes almost subliminal. And of course some editors simply were unconscious, or callous, or scoundrels. Yet this concern for community climate pervaded Southern journalism, conditioned its practices, and sharpened the editorial conscience of its better practitioners.

Lynching ended after a lot of crusading Southern journalists over four decades changed the climate of opinion and made it unrespectable and despicable. A really revolutionary school integration was carried out peacefully in the Black Belt of the Deep South in September, 1970, largely because journalists over the dozen years since Little Rock have created a climate of hostility to violence and extremism and their apostles and fellow travelers.

I can't help but wonder what Ralph McGill would have said had he lived to see it. For he more than any other single national figure embodied the Southern journalistic tradition I've been talking about. His life and career offer an abiding lesson for us today in journalism, as we re-examine our own practices and canons. It was a lesson he taught by precept and example: When hate propagandists and apostles of violence attack the democratic body politick, the journalist must be more than a passive channel of communication. He has got to be a crusader for a climate of reason in which ordered liberty and due process can work. For in a climate of hate, Truth, the journalist's god, is the first to perish. I read McGill every day for twenty years, and never saw him or his newspaper maintain any pretense of objectivity or passiveness whenever extremists jeopardized the peace and good order of their community, state or nation. In 1957, a pack of proto-Nazis bombed a Jewish temple here in Atlanta, and in thirty minutes he tapped out a column called "A Church, a School." He laid the blame squarely where it belonged: at the feet of the political leaders who spoke of "massive resistance," who justified defiance of lawful processes, who preached hate. His answer was that those who condone violence and who use violent language are as morally guilty as those who commit violence, and cannot wash their hands of responsibility when others act in harmony with the tone of their violent words. For that column, McGill won his Pulitzer prize.

I have found as I moved outside the South that the American journalistic tradition is divided and schizophrenic. The dominant tradition is that of the old Hearst & Pulitzer city editors. Around the turn of the century they were empirically developing definitions of "news" on the basis of street circulation sales. What makes people buy newspapers? Their instruments were headlines and reportorial enterprise in feature stories and sensation. Their criteria was

street sales and general circulation figures. Their laboratory was an indus-
trializing horse and buggy society just emerging into urban concentrations.

This "New Journalism," as Historian Frank Luther Mott called it, produced definitions and criteria of "news" valid for that day and that limited purpose of selling newspapers in that largely agrarian stable society. Unhappily,
those definitions and slogans became encysted in the sclerotic brains of city editors, copy desks and journalism schools, and taught by rote to new generations
of reporters functioning in a changed world. Journalism in the mid-Twentieth
Century has become enmired in a tradition trap.

Today the traditional practices are being increasingly challenged. On election day, 1970, we celebrated the 50th anniversary of the first radio news broadcast. This year, we are but 21 years into the era of transcontinental television
broadcasting. Television has had radical impacts we are only beginning to be
aware of. We know it has captured a vast fraction of the population's attention
span. It has also subtracted vast economic power from the print media. This
impact is marked by the graves of *Collier's,* the *Reporter, Saturday Evening
Post, Look* and *Life,* and a pernicious intellectual anemia in the newsrooms
whose brighter minds have too often in the past moved out in quest of higher
pay just as they began to mature. And from many quarters, ranging from both
our most recent presidents and the two vice presidents, to many within the journalistic profession, we hear warnings: the old canons and criteria are not adequate to the needs of our age. They are breaking down under the speedup and
complexity of modern life, and the twin threats of social sepsis or decay and
deliberate social demolition. Let's listen for a moment to one of the nation's
most distinguished and broadly experienced journalists, Douglas Cater, speaking in Washington in 1970:

> During the late fifties, our communication media failed to serve as
> an adequate early warning system for troubles already on the horizon.
> During the late sixties, the media failed to discriminate adequately
> among the troubles in our midst. Like a stuck burglar alarm in a
> department store, the jangling of the media threaten to stimulate either
> public panic or public apathy or both . . .

Cater points out quite correctly that it was not the media but President Lyndon B. Johnson, that excoriated "Head Pig" of the "Pig Establishment" of
"Amerikka" spelled with a double "k" that focused the nation's attention, and
media attention, on what had been "invisible" poverty in "the other
America." And Cater adds:

> Our communications media are not paupers. They can afford to do
> a larger share of the digging and the fitting together and the reporting
> in depth. I learned in my journalist days that the really important
> reporting is expensive in time and money. It is easier and much
> cheaper to play follow-the-leader journalism—to read the clip files,

think up a gimmicky new lead and practice armchair reporting. I watched a great deal of that kind while I was in the White House.

I marvel at the maldistribution of reportorial resources. Hundreds of reporters are dispatched to cover the inquest at Chappaquiddick. Less than a half dozen give any systematic coverage to the education crisis in America which affects the lives of millions of children . . .

I will be impressed when I see leaders from the press and television media, individually or in association, approach the universities and research institutes on better ways to organize intelligence about our society. We know, for example, that economic indicators have only limited value in revealing the social condition. Why aren't the media leading the effort to develop a set of social indicators that will provide reporters with meaningful yardsticks?

And Cater also raises a question that touches television newsmen on a sore spot that always causes them to yowl and chant slogans about repression, censorship, and the First Amendment. Cater says:

There is long tradition supporting Jefferson's tolerance for "error of opinion so long as reason is left free to combat it." Have time and technology changed Jefferson's principle? He wrote in an age when the dissenter's views reached only the range of his voice or the tiny circulation of the pamphlet press. If dissent made sense, it would be picked up and echoed by others. But how does network television apply that limitation? Does TV's coast-to-coast range give the dissenter publicity advantages which the voice of reason is unable to combat? This is surely one of the most weighty issues of our age. But the public has little evidence of how seriously the networks are weighing it. Network practice appears to vacillate one way or the other as the winds of opinion blow.

Talk to television reporters themselves and they express bafflement about the management of the nightly news roundups. What are the standards for allocating the precious seconds? Who provides the editorial review to make certain that bias and sensation don't dominate the news? Print media leave a record that everyone can examine. But television writes news in the air.

This—from Douglas Cater, a journalist not running for any office.

Can we afford to ignore such sober, thoughtful criticisms? Can we afford to ignore such a warning as that voiced by Dr. George Gallup in September 1968, *before* the present vice-president was elected and *before* he became "a household name"? Gallup told us then: "Never in my time have the media of communications been held in such low esteem" by the general public. Can we afford such thoughtless reactions as that of Sigma Delta Chi, whose national convention last November responded within hours of Vice President Agnew's first speech on television broadcasting? That response: sloganeering denunciations and cries of "repression"? Can we afford such reactions as that of the Association for Education in Journalism last August? Amid mindless cheering and without recorded dissent our journalism educators declared, "The present wave of repression is formidable for its sources among high officials and for its pervasiveness" and condemning "in the strongest possible terms the infringements on the First Amendment media freedoms being pursued under the leadership of President Nixon and Vice President Agnew." These knee-jerk reactions were of such a magnitude they must have registered on the Tokyo seismographs. Mr. Agnew may not be criticizing us for the right reasons. But he is a symptom, not a cause, of the megamedia crisis—and after all, we're supposed to look behind the surface of events and interpret their causes. It is significant to me that before anyone ever heard of Agnew, in July 1968 Vice President Humphrey was charging that television "has spread the message of rioting and looting" and "has literally served as a catalyst to promote even more trouble." As CBS newsman Roger Mudd subsequently pointed out, television is "a crude medium which tends to strike at the emotions rather than the intellect. TV has helped spread violence and extremist dissent." Indeed, I suspect the gargantuan reaction Agnew provoked would not have come from mature journalists secure in their positions and confident of their own roles and rectitude. And I believe we certainly have a right to expect more positive, forward thinking from our journalism educators, if not from the assembled leaders of the one professional association that represents both print and broadcast practitioners.

If the old practices and canons are inadequate, where shall we look for new principles?

We may draw from that other journalistic tradition, the agrarian and Southern response. As the canons of the "New Journalism" of Hearst and Pulitzer were carried into the South and Agrarian America, they underwent sharp modification, forced by the different circumstances. We can re-examine the tradition of the Editor as Establishmentarian and Peace-Keeper, the tradition of a Henry Grady, a Henry Watterson or William Allen White or Ralph McGill. This tradition was not wholly alien to the urban journalism of Pulitzer or Hearst; they, too, were establishmentarian and were community-minded. But this agrarian tradition reflected a different emphasis in values and priorities. Not merely selling newspapers, but a concern with tranquility and the quality of life and community, was dominant. It occupied a higher place on the scale of values.

News of conflict did not automatically displace news of consensus, as it tends to do in the dominant tradition. Indeed, if the cause of community peace seemed to indicate it, Southern editors learned automatically to seek the news of consensus and to tone down the news of conflict. It was not a matter of "distorting" or "censoring" but of "balancing" that amorphous entity we define as "news." If the situation demanded it, the deliberate agitators and professional rabble-rousers were targeted for lampoonery, impassioned editorialization, and every other weapon in the journalist's arsenal for isolating extremists and defusing hysteria. Such attention to the community's climate was seen as the essence of professional responsibility—the role of the journalist as peacekeeper.

We can see vividly and dramatically the modifications Southerners were forced to make, and the differences in the emphasis in the two journalistic traditions in the Atlanta race riot and its subsequent influence. Ironically—and sadly—you will not find this episode recorded in the standard histories and textbooks of American journalism prevailing in our journalism schools and newsrooms today. It is a lost lesson. But it deserves resurrection in this time of civil turmoil.

The Atlanta riot demonstrates truth that should be generally accepted, and certainly in an industry that lives off the advertising: That truth is that riots and mass violence *can* be created by climate-making propaganda in the mass media.

Moreover, there are those whose business it is to *plan* climate-making propaganda and to create climates of opinion through mass media operations. Some of them work for advertising agencies. And some of them work for foreign intelligence agencies. And some of them work for home-grown extremist organizations, ranging from the Weathermen and Black Panthers to the Maoist and pro-Soviet communist parties to the Ku Klux Klan. And television, given its aversion to "talking heads" and its insatiable desire for "action" shots, may be especially vulnerable. A single example illustrates what I mean: demonstrators who executed a plan to turn a Harvard "peace rally" into a riot carried baseball bats painted black so they would not show up in the film clips and so millions would not see what police were reacting to.

Unless free journalists develop our own goals and criteria for climate-making, and plans for doing it, we shall be passive patsies for others who *do* have such criteria and plans. And their goals are emphatically *not* the preservation of the First Amendment which we must have to live. We become mindless channels for their climate-making operations designed to exploit our own traditional criteria of newsworthiness toward our own destruction—the destruction of the ordered liberty and constitutionalism that are necessary components of the democratic ecology. I see no alternative but for America's journalists to assert ourselves, to examine anew our role and our canons of professional performance.

We face once more the kind of situation that moved Lincoln to say: "As our case is new, so must we think anew and act anew. We must disenthrall ourselves and save our country."

J. F. terHorst:

What the Press Must Do

AN AUTUMN OF MEANDERING across the country reminds this reporter that, even with Richard Nixon gone, many people continue to harbor a deep distrust of the news media. Time and again the questions keep coming up:

Why do the media "play God"? How come the press always goes after public officials but never seems to investigate unethical journalists or take on big business? Why do the papers and the networks still hound Nixon? Is reporting really an honest profession? Shouldn't reporters be licensed or regulated like doctors and lawyers? And, usually with a nudge in the ribs, didn't I finally discover the (awful) truth about the media during my tenure as White House press secretary?

The list of such inquiries is endless and perturbing. A substantial segment of the public seems to believe the media are not really telling it like it is, while an equally large segment is certain the press is telling too much.

Attacks on the media, of course, did not begin with Spiro Agnew and are not likely to end soon, not even if the First Amendment's guarantees of a free press were subjected, God forbid, to government or professional regulation. And yet, to be fair about it, the public's questions about the role of the news media deserve consideration. For if the press cannot adequately defend itself or admit to its own deficiencies and take corrective action, the concept of a free press may not long endure, even in America.

When I'm asked why the Washington press corps drove Nixon out of office, my reply is that it was not the media but his own miserable White House tapes. The press did not invent the Watergate burglary, the hush money or the cover-up lies that former Nixon aides now admit telling before the grand jury or in court.

Whenever I'm asked why we report so much bad news, I usually answer that news, almost by definition, concerns things that go wrong in our lives. A housewife chatting with her neighbor doesn't exclaim over the terrific breakfast she fixed. No, she is more likely to report that the toaster broke or that the bacon burned or that the morning paper was a rain-soaked mess.

Mr. terHorst is a syndicated columnist for *The Detroit News*. He was President Ford's first Press Secretary, who resigned after a short time at the post. This article is reprinted with permission from *Newsweek*, December 9, 1974. Copyright Newsweek, Inc. 1974

Some questions require candid admissions. As Bob Woodward and Carl Bernstein acknowledge in their splendid Watergate whodunit, there are times when reporters have resorted to sly tactics to get at a larger truth. And I also am forced to admit that the zeal with which the press pursued Watergate was considerably greater than the zeal it showed in unraveling the Bobby Baker affair during Lyndon Johnson's heyday, or Ted Kennedy's Chappaquiddick. The reason is not that the media are so liberal that they simply looked the other way when scandal touched these Democrats.

No, the reason was simply that neither the Baker case nor the Chappaquiddick tragedy involved Presidential decision-making at the White House. But, as a footnote, I believe my journalistic colleagues and I would give both of these matters much more intensive investigation were they to occur now—after Watergate. One Watergate lesson is that it's true what they say about icebergs.

What concerns me most about public suspicion of the media is not that it is unhealthy but that it is so often based on a misconception of the press's role. How do we go about clearing that up?

I would start with the late Alexander Bickel's reminder that, under the First Amendment, the press has been institutionalized by the Constitution as a part of the private sector that has a "governmental" role to play. It has a duty to inform the citizenry of governmental actions and thinking on public issues. That duty carries with it the corollary responsibility to examine the decision-making process and the motivations of the men and women who set public policy. If a free press ignores this duty it not only fails to inform but it *misinforms*. In the dissemination of information, it is really beyond the reportorial function of the press to consider whether such information is intrinsically good or bad news.

It is, obviously, within the *editorial* province of a free press to debate the merits of decisions on the editorial pages of newspapers or through the labeled commentaries on a network or local-station news show. I am old-fashioned enough to believe that the media's opinions should be reserved for these channels and should not be mirrored in their news reportage.

As President Ford's press secretary, I learned firsthand what I had always suspected—every President would like the press to serve as a cheerleader. But a truly free press does not have an obligation to support government policy; indeed, it has an obligation to refrain from support. Otherwise it is only a propaganda arm of government. As one of my predecessors, Bill Moyers, has so succinctly put it, the press's role is that of scrutinizing, debating and giving the public a chance to decide whether the government's decisions are right. Walter Lippmann put it best when he declared that the media have a responsibility to provide "a picture of reality on which men can act." But even Lippmann had doubts about the ability of a free press to communicate the "truth" about government or society. "News" and "truth" are not interchangeable words for the same thing, as he noted.

Several times during my short career as White House press secretary I was provided less than the whole truth by other Presidential advisers. Their mistaken attitude seemed to be that what I didn't know wouldn't hurt me, especially in view of Ford's promise of openness and my dedication to delivering it. I think the fear was that I might tell the press too much if I knew everything.

But on these few occasions when I was given less than the full story, the result was that I innocently transmitted "news" that was not wholly accurate. In each instance, including the Nixon pardon, the full story soon became available from me, but not without a price to the President. The media were reminded that they had a duty to remain skeptical of White House announcements, no matter how much individual White House reporters wanted the new President to succeed and wanted to be rid of letters from the public scolding them for not telling what is right about our country.

I'm convinced the press is constitutionally required to live in this kind of no man's land, subject to constant criticism of both government and public and loved by neither. The press need not be hostile, but it must remain an adversary—willing to test, investigate and challenge governmental decisions. It certainly would help if this concept of a free press were more widely understood and accepted by all three parties concerned—the government, the public and the media.

Simon Head:

The Super-Journalist

AMID THE HUGE Washington press corps there is a tiny élite of what might be called "super-journalists". They have better access to important officials than anyone else, and because they are rich (their salaries are, by British standards, enormous) they can entertain the Henry Kissingers of the world in the style to which they have become accustomed. Over and above their power and wealth they enjoy the confidence of the powerful not so much because they always slavishly follow the current Administration line, but because they are thought to be eminently "responsible": there is always a certain moderation in the way they

Mr. Head is a regular contributor to the *New Statesman*. This article is reprinted by permission from the *New Statesman* (August 24, 1973).

criticise government policy, even on Vietnam, and they can be relied upon not to divulge information which might jeopardise "national security." James Reston is the doyen of the super-journalists, and one would also have to include the Alsop brothers, Joseph Kraft and Rowland Evans.

There is of course nothing particularly virtuous about being a super-journalist. Indeed the best and most admirable journalists writing in America today are those who, after living through the Vietnam nightmare, have decided that the only possible way to write sanely about the US government is to keep a certain distance from it and to avoid those cosy relationships with top officials which are absolutely *de rigueur* for the super-journalist. I. F. Stone has practised this method for years, as now do Tom Wicker and Anthony Lewis of the *New York Times,* and James Wechsler, the distinguished columnist of the *New York Post.* But in terms of purely worldly power and status, the super-journalists are at the top of the ladder.

Usually the British correspondent in Washington does not rise to the great heights of super-journalism. He does not stay in Washington long enough and, sad but true, he does not have the money. Yet there is one British correspondent who, much to the chagrin of some of his peers, has become a sort of honorary super-journalist. Henry Brandon has now been in Washington for nearly 25 years, which gives him a very long head start over everybody else; his weekly article in the *Sunday Times,* usually about foreign affairs, gets as near to being a column in the American style as is possible in English journalism; and he is above all impeccably "responsible": the President and his advisers may make errors of judgment and they may be misinformed, but they are never foolish, corrupt, devious or plain evil.

Indeed this unshakable respectability gives Henry Brandon an advantage over even the super-journalists themselves; a columnist for the *Washington Post* or the *New York Times* is expected to be trenchant and opinionated; during a crisis like the Cambodian invasion he is expected to curse the President for his folly, or to praise him for his courage and wisdom. This makes it difficult for the American super-journalist to be "in" with everybody; liberals like Kraft and Reston will be welcomed by the Kennedys, kept at arm's length by Nixon and LBJ; vice versa for hawks like William S. White. But Henry Brandon, who chooses never to take sides in so crude and blatant a way, can be "in" with practically everybody: "in" with the Kennedys, John and Bobby both; on reasonable terms with LBJ (nobody who had been part of the Kennedy circle could be completely free of suspicion in LBJ's eyes) and most important, very much "in" with Henry Kissinger during the past four years.

Indeed during the first Nixon presidency Henry Brandon achieved some sort of apotheosis. The LBJ years were bleak for a journalist whose speciality was to write about foreign policy from the inside. Vietnam was the foreign policy story which overshadowed every other and as long as the "dope" was recounted by Walt Rostow, Dean Rusk, or LBJ himself there was a good chance that it would later turn out to be pure fantasy and invention. But as

Henry Kissinger became established in the White House, and as the "new diplomacy" with China and the Soviet Union superseded Vietnam as the number one foreign policy story, Brandonism flourished as never before. For one thing the inside story of the Nixon-Kissinger diplomacy was a subject ideally suited to the Brandon treatment; it was for once an inside story which was quite genuinely interesting, one which Brandon could recount in great detail without worrying too much about boring his readers to death.

It was, untypically, an American foreign policy initiative which was on the whole a good thing, and in contrast to the Vietnam story, the insider could wallow in the glory of being "inside," free of the unpleasant thought that he might be joining a bandwagon which could crash at any moment. Brandon has also benefited from being as close to Henry Kissinger as any Washington correspondent, American or foreign, has managed to get. Possibly this was because both were immigrants, Brandon from Prague, Kissinger from Southern Germany, and both seemed to share the same basic convictions about foreign policy. Brandon was also wise enough to go and talk to Kissinger while he was still a relatively obscure academic at Harvard, and this Kissinger has not forgotten.

One of the fruits of this special relationship is Henry Brandon's latest book, *The Retreat of American Power*. Predictably it suffers from certain fruits endemic to Brandonism. The passion always to demonstrate "in-ness" sometimes get completely out of control and one must wade through passages about life in the Nixon White House which sink to an almost unbelievable level of banality. There is, for instance, a large chunk describing the now notorious afternoon spent with Nixon and Kissinger in the rose garden at San Clemente, which, for some inexplicable reason, the *Sunday Times* saw fit to include in its serialised excerpts from the book. Some of the prose is pure *Woman's Own:* "We rushed through the rest of the meal and then went over to a little parking lot of electric golf carts, which seem to be the favoured means of transportation within the compound. Henry cautiously sat at the wheel and drove across toward a wide gate in a white stone wall and to the doors of the villa"—and so on. There is much more in the same vein. It is also probably inevitable that in trying to estimate the overall significance of the Nixon-Kissinger diplomacy Brandon takes on Kissinger's own version virtually *in toto,* and one gets very little sense of Brandon as an analyist with an independent viewpoint of his own.

But if the book is treated simply as straight narrative history, which is really what it is, then it does have real value. The fact that much of the information comes straight from Henry Kissinger himself is reason enough to take it seriously. But beyond that Brandon's descriptions of specific crises, particularly his account of the deliberations which led to the Cambodian invasion, and his account of the tortuous negotiations which preceded the SALT agreement go well beyond anything else which has so far been published, and reveal Brandon's talents as a reporter at their best.

For an example of Brandon at his most tricky, consider his reaction to Watergate. How was this perennial insider to deal with a crisis which made "insider journalism" as dangerous and risky as it had been in the days of Rostow and the Tet Offensive, since after all no self-respecting reporter could risk being regarded as a pliant conduit for the lies and deceptions of Ron Ziegler. The simple solution was to jump off the sinking ship as discreetly as possible, and to execute a shift of journalistic "line" with as much deftness and subtlety as a Gromyko or a Mikoyan introducing some new policy on the German question. A pure example of this singular method is afforded by comparing two articles Brandon wrote in the *Sunday Times,* the first on 1 April 1973, the second on 29 April. Both deal extensively with the same topic—the performance of the Haldeman-Ehrlichman regime—but the message of each is very different. The first is a typical example of the kind of bland, deferential "insider" journalism with which *Sunday Times* readers must have become all too familiar over the years. The reassuring glimpses of what the great are really like, to which only the insider is privileged: "Ehrlichman is more at ease with people than Haldeman, he exudes a cool charm, he smiles easily and he knows how to listen sympathetically." The authoritative put-down of gross rumours peddled by the plebeian press: "The occasional rumours of a rift between the two are without foundation." And most important of all, the assurance that all is well with the system: "The Germans (i.e. Haldeman and Ehrlichman) are a tightly knit group. Their emphasis is not on brilliance but on management, not on creativity but on stability, not on what appeals to the few but what pleases the majority. And who can blame them for a certain cockiness? After all they know what most appeals to Middle America."

What a surprise then that within a month Brandon should be mouthing the sweeping criticisms of the Haldeman-Ehrlichman regime which the Left had been urging for years, that suddenly he should wish to banish these worthy burgomasters to the innermost ring of hell: "[Nixon] surrounded himself with tough-minded managers and huckster-type public relations men . . . they believed in the arrogance of power rather than in its fallability . . . to enable them to deploy their power at will Haldeman and Ehrlichman surrounded themselves with young men, equally cynical and unscrupulous and also without political experience . . . They had little respect for the political system, for the game of politics or for politicians, they treated members of Congress and the cabinet accordingly"—and so on.

How come that these obvious truths, long self-evident to all but the most blind Nixon loyalists, had been so conspicuously absent in the article of 1 April? The answer is painfully simple. On 1 April the Haldeman-Ehrlichman regime was still intact, a functioning "establishment" with which the insider could still identify. True, there was the danger of McCord's impending disclosures, but it was as yet by no means clear exactly how far up the hierarchy these would penetrate. But by 29 April the system had completely disintegrated: McCord and Magruder had talked, Gray had resigned, the two Watergate factions (Mitchell and Dean versus Haldeman and Ehrlichman) were clawing each other to death, and Haldeman and Ehrlichman themselves were to resign the next day.

So what perfect symmetry between such an ebb and flow in the fotunes of the powerful and the twists and turns to be detected in the Brandon line! On 1 April Haldeman and Ehrlichman could still punish, boycott, and expel the insider who offended them, and therefore there were things which were better left unsaid. But by 29 April they were down and out and anything went. The accumulated resentments of four years could be shouted from the rooftops without fear of reprisal. No matter that the Wechslers, the Lewises and the Wickers had for years condemned the weaknesses of the regime, even when it was unfashionable to do so. They after all are not super-journalists.

Thomas Griffiths:

A Few Frank Words About Bias

NOTHING IRRITATES a journalist so much as to be told that he is biased, particularly when the charge comes from someone so blinded by his own prejudices that he wouldn't know evenhandedness if it smote him on both cheeks evenhandedly. The journalist is usually goaded into insisting that he isn't at all biased, an innocent state of mind impossible to prove. Better to admit from the start the inevitable subjectivity of journalism, and then to treat it as a necessary condition, not a right.

On the Seattle newspaper where I once worked, an only-the-facts-ma'am style of writing prevailed. In the areas we were allowed to report about, we were confined to the barren facts; the result was that the most conscientious reader hardly knew what was really going on in the city. Later I went to work for *Time* magazine. In its original prospectus, written twenty years earlier, two impish young men fresh out of Yale had proclaimed the impossibility of objectivity. They confessed to certain biases, such as a conviction that the world was

Mr. Griffiths, a former editor of *Life*, is author of *How True: A Skeptic's Guide to Believing the News*, from which this article is adapted. This article is reprinted by permission of Little, Brown & Co. in association with the Atlantic Monthly Press. Copyright © 1974 by Thomas Griffiths.

round and the cost of government rising too fast; they acknowledged a preference for the new, particularly in ideas, and a respect for the old, particularly in manners. These were engaging and undemanding admissions, but the principle itself was invoked in later years for some quite outrageous distortion of the news, which took *Time* years to live down. The assertion of nonobjectivity made possible the opinionated compression of the newsmagazines, which has proved a surprisingly durable form for fifty years. Slow to allow such bold appraisals of events in their news columns, newspapers still fastidiously label them "interpretation" or "analysis," as if everything else they printed had been subjected neither to analysis nor to interpretation.

Quite intelligent people can sometimes be heard saying that all they want from the press is the facts; they'll make up their own minds. T. S. Eliot once urged poets to "let the facts generalize themselves" but such advice is less helpful to journalists. Of course, "facts" such as stock market closings and batting averages can and do pass into print without comment, and traffic accidents can be reported "straight." If that were all journalism is about! Much else, and that which matters most, requires selection and judgment. Think of all that is said aloud every day the world over—of those Arab parliaments echoing with vituperation (which is the second leading export of Arab nations, after oil), of the stately nonsense and occasional late afternoon eloquence in the House of Commons, the windy indulgences that fill column after column of the *Congressional Record,* and then the jabber of a thousand city councils, school boards, library committees. All those egos! You can question a journalist's choice, but not his need to choose.

Not that selecting what is quotable out of the daily din of overstatement and contrived outrage is all that difficult. Most newsmen, confronted by a text, leap to the same passages. The best quotations may even have been pointed out in advance by a politician's press aide, for the canniest of politicians exist in their quotability. Spiro Agnew and his speechwriters, for example, worked hardest on those bombastic phrases in his speech that they knew would make the klieg lights turn on to record a minute's snippet for the evening television news. More qualified passages, suggesting that Agnew knew better, were buried in muted portions of his speech. And then, with the hypocrisy and gall that come so easily in public life, Agnew would sometimes argue that the "media" had played up only his more tendentious remarks.

That news is such an agreed quality—that deskmen at news agencies and in a thousand city rooms make up their minds so swiftly, and react in much the same way to the worth of a news story and the length it should be—says much about training and professional habits, but says more about the routineness of what passes for news. Practiced, no-nonsense deskmen know how to scourge copy of emotive words, at which point an editor is apt to congratulate himself on the objectivity of what he has wrought. When that mood steals over him is when he should be most on guard. An unaware bias, or a bias denied, is the worst kind. It suggests lack of imagination, and usually goes with the kind of journalism that isn't doing enough to serve its readers. That kind of look-no-hands objectivity has never quite recovered from Senator Joseph McCarthy, who taught journalists a hard lesson in responsibility. It wasn't enough to quote neutrally McCarthy's every lie and libel, reassuring oneself that "he said it, didn't he?" and "we can always print a later denial," for this was to give demagoguery a head start. As Mark Twain said, a lie can travel halfway around the world while the truth is putting on its shoes.

No, the real question of bias begins earlier, in what is pursued, or not pursued, as news. A news story originates in a collision of fact with an interested mind, and what makes one journalist "see" a story and another not has much to do with his own imagination, curiosity, and temperament. Other craftsmen, the copy editors, can later deprive the writer's words of any hint of feeling so that an article reads as if the reporter were as impersonally fashioned of metal as his typewriter. But the reader who thinks that the news can be delivered untouched by human hands and uncorrupted by human minds is living in a state of vincible ignorance.

SOME NEWS "HAPPENS," the rest is discerned. And it is this process of discovery of the news that is most mysterious, and most creative. Journalism is not an inexact science; it is not a science at all. Nonetheless, there are certain parallels to the scientific method.

In England in recent years a considerable debate has gone on about just how science makes its discoveries, and the argument is quite relevant to the journalistic practice of finding news. As Sir Peter Medawar, the biologist, has described the situation in *The Listener,* English science was for a long time under the spell of John Stuart Mill and his notions of inductive reasoning. The job of science was to observe nature objectively (it was assumed that objectivity was possible) and then to put these facts into sensible order. From this wrong conception of the scientist's role, Medawar thinks, came "the tragedy of the two cultures . . . the entirely erroneous belief that there is an enormous gap between people like artists and poets and writers, who work through the imagination, and scientists, who are, intellectually speaking, rude mechanicals."

The man who refined the scientific method is Sir Karl Popper, a Viennese intellectual who migrated to England after World War II. Popper challenges the notion of science as mere objective observation. Instead, he believes that all the basic discoveries of science originate in a hypothesis—an imaginative preconception of what the truth might be.

The scientific hypothesis should forecast what future observations or experiments will show, and must be put in such a way as to be tested, or, as Popper calls it, *falsified* by systematic attempts to refute it. In this testing, or second step of the scientific process, objectivity is not only possible but essential. If experiments go against the theory it is, of course, disproved; if they confirm the forecasts, the theory is still not said to have been proved, only to have passed a test successfully.

In a sense, science is a history of superseded theories. To Hermann Bondi, a theoretical astronomer at London University, a scientific theory is alive only as it lives dangerously, and must go on making further forecasts of what future evidence will show. "In science," Bondi declared over the BBC, "it isn't a question of who is right and who is wrong: it is much more a question of who is useful, who is stimulating, who has helped things forward. I like scientists who are quite passionate about their ideas. But they must always realize that the value of their ideas lies in how disprovable they are, in what tests they attract and in what discussions they stimulate."

It is easy to see how scientists find such an approach congenial to them. It gives imagination a central place in their work and dignifies the dogged corroboratory process as a step in further development, not merely as an attempt to shoot down a colleague's theory. The parallel to journalism of Popper's scientific method is one that a journalist must draw modestly, for the testing of his own ideas before he commits them to print can never be called scientific. Yet the process that Popper describes—of conjecture subject to verification—has much in common with how a journalist's mind works. He has a notion of something that needs looking into, usually in a gap he has spotted between what a situation is generally understood to be, or what someone claims it to be, and what he thinks inquiry will show. He senses a disparity between promise and performance, reads some figures that don't stand up, gets a tip from some dissenter within the ranks, and sets to work.

Now the second stage of Popper's process takes over and it becomes necessary to comprehend all the essential elements of a situation, to seek explanations from all who are involved, to check out the discrepancies between one person's version and another's, until the reality comes clearer. This is the cooler, more relentless process of verification. The most brilliant of journalists, those whose ideas are more audacious and invaluable, sometimes lack the stamina for patient detailed investigation or are reluctant to surrender an idea that didn't prove out; it is left to the more methodical members of the press to follow through. They may be eager to knock down a competitor's story, may lack some of the final neutrality of the laboratory, but this too adds something to the rigor with which assertions are tested.

Journalism, even more than science, is subject to Heisenberg's effect—the recognition that what is observed may be affected by the fact of observation. Once a pack of journalists goes baying after a scent, the pursuit takes on a momentum of its own; pressure builds up on those who have been silent or who have something to conceal; they may no longer be able to ride it out. Others, often out of partisan promptings, join in and keep the subject alive; grand juries or legislative committees elicit in sworn testimony answers that might have been refused a mere nosy journalist. Such a progression was most evident in the Watergate affair; the White House dismissal of it as a "thirdrate burglary attempt" might have prevailed but for the persevering efforts of two Washington *Post* reporters. Yet only when the law itself, an impatient federal judge, and an aroused Senate invoked their powers of subpoena, of grand jury testimony, and of televised hearings under oath did the full story begin to come clear.

In the end, issues of misfeasance or malfeasance are determined by the courts; if not, the final decision will come from the "court of public opinion," before which journalists as much as anyone else must plead their cases. That Court is not bound by the rules of evidence, nor by the objective standards of the scientific laboratory. Courts of public opinion hand down three kinds of verdict: guilty, not guilty, or not interested.

To ME, to be professional is not to be without bias (the self is always present in the seeing) but to be self-aware. There are newsmen who believe they should be untouched by what they see; not me. I know of no newsman at Dallas whose emotions weren't torn loose by President Kennedy's assassination; but with however big a lump in their throats, they got the word over the air, or steadied themselves down to gather all the facts for the stories they wrote. A big moment, even a tragic one, thrills a journalist, or he would be in some other line of work: it supplies the adrenalin he needs to get the story fast and tell it well. Suspect an indifference that calls itself impartiality; it is the pedestrian asset of second-raters.

Nor can ideas be judged by journalists who are without ideas of their own. Every good journalist I know has convictions; he also has a combative sense of right and wrong, and a shrewd intuition about which people in public life embody one or the other. Critics, discovering the presence of such attitudes in newsmen—and it is evident enough in their after-hours conversation—find this discovery proof conclusive that the journalist has his thumb on the scale. But a good journalist is an unreliable ally to any cause he believes in, as his friends in public life soon learn. His refusal to wear campaign buttons or to applaud speeches is but an outward demonstration of his belief that to enlist in any cause may be to prejudice his coverage. And it is in this capacity to separate his beliefs from his reporting that a journalist should be judged. Spiro Agnew thought it enough to label journalists as liberals in order to establish their untrustworthiness, which is the method of a smearer in all ages. In the 1972 campaign the Nixon people had gathered all the sticks of evidence they could find to show the bias of the liberal press, but never got the chance to light their fire. For along came Thomas Eagleton's concealed psychiatric treatment and George McGovern's disingenuous handling of it; reporters went in hot pursuit of the story, though it would result in the discrediting of their presumed favorite, Senator McGovern. That episode ensured the Nixon landslide, but never produced an acknowledgment by the Nixon Administration that the press can be trusted to forget its prejudices when a story cries for telling.

The true relationship between a journalist's beliefs and his reporting is something like that of a juror's desire to reach an impartial verdict. Jurors are not required to be empty minds, free of past experience or views; what is properly demanded of them is a readiness to put prejudices and uncorroborated impressions aside in considering the evidence before them. As much is asked of the journalist.

Journalists who once spoke of their objectivity now generally accept fairness as the criterion of their performance. This suggests that subjectivity is natural, and fairness a reasoned control of one's bias. The best of contemporary journalism meets this test, but I am not sure that in doing so the problem is fully resolved.

To me, bias is more elemental. It is really about sympathy given or sympathy withheld, and is so pervasive in everyone (we all "make allowances" for conduct in friends that we would deplore in others) that is is hard to root out. Journalists are not surgeons and our scalpels are not sterilized; we ourselves can be infected. In my own case, I find it difficult to write understandingly about the banal, the brutal, the greedy, and the craven; hard to sympathize with people who have everything and are discontent; hardest of all to give sympathy to those who give no sympathy to others. "To understand all is to pardon all" is a resonant French sentiment, but I don't share it. I think that I understand a lot that I don't pardon. These are prejudices of mine that exist at a level deeper than political partisanship, which one learns to compensate for.

Journalists are not eunuchs; they have views and sympathies; they are saved, when they are saved, by their skepticism and by their need not merely to theorize but to ground themselves in the particular. A similar alert skepticism is required of any reader if he would judge what out of all that wears the name of journalism is to be trusted or discounted.

Once a reader or listener asks himself whether he prefers columnists or commentators because their views are similar to his own, once he tests what he reads or listens to not by whether it dares to have a point of view but by whether that point of view properly reckons in all that might be said against its thesis, he may find himself revising his notion of what in journalism is most deserving of trust. And reading alertly and skeptically in this way, he might discover another impediment to getting the facts straight. For at this point he would be beginning the fascinating exploration of his own biases.

Barry Goldwater:

The Networks and the News

IN ANY BOOK TOUCHING on the news media and their relation to politics and government, room has to be made for focusing attention on a great new dimension—the powerful and oftentimes irresponsible major television networks.

As a candidate for President in 1964, I believe on this subject I can speak with even more authority than Vice-President Spiro Agnew. I yield to no other American politician for the dubious distinction of being a political candidate whose image was totally distorted by the television news medium. I know this phase of the media delinquency. Anyone who has had my experience, who has stood in front of the cameras as often as I have, and whose words have been reported on the evening news as often as mine have can attest to the fact that Vice-President Agnew's criticism of networks was anything but perfect—it didn't go nearly far enough.

What I am saying here is that Mr. Agnew has stirred up a hornet's nest over a situation which was a national disgrace. He raised thoughtful and penetrating questions about a medium whose influence over American lives has grown almost imperceptibly to the point where it now has become one of the most powerful instruments for the formulation of public policy ever devised. Every night—in fact, three times a day at a minimum—millions of American viewers are exhorted and influenced by a small, poorly chosen group of news commentators. In fact, these millions of Americans are to a very large extent captive audiences. Some of them get their news locally, but most of them are subjected to the outpourings of three major networks which share one thing in common—a liberal-leaning bias in political and government affairs.

Many times I have stopped to wonder why all Americans in public life, or all Americans aspiring to public life, should be required to pass muster with a group of individuals whose only assignment and whose only job is to record and recite the news. Nobody has endowed Mr. Huntley, Mr. Brinkley, Mr. Reynolds or any of the other network TV commentators with special powers. My feeling has long been that Mr. Brinkley's opinion is about as important as

Mr. Goldwater is a Republican senator from Arizona. This selection is reprinted by permission from the book *The Conscience of a Majority* by Barry Goldwater. © 1970 by Barry Goldwater. Published by Prentice-Hall, Inc., Englewood Cliffs, New Jersey.

that held by the boy who brings you your evening newspaper. Mr. Reynolds, who gives you his opinion on ABC every night, was not chosen by heaven, was not elected by the people, he was not even anointed by his fellow peers to be the beginning and end of all political wisdom and morality. Even that elder statesman, Eric Sevareid, is no better qualified than many other men who have spent 20 or 30 years in the news business. Yet all of these men not only announce the news, but they weigh it, judge it and punctuate it—sometimes with sneers and open ridicule. The viewer has no recourse but to sit and take it.

But every once in a while a viewer of some eminence, like the Vice-President of the United States, arrogates to himself the temerity to criticize the TV news medium. Vice-President Agnew's speeches on this subject are classics. They were long, long overdue. They would have been made long before this, and by myself, had it not been for the fact that as a defeated candidate for President my criticism would have sounded like sour grapes. But this should not in any way subtract from the fact that now that the ice is broken, now that a debate is ensuing, now that the objectivity and fairness of the TV news medium has become an open question, I have a considerable contribution to make. And I wish to emphasize again that in this field I hold special qualifications. I have been there. I have seen the whites of Sevareid's eyes just before CBS handed me a blindfold, offered me a consoling cigarette, and issued the order for my political execution.

I would caution the reader in appraising these comments to allow for a little healthy bias of my own. I believe I almost deserve it after the treatment I received at the hands of a lot of righteous, holier-than-thou commentators who insisted on sitting in judgment on every move and every comment I made in the political arena for a two-year period in 1963 and 1964.

One of the major revelations of Vice-President Agnew's campaign for truth in packaging for the news media is the reaction that followed his first two speeches. After the initial statements from the presidents of NBC, CBS and ABC, the networks participated in a virtual orgy of duologue discussions on nationwide television. I use the word duologue advisedly, and I do not want it confused with the word very popular with the network commentators which is spelled d-i-a-l-o-g-u-e. A duologue is where two people get together and voice their own opinions but don't listen to each other. A dialogue, on the other hand, is an exchange of views—a healthy process of verbal give-and-take used for an honest attempt to reach constructive conclusions between two different points of view.

The self-conscious way the networks have responded to the Agnew attack virtually proves Mr. Agnew's point. The reaction from the general public, which overwhelmingly endorsed the Vice-President's complaints, further drove home the validity of the critique. But let us concern ourselves here with the network officials and commentators themselves. For the first time ever, they were suddenly confronted with the kind of problem which they themselves hand out every night in the week to hundreds of men in public life. In other words, they were criticized. What a calamity. The righteous, the upstanding, the TV pure-in-heart, the "Dudley Do-Rights" of the networks, those men who believe themselves to be "stalwart, true with eyes of blue" all of a sudden became something less than a sacred institution and a medium commanded by mere mortals. For the first time in the history of television, the networks were confronted with a crisis. And in the few hours immediately following Agnew's hard-hitting criticism, they separated the men from the boys on the nation's visual airwaves. Let it here be recorded that in this crisis Mr. Goodman of NBC, Mr. Goldenson of ABC, and Mr. Stanton of CBS promptly stood up in front of the U.S. public and were measured for short pants. The commanders of the critics showed a fascinated nation that they could not take it. The bosses of those who dish it out to 60 million Americans 365 days out of the year yelled like a bunch of naughty children who had been subjected to their first spanking.

Their reaction was entirely lacking in intelligence on the one hand and appreciation for another point of view on the other hand. Their course was plain enough for anyone to see. They should have admitted very readily that they had made many mistakes and that their news operations were long overdue for a critical examation. They should have realized that every viewer with any awareness of, or appreciation for, public events can point personally to examples of lack of fairness on the part of the networks. If they had been really smart, they would have borrowed a leaf out of the book of the nation's large motion-picture producers back in the late 1920's when that entertainment medium came under heavy public criticism for the content of the product they were peddling to the American people. The moviemakers saw the handwriting on the wall and opted for self-censorship. The result was the establishment in Hollywood of the famous "Hays Office," which passed on movies for their contents and taste. In other words, the industry adopted a policy of policing itself; and instead of increased criticism, it got high marks from the general public for recognizing and accepting a responsibility which the industry growth had given.

But in the case of the networks, we are supposed to believe that the Vice-President of the United States is an irresponsible, spiteful and unprincipled politician who is out to dragoon and intimidate the major elements of one of the most powerful industries on earth. The fact that Mr. Agnew had the courage to call the shots the way he saw them, or in the parlance of the day, the courage to "tell it like it is," made him an instant enemy of an industry and a monopoly which, while still very young in terms of years, should be able to prove the fact that it had grown beyond the stage of adolescence. The fact that it did not has already been alluded to in my earlier comments about Messrs. Goodman, Goldenson and Stanton donning knickers for their public outcries.

The more you study the charges of "intimidation," "coercion" and "censorship" which have been hurled in the direction of TV's major critic, the more you come to realize how really irresponsible and lacking in maturity and poise is this new industry. In effect, the network officials and commentators made an immediate false assumption that the American public either (1) is stupid or (2) doesn't understand what it heard. *For a TV network to present a half hour of Mr. Agnew's calm, well-reasoned, thoughtful and penetrating analysis and then label it as an attempt to intimidate a multi-billion-dollar industry is ridiculous on its face.* If the network wanted to try and push this viewpoint, they should have begun by denying nationwide exposure to the Vice-President. It puts the networks in the place of a retailer who shows his customers a shining product and tells them that it's as dull as dishwater.

Of course, today a great deal of confusion exists over exactly what Vice-President Agnew had to say about the networks and how they cover the news. And with every passing day this is being further compounded by people with a special interest in confusing the whole issue of network responsibility with the news of the day. For this reason, I feel it might be important here to quote some parts of the Vice-President's very notable speech at Des Moines, Iowa, on November 13, 1969.

A week ago, President Nixon delivered the most important address of his Administration, one of the most important of our decade. His subject was Vietnam. His hope was to rally the American people to see the conflict through to a lasting and just peace in the Pacific. For 32 minutes, he reasoned with a nation that has suffered almost a third of a million casualties in the longest war in its history.

When the President completed his address—an address that he spent weeks in preparing—his words and policies were subjected to instant analysis and querulous criticism. The audience of 70 million Americans . . . was inherited by a small band of network commentators and self-appointed analysts, the majority of whom expressed, in one way or another, their hostility to what he had to say. . . .

Every American has a right to disagree with the President of the United States, and to express publicly that disagreement. But the President of the United States has a right to communicate directly with the people who elected him, and the people of this country have the right to make up their own minds and form their own opinions about a presidential address without having the President's words and thoughts characterized through the prejudices of hostile critics before they can even be digested. . . .

At least 40 million Americans each night, it is estimated, watch the network news. . . .

How is this network news determined? A small group of men, numbering perhaps no more than a dozen, . . . decide what 40 to 50 million Americans will learn of the day's events in the nation and the world.

We cannot measure this power and influence by traditional democratic standards, for these men can create national issues overnight. . . .

The views of this fraternity do not represent the views of America. That is why such a great gulf existed between how the nation received the President's address—and how the networks reviewed it. . . .

A narrow and distorted picture of America often emerges from the televised news. A single dramatic piece of the mosaic becomes, in the minds of millions, the whole picture.

The American who relies upon television for his news might conclude that the majority of American students are embittered radicals, that the majority of black Americans feel no regard for their country, that violence and lawlessness are the rule, rather than the exception, on the American campus. We know none of these conclusions is true. . . .

Tonight, I have raised questions. I have made no attempt to suggest answers. These answers must come from the media men. They are challenged to turn their critical powers on themselves. . . . And the people of America are challenged, too—challenged to press for responsible news presentation. The people can let the networks know that they want their news straight and objective. . . .

We would never trust such power over public opinion in the hands of an elected government; it is time we questioned it in the hands of a small and unelected elite. The great networks have dominated America's airwaves for decades; the people are entitled to a full accounting of their stewardship.

And the replies of the network presidents at the time would serve a useful purpose here, because I believe they show how inapplicable most of their remarks are to what the Vice-President had to say. First Julian Goodman, president of NBC:

Vice-President Agnew's attack on television news is an appeal to prejudice. More importantly, Mr. Agnew uses the influence of his high office to criticize the way a government-licensed news medium covers the activities of government itself. . . . Evidently, he would prefer a different kind of television reporting—one that would be subservient to whatever political group happens to be in authority at the time.

Frank Stanton, president of CBS:

No American institution, including television-network news organizations, should be immune to public criticism. . . . We do not believe, however, that this unprecedented attempt by the Vice-

President of the United States to intimidate a news medium which depends for its existence upon government licenses represents legitimate criticism. . . . Whatever their [newsmen's] deficiencies, however, they are minor compared to those of a press which would be subservient to the executive power of government.

Leonard Goldenson, president of ABC:

In our judgment, the performance of ABC news had always been and will continue to be fair and objective. In the final analysis, it is always the public who decides on the reliability of any individual or organization. We will continue to report the news accurately and fully, confident in the ultimate judgment of the American public.

It strikes me that the reaction of the TV network presidents was completely uncalled for and totally unresponsive. It is interesting, too, that the Vice-President's criticism of network bias struck a responsive chord among many, many people who called, telegraphed or wrote to express their agreement. There is nothing to suggest, however, that the tonal gradations of that responsive chord have penetrated deeply into the hushed chambers where TV network policy is made. It has been suggested that perhaps the executives of America's television networks suffer from tonal deafness and have developed what amounts to a dangerous inability to see faults in their own operations and to regard as a frontal challenge to freedom of speech every single word of criticism ever aimed in their direction.

I suggested earlier that it is possible that the television industry actually suffers from a delusion, a belief that it is beyond criticism. It certainly has always felt that it was beyond any kind of serious attack from anyone bearing conservative credentials.

Now I know this personally. I have had experience with network news that goes back a long, long way. Let me give you an example of what I think is complete network bias and irresponsibility. I know the details of it because it happened to me. It was some time in 1963 that a young man named Lee Coney, local representative of the Columbia Broadcasting System, came to me and asked if he could make an appointment for several officials of his network on a matter of extreme importance. I agreed to the appointment and shortly thereafter received in my office in Washington Mr. Fred Friendly, at that time in charge of all CBS news; Mr. Eric Sevareid, who was a CBS commentator and general analyst of news events, and Mr. Coney. Several members of my staff sat in on that meeting, and they could testify to the fact that I was asked to cooperate for a period of six weeks in an endeavor to obtain televised information for a documentary which was to be entitled "The Conservative Revival."

The CBS men asked if it would be possible for their camera crews to follow me around for this period of time and televise all of my activities, especially those which had to do with addressing public audiences. At the time,

I had a very heavy schedule, and I was not always speaking from textual material. Thus, it was something of a burden to realize that I had, at all times, the famous CBS eye recording everything I did and said in public. Now this may not seem like much of a mental hazard. But for a public official, it is more than just routine to have this kind of concentrated television attention directed at all of your endeavors.

However, I was a genuine conservative and much of my time was devoted to promoting conservative principles of this country. I saw no reason why I should not cooperate and to the fullest extent with any effort by a major network to come to grips with what I believed was a new American phenomenon, a conservative political revolution. The CBS team also got me to promise that at the end of this period of observation I would submit to two and a half hours of televised questioning by Mr. Eric Sevareid for use in the documentary.

You can easily see that the plan outlined to me was quite extensive, required a lot of work on my part, and also presaged a rather important documentary presentation to the American people. I faithfully kept all of my commitments. I subjected myself to televised coverage of all of my activities for a longer period than I like to think about. And then in a room in the United States Capitol, I sat for two and a half hours one afternoon and was questioned by Mr. Sevareid on every conceivable public position that I had ever taken or might take. As I recall that session, and it was televised, the first question started out by establishing the fact that my formal education did not include a college diploma. If my memory serves, Mr. Sevareid asked me if I felt in any way limited in my public role, even if it should involve seeking higher political office, by the fact that my formal education did not include a college degree.

From there on the questions got tough. At one point in the question, my press secretary spoke to one of the producers and asked, "Doesn't Sevareid have any nice questions to ask the Senator?" To this, he got the reply, "This is the kind of questioning that makes for a good show."

And here I believe we get right to the core of one of the big problems in TV presentation of the news. The producer was talking about theater; my press secretary was talking about politics. In other words, mean questioning, tough questioning, antagonistic questioning, of any public figure, especially a member of the United States Senate who had been mentioned as a possible presidential candidate, would be calculated to have a much more enthusiastic viewing audience than questioning which had to do with seeking to find out why there was a conservative upsurge in this country.

This did not seem to be the major motivating force behind the questioning which took place that afternoon. It was more like a concentrated and lengthy badgering of a conservative politician by a liberal expert. In all events, I put up with it in all good faith. Some time passed before one of the underlings at CBS contacted my press secretary to say that there was a program being shown that night which would include some of the material·from the Sevareid questioning. That little presentation turned out to be a special called "Thunder on the

Right.'' In it, CBS televised all the crackpot kooks of the radical right it could find, and then switched to Sevareid's questioning of me. He isolated a question involving the John Birch Society in which I refused to read them out of the human race, and very, very skillfully tied me in with every crackpot on the Far Right. Much time was given to the Minutemen organization. Much time was given to radical speakers who were showing their bigotry and racial prejudice. And then the switch to Goldwater. In other words, CBS managed to take all the kooks they could possibly lay their cameras on and in one short session, wrap them all around the neck of a conservative presidential possibility and leave them there. Needless to say, I was upset. I summoned Mr. Coney to my office the next morning and told him that I had never seen such a dirty, irresponsible, degrading attempt to assassinate an American political figure as CBS put on the night before. I told him that he had come into my office with his friends, Mr. Friendly and Mr. Sevareid, and completely and thoroughly misrepresented the CBS network's intentions. I not only did that, but I wrote Dr. Frank Stanton, president of CBS, outlined exactly what had taken place and told him that I felt that this was a typical example of total and complete irresponsibility and bias and prejudice on the part of CBS. As a result of my complaints, CBS finally televised a half-hour, carefully edited version of those two and a half hours of questions with Mr. Sevareid and presented it without fanfare and without advertising—not as a ''conservative revival,'' but as a conversation with Goldwater, or something to that effect. In other words, these CBS officials had come to me, a member of the United States Senate, and represented themselves as responsible people interested in doing a special television documentary report on a subject in which I was deeply interested. They obtained from me all the cooperation that I could possibly give them, even though I knew of their liberal bias, and even though I knew that Mr. Friendly and Mr. Sevareid did not share any of my political beliefs. I felt they were responsible news executives and businessmen. I was wrong. I have never experienced more shabby treatment at the hands of anyone in politics than I did from that particular team of CBS newsmen.

Now I recount this because I believe, and I am certain this is true, that at the time CBS could not have cared less. They had made use of a conservative who might possibly prove dangerous some time. They had done everything they possibly could to sink him politically on a nationwide basis. And they never, for one minute, suspected that the ''conservative revival'' which they had used to con me into cooperating was an actual fact, was a fact that would later come to fruition, would not only bring about the presidential nomination of the man they had victimized, but would also elect in 1968, a Vice-President who knew fully and exactly what their deficiencies were and would not be afraid to stand up and call his shots. In other words, I believe that the CBS officials, had they thought there was a chance that Goldwater would ever become President or even a candidate for President, would never have sanctioned this kind of operation. But they did not believe that. They had no belief in a conservative resurgence, and they played fast and loose with a Senator from a small, Far Western state to serve their own partisan purpose.

Now I want to make it clear that this was an operation by CBS nationally; and I want to say here that I am not condemning, because of this act, the entire network nor every station affiliated with CBS. In my home city of Phoenix, I get nothing but fine, honorable cooperation from the CBS outlet there. And in most other areas of the country, I have had fair and courteous treatment.

Only at the national level do the networks show their bias. And I might emphasize here that networks do not need to be licensed. There is a great deal of confusion on this particular score. To hear the network executives complaining about Mr. Agnew, you would think that they, as networks, were subject to regulation and to licensing by the Federal Communications Commission. This is not the case. Individual stations are subject to regulation; networks of stations are not. So it ill-behooves any network to complain that speeches by a government official threaten them with intimidation by a government.

Now to carry this CBS thing a little further, I think I may have surprised Dr. Stanton and his minions by not standing still for their type of operation. I accepted it for what it was and acted accordingly. I very often in my travels and in my speeches after that excluded, where it was possible, CBS newsmen from coverage. I didn't ask anyone's permission. I just made it very plain that I didn't like the way they handled public officials; I didn't like the way they handled politicians; I didn't like the way they handled the news and I was not going to assist them in any fashion. This attitude of mine continued and eventually became a matter for almost nationwide interest. And it continued until a good friend of mine named Walter Cronkite, a CBS news commentator, made a special effort. He came to Washington and spent an hour with me in my office. He outlined all of his views and said that he felt that a network as large as CBS should have at least one contact with a prominent Republican Senator who had been mentioned as a possible presidential nominee of his party.

As a result of this conversation, I became the first public official interviewed by Mr. Cronkite when his program was extended from a 15-minute segment to a half-hour segment each evening. I might say this, that all my relations with Mr. Cronkite and with many other CBS newsmen, Harry Reasoner, for one, have been completely amicable. They do not agree with all my political beliefs. I do not share all their views of public events, but we do not try to double-cross each other. We have an honest respect for each other's opinions, and this is the way I think it should be.

However, my friendship with Mr. Cronkite was sorely tried in the immediate aftermath of President Kennedy's assassination. During the confusion of constant television reporting of the events surrounding that tragic event, Mr. Cronkite commented that of the many notables who had expressed their shock and grief, the name of Barry Goldwater was missing. The Arizona Senator, he reported, was en route to a political rally in Muncie, Indiana, and had not been heard from. The fact of the matter was that a telegram of condolence had been sent to the White House long before Mr. Cronkite's comment, and my trip to Muncie was not designed for political purposes. I was accompanying my wife on the sad journey to her mother's funeral.

No sooner had Mr. Cronkite made his remarks than the CBS switchboard began receiving calls of protest from friends of mine, including Arizona Governor Paul Fannin, who knew the true state of affairs. Some time later the mistake was corrected; and in a letter to me, Mr. Cronkite explained that he had been handed the information about me on "a little piece of paper" which was handed up to him by someone on his news desk. He readily admitted the error and said he hoped that I was not only a forbearing but a forgiving man.

I don't want to appear churlish or unduly sensitive to such mistakes. I believe they can happen, especially in the kind of confusion that is bound to prevail in all newsrooms at the time of a presidential assassination. Because of this, I was willing to accept Mr. Cronkite's apology in good faith. However, no politician who had been subjected to the kind of treatment that I had received at the hands of CBS previously could help but wonder about that "little piece of paper" and who was responsible for writing it and handing it to a man who was talking to a badly shaken nation of millions of politically sensitive people. Any conscientious editor who wanted to take the trouble to check the wire service news could have easily established the true facts about my activities and my whereabouts. In fact, the trip to Muncie had received unusual attention earlier in the day from political reporters, because I had been forced to cancel a meeting in my office with Governor William Scranton of Pennsylvania. Mr. Scranton had made the appointment to talk with me about delegates to the Republican National Convention from his state. The projected meeting was regarded as "hot" political news prior to its cancellation.

Now, lest this appear to be too heavily weighted on the critical side, let me explain that all of my experiences with all newsmen, or even with all CBS newsmen, were not unhappy ones. Quite the contrary. Most of my relations with the press were congenial and fair. I did not ask for, nor expect, any special treatment or consideration from any segment of the communications media. All I wanted was fair treatment, not only from CBS, but from all newsmen covering my activities. I had had sufficient exposure to be able to appraise the treatment I received long before I became a presidential candidate. I had, of course, been covered as a member of the Senate from Arizona, as chairman of the Senate Republican Campaign Committee for a number of years, and as a spokesman for a large segment of the Republican Party, the conservative wing.

It is important, I believe, for the casual reader to understand that the men covering political campaigns are assigned primarily to work as reporters, not as judges. The ones assigned to me during my presidential campaign filed reports to their newspapers and went on the air over television and radio several times a day. Their job was to record, if you will, what happened and report it fairly to the American people. Where this was done, I had no objection. Even when I made mistakes, when I blundered, when I make ill-considered remarks and they were recorded and reported, I had no objection. I had no objection at all to the truth. My objections were reserved completely for dishonest or slanted coverage, for misquotation and misrepresentation of my remarks, for special parceling-out coverage. By this I mean, coverage which was performed by the deliberate selection of particular items in a day's events to show the candidate or the subject in the worst possible light. I also resented being judged by newsmen who were not elected or chosen to pass as critics on everything and anything that a politician had to say but who every day constituted themselves as "experts par excellence" and whose word was final. This was just plain nauseous to informed politicians and public officials who listen to newscasts knowing full well how poorly informed are the newsmen doing the reporting on particular situations.

Now let me bring things up to a real climax, or to two climaxes, where CBS is concerned. During the Republican Presidential Nominating Convention in San Francisco, in 1964, a special CBS program was televised, I believe the date was July 12, from somewhere in Germany. CBS newsman Daniel Schorr took it upon himself to put on a news report which did its best to portray the idea that I was trying to forge links with far rightist neo-Fascist groups in Germany. As correspondent Schorr reported:

"It is now clear that Senator Goldwater's interview with *Der Spiegel* (sometimes called Germany's equivalent of *Time* magazine) with its hard line appealing to right-wing elements in Germany was only the start of a move to link up with his opposite numbers in Germany."

Schorr dealt heavily in false facts which neither he nor CBS newsmen in this country made any attempt to check with my office. He said I had accepted an invitation to speak at an Evangelical Academy near Munich and tried to imply that this school was a gathering place for neo-Nazis. The fact is, I had neither received nor accepted any such invitation to speak in Germany. I had never heard of the academy in question, although I later discovered that Chancellor Adenauer, among other respectable public officials, had spoken there.

Mr. Schorr's broadcast, including his innuendos and his outright declarations that "it is now clear," was false.

All by itself, Schorr's TV report, coming at a time when the Republican National Convention was in progress, was bad enough; however, *The New York Times*, in a special unchecked dispatch from correspondent Arthur J. Olsen, promptly headlined "Senator in Touch with Bonn Right." If there ever was any truth in the belief that *The New York Times* is meticulous about checking all the news "that's fit to print," Olsen's report was a distinct departure from policy.

Without any apparent effort to check Schorr's information, Olsen, enlarged on the CBS line with completely false details. He said I had been "in 'frequent and friendly' correspondence for some time" with the Sudeten leader Hans Christoph Seebohm, who had recently figured in a dispute over "militant" statements, and "other conservative West German politicians." Olsen further contended that I had given an interview to the *Zeitung und Soldaten Zeitung,* an extreme rightist weekly.

There was only one thing wrong with Olsen's story. It was 100 percent false. I had never corresponded with anyone named Seebohm. I had never heard of his name nor of the controversy over militant statements. I have never corresponded with any West German politician, conservative or otherwise, and I had never granted an interview to the *Zeitung und Soldaten Zeitung* newspaper.

Needless to say, the CBS program from Germany in the midst of the Republican Convention was picked up and carried far and wide by other segments of the news media. And then later, when I had been asked about it and branded the whole thing a lie, *The New York Times* had this to say about it on July 13, and I quote:

"Senator Goldwater has decided not to take a post-convention vacation in Germany. One reason was a Columbia Broadcasting System news report yesterday that asserted Mr. Goldwater's trip signaled a link between the right wing of the United States and that of Bavaria. . . .''

Now this charge by the CBS which was widely picked up by the newspapers was also used by my opponents at the convention. For example, Governor Scranton, who was publishing a daily tabloid of news for convention delegates, reproduced almost every bit of these charges even though they were known, by people right in Governor Scranton's campaign camp, to have no basis in fact whatsoever. Five days later, *The New York Times* carried this so-called "clarifying statement'' broadcast by CBS news correspondent Daniel Schorr:

"In speaking the other day of a move by Senator Goldwater to link up these forces, I did not mean to suggest conscious effort on his part, of which there is no proof here, but rather a process of gravitation which is visible here.''

Of course, the "clarifying statement'' was never seen by most people. And this deliberate smear in the midst of a political convention was allowed to stand for all important purposes. I suggest that the timing, the motivations, the presentation and the material used all add up to deliberate bias based upon deliberate falsehood. I know of no other way to characterize that particular program from Germany and by that time in 1964 I had concluded that there was no way for a Republican candidate named Goldwater to do business with CBS without being distorted and presented in a completely false and unfavorable light. Therefore, I decided that CBS would not be any part of my campaign plans.

Thus it was on the night I was nominated as the Republican candidate for President of the United States in San Francisco, I agreed to appear before the television cameras and make a statement regarding my selection. This scheduled appearance before the TV cameras and microphones the night of the action which nominated me as presidential candidate was arranged in response to a request by the networks to present something live from the newly selected

Republican candidate prior to the time when I went before the convention to make my acceptance address. In other words, in my acquiescing to this plan, I was not only presenting an image to the entire voting population of the United States, which was of no mean consideration, but I was also providing the networks with a service.

And I concluded that that service did not necessarily have to include CBS. I decided that a network irresponsible enough and biased enough to deliberately present a program like the Daniel Schorr program from Europe in the midst of a nominating convention was not responsible enough to be considered. And make no mistake about it, that program was designed to make Barry Goldwater look exactly like a politician with neo-Nazi leanings. I had no illusions about this, and the people who saw the program had no illusions about it. I found it absolutely astounding that a major network would permit such a thing to go out over their stations without absolute assurance that every word and innuendo was correct. Apparently no effort, at least none I was aware of nor my staff was aware of, was ever made to check the Daniel Schorr program.

Therefore, on the night of my nomination, with the entire country waiting, I gave my press representatives orders to have the cameras set up on the fifteenth floor of the Mark Hopkins Hotel. I said that I would appear before the cameras and the microphones but only if CBS was not included in the plans. I was absolutely sincere in issuing that directive, and it is impossible to describe the kind of scurrying and pressuring and telephoning that went on prior to the time set for my appearance before the microphones.

It just so happened that about five to ten minutes before the scheduled appearance word reached me to the effect that the network officials might try to blame their local CBS correspondent and that Robert Pierpoint, the man who had traveled with me many weary miles during my campaign for the nomination, was to be held responsible. And this was the only reason—and I repeat—this was the only reason that CBS was included in one of the most important television appearances of my entire political career. And it was easily the most important political telecast of that particular month. Needless to say, I was amused at some of the arguments used in that last-minute scramble to get CBS included in a television presentation that was going to easily carry every major station in the country. And they went along these lines: "After all, you can't exclude a major network." "After all, CBS is an important part of the communications media." "After all, CBS is one of the three largest TV networks." And my reply in each instance was "Yes, but after all, CBS has shown itself very, very clearly to be irresponsible in the presentation of political news. It has been irresponsible in the presentation of political news regarding my candidacy. I see no reason to include it in another episode of television history."

As I say, the decision was reversed merely because I was afraid that some innocent bystander, a young man who had to my knowledge and to my way of thinking done a fairly good job to be objective for a very biased team of news television commentators, would be hurt. It was only my belief that this young man might be held accountable that in any way influenced me to alter my decision. In all events, CBS like ABC and NBC finally was admitted to the television studio room and was able to televise my remarks, my appearance with my wife Peggy, and my replies to questions put to me by TV commentators at that particular time in my career.

I recount these things to illustrate to the reader that I am not dealing in generalities nor do I think Spiro Agnew is dealing in generalities when he says that the TV networks need to reexamine their handling and presentation of the news. I know what was done to me by the Daniel Schorr broadcast. I know that nothing in the way of correcting that was accomplished by the statement that was televised by CBS five days after the fact and which had a lot of gobbledygook words from Mr. Daniel Schorr about something called "a process of gravitation." Another point I wonder at is what chance there would have been to obtain even a clarification five days later from CBS if the subject of their report from Germany had not by that time conclusively sewed up the Republican nomination for President. I am fearful to speculate on this because I have a feeling that the people who were then in charge of CBS news had not the slightest interest in being fair or objective in any way. I have every reason to believe they were motivated only by partisan self-interest. I have no reason to believe that their objective was to inform the American people or to present a clear, unbiased report on a presidential candidate. I think their consideration was for public image of CBS, for their ratings, and for their own particular political preference. This is the only conclusion I can reach about a network that would go on the air in the midst of a national political convention with a program apparently designed to influence the rejection of a particular candidate. I repeat, I'm not dealing in generalities, nor in suspicions, nor in any of the other allegations or types of allegations that go with charges that the networks slant the news, present biased news, present prejudiced news. I am talking about deliberate efforts at political tampering by a major network and by the reporters for a major network. I am not speaking from hearsay. I am speaking from bitter personal experience.

And while I am speaking of the 1964 campaign, I might mention that it was another network television broadcast which served to launch one of the really major falsehoods of the entire campaign. This happened on May 24, 1964, on American Broadcasting Company's "Issues and Answers" program. But I want to make it very emphatically clear that neither the network nor the program participants were guilty of any kind of bias or distortion or misrepresentation of the facts. All these things came later in news stories based on that interview, which perhaps will go down in presidential campaign history as the "defoliation issue."

It came about while I was being interviewed by ABC's correspondent Howard K. Smith, who asked for some suggestions on how the war in Vietnam might successfully be prosecuted. I mentioned bombing bridges, roads and other routes by which the Communists moved troops and supplies into South Vietnam. Then I added, and these were my exact words:

"There have been several suggestions made. I don't think we would use any of them. But defoliation of the forests by low-yield atomic weapons could well be done. When you remove the foliage, you remove the cover.

"The major supply lines, though, I think would have to be interdicted where they leave Red China, which is the Red River Valley above North Vietnam and there, according to my studies of geography, it would be a difficult task to destroy those basic routes."

That interview occurred on Sunday. By Monday morning, the newspapers had me suggesting the use of nuclear bombs in Vietnam. Even one of the usually reliable wire services moved such a story based on the ABC interview. When its editors got a look at the transcript of the show, however, the Associated Press quickly put out a correction. The fact that the correction never caught up with the original incorrect account is still evident to this very day. Not many weeks ago, a friend of mine called to tell me that he had heard once again a TV news commentator state flatly that Goldwater had suggested the use of nuclear bombs to defoliate the jungles of Vietnam.

This incident, among many others, shows how important it is for news correspondents, especially those whose reports are carried to millions of readers and viewers, to be absolutely sure of their facts before they give them glib public expression. Because it is a political fact of life that a "clarified" TV report (such as was belatedly put out by CBS in the Daniel Schorr incident) or a newspaper correction never catches up with the original allegation. And this is particularly true when the first news account is of an especially sensational nature. And, of course, it is always true that media people—especially newspaper editors—will give big black headlines to a sensational story and very small, carefully hidden display to a later correction.

The *San Francisco Examiner's* handling of the defoliation interview was as irresponsible and as prejudiced as anything I have ever seen. Its front-page headline on May 25, 1964, screamed:

GOLDWATER'S PLAN TO USE VIET A-BOMB

The subhead presumed to be a quote of mine. I read:

"I'd risk a war"

The headline inside the paper where the sensation mongering tale was continued from page one carried this neat little example of editorial misrepresentation:

BARRY'S PLAN: USE A BOMB

The above account might be entitled "The Anatomy of a Political Lie," because it is fairly typical of how newsmen with a built-in bias will jump to place the worst possible construction on the statements of a candidate with whom they disagree. The whole treatment given to that interview by liberal newspapers throughout the country I believe, was an accurate measurement of how extremely uninterested some liberal journalists were in 1964 to get at anything resembling the truth.

This defoliation incident was misinterpreted so far and so wide that I feel it is important to explain it in my own words even at the risk of being unfair to Mr. Howard K. Smith. I have known Mr. Smith for a long time. I know that when he began his news career he was almost unreasonably liberal. It will be remembered that he figured in the famous ABC-TV show that presented a requiem for the political career of Richard M. Nixon after his defeat for Governor and included on his panel none other than the notorious Alger Hiss, whom Mr. Nixon had investigated during his House career and prior to Hiss's conviction for perjuring himself in a celebrated Communist spy trial 20 years ago.

But Mr. Smith represents something special to me these days. The best way to describe it is that I believe he can be called an "honest liberal with an open mind." There is no other way to account for his widely publicized conclusion, following Vice-President Agnew's criticism, that there "is a network news bias" in favor of liberal causes. Not only did ABC's Smith say that he agreed with much of what Mr. Agnew said, but he actually claimed credit for saying it before the Vice-President did. In an interview in the magazine *TV Guide* published February 28, 1970, Mr. Smith described himself as being "left of center." But he added: "Our liberal friends today have become dogmatic. They have a set of automatic reactions. They react the way political cartoonists do—with oversimplification. Oversimplify. Be sure you please your fellows, because that's what's 'good.' They're conventional, they're conformists. They're pleasing Walter Lippmann, they're pleasing the *Washington Post,* they're pleasing the editors of the *New York Times,* and they're pleasing one another."

Touché. No conservative could have described the kneejerk liberals of the communications industry any better or with more accuracy. In fact, he gives special mention to the TV news media's attitude on conservatives. He put it this way in that *TV Guide* interview:

"If Agnew says something, it's bad, regardless of what he says. If Ronald Reagan says something, it's bad, regardless of what he says. Well, I'm unwilling to condemn an idea because a particular man said it. Most of my colleagues do just that."

I am almost inclined to say "thank heavens" for at least one honest liberal in the news media. In my travels I have actually overheard newsmen say to each other, "That wasn't a bad idea, I wish it wasn't Goldwater who had said it."

What I am getting at here, what Vice-President Agnew has been working on, and what the American people are beginning to understand is that, politically, where much of the TV medium is concerned, the crime is of an ideological hue. In the oversimplification which Mr. Smith speaks about, it adds up to a belief that conservatives are "devils," but they are devils who should not be given their due at the hands of the media. The consideration becomes, not what is said, but who said it.

This is a disgraceful situation to exist in a large, vital segment of the American economy like the television industry. It has been getting away with murder—political murder, that is—for much too long a time. Mr. Agnew was absolutely correct in calling the industry to account and I for one am not going to stand by and let the whole thing get obscured under false charges of threat to the freedom of the press. It was for this reason that I challenged a statement made on March 11 by Mr. Julian Goodman, president of the National Broadcasting Company. Addressing a Sigma Delta Chi Foundation lecture at the University of Texas in Austin, Mr. Goodman asserted that "Not since 1789—when newsmen were sentenced to prison under the Sedition Act for statements displeasing to the government—has American journalism been under greater attack." Mr. Goodman saw what he calls a "clear and growing danger to freedom of information" in almost every action and statement made by government officials since President Nixon took office. He literally issued orders to the government with this ringing declaration:

"The government must stand back from the press. The use of subpoenas on the news media—especially for off the record or similar unpublished material—should be abandoned by both Federal and state officials as a matter of constitutional self-restraint."

Mr. Goodman's intemperate and irresponsible declaration struck me as interesting. If such a great danger existed to freedom of the press from statements by Mr. Agnew, one wonders why Mr. Goodman waited until he was asked to lecture to the Sigma Delta Chi four months after the Vice-President's criticism of television news treatment to raise this vital question. Being an important policy maker in television, one would have expected Mr. Goodman to be fighting such a threat on a daily or at least a weekly basis if he felt it were so dire.

In all events, in talking to a Young Republican Leadership Training School in Washington on March 12, I called attention to Mr. Goodman's sensational charge and remarked:

> For a responsible industry executive to expect the American people who watch a steady stream of criticism aimed at the Republican administration on TV newscasts everyday to believe a great threat exists to the freedom of the press is downright ludicrous.
>
> Mr. Goodman coupled his irresponsible charge with a call on Federal and state officials to abandon serving subpoenas on the news media.
>
> I think it's time to ask just who these TV news people think they are. If one of their employees has information or material that would be useful to a grand jury or a district attorney in legal proceedings, why shouldn't he be asked to produce the items requested? Are we to take Mr. Goodman's word for the fact that the news media is above the law? That's not my understanding of freedom of the press. I strongly believe in freedom of the press, but I also believe that it carries with it a very heavy responsibility for members of the press to be civic-minded and helpful to law enforcement agencies.

The treatment my remarks received on Mr. Goodman's major news telecast—the Huntley-Brinkley Report—that day was typical. Mr. Brinkley quoted from my speech saying that Barry Goldwater had noted that "liberal comments about the Nixon Administration have taken on an edge of desperation and hysteria since the Vice-President began to give voice to some of the pet peeves of the "Silent Majority." Mr. Brinkley then assured his nationwide audience that the Senator had given no examples or explanations of what he meant. Neatly ignored was the following sentence in the prepared text of my speech which read, "For example, only this week Mr. Julian Goodman, president of NBC, became the author of one of the most dishonest and ridiculous statements of the new decade. In a speech at the University of Texas in Austin, he characterized recent criticism of the news media as the greatest threat to freedom of the press since the Sedition Act of 1798 when newsmen were jailed for making statements which were displeasing to the government."

While Mr. Brinkley carefully left his viewing audience with the impression that I had made a wild, unsubstantiated charge, he smiled smugly and went on to say that he couldn't help but observe that TV officials seldom receive complaints from politicians whom the medium had praised.

This, of course, was designed to be cute, but upon examination it makes one really appreciate Mr. Brinkley for being a "master of the obvious" in some respects.

It is interesting to ponder what NBC viewers who heard Mr. Brinkley thought the next morning when the news report on the NBC "Today" show carried a film clip of my criticism and reported on a letter which Mr. Goodman wrote to me in response to my published remarks to the Young Republicans. I can only say that one newspaper, the *Arizona Daily Star,* in its March 13, 1970, issue, carried an account of Mr. Goodman's letter to me with a subhead which accurately summed it up. It said, "Goodman Denies He's Ridiculous." Actually, what the NBC president said was that he was sorry to find me in sharp disagreement with him, but he had no intention of entering into a debate. He made two points which I want to record verbatim in an exercise of courtesy which I am glad to extend to the NBC president, but which his employee, Mr. Brinkley, refused to accord me. Mr. Goodman's two points are as follows:

> First, my reference to the Sedition Act was as follows: "Not since 1758—when newsmen were sentenced to prison under the Sedition Act for statements displeasing to the Government—has American journalism been under greater attack." That is my own judgment, based on more than 20 years in journalism and my knowledge of the history of the profession. I believe it was a fair statement, and not a ridiculous one, as you chose to characterize it.
>
> The other, is that I felt I made clear in my Austin speech that I was referring to subpoenas that compromise news sources or prejudice further news access. I base this view on the Constitutional guarantee

of press freedom, and I suggested that Constitutional self-restraint should discourage Government from 'the broad use of subpoena powers.' I did not and do not suggest that the news media should be above the law. On the contrary, I have been emphasizing the Constitutional protection of press freedom, which is such a basic part of the law. In taking this position, the press is defending the nation's basic law, and those who are in opposition are in fact undermining it.

*Gabe Pressman, Robert Lewis Shayon,
Robert Schulman:*

Ethics in Television Journalism

WILBUR SCHRAMM once observed that news exists in the minds of men, that news is not the event itself but something perceived after it has occurred, "an attempt to reconstruct the essential framework of the event—essential being defined against a frame of reference which is calculated to make the event meaningful to the reader." * The observation is useful, yet the substitution of *viewer* for *reader* introduces new conditions and intensifies old arguments related to the reporter's functions, responsibilities, and ethics.

As television's journalists well understand, their often cumbersome methods of reconstructing the essential framework of events, by camera and microphone, have complicated the tasks of getting the story. Further, they have revealed levels of human interaction within news happenings that no other medium can expose. Such possibilities of revelation emphasize the matter of reportorial taste and judgment, as well as the respect for the individual in an open society. Since Dallas many have voiced their concern about these issues; Dr. Frank Stanton recently proposed an independent study by which might be

---

Mr. Pressman was a newsman for WNBC (New York) and Mr. Schulman was director of Special Features for KING-TV (Seattle) at the time of this interview. Mr. Shayon is an author and critic. This article, which appeared in *Television Quarterly,* the official journal of the National Academy of Television Arts & Sciences (Spring, 1964) is reprinted by permission.
* In "The Nature of News," *Journalism Quarterly* (September, 1949), p. 259.

explored and recommended some ground rules for the fair and forthright recording of change in our civilization.

In the following exchange of opinions by critic *Robert Lewis Shayon* and TV newsmen *Gabe Pressman* and *Robert Schulman,* the morality of the journalist comes under consideration.

> *Gabe Pressman and Robert Lewis Shayon met in the offices of the Academy's New York Chapter. Their conversation was recorded and a copy of the transcript forwarded to Robert Schulman in Seattle for his comments.*

Conversation in New York

Mr. Shayon, Gabe, in all the discussions about broadcast journalism there seems to be an assumption that newsmen on television and radio don't have a code of ethics. It seems highly improbable. You're a working newspaperman; you've been in the business a long time. I would suppose you have basic philosophical assumptions about what you do.

Mr. Pressman: I think that a code of ethics is something a working newsman probably seldom gives enough thought to. As a group, reporters have never really formalized their ethics. Yet I think the best of them have always followed the strictest code of ethics, a code that would compare with what the medical or the legal professions have established. It's a dedication to uncovering the truth, to communicating information to people—information they're interested in getting, information with which they can most closely identify within their own lives. It's a dedication to getting information to them rapidly and accurately, to reporting the news without prejudice.

Mr. Shayon: When you report a story, or when you have reported stories in the past, are you ever confronted with ethical dilemmas, or is it all just open and shut? Do you have any pangs of conscience, or hesitations and reflections about whether or not a certain thing should be done?

Mr. Pressman: I think so. If a problem arises in relation to the general idea of public interest and concern, this is the primary ethic; and any means that you can use to avoid hurting people who are innocent are, I think, proper means. There's a great danger, however, in exerting too much self-censorship. Self-censorship can be as evil as that kind directed from some authority which impedes the pursuit of the news.

Mr. Shayon: Have you ever inhibited yourself when doing a story?

Mr. Pressman: Yes. A case that comes to my mind right now involved a wildcat strike in a city department—a recent strike by employees of New York. A group of drivers of police department vehicles—wagons used to load and unload prisoners—went on strike along with other city employees. The police commissioner, feeling that they were in a special category, immediately suspended them and served notice they would be fired.

A group of pickets were at City Hall on a particular day, and our primary interest was treating a part of the story involving this particular group of 14 or

15 drivers. A couple of the drivers were on the picket line. They had just been fired, and I went over to talk to two of them on camera. One of the leaders of the union came over to me and whispered to me: "Look, I don't mind you talking to these guys but for God's sake, please don't ask them questions which might lead them to insult the police commissioner—because you and I have been through strikes before and you know that somehow this is all going to be settled. The mayor is going to step in and there'll be an amicable settlement. And I don't want these guys to burn their bridges completely. If they don't get jobs as police department drivers, they'll be put on as drivers somewhere else in the city. If they say a lot of insulting things about the commissioner, it's going to be very difficult." I replied, "Don't worry, I won't ask them any questions like that. I understand they've got wives and kids and I don't want, for the sake of a sensational kind of charge about the police commissioner, to get them into any trouble. But I do want to know how they got the news that they were fired and whether they regret going out on strike." So, to that extent, I limited myself on that story as I guess I have done on many other stories. There was no point gained in trying to get those guys worked up to say what was perhaps really in their hearts, to recite their emotions at that moment.

Mr. Shayon: There are many talmudic rabbis, and philosophers, who say that you can never tell the whole truth—that you are always withholding part of the truth. What you just told us seems to indicate that you, too, apply this principle. There are times when the reporter is not waving a banner and crusading for total truth.

Mr. Pressman: I think you raise an intriguing philosophical question. When I use the word truth, I don't use it in the absolute concept. I think that we can't pretend, as reporters, to any divine insight into life and its problems, or to the contemporary history we're engaged in covering.

Mr. Shayon: So then we're dealing with relative truth—an area of judgment. This is precisely what we're talking about, isn't it? You've given us an example of where you exercised restraint in the interests of good taste.

Mr. Pressman: Well, I don't know whether it was a question of good taste. I think my restraint was also in the interests of humanity.

Mr. Shayon: You recognized a higher principle than the immediate story. Was there ever a case when it worked the opposite way—when you can say now, looking back on it, that you broke the bonds of responsibility? This is a tough one, but be candid with it.

Mr. Pressman: I remember a case when it was done. I didn't have any part in it. It was an airplane crash and the victims were out at sea. All were lost, and relatives had been waiting at International Airport for their loved ones. The man with a camera crew went to the airport to talk to these people, and his interviewing was a distressing thing to see on the air. With hindsight, I would say that it was bad taste, that it unnecessarily capitalized upon sorrow. Not that I think that television should not cover human sorrow. Emotions are a part of life. They are part of what journalism is all about, and television has the capacity to portray these emotions, in many cases more vividly than the printed word. I don't think we have to shy away from using this power. In this case, I'd say it was wrong.

Mr. Shayon: But this is a case in point dealing with another reporter. There are times while I've watched you, and I watch you very regularly with my family, when I have winced at some of the things you've done.

Mr. Pressman: For example?

Mr. Shayon: I remember a situation where a man had committed a crime and had been apprehended by the police. He was being put into a van and you and some other reporters were very aggressive in your determination to get a statement from him. While he was in transit, you stuck a mike in his face—while he was being loaded into the van—and you kept firing questions at what appeared to me to be a pathetic, perhaps mentally disturbed individual—asking him questions which, had he answered, might have affected his right to a fair trial later when he got into a courtroom. And I thought that in your desire to get a story you pushed beyond the bounds of good taste. Do you recall this?

Mr. Pressman: There have been many cases like that one, about which I have evolved an ethic in my own mind. Let's start, first of all, with the whole question of the coverage of legal proceedings.

Mr. Shayon: Are you talking about legal proceedings or police apprehension?

Mr. Pressman: It's all part of the same picture. If a man is arrested and he's booked, he's taken to police headquarters and mugged. He's then taken for arraignment to a court and subsequently he's tried in the court. First of all, let me say that television is now the primary source of news to the American people. This wasn't so nine years ago when I left the newspaper business and went into TV, but it's true now. And the Constitution guarantees every person the right to a fair trial. Perhaps the greatest violation of that right occurs during the many hours a prisoner spends in a police station without a lawyer—incommunicado—being interviewed first by the police, then by an assistant district attorney, or by the D.A. himself in rare cases that are sensational in nature.

I feel, of course, that it's possible for us to violate a defendant's rights by conducting an exhaustive interrogation. I also feel, however, that it's in keeping with the best interests of justice to give a man a chance to say *something*. Over the years, my own thinking has evolved to that point where I feel the simple question "Do you have anything to say?" can at least give a man an opportunity to state that he was not permitted to call a lawyer, or that he was being questioned, or beaten. He may simply want to say he's innocent. But what he *does* say might hold significance in relation to the fairness of the arrest procedure. I don't think that exhaustive questioning should be allowed. I'm not trying to rationalize the fact that this business of questioning prisoners by reporters has grown up with television.

The Appellate Division of New York State recently made a ruling which the police department has interpreted in such a manner as to prevent us from interviewing prisoners in the future. This part of the story still has to be played out, of course, and I don't know how it's going to be applied. But we have to face the fact that although we have reporting tools—the camera and the microphone—we are constantly thwarted and frustrated in our efforts to use them. In Great Britain perhaps they have a much finer system. The British system doesn't allow for any coverage from the time a man is arrested until he's brought to trial. Why, you may wonder, has this blown up in America—this business of chasing people in the streets and in corridors outside courtrooms? Why do we do this? Because these are important stories. We want to use our tools, but we're not allowed in the courtrooms. And now we've been barred from court buildings. As TV newsmen we are not a rabble bent on digging out sensationalistic approaches to news. But, basically, we want to get a piece of the story. We want to show people what the guy who has been arrested looks like because they're interested. The newspaper reporter with his pad and pencil is allowed in the courtroom; we're not. Properly, we should be in the courtroom, not in the corridors. We shouldn't be interviewing prisoners in the streets. There should be invisible cameras. There should be an electronic transcript of *every* public proceeding and this would obviate—would eliminate—all the razzle-dazzle circus atmosphere.

I think you referred, in your example, to the Martin Epstein case, where the State Liquor Authority Chairman had been arrested. He was sick, and was taken from the D.A.'s office in an ambulance. The D.A.'s office and the police knew we were out there. They did nothing to stop us or even to organize the event. There were more photographers and reporters than there was room for, and the shuffling that went on resulted from cameramen who were all trying to get a clear shot so their office wouldn't say: "Why didn't you get the picture?" This congestion included not only TV newsmen, but newspaper photographers; and although the *New York Times* carried an editorial about this rabble and such disgraceful exhibition, they had not only one photographer, I believe, but two—and a reporter—at the scene. They were part of that mob and I don't blame them for being there. That's journalism. Unfortunately, it's gotten more complicated, and public officials have not always troubled to consider the new conditions and physical problems.

Mr. Shayon: You've made a number of points; let me comment on them. You said this is journalism, and seem to postulate a premise that journalism has certain principles of its own which must be obeyed, often at the risk of laws or other aspects of our society. You said the police didn't make an effort to stop it. We're not talking about police responsibility.

Mr. Pressman: No, not to stop it—to organize it.

Mr. Shayon: Even to organize it.

Mr. Pressman: To do it properly, then. They brought this man into and out of the building without any warning, without trying to organize matters and say, "Look fellows, stand behind this barrier; everyone will get a shot."

Mr. Shayon: This is like the Oswald Case and the behavior of the Dallas police. But we're not talking about the negligence, alleged negligence, or responsibilities of police. We're talking about the reporters. You made a significant point when you said that you stick a mike in a man's face to give him an opportunity to say something that may be for his own protection. You're obviously thinking of Star Chamber proceedings, to avoid which we started our whole system of rights under English law. The right of the defendant to a fair trial is different from the right of the public to hear the trial. A courtroom is in itself sufficient to do away with Star Chamber proceedings. So long as people can come to a courtroom while a man is on trial, the law—our Western law—may assume that this man's rights are protected from Star Chamber proceedings. But this is entirely different from the right of the public to hear and see what's going on. In other words, law was not designed for the protection or for the interests of the public; it was designed for the protection of the defendant. And it seems to me that the rights of the defendant are not well served when the public, through the apparatus of television, comes in and perhaps distorts the proceedings.

Mr. Pressman: Have you ever been to night court in New York?

Mr. Shayon: Yes.

Mr. Pressman: What do you think of the judicial proceedings there? The legal proceedings?

Mr. Shayon: Sometimes they're very sloppy.

Mr. Pressman: I think that very often they're a disgrace.

Mr. Shayon: Yes.

Mr. Pressman: I think that journalism has a crusading role to perform in our society, and one of the most salutary and immediate benefits to be derived from cameras in courtrooms is to let people see how our lowest courts are conducted. I think this is a scandalous part of our society, and journalism has a watchdog role to execute. The judicial branch of government is not immune to criticism or public exposure. Put a camera into night court, or into some of the other lower courts where the procedures, as you say, are often sloppy and where some of the people who mete out justice fall far below standards that we should expect. This would hold a salutary value for society.

Mr. Shayon: I happen to agree with you—although I think it's a very sensitive problem—on this Canon 35 question of reporting court cases. I'm in favor, under proper organization, of cameras being permitted in courtrooms and legislatures. I'm entirely in sympathy with that. We're talking about another thing. We're not talking about journalism reporting in an organized way the processes of law and order. We're talking about the nebulous state which exists *before* these processes come into full and organized play—in those free-wheeling moments when a man has been arrested. Most of the time this is when the failures to observe good taste occur.

Mr. Pressman: I agree there have been lapses in taste. I don't try to excuse them, but I've tried to explain them. They're an outgrowth of the proper zeal we have to exert in covering stories—and of the frustration we encounter as compared to the newspaper reporters and photographers who are doing the same thing.

Mr. Shayon: Then we've identified the fact there are lapses of good taste—you've been candid enough to admit them and you've explained why they occur. Let's talk about a few more specific cases and try to proceed to some generalities and conclusions. I was watching CBS News last night and I saw a CBS reporter and cameraman, unannounced and without warning, walk into the headquarters of the John Birch Society. The reporter began to question the people there and they told him to get out immediately. They hid their faces from the camera. He kept throwing questions at them until the last possible moment. Now I have my own feelings about the John Birch Society, but I was impressed with the poor taste of this journalistic venture into the privacy of a group. No matter what the man was saying, he was already on the record. He was making a public impact. Will you comment on that?

Mr. Pressman: I'm at a disadvantage for two reasons. First, CBS is a competitor of my company, and normally I would be hard put to defend them. Second, I didn't see the film. But I will ask you this: If a newspaperman with a pad and pencil did the same thing, and wrote a story about how he was thrown out of the office, would you consider that bad taste?

Mr. Shayon: I probably wouldn't and yet I'm curious to know what the difference is. Why am I disturbed when the reporter with the camera walks in? I think, of course, that the much-touted impact of the camera has much to do with it. I'm aware of the fact that my eye cannot avoid the story on TV as it can avoid it on a printed page. Somehow TV coverage placed the people in this adventure in journalism at a terrible disadvantage. It seemed to detract from their dignity as individuals. This is the special uniqueness of television. This is what we talk about and worry about all the time—the impact.

Mr. Pressman: I think you chose a bad example. A political organization like the John Birch Society has got to be ready for controversy. It's an extreme group. Any political group is always putting its neck on the block, and has to expect to be questioned. If the reporter went into a private home with a camera, I would question the taste. But in this case, I would be inclined to defend the film. I feel that the newness of our medium may make it irritating. The camera is used as a newspaperman uses his pad and his pencil. And yet, the camera is the most faithful reporter we have. The video-tapes don't lie and the film doesn't lie. The camera gives you a very real insight into people as they really are, into personalities. It never distorts a quote. It's a pretty accurate form of reporting. So I would respond to your concern about barging into a political headquarters and talking to people by saying that that's what politics is about. It's controversy.

Mr. Shayon: But usually political groups welcome publicity and attention. This is a group which definitely doesn't welcome it.

Mr. Pressman: They carried a big full-page ad in the *Times* recently. Apparently—

Mr. Shayon: On their own terms.

Mr. Pressman: Yes.

Mr. Shayon: They preferred the publicity in the controlled situation of a newspaper ad.

Mr. Pressman: They are *controversial*. The public is interested in them. I think that what CBS did, however, is not objective journalism—it's slanted. If it's clearly labeled as such, if they take an editorial position and they segregate this from other news coverage—

Mr. Shayon: But they didn't. They merely said our reporter got the brush-off at the John Birch Society today and they showed you *how* he got the brush-off.

Mr. Pressman: I think that within the context of investigatory crusading journalism, as distinguished from spot news reporting, this is a permissible tactic. If it was done with good taste within the framework of the kind of effort it was—which was, apparently, to find out what kind of people are in the John Birch Society or what kind of people run their office—then I would approve of it. Speaking clinically, I don't think it's too hot a story, but I would still defend their right to do it.

Mr. Shayon: Let's not belabor this particular story. There are many others. Before we get into them, let me say that admirers of television's better moments of broadcasting journalism can never forget the service TV did in the McCarthy case where, subject to your own bias, many people felt that the camera did render a great public service by exposing things that needed to be exposed. So we are well aware of the fact that the camera can make decisive, positive contributions as well as negative—depending upon which side of the line you are politically. But here, I think, we are groping for principles which would help us establish some distinctions between aggressive newspaper reporting and the public interest. What do you think about the much publicized Oswald incident and the editorial comment to the effect that the networks and the reporters who covered this killing were responsible for Oswald's death?

Mr. Pressman: I think that's an atrocious distortion. I wasn't there, but it seems to me that the police were responsible for the safety of this prisoner. The newsmen naturally wanted to get a picture of him because the whole nation—the whole world—wanted to see what this man looked like. Ruby was a man who was known to the Dallas police. I don't have the details of the investigation, but apparently he was a police buff. He could well have been on the premises anyway, even if the newsmen hadn't been there. Whatever happened there, Ruby did get in. Whether or not he would have gotten in had the press not been allowed in that courtyard is, I think, an academic question.

This is an example of how TV's detractors or haters come after us when something goes wrong. It reminds me of the attitude held by some members of the bar toward the admitting of broadcast journalists into the courtroom. The lawyers of the A.B.A. with whom I've met in various cities of the country—I'm on their standing committee on broadcast journalism—and the media representatives always wind up in a stalemate. The lawyers on this committee listen to us politely, and then continue Canon 35 without modification. They admit that we could plan a courtroom where the machinery is unobtrusive, where the TV cameras or the newspaper photographers could be invisible. But they insist there still would be a psychological barrier to a fair trial because the lawyers, judges, and everybody would ham it up because the cameras are present.

Now this is a question that involves the ethics of the bar, and in the case of Dallas or anywhere else, it also involves the ethics of the police. Because we have the capability of telling a story efficiently, dramatically, and with a maximum amount of impact—because we have the ability to satisfy the need of the American people for instantaneous journalism in this modern age—does it follow that we have to be penalized because people react badly? They've got to, you know, clean up their own houses. It's not our fault.

Mr. Shayon: You talk about the need of the American people for instantaneous news. That's not the sole American need. The greater need of the American people is to perpetuate their hard-won systems of justice which defend the rights of the individual.

Mr. Pressman: Absolutely.

Mr. Shayon: And these two needs often come into conflict, as they did in Dallas. You speak of the people who criticize the role of the television reporters in Dallas as being proponents of the Hate TV School. This month *Variety* published a long, eloquent letter written by a man who said that television was directly responsible for the murder of Oswald. It was signed by William T. Bode, WCAU-TV, Philadelphia. This man is not an outsider, he's an insider.

Mr. Pressman: I don't know if he was there. I don't think he was, was he? Did the letter say he was there?

Mr. Shayon: No, it doesn't. But that's not the point. The point is that many people are concerned about this, and not because they hate TV. Many people who admire TV are also concerned.

Mr. Pressman: But why should TV be blamed because of the negligence of the police in protecting Oswald? I saw the pictures of Oswald and his bodyguards and escorts. The police were looking at Oswald or they were looking at the camera. They were not looking around.

Mr. Shayon: They were not even thinking they had exposed him: "Look we're all stars on television, and here's the main one."

Mr. Pressman: They appeared to be mugging for the cameras. I wasn't there, and I say again that without having actually been there I can't speak knowledgeably about it. Yet it appears to me that the police were, perhaps to some extent, hamming it up. This is a human quality. I think we're all hams. Maybe even some magazine writers are hams. To blame TV for the ineffectiveness of the police in protecting this man just doesn't make any sense. Our job there, and the job of the newsmen from other media, was to get a picture of this fellow—to tell the story of how he was being transported from one place to another. The duty of the police was to escort him safely.

Mr. Shayon: Let's look at it in this way. You're saying, "We are not culpable because the responsibility lay with the police. Once they made the decision to transfer Oswald in public, we had a right to cover that story." It's true, of course, as we were informed, that the police changed the time of the transfer to suit the requirements of the television coverage. Initially, they meant to transfer him secretly, but the TV men insisted that it be done in public. My question to you, without prior condemnation but just for exploratory purposes, is: Assuming that the police had made the wrong decision, should you not have exercised restraint and said, "Although this is not our fault, we *still* must realize what we're doing here and not cover this"?

Mr. Pressman: I'm sure that you're aware, as I am, of the breath-taking evolution of events during that tragic weekend. I'm sure you're also aware that all newsmen work under discipline; you do, on the magazine you work for. I do; we all do. There are men at desks in offices who give orders to men who are on the scene. I don't understand what you're driving at. Are you saying that the men on the scene should have realized that this was a desperate situation, that there was a possibility that someone would come forward in the confusion and kill Oswald? Should the working reporters have predicted the assassination and said, "We can't cover this because it's too much of a mob scene and this guy may get killed"?

Mr. Shayon: That kind of directed thinking and restraint in such an emotional moment would be superhuman. What I am saying is that this tragic event might cause, I would hope, broadcasters to consider how to behave in such future situations. Because what we had in Dallas was a situation of heat, of instantaneous emotional explosion in which human beings are forced by their jobs to act in a certain way—a kind of behavior which, when you look at in hindsight, is destructive of great traditional values. Somehow the industry ought to bring out of this a desire to re-examine its own values—an effort to discover if it's possible *not* to contribute to these things in the future. This is what I'm asking—that we begin to question—

Mr. Pressman: Are you saying that tenacity, persistence and a desire to break down official red tape are qualities newsmen should not have?

Mr. Shayon: No, I'm saying that newsmen should also have values by which they *measure* their tenacity and their desire to break down red tape. In other words, nothing exists in a vacuum. There are no absolutes. The freedom of journalism is not an absolute freedom.

Mr. Pressman: How could this bolt from the blue have been anticipated? I mean, how could anyone foresee that, in the transfer of a prisoner from one place to another, he would be assassinated?

Mr. Shayon: He was perhaps the most lynchable human being in America at that moment, and if the TV editors, news directors and reporters prevailed upon the Dallas police to change their schedule of moving this man at 3 A.M.—in secret and under great protection—to a time when he could be transferred in full view of a vast American audience, then both TV *and* the

Dallas police are certainly equally responsible. Both had better do some profound soul-searching.

Mr. Pressman: There are many times when people are running targets. Every time an important public official moves, and every time anyone is arrested for an atrocious crime, they become targets for a mob. Does that mean that we should move people secretly—that we should engage in totalitarian methods?

Mr. Shayon: No, I think that is an extreme!

Mr. Pressman: There's a way of covering news in a democracy and of doing it under safeguard. This was a happening that no one anticipated. Apparently the police were delinquent in not giving this man adequate protection. Even if they had, maybe Ruby would have found a means of getting through anyway. But you can't say that because this terrible thing happened, you're going to exclude television newsmen from covering a hot story. That doesn't make sense. It doesn't add up.

Mr. Shayon: Let me ask you what I think is a fair question. Granted that the past is gone. If a similar situation should arise, and if you are a newsman covering the transfer from one jail to another of an alleged assassin, would you press for the story just as much or would you say, "This man is in danger of being killed or lynched. Let's hold off. Let's have the transfer made in secret even though we lose the story"?

Mr. Pressman: I would press for the story just as much because it is important that this man be seen. That's my mission as a newsman. I'm not a law enforcement officer. It's not my job to protect this man. The law is fully capable of protecting a man, and if there was a conflict between the security of the man's life and our getting a picture of him, naturally the man's life comes first. But that is not our function. Our function is to try to get the news. If you've been on a police story where you were denied knowledge of what was going on for 12 hours, you would see how basic this drive is. You try cajolery and other indirect methods of getting at the story, and perhaps, finally, you're forced to a position where you have to say: "Look, we're going to say that you're not talking to us. We're going to say this on the air, and we're going to say that we can't get the information from you." That's blackmail, isn't it? But sometimes a newsman has to resort to extreme measures in order to ferret out the story. Public officials are prone in many cases to withholding news, to running the show in their own way. I had a city editor once who said that all public officials are guilty until proven innocent. This was his motto. And while I wouldn't buy anything as extreme as that, I do think that we *are* watchdogs. We have got to see as much as we can so the people are informed. That's our function. We cannot worry about the way other people are conducting their jobs.

There was no reason why pictures could not have been taken of Lee Harvey Oswald while he was given adequate protection. The only unfortunate factor is that he got *inadequate* protection. He wasn't shot by a newsman. Sometimes, hearing this controversy, I get the impression that people are blaming one of us for shooting him. He was shot by a man known to the Dallas police department, who hung around the police, was a police buff, and who might very well have been there anyway.

Mr. Shayon: Gabe, we're not moving each other in our views. As I see your point of view, what you're stressing is that the responsibility of the newsman is to get the story and not worry about any other person's responsibility. What I am suggesting is that, as you admit and as the whole industry admits, the impact of television has become so great and so powerful that it has perhaps gotten to a point where it not only gets the story but, by influencing the developments, it *makes* the story. If this is true, then TV may distort our whole system of the protection of the defendant. This is what I'm saying to you.

Mr. Pressman: I have faith in our democratic institutions and our traditions, and I feel that this is an alarmist's viewpoint. I believe that members of the judiciary, the executive branches of the government, the legislature—all three co-functioning branches of government—are fully capable of weathering the newness of television, of resisting that tendency to be a ham which, perhaps, all human flesh is heir to.

Furthermore, I think that television can be a great aid in a society of checks and balances by operating as a check on these branches of government, on the police and on all officials who are entrusted with the welfare of the public as a whole, as well as of individuals who come under their protection, their scrutiny, or their custody. I think that it's always dangerous to exert censorship, whether it comes from above, whether it comes by direction from a government department or official, or whether it's voluntary.

Mr. Shayon: Aren't you then postulating the freedom of the newsman as an absolute value? Free, even, from his own sense of restraint?

Mr. Pressman: No. I think restraint is very important, as is any reporter's own sense of taste.

Response from Seattle

Mr. Schulman: It is puzzling to find a discussion about ethics beginning with mention of an assumption that broadcasters in television and radio lack a code of journalistic ethics. Credit Bob Shayon with conceding that the assumption seems improbable. The fact is that the conscientious and competent newsman in radio or television—and I would emphasize those adjectives—is motivated by precisely those same dictates and guidelines that have for many decades motivated the newsman in newspapers and magazines. These are—and Gabe touches on some of them—accuracy, fairness, an informed sense of judgment combined with good taste, and a sensitivity to the appropriate rights of the individual, including the right of privacy. In television we share with the print media the day-to-day problem of balancing, on one hand, the perennial zeal for getting the story and, on the other, the commands of restraint and good judgment.

It was more than a quarter-century ago, when I was a cub on the *St. Louis Post-Dispatch,* that I was engaged in what was known as "picture chasing." This involved beating the competition to the homes where some great disaster had struck in order to get snapshots or photographs of the survivors. On one such occasion I arrived at the home of a newly-made widow and found myself, in effect, bringing her the first word of the death of her husband. Because she was an expectant mother, she almost suffered a miscarriage on the spot. Had the newspaper known in advance of the situation, I am certain that we would have employed somewhat more cautious procedures.

Yet today the newspapers and many radio and television stations continue to traffic in the reactions of next of kin of disaster victims. This is the part of the stuff of news. It seems to me that value judgments must be made, in each case, on the way in which a situation is to be handled. In light of a pronounced trend in broadcasting toward the employment of newsmen *as* newsmen (either from the printed media or out of the colleges) it is difficult to understand how any thoughtful observer of the broadcasting scene would fail to see that we are moving toward more restraint and evaluation in day-to-day news operation. Perhaps this is not moving at the rate that some of us would like, but it is nonetheless happening.

I would agree that, because of the impact of the camera, our responsibility in broadcasting news may be greater than in print. I can recall some personal misgivings when our local newsmen recently interviewed a teenager being released from a mental hospital. The boy had undergone several years of treatment following the pathological murder he committed at the age of 12; the interview had been arranged by the law enforcement officials who were overseeing the return of this youth to the community. It was, for me at least, painful to see a boy interrogated on how he would deal with the world awaiting him after this period of confinement. I confess that I would have been disposed to forego the opportunity for questioning him. It was legitimate in this instance to ask what was being served by subjecting this boy to a grilling of this kind, especially at this early stage in his return to society.

To have abstained from this interview would have involved the kind of exercise of judgment and conscience which Bob Shayon has referred to. Yet I am certain that such exercise is not disavowed by Gabe Pressman, or by any other broadcast newsman of his stature and devotion. I prefer not to get into the Oswald question, but it seems to me that Shayon does a disservice to Pressman when he attempts to define that responsibility in terms of that unusual case.

In my opinion, Gabe is absolutely correct when he terms it atrocious for anyone to assume that television could be held responsible for the killing of Oswald. As he appropriately suggests, the Dallas police officials at no time presented the newsmen—and they included the print media as well as television and radio—with the possibility that taking Oswald to the County Court House under public conditions might pose problems too difficult for their security measures to contend with. As Pressman points out, if they had indicated such concern then an ethical decision would certainly have been called for. But even under those circumstances it would have required, in my judgment and I am sure in Gabe's, some considerable reflection. I think we need to bear in mind, in terms of the open society to which all of us are committed, that office-holders and politicians can always attempt to use inadequate security or other stratagems as devices for interfering with the free flow of important public information.

It is the primary responsibility of law enforcement officials, judges and attorneys to protect the security and the legal rights of defendants and violators. It is the responsibility of newsmen, whether in broadcasting or in newspapers and magazines, to press for the story—subject only to these measures of restraint and common sense that we are all mentioning. The interplay between these forces is part of the system of checks and balances which undergird our democratic society. To say, therefore, that television may be in danger of distorting our whole system of the protection of the defendant is alarmist at the least. If it is true to say that television and radio "make the news," it is also necessary to recognize that this function has been executed almost since the time when the first printing press was developed. The difference is simply that television is doing it with greater impact and, inasmuch as the camera records with an authority which even the most consumately gifted reporter cannot hope to achieve, more faithfully.

It is precisely in this sense that television and radio can complement the contributions of newspapers and magazines to American life and our understanding of public issues. While more of us might show greater awareness of the enormous power of the tools which we are given to use, it seems to me that Bob Shayon has yet to recognize the potential social benefits these tools might reap.

Must we not consider the possibility that emotion is a fundamental element of the understanding of public events and issues, and movements? Is there any fundamental difference between a written report that a widow shed copious tears and a camera's exhibit of those tears? Do not, indeed, many of our existing social problems stem from a trend in recent years toward depersonalization of events in American life? It is this depersonalization which television is uniquely equipped to offset.

Two years ago on our stations in the Pacific Northwest, we devoted one hour to a first-person documentary account by a convicted killer. It was a story of the ways in which society and society's apparatus failed to meet his psychiatric and social needs. We went to great lengths in the program to stress that we had no intention of trying to influence the fate of this man. Rather, we were attempting, through his own telling of this story—with approval of his attorneys—to shed light on the social lessons to be learned from that human tragedy. Yet I regret to say that after the film was shown in New York City, Jack Gould of the *New York Times* was, in my judgment, insensitive enough to describe this documentary as the display of the agonies of a wounded animal to television's curious mob. This criminal's fate is now being weighed by the Governor of the state in which he resides, and among the material submitted to the Governor is an affidavit from the man's attorneys attesting to the broad-scale corrective social actions that were stimulated by the telling of this story— the telling of this *emotional* story. Still another intriguing outcome of the program is a report from psychiatrists to the effect that, as a result of the participation of this man in a television documentary, he has undergone what is regarded as a kind of instant and surprising psychoanalysis which appears to have brought him at least part-way out of his mental disturbance.

As the man's life hangs in the balance, we are being inundated with requests to rerun the documentary. Messages are coming from those who feel that it would influence a decision in favor of commutation of the death sentence. Our intention is to refrain from a rerun of the show because it would impose added pressure on those who must make the decision—a judicial decision. I suppose this is what Bob Shayon might call an example of higher judgment, or social responsibility. It is our assumption, or at least our hope, that more and more stations throughout the country would do the same if placed in our position.

Many of us believe that television and radio broadcasting, especially at the local level, must move at an accelerated rate toward the exercise of social responsibility. Many of us also would agree with Bob Shayon that, by and large, television news continues to be somewhat overweighted with reports of robberies, small crimes, and fender dentings. Yet I suppose that every competent newspaperman agrees in his heart that the efforts toward a more balanced diet of news and away from preoccupation with the cheap, the maudlin, and the superficial is a challenge to all of us.

There is no question that the red eye of the television camera or the whirl of a film camera brings out the "ham" in many public officials, but when was there ever a public official who did not begin to "tailor" his statements upon the appearance in his office, or in his courtroom, or in his legislative chamber, of a real live reporter. The timing of public statements to catch the Sunday newspapers is as old as the feather duster.

From the earliest days of TV, legislators have feared the presence of the camera. We have often attempted to defer to this fear by turning off the red light of the cameras. Yet a proper exercise of decorum and a lack of ostentation by television crews, combined with a gradual acceptance of the camera by the legislator, does cause "adjustment" to occur. Already we have seen instances where votes that might have been thrown behind a bill of special interest were not so cast. To be sure, there have been other instances where a vote which required a degree of courage in the public eye was not cast for a desirable piece of legislation; the presence of the cameras may have inhibited such action. Yet, surely, we must take the optimistic position that a society will stand only to the extent that all of us can learn to live with exposure, public performance and truth.

Nat Hentoff:

How "Fair" Should TV Be?

LAST FEBRUARY, ABC-TV refused to televise an already-taped Dick Cavett show with guests Abbie Hoffman, Jerry Rubin, Tom Hayden and Rennie Davis. In response to queries from newspaper reporters, ABC's management explained that the network "had an obligation to insure fairness and balance under requirements of the Federal Communications Commission." And Cavett's four guests, ABC management continued, "made controversial remarks about the U.S. judicial system, continuing hostilities in Southeast Asia, Watergate scandals and the use of revolutionary tactics."

The offending program would be aired, ABC said, only if Cavett sliced a half-hour out of it and, in accordance with what's known as the Fairness Doctrine, used that time to interview one or more people who are manifestly conservative in their views.

Cavett at first refused, then succumbed reluctantly after the network canceled the original show. When it was finally aired on March 21, it not only had been altered slightly, but for rebuttal purposes two right-wingers—Jeffrey St. John, a CBS political commentator, and Fran Griffin, Illinois chairwoman of Young Americans for Freedom—had been tacked on.

The Fairness Doctrine became law in 1959, when Congress amended the 1934 Communications Act to insist on the obligation of broadcast licensees "to afford reasonable opportunity for the discussion of conflicting views on issues of public importance." The air, after all, is public; and the public should have access to broadcasting facilities using its air.

Mr. Hentoff is a columnist for the *Village Voice* of Greenwich Village and is on the faculty of the Graduate School of Education, New York University and The New School for Social Research (New York). This article is reprinted here by permission from *Lithopinion* No. 34, the graphic arts and public affairs journal of Local One, Amalgamated Lithographers of America (New York), © 1974 by Local One, A.L.A.

Television- and radio-station owners, and not a few news reporters and analysts in broadcasting, objected. Nobody, they reasoned, certainly not the government, can force a newspaper or magazine or book publisher to give space to those who consider a particular article or book "unfair." So why shouldn't television and radio, like the print media, have the same inalienable First Amendment rights to voice views freely?

In 1969, the Supreme Court appeared to have answered that question for some time to come. In its *Red Lion* decision, the Court proclaimed that "a licensee has no constitutional right . . . to monopolize a radio frequency of his fellow citizens." Furthermore, the Court emphasized, "It is the purpose of the First Amendment to preserve an uninhibited marketplace of ideas in which truth will ultimately prevail, rather than to countenance monopolization of that market . . . [by] a private licensee."

Almost Everybody Approved

The *Red Lion* decision caused general rejoicing among liberals, most centrists and even a sizable number of conservatives who, while usually of the view that private enterprise and government regulation are antithetical, decided that in the matter of the public air-waves, only the government can effectively mandate that there be a real public forum for clashing ideas. (Many conservatives, after all, hold it as an article of faith that broadcasting is dominated by "left-leaning" reporters and analysts, and the *Red Lion* decision gave promise of some "balance" on the people's air.)

As a civil libertarian, I too was among the rejoicers. One of my own articles of faith has long been that owning a radio station, and especially a television station, amounts to having a license to make a hell of a lot of money. The least that broadcasting ownership can do to justify all those profits is to give dissenting citizens free and fair access to their channels.

My "heresy," with regard to the Fairness Doctrine, began to take shape in November 1972, when I read a dissenting decision by David Bazelon, Chief Judge of the United States Court of Appeals for the District of Columbia Circuit. Bazelon, who warred frequently with Warren Burger when the latter was on that appeals court, is a pre-eminent civil libertarian. He is also one of the few judges in the country who, like William O. Douglas, writes with marvelous and witty lucidity. We all have our prejudices, and one of mine has been best summarized by J. Mitchell Morse in *The Irrelevant English Teacher* (Temple University Press, 1972): "Style is a matter of intellectual self-respect. To write well, a certain moral courage is essential."

I would pay more attention, for instance, to William Buckley if he were finally to recognize that ormolu rococo reveals a talent for self-inflation but has little to do with writing or thinking well.

It was not, however, on aesthetic grounds that Judge Bazelon's decision in *Brandywine-Main Line Radio, Inc.* v. *Federal Communications Commission* shook me up. What Bazelon was saying made unnerving sense—both common sense and constitutional sense.

The case at issue concerned the FCC's refusal to renew the license of radio station WXUR in Media, Pa. The station was under the control of Rev. Carl McIntire, a fustian preacher whose views are well to the right of those of, let us say, Barry Goldwater and Savonarola. The FCC claimed that WXUR had failed to adhere to the Fairness Doctrine, pointing out that in decapitating WXUR, it was only doing what the Supreme Court, in the *Red Lion* decision, had mandated it to do.

Bazelon's dissent is worth close attention because it gets to the core of a rather complicated question. The First Amendment is designed to allow the citizenry as wide and robust a range of views as partisans can come up with. Accordingly, the Fairness Doctrine would appear to be eminently in line with the First Amendment. The people's right to hear diversity of opinion, and to express their own opinions, must surely have primacy over the First Amendment rights of those who own radio and television stations and of those who are regular staff reporters and commentators.

The Right to Be Disruptive

It is not, however, all that simple. First of all, Bazelon noted, the FCC, by forcing WXUR off the air, had deprived its listeners of *that* station's ideas, "however unpopular or disruptive we might judge these ideas to be." (Or, as Justice Douglas has pointed out, "Under our Bill of Rights, people are entitled to have extreme ideas, silly ideas, partisan ideas.")

Hold on, though, Let us grant that those who determine policy for a station do have the right to express even such noisome ideas as those of Rev. McIntire. What, then, can be wrong with forcing such ownership at least to share its channel with those who oppose its ideas?

Bazelon answers by observing that it is very difficult for a station such as WXUR to be held firmly and continually to the Fairness Doctrine, since "the monitoring procedures which the FCC requires for identification of controversial issues are beyond the capacity of a small staff, or a shoestring operation." This burden of equal time, he added, involves ". . . very critical First Amendment issues indeed. The ratio of 'reply time' required for every issue discussed would have forced WXUR [if the FCC had allowed it to continue, in strict conformity to the Fairness Doctrine] to censor its views—to decrease the number of issues it discussed or to decrease the intensity of its presentation. The ramifications of this chilling effect will be felt by every broadcaster who simply has a lot to say."

A specific example which Judge Bazelon might have cited has to do with a complaint filed with the FCC in 1971 against KREM-TV in Spokane, Wash. The viewer invoking the Fairness Doctrine was Sherwyn M. Hecht, who was irritated by the unfairness, as he saw it, of KREM-TV's failure to provide sufficient air time to those citizens of Spokane opposing a local bond issue to raise money for a projected "Expo '74" undertaking.

Ultimately, on May 17, 1973, the FCC decided that Mr. Hecht's complaint was unwarranted. In the meantime, however, the station had to spend some 480 work-hours of executive and supervisory time satisfying the FCC that it had indeed been fair on that issue. This did not include supporting secretarial or clerical time. As a station official said rather wearily, "This represents a very serious dislocation of regular operational functions and is far more important in that sense than in terms simply of the dollar value of the salaries of those engaged in our self-defense."

That's too bad, an advocate of the Fairness Doctrine would say, but this kind of expense and dislocation is a necessary part of the cost of being a responsible—and responsive—broadcaster. If there is indeed a danger that some small stations might go under because of this financial weight, it could be possible for non-competing stations (stations in different cities) to share expenses in hiring a full-time team of people expert at responding to FCC inquiries.

Dig We Must

In any case, this economic argument against the Fairness Doctrine surely can't apply to metropolitan stations or to the networks. However, Richard Salant, head of CBS News, disagrees. In an interview with writer Fred Powledge for the latter's American Civil Liberties Union report, *The Engineering of Restraint: The Nixon Administration and the Press,* Salant spoke of network economic and dislocation problems inexorably linked to the Fairness Doctrine, no matter which administration is in power: "We get a letter [from the FCC, notifying the network of a complaint from the public] and everybody has to dig. The reporters, the producers of the show, everybody has to dig out stuff and try to reconstruct why they did what they did . . . If nothing else, it takes you away from your work. And when it is the government, through the FCC, moving into areas of program content, the effect is *chilling*. We have more lawyers than we have reporters."

It is when broadcasters, including reporters, argue against the Fairness Doctrine on the ground of its "chilling" effect that we move from matters of economics and personnel disarrangement to a fundamental First Amendment question. As Judge Bazelon emphasized in his dissenting opinion on the FCC's expunging of WXUR, "In the context of broadcasting today, our democratic reliance on a truly informed American public is threatened if the overall effect of the Fairness Doctrine is the very censorship of controversy which it was promulgated to overcome."

Is there evidence of a chilling effect because of the Fairness Doctrine?

Louis Seltzer, president of WCOJ, a 5,000-watt radio station in West Chester, Pa., wrote the American Civil Liberties Union last year in an attempt to persuade it to stop supporting the Doctrine. "The Fairness Doctrine," Seltzer argued, "is *unfair*. As a practical matter, I know that it has served to muzzle this station for 25 years. An example: We aired only one or two [shows] of a well-produced series put out by the Anti-Defamation League of the B'Nai B'Rith on 'the Radical Right.' Why? Simply because airing these programs would open the floodgates to a paranoid response from the 'nut' groups . . . True, we could refuse to run the reply programs on the basis of their patent untruth, but this would cost us a $10,000 lawsuit up to the Supreme Court of the United States, and even then there would be a possibility of losing . . . This station is not small, but it is not that large. We have neither the time nor the money to devote to such Joan-of-Arcian causes."

One obvious response to Mr. Seltzer's words is that the First Amendment exists for the benefit of "nut" groups too, but the point is that he did decide not to run the full series rather than get embroiled in a lawsuit.

A Chilling Balance

Another illustration of the Fairness Doctrine's negative effect was that Cavett show decision. Richard Salant, who on the basis of his doughtily independent record would not, I think, have censored that program, has observed in answer to another request for the kind of "balance" that ABC-TV asked Cavett: "Suppose the English governor had told Tom Paine that he could go ahead and publish all he liked, but at the back of his pamphlets he would have to allow the governor's assistant to publish *his* views to guarantee that the pamphlet had given the other side. That would have preserved Tom's right of free speech, but far from being an implementation of the First Amendment, it would have been just the opposite. You would have to consider it a restriction upon speech, if, in order to print a broadside, Tom Paine had to present not only his own views but also those of someone arguing on the other side."

During the same week in which ABC-TV, in fear of the Fairness Doctrine, exercised prior restraint on Dick Cavett and his four controversial guests, a number of radio stations throughout the country refused to broadcast a new recording by the singing team of Seals & Crofts. The song, *Unborn Child*, argued against abortion. The station executives who censored the song from the public air explained that they did not want the hassle of providing equal time to pro-abortion spokespeople.

A recurring point made by Salant is that the *publicized* examples of station and network self-censorship are only a small percentage of such management decisions which no one ever gets to hear about. "When one's very survival in one's business—broadcasting—depends on licensing by the government; when the penalty for error and for government disagreement is not a fine, but capital punishment [the loss of your operating license], does anybody think for a moment that there are not those who have said, 'Let's skip this one, let's not make waves, let's stay out of trouble'?"

Even in his own organization, Salant, who is more supportive of his investigative reporters than any other network news chief, has "a constant fear that somebody down the line—reporters or producers or somebody—will think 'Gee, we've caused such headaches to management, or to ourselves, in having to dig out all this stuff, when the lawyers come around, I'll play it easy for a while.' " Salant even sent a memorandum to his news staff telling them he considered self-censorship a "high crime."

Salant may not know it, but the memorandum didn't work in all cases. An official at WCBS-TV in New York has said—not for attribution, of course—"Sure, there are enough pressures in this business; who needs trouble from the FCC?"

A classic case of FCC interference with a network news operation began with a complaint by a small but vigorous organization called Accuracy in Media (AIM), accusing NBC-TV of not being fair in its 1972 documentary, *Pensions: The Broken Promise.* AIM told the Federal Communications Commission that the program had been unbalanced, focusing on the deficiencies of private pension plans and not providing equal time to those pension plans that actually do protect the retired worker. The FCC agreed, and in May 1973, wrote NBC: "It does not appear that you have complied with your Fairness Doctrine obligation" to give both sides of controversial issues.

How to Beat the Bland

NBC is appealing that decision, maintaining that if the FCC ruling stands, investigative reporting on television will be markedly curbed. Attorneys for the network have emphasized that "to the extent the FCC staff's opinion requires ever greater accountability to the government itself, it is simply inconsistent with the long history of disassociation and even antagonism that has characterized the relationship between government and press in our country." Television journalists, NBC went on, would be forced "to engage in a kind of thinking and practice which has nothing to do with journalism. It would impose, as well, a variety of other less-obvious sanctions—the inhibiting effect upon television journalists and producers of being obliged to justify to their superiors and to the Commission the work they have done; the immense amount of time required—time better spend in preparing new programming—in preparing a 'defense' to similar charges; the ever-present threat to license renewals inherent in such rulings; and the like. In short, the issue is not alone whether television journalism will be too bland; it is whether it will be free enough not to be bland."

Ironically, in a footnote to its decision affirming the complaint against NBC by Accuracy in Media, the FCC staff had accurately observed that "for years prior to the broadcast of *Pensions,* neither NBC nor the other networks, to the best of our knowledge, had telecast any program dealing extensively with private pensions. There was little discussion in any general circulation print media and [there were] no widely distributed books on the subject. In fact, there was no apparent public discussion, much less controversy, apart from that of a relatively small number of experts, businessmen and government officials who take a professional interest in the subject. There had been hearings in the last Congress on the subject, but NBC was breaking new ground journalistically on a subject about which the public, at that time, had little knowledge.''

So, by way of encouraging new groundbreaking by television journalists, the FCC thereupon demanded that NBC give time to ''the other side.''

Meanwhile, Abraham Kalish, Executive Secretary of Accuracy in Media, wrote a letter to stations affiliated with NBC, reminding them: ''If you carried *Pensions: The Broken Promise* and you have not given your audience a program that showed the other side of the issues, you have not fulfilled your obligation under the Fairness Doctrine. I am sure that you are anxious to fulfill that obligation. NBC may wish . . . regrettably . . . to challenge the FCC on the Fairness Doctrine issue, but it is the licensee, not the network, that *may have this used against him in any challenge to a license renewal*. NBC has an obligation not to play games with your license. We urge you to tell NBC that.'' [Emphasis added.]

Antediluvian Entrepreneurs

The message was well-aimed. As a network correspondent—again, not for attribution—notes, ''All along the line there are individual owners of affiliated stations who are antediluvian, moneymaking, conservative-thinking entrepreneurs. The network sends them something like CBS's *The Selling of the Pentagon* or NBC's *Pensions: The Broken Promise,* and they get very very worried.''

Richard Salant, for attribution, puts it even more starkly: ''The affiliates have the perfect right under the law to turn down everything from the network that they don't want. They can put those of us in news completely out of business by turning the faucet. The government knows it can scare the pants off almost any broadcaster—certainly the affiliates. It takes an awful lot of guts for management to ignore these attacks because they can literally mean station owners will lose their economic life.''

In one of the affidavits included in NBC's petition with the Court of Appeals for the District of Columbia, in its attempt to have the FCC decision on *Pensions* overturned, the network points out that this particular program won the prestigious George Peabody Award for public service in television as ''a shining example of constructive and superlative investigative reporting.'' Furthermore, in March 1973, *Pensions* received a Christopher Award for ''television news calling public attention to a much-neglected social issue.'' In May of that year, there was also a National Headliner Award for the program, followed in June 1973 by a Certificate of Merit of the American Bar Association.

Nonetheless NBC—unlike, let us say, THE NEW YORK TIMES if it had printed a similar report on pensions—has to defend itself against the government. Reuven Frank, an NBC News executive with a remarkable track record for investigative journalism on television, says mordantly that the FCC's decision means that "we in television news must never examine a problem in American life without first ascertaining that we have piled up enough points on the other side—a little bank account of happiness to squander on an area of public concern. Otherwise, we should be overdrawn, and would have to schedule a program in payment of the debt.

"Must I and others charged with the responsibility for documentary programs," Frank continues, "review each proposed subject to see not only if it needs doing and can be done but whether we are *entitled* to do it? Must a search be made each time of the entire history of the network and its programs to determine whether enough has been presented saying there is no problem, so that we can be licensed to do a program saying there is a wee problem after all? Anyone I could hire for this would not be worth having. On the other hand, it will be a boon for travelogues."

David Brinkley adds: "To be found guilty of 'unfairness' for not expressing to the government's satisfaction that most people are not corrupt or that most pensioners are not unhappy is to be judged by standards which simply have nothing to do with journalism."

A Wet Blanket on Boldness

And Bill Monroe, Washington editor of the NBC News' *Today* program, articulates the anxieties of many news broadcasters on other networks and independent stations: "The very knowledge that the obstacle course seen in the *Pensions* ruling exists has an inevitable wet-blanket effect on reporters and producers. The FCC, while speaking for boldness, turns around and punishes those who practice it. It is thoroughly understood in the industry that the most likely outcome of bold journalism is trouble with the FCC: a penalty, amounting to harassment, in the form of an official request for justification, in 10 or 20 days after a program has been aired, that the program is in compliance with the Fairness Doctrine. Any newsman who has seen the effort a broadcast executive and his staff must make to prepare an answer to such an official request can only assume that his boss, as a human being, would have a desire to minimize such official challenges in the future."

Joining in NBC's petition to the Federal District Court was J. Edward Murray, associate editor of the Detroit *Free Press* and a past president of the American Society of Newspaper Editors. By way of example of how inhibiting a fairness doctrine applied to print media would be, Murray says: "Newspapers, including the Detroit *Free Press,* investigate and expose policemen who are on the 'take' in the dope rackets. If an equivalent weight or time must be given to policemen who are not on the 'take,' the whole campaign becomes so unwieldy and pointless as to be useless. Must the good cops get equivalent space with the bad cops?''

As of this writing NBC's case for First Amendment rights for its news staff is still in the courts. "Even if we win," an NBC reporter observes, "you can be sure that the next time someone comes up with an idea for a tough exposé, the brass is going to think quite awhile before it gives us the go-ahead, and then they'll probably impose their own 'fairness doctrine' on us."

Whatever the courts do decide, those who fervently support the Fairness Doctrine continue to argue that broadcast and print journalism cannot be equated because anyone can start a newspaper but radio and television channels are limited. Therefore, there *has* to be government supervision of "fairness." This is a venerable contention, but it no longer is germane to the real world of communications. In his dissenting opinion in the WXUR case, Judge David Bazelon pointed out that as of September 1972, the number of commercial broadcasting stations on the air was 7,458. By contrast, as of Jan. 1, 1971, there were only 1,749 daily newspapers in the country.

"Nearly every American city," Judge Bazelon wrote, "receives a number of different television and radio signals. Radio licenses represent diverse ownership; UHF, local and public broadcasting offer contrast to the three competing networks; neither broadcasting spectrum is completely filled. But out of 1,400 newspaper cities, there are only 15 left with face-to-face competition."

The Cable Revolution

Starting a new daily paper now requires an enormous amount of money and an extraordinary leap into faith. "Who at this time," Justice Douglas asks, "would have the folly to think he could combat *The New York Times* or Denver *Post* by building a new plant and becoming a competitor?" The prospect, in fact, is for fewer rather than more daily newspapers in the years ahead. On the other hand, the already markedly larger number of television choices available to the citizenry is going to increase significantly. "It is predicted," Bazelon observed, "that in perhaps 10 years it will be possible to provide to the television viewer 400 channels; that by 1980 half the nation will be on cable television; and that a host of educational and public services will accompany the cable revolution which are simply mind-boggling. Thus, even now we possess the knowhow necessary to do away with technical scarcity through CATV [cable television]. . . . Is it not a little ironic that we still adhere to our fears of monopoly and limited access? Ought we not instead focus our attention on how we can make the cable medium economically accessible to those who assert a right to use it?''

I would add that those undeniably well-intentioned groups now striving to expand the Fairness Doctrine—thereby unwittingly "chilling" the potential for more controversial broadcast journalism—might better expend their energies in trying to implement the American Civil Liberties Union's conviction that "cable television should be operated on a common-carrier basis. This means channels of the cable service should be open to anyone willing to lease them, just as the telephone lines are open to anyone willing to pay to make a telephone call."

Testifying before the FCC in 1971, Irwin Karp, a member of the ACLU's Communication Media Committee and also attorney for the Authors League and the Authors Guild, stated: "The ACLU believes that the adoption of a common-carrier policy is essential because it will provide a system of communication that fulfills the needs of the First Amendment, avoiding public and private restraints on freedom of expression; and assuring full access to a meaningful marketplace of ideas. The ACLU also believes that a common-carrier approach will provide the greatest diversity of programming and the most efficient service of which the medium is capable."

Keeping in mind the number of channels which can be made available through cable television, there is the further point that—as a recent Rand Corporation study, *New Television Networks,* demonstrates—right now it is possible to "drop in" at least 67 major TV stations in the country's 100 largest urban centers. There are stations that could be seen even if you don't have a cable television. It is not at all fanciful, in sum, that in a decade or so, *TV Guide* will, as a television researcher says, be "as fat as a telephone directory."

The Role Government Should Play

The scarcity argument—that Federal officials have to insure "fairness" in television because there are so few channels—is no longer tenable. Does the government, then, have any legitimate function in television? Sure, says Justice William O. Douglas. It has a duty with regard to television—as it has concerning the printed media—to prevent monopolistic practices. That it has largely failed in this responsibility in relation to newspapers (most recently, through the Newspaper Preservation Act, which gives them limited but substantial exemption from antitrust laws) does not mean that the government ought to abdicate this duty concerning television. If, for example, one group of station owners is a predominant force in a particular region, that ownership should be divested of some of its telecasting facilities.

Federal authorities are also, Justice Douglas notes, responsible for "promoting technological developments that will open up new channels. But censorship or editing or the screening by government of what licensees may broadcast goes against the grain of the First Amendment."

Another necessary function of government is to make sure that channels don't intersect. Seeing to it that Channel 2 in any given city doesn't cut into Channel 4's picture has nothing to do with the First Amendment. In this respect, the government's role is like that of a traffic cop keeping motorists in their proper lanes.

There is also nothing destructive of the First Amendment in the current ef
forts of various groups to see that fair-hiring practices—including equality of
access to broadcasting jobs by minorities and by women—are adhered to by
television stations. That kind of pressure is also being applied to newspapers,
and it is entirely constitutional.

My thesis—that those who would also have the government intervene in
programming to assure "fairness" are wrong headed—has another dimension.
Emboldened by these forays into broadcasters' First Amendment rights, people
who decry the "unfairness" of newspapers are pressing for "access" to print
media.

On Feb. 4, 1974, Senator John McClellan of Arkansas suggested that
Congress consider mandating that newspapers publish the replies of public figures who are attacked. Let the head of *that* camel get into the tents of newspapers and magazines, and those editors who are already timid—and they are not
few—will make sure that their reporters stick to "safe" stories, like "color"
features attendant on the annual Indianapolis Speedway race. In 1972, David
Burnham of *The New York Times* wrote a long, devastating article on police
corruption in New York City—a piece that forced an extremely reluctant Mayor
John V. Lindsay to establish the independent Knapp Commission to dig into
the subject of cops on the "take." Would that story have had nearly as much
impact if the *Times* had been compelled to give equal space and position to a
story quoting the Police Commissioner about how many honest cops there were
on the force? Furthermore, that kind of requirement might well persuade a less
independent newspaper than the *Times* not to publish a story on police corruption in the first place.

Florida's "Right to Reply" Law

There is, in fact, a state law—in Florida—that *does* require newspapers to
print the replies of political candidates to critical editorials. In the fall of 1972,
when Pat L. Tornillo was a candidate in the Democratic primary for the Florida
House of Representatives, The Miami *Herald* referred to Tornillo in an editorial as a "czar" and a lawbreaker who engaged in "illegal acts against the
public trust." A few days later, the newspaper published another editorial
which also considerably annoyed Mr. Tornillo.

The alleged "czar" asked the newspaper to print his rebuttal—verbatim
and free, as the Florida statute permits. The *Herald* refused; a lawsuit followed; and the Florida Supreme Court, reversing a lower court decision, held,
in a highly disturbing 6-1 ruling, that the state "law of reply" is indeed constitutional.

In a brief that asked the United States Supreme Court to reverse the ruling
of the Florida Supreme Court, the American Civil Liberties Union reminded the
nine Justices of a previous statement by one of them, Potter Stewart, that the

Constitution clearly commands "that Government must never be allowed to lay its heavy editorial hand on any newspaper in this country."

Should the Supreme Court uphold the Florida "right of reply" statute,* Sen. McClellan will surely be joined by other legislators in concocting all sorts of "fairness doctrines" to be invoked against print journalism. Justice William O. Douglas, in arguing for full First Amendment rights for television and radio broadcasters (*Columbia Broadcasting System* v. *Democratic National Committee*), has usefully reminded us: "In 1970 Congressman Farbstein introduced a bill, never reported out of the Committee, which provided that any newspaper of general circulation published in a city with a population greater than 25,000, and in which fewer than two separately owned newspapers of general circulation are published, shall provide a reasonable opportunity for a balanced presentation of conflicting views on issues of public importance and giving the Federal Communications Commission power to enforce the requirement."

And Congressman Leonard Farbstein, from New York City, was generally considered a liberal!

With any encouragement from the Supreme Court, such a bill might find it a great deal easier to emerge from committee in 1974 or 1975. In this regard, it is important to remember that not only the Nixon Administration has been given to pressuring the press. As Richard Salant has noted, "We have learned by now that each administration improves on its predecessor in its ability to try to get at us."

Imagine John F. Kennedy's delight, or Lyndon Johnson's, if either had been able to exercise leverage on what newspapers print. Or, for that matter, the delight of Chicago's Mayor Daley or California's Governor Reagan or your own local politician-target of a critical press.

The Damned First Amendment

I am afraid, for further illustration of the vulnerability of the First Amendment, that if a national plebiscite were held now as to whether a "fairness doctrine" similar to the one now operative against radio and television should be applied to newspapers and magazines, the results would be largely in favor of such governmental controls—the First Amendment be damned.

The grail of "fairness" is an enticing one; but unless editors are allowed to edit on the basis of their own judgment—however quirky and infuriating that judgment may be to many citizens—newspapers and magazines will be saddled with a fairness doctrine which, as William O. Douglas says of the doctrine presently imposed on television, "is agreeable to nations that have never known freedom of press and tolerable in countries that do not have a written constitution containing prohibitions as absolute as those in the First Amendment."

* The U.S. Supreme Court unanimously overturned the Florida decisions in a 1974 ruling (Miami Herald v. Tornillo).

Even Chief Justice Warren E. Burger, who believes in the constitutionality of a fairness doctrine for television, is apparently beginning to wonder about what he and the majority of his brethren on the High Court have wrought.

"For better or worse," the Chief Justice said last year, "editing is what editors are for; and editing is selection and choice of material. That editors—newspaper or broadcast—can and do abuse this power is beyond doubt, but that is no reason to deny the discretion Congress provided. Calculated risks of abuse are taken in order to preserve higher values."

Ben Franklin, when he ran a newspaper, put it more bluntly. "My publication," he said, "is not a stagecoach with seats for everyone."

In any case, print journalism, despite its partial redemption in terms of public confidence as a result of Watergate, is not out of danger of government incursion into its First Amendment rights. And the broadcast media are going to have to struggle mightily to shed themselves of what I—and more importantly, to say the least, Justice Douglas—believe to be the unconstitutional Fairness Doctrine. But broadcasters are gradually getting some heretical allies. Most of the "good government" and civil liberties groups are still in favor of the Fairness Doctrine; but in 1973, the research branch of the Association of Trial Lawyers came to the conclusion that "Congress and the courts must return to the First Amendment and apply it for the benefit of all the media . . . Diversity of expression is not to be found in a tightly regulated medium, where fears of censorship, governmental interference, and the possibility of losing one's license reduce creativity to a common blandness, so as not to incur the wrath of the regulator."

Towards Deeper Muckraking

Will television become less bland—at least in its news and documentary divisions—if it is emancipated from the Fairness Doctrine? There are no guarantees, but the strong likelihood (and I speak from many years of coverage of television journalism) is that those with a taste for muckraking—Richard Salant, Reuven Frank, Paul Altmeyer at ABC-TV, and many others—will feel a lot freer to dig a lot deeper.

I asked Richard Salant that question while researching this article. "If we had full First Amendment freedoms," he said, "the benefits to the public would be precisely the same benefits it now receives from the full application of the First Amendment to print journalism. For papers run by timid, lazy or greedy entrepreneurs, the First Amendment may not do a hell of a lot of good. So, too, in broadcasting.

"But at least," Salant added, "no timid broadcast management could cop out on the ground that they might get into Fairness Doctrine problems with the FCC, or risk a lot of lawyers' fees, or even run the danger of losing their license.

"Whether the Fairness Doctrine is a real or an imagined Sword of Damocles—and it's real enough for a lot of broadcast journalists—it also serves as a shield for some broadcasters who want to duck hard investigative reporting. I am persuaded, but obviously cannot yet prove, that the brooding omnipresence of the Fairness Doctrine *does* indeed affect the state of mind of some reporters, some editors, some news executives, if only because they know that if they don't watch out, they're going to have to spend an enormous and unfruitful amount of time and money transcribing old broadcasts and searching them out to provide material for the lawyers who have to respond to complaints and to FCC 20-day letters.''

There can be no concrete proof of how much bolder and braver television journalism may become if it finally is fully protected by the First Amendment, but surely it's an option worth taking, particularly since, as Judge Bazelon emphasizes, ''Most Americans now consider television and radio to be their most important news sources. Broadcast journalists have grown up. They see it as in their interest to be guided by the same professional standards of 'fairness' as the printed press. There is no factual basis for continuing to distinguish the printed word from the electronic press as the true news media.''

And that analysis, I contend, is fair enough—for all.

Roy Danish:

Broadcast Freedom: Is It Still There?

IN AN AGE WHEN the fundamental institutions of our society are vigorously questioned, no public institution can expect to hide quietly in the shadows, protected and inviolate. A truly free society, responsive to the changes brought on by growth, would not allow it.

Television—so visible, so pervasive, so much a part of American life—has drawn, almost from its first flickering, the fire of the right, left and center, of high-brow and low-brow, of the political ''in's'' and the would-be ''in's.'' But today, as the entire society grapples with new problems and often grasps too

Mr. Danish is director of the Television Information Office. This article, from a speech delivered to the Poor Richard Club in Philadelphia Nov. 9, 1971, is reprinted by permission of the Television Information Office.

quickly for simple answers, the assault has escalated. In fact, the basic theory and structure of our industry is clearly threatened.

Five areas are of particular concern to broadcasters: journalism, advertising, program content, access to air-time and the stability of licensees. All five are being reexamined, from both within and without the industry, and that process can be healthy, of course. But there are too many moments when the examiners seem to be using pick-axes instead of stethoscopes.

In those five areas, have we failed so miserably that large-scale attacks are justified?

The public clearly does not think so. Take note of the Roper reports, which show that the majority of Americans trust television news more than news given through any other medium. Take note of viewing statistics, which indicate that the average set is in use over six hours a day—more than ever before. In those evening hours which we refer to as "prime-time," 65 to 70 per cent of the homes in this country have their sets turned on. And look at the sales figures which show that over 12 million new television receivers were bought in 1970 alone.

Are these reactions of a public which is dissatisfied with our performance?

Not even the President of the United States is insensitive to television's tremendous appeal. When he selects prime-time for his most important speeches to the nation, he is careful to avoid conflict with the most popular entertainment offering. No one who needs all the friends he can make would want to face a *Marcus Welby* backlash.

And yet, despite this proven popularity, there are Congressional committees, government agencies, courts and a few citizens' groups who seem to be in hot pursuit of us. Each has an idea of what ideal broadcasting might be and, often, their ideas are valuable. But they are valuable only so long as they are couched as rational suggestions, not as mandates.

Let me take the five areas I have mentioned and outline briefly the dangers we face as an industry and the consequences for our viewers.

First, there is the question of journalism. Of all our problems, it has received the most attention in recent years. And note also that not only television journalism has been threatened; newspapers, which have not always been numbered among our best friends, have certainly found themselves in our corner on this one issue.

It is fitting that they should. We're both being shoved into the same leaky boat. We both fall heir to the prejudice expressed in the following quotation: "A newswriter is a man without virtue who lies. . . . . for his own profit." Long before our Vice President took to the hustings,* those words were written

---

* Mr. Danish's speech, delivered during a time of considerable stress between the Nixon administration and the television industry, contains reference to—among other things—specific areas in which the industry felt the pressures of politically-inspired government campaigns for control sanctions over television news and commentaries. Though *some* threats seemed to have eased by 1975, some had not and the possibilities for recurrence, in any event, may never be far distant. EDITORS.

by the English critic, Samuel Johnson. But if he were alive, we might find his sarcasm supporting our side. Because I think that we, like him, home in toward the truth of the matter. We can't help it. That's the nature of the medium. Inevitably, we puncture pomposity, even when we don't mean to. We show the ugliness beneath a polite lie, or the tragedy that no one is willing to face, simply because of the peculiar nature of the mechanisms through which we work.

But this great achievement is also our most pernicious danger. We can be, we think we are, a powerful instrument for information. In the wrong hands, in the hands of any one interest group or government agency, we could become the most horribly effective medium for propaganda the world has ever known. Believe me, we know the inherent dangers better than anyone else. I want to say quite strongly, we must allow no one to enjoin us from showing the world as it is.

Of course, we make mistakes; we are subject to limitations which are technical and all too human. But we respect the judgment of the average viewer; he is no slave to our errors. At this stage in the development of our art, he has a sophisticated awareness of television techniques. He knows, as well as you and I, what film is and how it can be cut. He can recognize the nuance in the announcer's voice. He is quick to sense what might lie behind the camera's selective eye. And you can be sure he lets us know, loud and clear, when he suspects we are guilty of tampering.

You see, we believe the public will defend itself. Over 1700 daily papers and thousands of weeklies and monthlies are there to protect the viewer against bias—be it wilful or not. And it is obviously in our own best interest to serve the viewer in a manner that he will respect. Even when we fail in that attempt, I cannot believe that the majority of our citizens will stand for any form of censorship of the news. But will we work fast and effectively enough to enlist them in our cause? Most important, can even the American public help us throw off those subtle, unspoken pressures which operate when those high in government drop hints about possible future restrictions?

There are White House staffers who accuse us of paranoia. But even a paranoid might have real enemies. I suggest that we are no more paranoid than those men who sat down in this city and wrote, "Congress shall make no law . . . abridging the freedom of speech, or of the press."

Clay Whitehead, director of the White House's Office of Telecommunications Policy, spoke to a luncheon meeting of the International Radio and Television Society in New York last October. With some feeling, he protested that we in the industry who fear government intervention have saddled the administration with an insulting suspicion of "maliciousness and stupidity."

I can assure you that we are willing to be proved wrong. But we will not rest easy when the FCC hints at new rulings about so-called offensive material. It would take no Constitutional amendment to bring the six o'clock news under that kind of ruling.

Nor can we relax when the Justice Department, Congressional committees and high administration officials move toward actions which would restrict our freedom to explore for information without fear of reprisal. In the last 30 months, for example, ABC, CBS, and NBC have been served with over 170 subpoenas for materials which were not even broadcast. News departments now labor in an atmosphere that CBS Vice Chairman Frank Stanton aptly labels ''a climate of subpoenability.''

In addition, the atmosphere in which broadcast journalists work (and print journalists, too, for that matter) has been clouded since the Vice President added the criticism of reporting to his other duties. Like every other citizen, Mr. Agnew has the right to be critical. But unlike those who do not share the power of high national office, he can have a very special impact when he suggests a visit to the woodshed. Television broadcasters are licensed by the federal government; Federal Communications Commissioners are appointed by the White House.

Certainly, as an individual and as a political partisan, the Vice President is bound to be upset by some of the news he hears and sees and reads. No one who holds strong views or has firmly-rooted attitudes about public matters can be unaffected by an instance of reporting which seems to undermine his positions or beliefs. But it is true of free journalism that in time it will rub each of us the wrong way. And we remember what irritates or angers us far longer than what pleases us.

In the last analysis, the over-riding obligation of journalism is to serve the citizen's right and need to know what is happening. Competition among networks and stations and the other voices of a free press is the best guarantee that all of us will be fairly served. Because today's ''in's'' may be tomorrow's ''out's,'' it would be tragic if our news media swung with the pendulum of political change. The low esteem in which government-guided journalism is held in other countries is ample warning to us.

Should we ever encounter widespread public distrust of the broadcast journalist, this nation would face a potentially dangerous situation: the broadcast journalist's loss of credibility. With it would be lost the most popular medium of information exchange—and not just between broadcaster and viewer, but between government and viewer, as well. As happened with French television under De Gaulle, few would believe its news content and government handouts would be as suspect as all other kinds of news. Those who would contribute to this doubt by intemperate and ill-considered public outbursts issued from seats of authority are undermining, inadvertently or not, the free flow of information and ideas. Responsible leaders will see the value, the necessity, of an unhampered press, even when their own oxen are gored. Whatever its excesses or mistakes, the free system of broadcasting is infinitely preferable to the controlled one.

Surely, the point is non-debatable. And that is all the more reason, if there are still those who don't understand it why we have reacted with shock and outrage to this recent rash of officially-sanctioned harassment.

A second major area of concern is advertising. And it is not improper product claims or deceptive demonstrations that hold the center stage. The occasional excesses which sometimes slip through the continuity acceptance screens have been joined by a formidable newcomer: the so-called controversial spot announcement. And here, the word "controversial" has the same meaning as it does when the FCC's Fairness Doctrine is brought into play by news programs or documentaries.

Take a most recent case in point. An advertisement for a large automobile brought on a request for free time to criticize large cars because they are presumed to be more likely to pollute the air than smaller cars—or no cars at all. The FCC rejected the complaint on the grounds that the Fairness Doctrine was not intended to apply to product commercials. But, when the case was brought to the D. C. Court of Appeals, that body ruled against the FCC decision. Unless further FCC proceedings produce a different rule, the broadcaster appears obligated to provide time for what are in effect anti-product commercials or programs—and at no cost for that time.

This is a direct extension of the principle that the FCC first applied to cigarette advertising in a decision that was labelled by the FCC as unique, one which was meant to set no general precedent. But, the Appeals Court used it as the precise precedent for its decision in the matter of the large car.

Think for a moment of all the product advertising that might be used as a springboard for similar requests for free antiproduct commercials. Whoever looks to advertising to market merchandise or services is apt to disappear through Alice's looking glass. And so, I'm afraid, will we in broadcasting. Our objection is not to consumer criticism, but to misguided and over-zealous government attempts to answer that criticism. We worry about the temptations for a government agency to justify its own existence at the expense of ours.

Meanwhile, the current Federal Trade Commission hearings on advertising give promise of producing guidelines—the kindest word I can think of—which may alter all our conceptions of what we can properly do to promote perfectly acceptable, useful products. These guidelines would rest on the basic premise that because some advertisers have overstated their claims, it is likely that all will do the same.

This is not a happy relationship between a government and its citizens.

But the presumption of prior guilt is a small thing in comparison with the implications of a recent decision by that same D.C. Court of Appeals. With a ruling that combines the Fairness Doctrine and the newest concepts of another area of concern—access to airtime—the court, in a very real sense, encourages us to incriminate ourselves while, simultaneously, we leave ourselves open to the penalties.

This is how it works, and let me emphasize again, we are dealing with no Orwellian fantasy, but with fact. In this case, separate rulings by separate bodies combine to hamstring us. First, the FCC, under the Fairness Doctrine, has held that when a station presents one viewpoint on a controversial public issue, the public interest requires that reasonable opportunity be afforded for the presentation of opposing viewpoints. Taking a step further and, we feel, off course, the D.C. Court of Appeals has ruled that a broadcaster may not have a policy which excludes all paid "editorial advertisements" setting forth partisan viewpoints on public issues.

You can see the point. We can be forced to sell air-time, regardless of the completeness and balance of our own news coverage, to a group that approaches us. And by so doing, we can, in turn, be forced to provide time, free of charge, to that group's opponent or, as in most cases, to many opponents. Just consider the possible consequences of provocation, response and counter-response, ad infinitum—with the broadcaster trapped on a treadmill he could not escape.

Ironically, these trends do not result from the insidious actions of stupid or vengeful men. On the contrary, the nine jurists of the D.C. Court of Appeals are regarded by most as distinguished and scholarly. But, as in other areas of public life these days, power has somehow shifted from one branch of the government to another. The imbalance could be dangerous; it has already been detrimental. As one lawyer has said about the court, "These guys second-guess the Commission. They've been called upon to act in so many broadcasting cases that now they substitute their own philosophies, instead of just ruling whether the FCC acted within its discretion."

Our third problem is program content control. What will happen when such a slippery issue is thrust into this gray area of vague and conflicting regulation? There will be chaos, for there is no common agreement on the rights of the broadcaster, the responsibilities of the FCC and the scope within which the courts should operate. Ideally, these three forces should work as a single system of checks and balances, but this has not happened.

One example of what we face is the very real possibility that the FCC will decide to impose stringent controls on children's programming. Under pressure from a Boston group known as ACT, the FCC has under consideration a plan which, in itself and in its implications, would bring us close to total economic breakdown. ACT has proposed that all television outlets in the nation devote two hours of each day to commercial-free programming for children. We are being asked to move from the field of commercial broadcasting and to sustain the full costs of specifically and narrowly defined non-commercial, educational programming, while at the same time we forego the prospect of revenue for a substantial portion of each day. In addition, it is proposed that we be "encouraged" to improve the quality of children's programs. I like that word, "encouraged." Coming from the agency which licenses all our activities, it has a certain solid ring.

But we first ask, who will be the judges? Already, that agency has hired two children's experts, and you can readily infer the possibilities.

I wonder if they are aware of the economic track record of so-called quality programming for youngsters, for it is dismal, indeed. One of the most highly respected of such programs, *Captain Kangaroo,* lost CBS millions of dollars in its early years. One network, after two years of concerted efforts to experiment with the introduction of critically respected programming, is still licking its wounds.

And this should be no surprise, if we realize that children, like their parents, tend to use television as a medium of entertainment. Although we have been accused of being pernicious taste-makers, of corrupting the child, it is now obvious that we have no such power. Clearly, we cannot demand their attention. Programs like *Take a Giant Step* or *Curiosity Shop* or *You Are There* must make their own way in attracting young viewers.

Other new programming is on the air or in the planning stage. Although these programs are designed to combine learning with entertainment, they will, like all programs, sometimes succeed and sometimes fail. If the ACT proposal is rejected, the revenues attracted by the programs children like will pay for the losses of the failures. Each new effort promises greater diversity, but for many youngsters, pure entertainment has stronger appeal and who is to say they should have no choice in the matter?

This subject bumps us directly into our fourth area of major concern—public access to air-time. It is a concept which finds some legal justification in the Fairness Doctrine and, on paper, it does not sound unreasonable. When a station airs an editorial on a topic of general community concern, the FCC requires that the qualified representative for an opposing point of view be given time to reply. Further, in accordance with one of the fourteen programming guidelines laid down by the FCC, and also because it makes good sense to do so, television broadcasters devote several hours a week to public affairs programs. Some may be political in nature; most deal with broader topics.

It is not this concept with which we disagree. But we do fear the tendency toward regulation which would force us to give away so much air-time that we could no longer function as a commercial medium. And you must believe that I am not creating a straw man, as you will see if we go a further step beyond the ACT proposal for children's programs. At its heart is the demand that government formally mandate the number of hours that are to be programmed for a special category of viewers—in this case, children. But why not mandate additional hours to serve the special needs of other large and apparently homogeneous groups? Why not for certain ethnic groups, or the elderly, or for religious and charitable movements which can claim a wide membership, or for political parties?

Divide the society by age and persuasion, by race and belief, and you find a myriad of large, responsible groupings. Can we give each an hour of prime-time programming? Of course not. Not if there is to be an economic base to support the general entertainment and information programming that prompted viewers to buy their sets in the first place. After all, how many advertisers can afford the outlay necessary for a national hook-up when they are asked to sponsor a program which will only reach a narrowly self-selected portion of the total viewing audience?

If all four problems I have discussed are taken together, however, they fall short of the most pressing of all. Put simply, it is this: how long can a licensee hope to retain his privilege to broadcast? The road has become rockier every day since the 1960's. The days when a station's renewal hinged on its fulfillment of the promises in its license application seem ancient history.

Today no licensee, regardless of how conscientiously he has served his community, can approach license renewal time with complete confidence. Instead, he may find himself in contest with special interest groups who want to strip him of his license for any of a growing number of reasons. These range from allegations of unfair hiring practices and criticisms of program schedules to demands for program control by non-broadcasters who often represent only a handful of dissenters.

The D.C. Court of Appeals, reversing years of FCC precedent which recognized the merits of past performance, has said that a licensee's record of service gives him only questionable advantage against the promises of contesting applicants. And as the FCC wrestles with the renewal problem once again, what is the position of the licensee? Should he make long-term commitments for needed physical facilities? Is he best advised to try to drain maximum profits during his three-year license term and then take his much-diminished chances to get a renewal? Should he change his promises at each renewal date to please the tastes of a constantly changing FCC? (His competitors for the channel are *certain* to do just that.)

It now appears to most of us in broadcasting that our hope for clearer answers lies with the Congress itself. It was in Congress that the words "interest, convenience and necessity" were written to describe the basic elements in proper broadcast services. And we must look to that body for recognition of a simple principle: good performance, ·promised and delivered, should be rewarded with renewal.

The recital of mutations you have heard today is the clearest illustration of how slippery an over-simplified Congressional mandate can become. After 50 years of broadcasting experience, a firmer and fairer yardstick is needed, and needed immediately.

Let me stress that what is at stake here is not simply the station owner's reasonable wish to continue in an exciting and responsible and usually profitable business. After all, his success as a broadcaster hinges on his capacity to meet the needs and desires of viewers, if for no other reason than that no television broadcaster is a monopolist. For example, according to A. C. Nielsen Company: 97 per cent of U.S. television households can receive at least 3 signals, 79 per cent can receive 5 signals, 53 per cent can receive 7 and 26 per cent can receive 9 signals.

Given this highly competitive marketplace, what the television broadcaster requires most is elbow room to make the judgments his experience dictates. Unreasonable encroachments on this flexibility will inevitably lead to a loss of audience attention and advertising revenue. Flowing from these, there will obviously be need for adjustments to maintain economic stability. Just how each broadcaster will accommodate himself to the need for change is, of course, unpredictable. But, inevitably, both at the network and local levels, resources available for programming will shrink and the net result cannot help but be reflected in diminished service to viewers.

Today, the industry can bear the operational and monetary strains that fast-breaking news events impose. Television programs of special interest and high cost can be offered without hope of profit. But will that be true if the economic base of the medium is sharply narrowed? I seriously doubt it. In study after study, viewers by a margin of 8 to 1 say they consider the presentation of commercials a fair price to pay for the programs they watch. They have come to expect, and with good reason, that no important news event will go uncovered by television—whether it be a moon shot, a Pope's visit, or a Presidential address. For these viewers, the threat is very simple—less, perhaps much less of what they now enjoy.

In the five major areas I have mentioned, we are facing proposals which would radically alter the present concept of commercial television. They are discriminatory, because no one has moved in this manner to restrict the performances of the other media. They are counter-productive, because they do not lead toward the increased pleasure or enrichment of the vast audience of viewers we now serve. They are anti-democratic, because they would bring about increased government control of an industry which is healthiest when it must sail through the winds of change in public opinion and public taste and public need.

Take these proposals, piece them together, and look at the picture. Perhaps you'll see what former Federal Communications Commissioner Lee Loevinger did.

He has studied the trends toward government control of broadcasting and has offered a jolting prediction, the possibility of a FEDCAST. As he puts it, FEDCAST would be "the federal corporation set up to take over the operation of all commercial broadcasting stations after their economic viability has been destroyed by federal rules choking off advertising, and their freedom of programming has been constricted to the scope desired by those in control of the FCC."

As you can see, trouble is here and more seems to lie ahead. We want you to know it. We want you to understand.

In five areas that involved the basic elements of broadcasting, government is telling us what we can do, but this control extends through our industry to the American people—and, in effect, it is their lives which are regulated when our freedom is restricted. For they will be told what they can see and hear on the news, what they can see and hear in entertainment, what opinions they can hear on the air, what products they can be sold on the air, and what kind of performance will be demanded—presumably in their behalf, if not to their tastes—from the broadcasters who serve them.

As Walter Cronkite said at a recent Senate hearing, our "freedom has been curtailed by fiat, by assumption and by intimidation and harassment.'' He is an experienced and fair-minded man, as you know. And it is to his statement that our problems come home. They merge at this simple concept—the freedom of the responsible broadcaster to serve the public on the public's own terms.

Our course is clear, but we need the cooperation of men and women who work in advertising and marketing and other media, just as we need fair-minded appraisals from the regulatory agencies, and just as surely as we need, and sincerely want, the active discussion of enlightened viewers among the general public. And if we do not succeed, if we cannot gain the support of concerned citizens who believe in the basic concept of a free broadcasting system operating within a free society, if we cannot count on the good will of elected officials, independent commercial broadcasting will disappear from the scene.

It won't be murder by conspiracy. It will just happen, as the worst things can happen, because several actions taken in several places will suddenly come together, almost by chance—but no less disastrously for the lack of ill will and malicious intent. It will happen because we did not state our case loudly and clearly enough or because no one listened.

If I have persuaded you that we have a common stake in maintenance of free and self-supporting television broadcasting, what can you do?

Certainly those of you who are involved in the production and distribution of consumer products can work singly and through your business organizations to make your concerns known to Congress. Television has served most of you well; if its capacity to inform about legitimate goods and services should be diminished, so, too, will be your effectiveness as a part of the marketing system.

If you are in publishing, whether as businessman or journalist, the long-range implications of the threats to one mass medium must be clear to you. The First Amendment protection we now enjoy was fought for in the courts during our own Hundred Years' War against censorship. What was gained can be lost—and not just to us, but to the people whose right to know we serve. Use the medium you work in to make your readers and their representatives aware of the threats we face.

If you have no direct interest in media or distribution or advertising, you still have great self-interest in the television and radio stations, and in the newspapers and magazines that entertain and inform you in accordance with your needs. If legislation or regulation should whittle away their freedom and economic stability, you, like every other American, will surely be the loser. I urge you to look for opportunities to let your own views be heard among your friends, associates and public officials.

Let me say, again and finally, that I beg your support. Please join with us, lend us your influence, plead our cause because I am asking you, simply, to head off the dangers that threaten some of our basic American freedoms.

Aldous Huxley:

The Arts of Selling

THE SURVIVAL of democracy depends on the ability of large numbers of people to make realistic choices in the light of adequate information. A dictatorship, on the other hand, maintains itself by censoring or distorting the facts, and by appealing, not to reason, not to enlightened self-interest, but to passion and prejudice, to the powerful "hidden forces," as Hitler called them, present in the unconscious depths of every human mind.

In the West, democratic principles are proclaimed and many able and conscientious publicists do their best to supply electors with adequate information and to persuade them, by rational argument, to make realistic choices in the light of that information. All this is greatly to the good. But unfortunately propaganda in the Western democracies, above all in America, has two faces and a divided personality. In charge of the editorial department there is often a democratic Dr. Jekyll—a propagandist who would be very happy to prove that John Dewey had been right about the ability of human nature to respond to truth and reason. But this worthy man controls only a part of the machinery of mass communication. In charge of advertising we find an anti-democratic, because anti-rational, Mr. Hyde—or rather a Dr. Hyde, for Hyde is now a Ph.D. in psychology and has a master's degree as well in the social sciences. This Dr. Hyde would be very unhappy indeed if everybody always lived up to John Dewey's faith in human nature. Truth and reason are Jekyll's affair, not his. Hyde is a motivation analyst, and his business is to study human weaknesses and failings, to investigate those unconscious desires and fears by which so much of men's conscious thinking and overt doing is determined. And he does this, not in the spirit of the moralist who would like to make people better, or of the physician who would like to improve their health, but simply in order to find out the best way to take advantage of their ignorance and to exploit their irrationality for the pecuniary benefit of his employers. But after all, it may be argued, "capitalism is dead, consumerism is king"—and consumerism requires the services of expert salesmen versed in all the arts (including the more insidi-

A. Huxley (1894–1963) was born in England and died in California. He was a writer and journalist of great versatility and international reputation. This article is reprinted here from his *Brave New World Revisited*. Copyright © 1958 by Aldous Huxley. By permission of Harper & Row, Publishers, Inc.

ous arts) of persuasion. Under a free enterprise system commercial propaganda by any and every means is absolutely indispensable. But the indispensable is not necessarily the desirable. What is demonstrably good in the sphere of economics may be far from good for men and women as voters or even as human beings. An earlier, more moralistic generation would have been profoundly shocked by the bland cynicism of the motivation analysts. Today we read a book like Mr. Vance Packard's *The Hidden Persuaders,* and are more amused than horrified, more resigned than indignant. Given Freud, given Behaviorism, given the mass producer's chronically desperate need for mass consumption, this is the sort of thing that is only to be expected. But what, we may ask, is the sort of thing that is to be expected in the future? Are Hyde's activities compatible in the long run with Jekyll's? Can a campaign in favor of rationality be successful in the teeth of another and even more vigorous campaign in favor of irrationality? These are questions which, for the moment, I shall not attempt to answer, but shall leave hanging, so to speak, as a backdrop to our discussion of the methods of mass persuasion in a technologically advanced democratic society.

The task of the commercial propagandist in a democracy is in some ways easier and in some ways more difficult than that of a political propagandist employed by an established dictator or a dictator in the making. It is easier inasmuch as almost everyone starts out with a prejudice in favor of beer, cigarettes and iceboxes, whereas almost nobody starts out with a prejudice in favor of tyrants. It is more difficult inasmuch as the commercial propagandist is not permitted, by the rules of his particular game, to appeal to the more savage instincts of his public. The advertiser of dairy products would dearly love to tell his readers and listeners that all their troubles are caused by the machinations of a gang of godless international margarine manufacturers, and that it is their patriotic duty to march out and burn the oppressors' factories. This sort of thing, however, is ruled out, and he must be content with a milder approach. But the mild approach is less exciting than the approach through verbal or physical violence. In the long run, anger and hatred are self-defeating emotions. But in the short run they pay high dividends in the form of psychological and even (since they release large quantities of adrenalin and noradrenalin) physiological satisfaction. People may start out with an initial prejudice against tyrants; but when tyrants or would-be tyrants treat them to adrenalin-releasing propaganda about the wickedness of their enemies—particularly of enemies weak enough to be persecuted—they are ready to follow him with enthusiasm. In his speeches Hitler kept repeating such words as "hatred," "force," "ruthless," "crush," "smash"; and he would accompany these violent words with even more violent gestures. He would yell, he would scream, his veins would swell, his face would turn purple. Strong emotion (as every actor and dramatist knows) is in the highest degree contagious. Infected by the malignant frenzy of the orator, the audience would groan and sob and scream in an orgy of uninhibited passion. And these orgies were so enjoyable that most of those who had experienced them eagerly came back for more. Almost all of us long for peace and freedom; but very few of us have much enthusiasm for the thoughts, feelings and actions that make for peace and freedom. Conversely almost nobody wants war or tyranny; but a great many people find an intense pleasure in the thoughts, feelings and actions that make for war and tyranny. These thoughts, feelings and actions are too dangerous to be exploited for commercial purposes. Accepting this handicap, the advertising man must do the best he can with the less intoxicating emotions, the quieter forms of irrationality.

Effective rational propaganda becomes possible only when there is a clear understanding, on the part of all concerned, of the nature of symbols and of their relations to the things and events symbolized. Irrational propaganda depends for its effectiveness on a general failure to understand the nature of symbols. Simple-minded people tend to equate the symbol with what it stands for, to attribute to things and events some of the qualities expressed by the words in terms of which the propagandist has chosen, for his own purposes, to talk about them. Consider a simple example. Most cosmetics are made of lanolin, which is a mixture of purified wool fat and water beaten up into an emulsion. This emulsion has many valuable properties: it penetrates the skin, it does not become rancid, it is mildly antiseptic and so forth. But the commercial propagandists do not speak about the genuine virtues of the emulsion. They give it some picturesquely voluptuous name, talk ecstatically and misleadingly about feminine beauty and show pictures of gorgeous blondes nourishing their tissues with skin food. "The cosmetic manufacturers," one of their number has written, "are not selling lanolin, they are selling hope." For this hope, this fraudulent implication of a promise that they will be transfigured, women will pay ten or twenty times the value of the emulsion which the propagandists have so skilfully related, by means of misleading symbols, to a deep-seated and almost universal feminine wish—the wish to be more attractive to members of the opposite sex. The principles underlying this kind of propaganda are extremely simple. Find some common desire, some widespread unconscious fear or anxiety; think out some way to relate this wish or fear to the product you have to sell; then build a bridge of verbal or pictorial symbols over which your customer can pass from fact to compensatory dream, and from the dream to the illusion that your product, when purchased, will make the dream come true. "We no longer buy oranges, we buy vitality. We do not buy just an auto, we buy prestige." And so with all the rest. In toothpaste, for example, we buy, not a mere cleanser and antiseptic, but release from the fear of being sexually repulsive. In vodka and whisky we are not buying a protoplasmic poison which, in small doses, may depress the nervous system in a psychologically valuable way; we are buying friendliness and good fellowship, the warmth of Dingley Dell and the brilliance of the Mermaid Tavern. With our laxatives we buy the health of a Greek god, the radiance of one of Diana's nymphs. With the monthly best seller we acquire culture, the envy of our less literate neighbors and the respect of the sophisticated. In every case the motivation analyst has found some deep-seated wish or fear, whose energy can be used to move the consumer to part with cash and so, indirectly, to turn the wheels of industry. Stored in the minds and bodies of countless individuals, this potential energy is released by, and transmitted along, a line of symbols carefully laid out so as to bypass rationality and obscure the real issue.

Sometimes the symbols take effect by being disproportionately impressive, haunting and fascinating in their own right. Of this kind are the rites and pomps of religion. These "beauties of holiness" strengthen faith where it already exists and, where there is no faith, contribute to conversion. Appealing, as they do, only to the aesthetic sense, they guarantee neither the truth nor the ethical value of the doctrines with which they have been, quite arbitrarily, associated. As a matter of plain historical fact, the beauties of holiness have often been matched and indeed surpassed by the beauties of unholiness. Under Hitler, for example, the yearly Nuremberg rallies were masterpieces of ritual and theatrical art. "I had spent six years in St. Petersburg before the war in the best days of the old Russian ballet," writes Sir Neville Henderson, the British ambassador to Hitler's Germany, "but for grandiose beauty I have never seen any ballet to compare with the Nuremberg rally." One thinks of Keats—"beauty is truth, truth beauty." Alas, the identity exists only on some ultimate, supramundane level. On the levels of politics and theology, beauty is perfectly compatible with nonsense and tyranny. Which is very fortunate; for if beauty were incompatible with nonsense and tyranny, there would be precious little art in the world. The masterpieces of painting, sculpture and architecture were produced as religious or political propaganda, for the greater glory of a god, a government or a priesthood. But most kings and priests have been despotic and all religions have been riddled with superstition. Genius has been the servant of tyranny and art has advertised the merits of the local cult. Time, as it passes, separates the good art from the bad metaphysics. Can we learn to make this separation, not after the event, but while it is actually taking place? That is the question.

In commercial propaganda the principle of the disproportionately fascinating symbol is clearly understood. Every propagandist has his Art Department, and attempts are constantly being made to beautify the billboards with striking posters, the advertising pages of magazines with lively drawings and photographs. There are no masterpieces; for masterpieces appeal only to a limited audience, and the commercial propagandist is out to captivate the majority. For him, the ideal is a moderate excellence. Those who like this not too good, but sufficiently striking, art may be expected to like the products with which it has been associated and for which it symbolically stands.

Another disproportionately fascinating symbol is the Singing Commercial. Singing Commercials are a recent invention; but the Singing Theological and the Singing Devotional—the hymn and the psalm—are as old as religion itself. Singing Militaries, or marching songs, are coeval with war, and Singing Patriotics, the precursors of our national anthems, were doubtless used to promote group solidarity, to emphasize the distinction between "us" and "them," by the wandering bands of paleolithic hunters and food gatherers. To most people music is intrinsically attractive. Moreover, melodies tend to ingrain themselves in the listener's mind. A tune will haunt the memory during the whole of a lifetime. Here, for example, is a quite uninteresting statement or value judgment. As it stands nobody will pay attention to it. But now set the words to a catchy and easily remembered tune. Immediately they become words of power. Moreover, the words will tend automatically to repeat themselves every time the melody is heard or spontaneously remembered. Orpheus has entered into an alliance with Pavlov—the power of sound with the conditioned reflex. For the commercial propagandist, as for his colleagues in the fields of politics and religion, music possesses yet another advantage. Nonsense which it would be shameful for a reasonable being to write, speak or hear spoken can be sung or listened to by that same rational being with pleasure and even with a kind of intellectual conviction. Can we learn to separate the pleasure of singing or of listening to song from the all too human tendency to believe in the propaganda which the song is putting over? That again is the question.

Thanks to compulsory education and the rotary press, the propagandist has been able, for many years past, to convey his messages to virtually every adult in every civilized country. Today, thanks to radio and television, he is in the happy position of being able to communicate even with unschooled adults and not yet literate children.

Children, as might be expected, are highly susceptible to propaganda. They are ignorant of the world and its ways, and therefore completely unsuspecting. Their critical faculties are undeveloped. The youngest of them have not yet reached the age of reason and the older ones lack the experience on which their new-found rationality can effectively work. In Europe, conscripts used to be playfully referred to as "cannon fodder." Their little brothers and sisters have now become radio fodder and television fodder. In my childhood we were taught to sing nursery rhymes and, in pious households, hymns. Today the little ones warble the Singing Commercials. Which is better—"Rheingold is my beer, the dry beer," or "Hey diddle-diddle, the cat and the fiddle"? "Abide with me" or "You'll wonder where the yellow went, when you brush your teeth with Pepsodent"? Who knows?

"I don't say that children should be forced to harass their parents into buying products they've seen advertised on television, but at the same time I cannot close my eyes to the fact that it's being done every day." So writes the star of one of the many programs beamed to a juvenile audience. "Children," he adds, "are living, talking records of what we tell them every day." And in due course these living, talking records of television commercials will grow up, earn money and buy the products of industry. "Think," writes Mr. Clyde Miller ecstatically, "think of what it can mean to your firm in profits if you can condition a million or ten million children, who will grow up into adults trained to buy your products, as soldiers are trained in advance when they hear the trigger words, Forward March!'' Yes, just think of it! And at the same time remember that the dictators and the would-be dictators have been thinking about this sort of thing for years, and that millions, tens of millions, hundreds of millions of children are in process of growing up to buy the local despot's ideological product and, like well-trained soldiers, to respond with appropriate behavior to the trigger words implanted in those young minds by the despot's propagandists.

Self-government is in inverse ratio to numbers. The larger the constituency, the less the value of any particular vote. When he is merely one of millions, the individual elector feels himself to be impotent, a negligible quantity. The candidates he has voted into office are far away, at the top of the pyramid of power. Theoretically they are the servants of the people; but in fact it is the servants who give orders and the people, far off at the base of the great pyramid, who must obey. Increasing population and advancing technology have resulted in an increase in the number and complexity of organizations, an increase in the amount of power concentrated in the hands of officials and a corresponding decrease in the amount of control exercised by electors, coupled with a decrease in the public's regard for democratic procedures. Already weakened by the vast impersonal forces at work in the modern world, democratic institutions are now being undermined from within by the politicians and their propagandists.

Human beings act in a great variety of irrational ways, but all of them seem to be capable, if given a fair chance, of making a reasonable choice in the light of available evidence. Democratic institutions can be made to work only if all concerned do their best to impart knowledge and to encourage rationality. But today, in the world's most powerful democracy, the politicians and their propagandists prefer to make nonsense of democratic procedures by appealing almost exclusively to the ignorance and irrationality of the electors. ''Both parties,'' we were told in 1956 by the editor of a leading business journal, ''will merchandize their candidates and issues by the same methods that business has developed to sell goods. These include scientific selection of appeals and planned repetition. . . . Radio spot announcements and ads will repeat phrases with a planned intensity. Billboards will push slogans of proven power. . . . Candidates need, in addition to rich voices and good diction, to be able to look 'sincerely' at the TV camera.''

The political merchandisers appeal only to the weaknesses of voters, never to their potential strength. They make no attempt to educate the masses into becoming fit for self-government; they are content merely to manipulate and exploit them. For this purpose all the resources of psychology and the social sciences are mobilized and set to work. Carefully selected samples of the electorate are given ''interviews in depth.'' These interviews in depth reveal the unconscious fears and wishes most prevalent in a given society at the time of an election. Phrases and images aimed at allaying or, if necessary, enhancing these fears, at satisfying these wishes, at least symbolically, are then chosen by the experts, tried out on readers and audiences, changed or improved in the light of the information thus obtained. After which the political campaign is ready for the mass communicators. All that is now needed is money and a candidate who can be coached to look "sincere." Under the new dispensation, political principles and plans for specific action have come to lose most of their importance. The personality of the candidate and the way he is projected by the advertising experts are the things that really matter.

In one way or another, as vigorous he-man or kindly father, the candidate must be glamorous. He must also be an entertainer who never bores his audience. Inured to television and radio, that audience is accustomed to being distracted and does not like to be asked to concentrate or make a prolonged intellectual effort. All speeches by the entertainer-candidate must therefore be short and snappy. The great issues of the day must be dealt with in five minutes at the most—and preferably (since the audience will be eager to pass on to something a little livelier than inflation or the H-bomb) in sixty seconds flat. The nature of oratory is such that there has always been a tendency among politicians and clergymen to over-simplify complex issues. From a pulpit or a platform even the most conscientious of speakers finds it very difficult to tell the whole truth. The methods now being used to merchandise the political candidate as though he were a deodorant positively guarantee the electorate against ever hearing the truth about anything.

George N. Gordon:

The Making of a Consumer

THE CONTEMPORARY art of salesmanship is an ever-acute and significant manifestation of American genius. Without its present development, it is doubtful, to this writer at least, that either technology, invention, contemporary education or popular democracy might have functioned as efficiently as they have during our short history, granting, of course, their many and serious imperfections.

Dr. Gordon is Director of the Communications Center, Hofstra University. This article is reprinted by permission from his *Persuasion: The Theory and Practice of Manipulative Communication* (New York: Hastings House, Publishers, © 1971).

Most economists grudgingly agree that our peculiar (and sometimes apparently irrational) methods of marketing, sales and advertising are as important as any other factors in the function of the contemporary technological state. At least, few of them would be willing arbitrarily to recommend that these methods be severely modified without sounding dire warnings of possible devastating economic results. Their trepidations might be greatest in the matter of advertising where cause and effects and mechanistic relationships between output and public behavior are difficult to analyze and predict with precision.

The institution of advertising has had a curious social history and occupies a colorful corner of American cultural life. Words like "schizoid" and "ambivalent" may fairly be applied to general attitudes towards it in all of its manifestations. Commercial persuasion—the essence of most advertising—emerges so obviously and deterministically from the growth of competitive industry, the accumulation of personal wealth, mass production and modern materialism that one might expect it to be as broadly accepted—and acceptable—in a culture like ours, as sewers, traffic lights and roadways. Yet, advertising has been, and is, a topic of continual social controversy and literary exploitation about which feelings run high. Some years ago, at the end of a broadcast concerning advertising hosted by the writer, one of the then most respected consultants in the advertising industry noted aloud, "I have never been able to figure out why advertising, that devotes itself to selling other people's wares, has about the worst image of any industry in the country!"

Advertising and Morals

For all of his experience, he need not have wondered. The history of his own profession provides answers, not necessarily justified or rational, but answers nevertheless.[1]

First, advertising of some sort has almost always been intimately related to trade and commerce, neither of which, from the beginnings of mercantilism, ranked high in the strata of respectable occupations in the West, until the heroes of invention and production, like Thomas A. Edison and Henry Ford, began to capture the fancy of the public at the beginning of the twentieth century. Politics, education, warfare and medicine were socially acceptable. Business, unless it was carried on under the guise of statesmanship or philanthropy, was fit for Jews, the uneducated, the gross and uncultivated who had neither the time nor inclination to participate in better facets of Culture. Even such recent developments as the opening of the Harvard Graduate School of Business after World War I did little to improve a stereotype that had associated money-changing with usurers, factories with exploiters, and counting-houses with Scrooges.

Second, advertising could not claim even the status that business itself assumed (in the words of its own enthusiasts) because, apparently, it produced nothing: neither tangible goods nor significant consumer services. True, it did employ people, circulate currency, help to defray publishing costs, and provide the market with rough and capricious schedules of available items and reasonable prices, but its exact relationship to the marketplace was never clear—nor is it to this day. How many times has the statement been made (attributed to John Wanamaker, Lord Leverhulme and others) that "three-quarters of the money I spend on advertising is wasted, but I'll be damned if I know which three-quarters!"

Advertising's reputation for wind merchantry has been compounded in many ways. It is, for instance, axiomatic among most students of our current society that *all* consumer goods, if they are to be distributed to a national market and succeed in capturing the public's fancy, *must* advertise or fail in the market. Yet, the single exception to this rule is to some breathtaking. Aside from a short time during World War II (and for reasons having nothing to do with merchandizing), the Hershey chocolate bar has never been advertised via any instrument of mass communication, in any manner, in the United States.[2] Brilliant advertising strategies, like the scientific analyses that preceded the birth of the Edsel, have failed in odd ways, and in the face of much generally accepted advertising mythology.[3]

Rules, laws and stratagems of advertising all admit of exceptions and provide an impression that caprice and charlatanry run rampant in the profession, and that, in the absence of hard-core production imperatives and irrefutable marketing tests (the best of which are presently equivocal), the advertising industry is corrupt—printed codes of ethics, industry protestations and published analyses notwithstanding.[4] And the impression, of course, is not entirely misconceived—nor is it generally true enough to derive from it dire moral consequences, or to sustain the weight of the fancies that have been spun upon it.

Third, advertising by its nature (including even such neutral announcements as those found in classified sections of newspapers), must always be selective, and often, to certain perceptions, distortive. Wherever one finds advertising of any kind, in picture or narrative and regardless of the instrument by which it is purveyed, one also discovers drama or communication by re-enactment. When effective drama is employed, it utilizes showmanship, and the latter almost invariably requires a certain measure of hyperbole and deception, even when it may be regarded legitimately as dramatic license. All actors are, to the hard-nosed realist, liars, and so are novelists, painters, poets and advertisers.[5]

The result of this (perhaps) inevitable state of affairs, therefore, is that advertising must, at present, involve deception to some degree, no greater, in many instances, than those deceptions employed in other commercial affairs, in most education and in modern government. But deception it is, in fact, that encourages a vast number of otherwise sensible citizens to degrade both the nature and purpose of advertising and to maintain attitudes of aloof ethical superiority to it, even though they may personally be engaged in activities as shady as, or even more deceptive than, advertising. A physician who might not think twice about "covering" a colleague's ineptitude, or offering a precise but bogus physiological diagnosis and placebo for a condition he knows merely to be caused by nerves, may snoot at a mild omission (like rate of gas consumption) in an advertisement for an automobile. A college professor whose wife marks his term papers (unknown to his students) may criticize an actor who mouths a hair tonic testimonial for cold cash. A politician whose atheism does not prevent him from evoking God's blessing upon his party's platform may protest to his friends the irrelevancy of a windjammer in an advertisement for Scotch Whisky.

Hoist on their own petards of deception, advertising personnel usually resent this sort of hypocrisy with considerable justice, particularly in the light of their belief (never proven incorrect) that the capitalistic market owes much of its vigor and apparently unending potential for expansion to them. Their seeming ability to channel goods, create—within limits—demands for consumer goods and services and facilitating power for activating public faith in the economy are, to them, positive cultural contributions deserving of the same sort of laurels that are given to other captains of industry and public benefactors. Only their self-evident self-guilt keeps them from protesting more than occasionally in trade newspapers and letters to the editor. The advertising professional is rewarded financially a good deal more benevolently, after all, than he might reasonably expect for services that, when boiled down to essence, are not (compared to other artistic and literary skills) either difficult or demanding creatively, industry protestations notwithstanding.

Packard has, in an over-stated polemic,[6] hit upon the major cultural problems of contemporary advertising persuasion. Simply stated, it is the peculiarity of responsible segments of this industry—or profession—that they have come somehow to believe their own myths, to credit with truth their own deceptions, and to swallow the rationalization of their own uses of sciences, particularly those derived from sociology and psychology, usually employing surveys, demographic studies and elaborate statistical computer print-outs. Add also the fact that some (but far from all) advertising practitioners have also accepted and postulated pseudo-Freudian techniques, unique selling propositions, bogus semantic notions, communications theories and human relations mystiques that belie the supposed ivy-league educations of the fish who swallow their consultants' and resident experts' bait.

A skilled magician usually does not believe in supernatural magic precisely *because he can* (apparently) perform supernatural feats, read minds, and, for that matter, make water flow upwards. He therefore knows how the tricks are done, and that they are tricks, not miracles of nature.[7] Commercial advertisers, for reasons irrelevant here, are not nearly as realistic. They feel constrained to pay obeisance to their success gods by defending the value of advertising for culture, not in sensible, justifiable, objective, economic and historic terms, but rather in dubious moral and spiritual ones. In short, they want not only to be important, well-remunerated people; they want also to be virtuous, beloved and cossetted, which is asking a lot in twentieth century America.

This situation appears to extract its greatest penalties in the psychological fallout from self-deception which sometimes renders skilled advertising professionals useless for any other human purposes. Certainly, the demeaning nature of their work does not cause this characterological erosion, because the labor is not all that demeaning. Many of us who suffer more menial labors than writing odes to laundry soap are able to surmount the tedium of our work. Advertising people (with notable exceptions) rarely do, probably because the impetus of professional justification and rationalization requires an interiorized world-view which spills over from their working hours into the rest of their lives. And the individual obsessed with self-justification is not likely to relax long or well enough to employ his energies and talents wisely, especially if he carries also the burden of the guilt of unmerited affluence, a syndrome frequently displayed by the new rich.[8]

Advertising and the Marketplace

Criticism and denigration of the quality of American commercial persuasion, and advertising everywhere, for that matter, has long been a favorite international indoor sport. It is as old as the profession itself, but was given new currency in the United States after World War II with the publication of Frederic Wakeman's impressive novel *The Hucksters,* and by the development of the television commercial which managed, in its earliest days particularly, to carry quickly to absurdity everything jejune, insipid, and simple-minded that all other forms of advertising had painfully and slowly developed in a century and a half. These dispositions were deepened by the mythos of the advertising industry itself that its own exponents spread. It reflected as well an industry-wide guilt reaction and heightened sensitiveness among advertising personnel, amusing to behold, to criticism of any kind.

Other factors were also involved. With their almost limitless belief in the power of education and rational potential of the average man in the street, Americans have long cherished numerous colorful suspicions that a modern version of the classical Italian hand is everywhere at work in our culture. By and large, it is possible to sell much of the public almost *any* conspiracy notion, particularly if it is foreign, preferably Mediterranean. Despite our gullibility, the *idea* of mass persuasion for profit is repellent to most Americans on its face—theoretically a not unwelcome insurance policy against demagogery, except that the clever demagogue usually poses as an honest man exposing a conspiracy. Because ostensible competitive advertising is in fact so uniform in content, the possibility of a conspiracy of persuaders causes a cultural undertow that it is difficult *not* to feel when looking at our current marketplace with its imitative, repetitive numerous consumer brands, almost all identical except for packaging, and sold at similar prices and advertised in the same ways.

Numerous economists regard this problem in a different manner, but arrive at much the same conclusions using similar and more precise data. Large corporations, all with easy entry into the marketplace (the economists claim), utilize advertising merely to keep prices high and lure customers from one brand to another; in fact, to share their potential market (and wealth) between themselves. The consumer's choice is narrowed down to which product he buys. And his consumption is stimulated by minor model changes (as in automobiles, or proliferating, near-identical, lines of breakfast foods) that then become exploitable themes for advertisers who stimulate more—and unnecessary—consumption. Advertising is, on one hand, a system of corporate checkmate, and, on the other, a device for maintaining high prices and continually increasing consumption. It is, from this viewpoint, economic blubber, essentially wasteful, costly to consumers, and, if it were all eliminated in one instant, not essentially destructive to those large corporations that now spend millions (in costs passed on to the consumer) by simply maintaining an economic standoff with their competitors.

The construction of our marketplace above is obviously not a dynamic one, and does not take into account the interplay of many unseen variables that maintain our social and economic life. Galbraith's construction of the role of advertising in our present culture is far more sophisticated—and probably accurate—although it has appeared to have little effect upon contemporary attitudes and the thinking of most economic theorists.[9]

First, he says, demand is rarely static in a constantly evolving technological nation. In effect, both quantity and quality of consumption may be force-fed up to a point. A family that owns one car may be able to afford—and use—two. An individual used to hanging cheap, framed reproductions on his wall may be encouraged to purchase original charcoals—or to begin painting himself, for better or worse. A family may be encouraged to take a so-called "budget" vacation to Europe instead of a cheaper hegira to the local seaside. Advertising is probably the easiest and cheapest mechanism to affect consumer changes of these sorts.

Second, Galbraith notes that the homeostatic concept of brand loyalty obtains for a time, but gives way eventually to a form of operational "games theory" between competing advertisers with similar goods or services. Such strategy involves, of course, continual modifications of advertising that mean little. But it also may include changes in product design, services, value for price, voluntary price control, and even—at times—modifications in the fundamental nature of the product itself. These changes are far from meaningless; they are essential to the dynamism of the market, and, in many ways, also directive of cultural life.

A recent example (too grotesque and overt to serve as more than a caricature of the process) is the competition in both advertising and product between *Hertz* and *Avis* car rental services, although most similar "games" involve many more than two players and therefore have greater economic ramifications. Within its parameters, however, the *Hertz-Avis* gambit was both interesting and productive. Games like these also may rectify temporary slumps in business by producing new formulas for sales, with resultant stabilizations of industrial expenses, although the entire market still remains vulnerable to overall economic cycles.

Third, Galbraith regards this sort of management of demand as a subtle but effective social control, with the consequence that, "while goods become ever more abundant they do not seem to be any less important . . . Yet it might not have been. In the absence of massive and artful persuasion that accompanies the management of demand, increasing abundance might have reduced the interest of people in acquiring more goods. They would not have felt the need. . . ," [10] (a need induced, in part, by commercial persuasion) for the apparently unlimited profusion of goods which circulate in the market. This need is necessary for the maintenance and expansion of the industrial system, as well as the sustenance—in a highly competitive world—of the morale, prestige and health of the total culture itself.[11]

Galbraith concludes:

> For advertising men it has long been a sore point that economists dismissed them as so much social waste. They have not quite known how to answer. Some have doubtless sensed that, in a society where wants are psychologically grounded, the instruments of access to the mind cannot be unimportant. They were right. The functions here identified may well be less exalted than the more demanding philosophers of the advertising industry might wish. But none can doubt their importance for the industrial system, given always the standards by which that system measures achievement and success.[12]

Our next problem, from the point of view of the consumer and citizen, is the close consideration of these standards, the persuasion used to maintain them and their relevance to those facets of culture that reach beyond the marketplace.

Consumer Culture

Before our cultural critics consign the contemporary marketplace to oblivion (as they often do), we had best ponder carefully the complexity of the contemporary technostructure. Since World War I, it has simply been too easy to fixate upon a few, certain aspects of culture in the West that show signs of inner rot, or worse, extended adolescence, and blame materialism and competitive capitalism for them. The later works of Freud combined with simplistic constructions of Marxist materialism have produced a strange and powerful fusion in modern thought.[13] Many of us who survived the ravages of the past generation salted our popularized Freud with fashionable socialistic discontents that were confirmed by paperback nay-sayers and the prophets of alienation.

The simplicity with which commercial culture and mass culture were equated one with the other as symptomatic of the failure of capitalism to provide for our people a humane psychological environment need neither be stressed nor repeated here. If we believed that popular culture was vulgar, the forces of commerce and the perversions of cash were the instruments vulgarizing it. The possibility that state-supported culture (Public Television, for instance) might one day be more vulgar than the commercial variety did not occur to us, mainly because we were not exactly sure of what vulgarity *was*. The theatre, arts, literature, films, social life, even education were apparently being destroyed by heathens of the marketplace. Avaricious movie producers, publishers and broadcasters were prototypical capitalists in high hats, smoking enormous imported cigars. They spit in the face of the masses and forced their peculiar commercial opiates down the public gullet, or so many believed.

The viewpoint had (has) the advantages of simplicity and naïveté. Like all such systemic discontents, it produced "good guys" and "bad guys," and its shallowness only becomes apparent after searching and careful study of the "good guys," and mature reflection on the "bad" ones. Whenever government and public spirited foundations did, in fact, begin to assume a tentative directive force in American cultural life, neither the quality of that culture nor the nature of life changed noticeably for the better. If anything, it became worse, in the opinion of many.

Eleemosynary high, low or middle-brow culture may lack the strident groping after popularity that marks much consumer-oriented culture, but it also lacks its verve, originality, daring and spirit. The American drama was not saved by public works; if any drama is being created today in the USA it is probably in the commercial crucible of off-Broadway free enterprise productions. Our proclivities for preserving the better things in life in public museums have stimulated the creation of far less significant pictorial art than the commercial galleries on New York's 57th Street. Municipal orchestras have commissioned countless symphonies, but important developments in American music are probably being made by the many commercial types who feed our burgeoning recording and hi-fi industry. And so it goes, in almost every corner of American life: the cultural output of the United States Government Printing Office, the Office of Education and similar arms of government—free from the pressures of the commercial market—are models of unimaginativeness. Foundation-supported culture analysts and political scientists pour out pedantic nonsense (neatly parodied in the spoof, *Report From Iron Mountain*), while the men who man the newsrooms of our networks and who slapdash together our many newspapers (in continual competition one with the other) limn for us, daily, a remarkably sensible appraisal of the world's newsfronts—better usually than we credit them, especially when we compare their output with their opposite numbers in nations with state controlled news services.

To many, however, advertising still epitomizes the vulgarization of art and culture in the service of commerce and is accepted this way with neither study nor qualification. Certainly, much truth lies in the conceptual fusion of commerce and mass culture as cheap, low culture, almost by definition of either or both. But much popular culture is highly satisfying, apparently harmless and technically excellent, even if it does not satisfy the need of refined sensibilities for special experiences. Advertising, on the other hand, appears (and has always seemed) to possess none of the spontaneity of the best of mass culture. It is usually damned on its face and withheld *a priori* from serious consideration as art or culture of any kind.[14]

The basic reason, of course, results from the assumption that commerce simply *could not and cannot* produce "Culture," at least Culture in the refined sense of the European leisure class and university world of the past century. It has been forgotten (or never known) that commerce has been involved in producing—quite directly—most of the fine Culture of the past: the Parthenon, the Mona Lisa, the Elizabethan theatre, Italian Grand Opera and the best of French Impressionism; that the greatest artists in our history (from Cellini to Shaw) have often been the greediest and sharpest commercially; and that many (or most) of man's most significant cultural advances have been motivated by private profit and the yearning for personal glory. But the secret could not be kept, because the artistic grandeur of contemporary technology was too enormous to contain and too obvious to hide. The Golden Gate and Verrazano-Narrows bridges were too impudently magnificent to ignore; a banking Boeing 747 was too dignified and thrilling to deny; and (most important) the Volkswagen magazine ad or the airline commercial on television was too clever, articulate and intelligent to bypass with condescension as nothing more than a sleazy by-product of commerce.

All of this is relatively recent history. And it is not the author's purpose to lionize advertising as the flower of a contemporary renaissance in design or high art. The problem is one of relative values, centering mostly upon the question of whether the truly public arts (highways, housing developments, stadiums, bridges, post offices, schools, etc.) bear a noticeable and distinctive superiority to the arts involved in commerce—particularly advertising—on view in contemporary life. The writer simply suggests that quite the reverse is frequently true: that the landscaped roadside, for instance, planted along a new highway is frequently inferior as design, art or culture (but obviously not as nature) to much of the old billboards and poster art that it presently replaces, and that it is undeniably far more tiresome for the driver to suffer and less diverting and/or amusing.[15]

To the eye of the contemporary Gnostic, however, postulating, as he does, that the market is corrupt, everything that emerges from it must also be tainted with corruption. His viewpoint is not unlike that fostered upon Soviet artists in the Stalinist era and upon Germany by Hitler—the latter, a man, by the way, who not only knew what he liked but also knew a good deal about art. To the determinist, particularly the Hegelian (be he Socialist, Fascist or voluntarist with naïve beliefs of human relations and brotherly love), one must first consider the source of an artifact before one evaluates it. To the social determinist, a play with a so-called "message" is superior to a play without one (or with the incorrect one), regardless of the skill manifest in conception or performance. To Stalin, expressionist art (at a certain period) was decadent, because it evolved in capitalist nations and expressed what he considered degenerate ideas. To Hitler, Jewish writing was corrupt, because it was Jewish. Intrinsic qualities, to the determinist, have nothing to do with quality. Life, for him, is literally lived on an extrinsic level.

Little wonder, therefore, that advertising's persuasion has been regarded as a ubiquitous evil in the West, likened by many to an epidemic, and symptomatic, supposedly, of a degraded culture and public obsession with materialism, especially, it must be added, by the guilt-ridden advertising industry itself. The culprits are, accordingly, forever trying to expiate their sins by attempting public service work that might often better be accomplished by public servants, and by giving each other awards. In this respect, they are not unlike educators, movie makers and architects. (The latter are probably the busiest award givers and receivers in the West.)

An *extrinsic* view of commerce, capitalism or technology necessitates an unrealistic, negative attitude towards, particularly, their (apparently) nonproductive aspects, particularly in their most competitive, simplistic and standardized modes. While it appears not to be difficult to use and exploit the material benefits of capitalism and, at the same time, to deride the system that created them (like a Ford Foundation grantee expounding an elegant economic and social theory that mass production discourages the study of social theories), it is far more difficult to admire advertising and, at the same time, equate capitalist technology with sin.

What is even worse (from the extrinsic perspective) is the apparent truth that quite a number of intelligent people in contemporary Western society enjoy advertisements—or, at least, do not mind them. Fairfax M. Cone [16] reports a Roper study of the audiences of television commercials that indicates a number of things, among them the finding that about two-thirds of the viewing public seems not to mind commercials. One quarter finds them annoying, and ten per cent actually dislike them, presumably not enough to stop watching television because of them. Cone is an unusual advertising mogul, in that he occasionally punctures some of his industry's myths and treats his craft realistically. He notes that these same statistics indicate also that, while two out of three people show favorable attitudes towards television commercials, seven out of ten "find at least some commercials objectionable," which is exactly what the survey (made for the television broadcasters' persuasion front, the Television Information Office) does indeed indicate.

Granting even that three out of ten people *like* television commercials (the least inventive, amusing or interesting part of the advertising industry, in the opinion of many) one wonders what percentage of the public *likes* newspaper and magazine advertisements, billboards, car cards and radio spots (which are becoming increasingly interesting and clever). Certainly, a good portion do—or enough to justify the observation, made at many times and in many places that, were advertisements taken from the American scene, most of us would miss them sorely.[17] Popularity of this sort, in the face of all of the cultural artifacts which social ameliorists *know* are far better for the health, education and welfare of our populace than advertisements, is, from an extrinsic view, inexcusable, and explains also the general cultural status of commercial persuasion today.

How defensible is this enormous cultural attention paid to advertising, and the possibility that it is, in some ways, the single most popular aspect of mass culture? Not defensible at all, if one thinks of it—as is often done—in terms of the displacement of other experiences. But does it really displace them, or does the general current of advertising serve merely as a vehicle of acculturation to a highly complex society where much special knowledge is demanded for basic survival? And who knows what role this orientation plays in the steps all of us must take in learning to sever the honest from the dishonest, persuasion from fact, and junk from gold.[18] As the movie critic, Pauline Kael has noted, ''I don't trust any of the tastes of people who were born with such good taste that they didn't need to find their way through trash.'' [19] Many of us are open to the accusation that we have not progressed far in the cultivation of taste *beyond trash,* if we defend seriously commercial advertising's positive cultural functions. Perhaps. But, at least, we are progressing beyond patent satisfaction with sheer kitsch, and so may many millions of people, further and faster than even apologists for advertising's sins dare suggest.

Friendly Persuasion

Good or bad as culture, advertising is the merchant of consumerism, and our present consumer technology could probably not exist without it. When relevant arguments, therefore, are presented against advertising, they are not directed against persuasion itself, but instead, usually, against the need to consume as we do. Krutch, for instance, makes the simple and intelligent point [20] that man has not, in his long history, been primarily regarded as a consumer by humane arbiters of his social order. As the world became more materialistic, so the productive capacity of man and his talent for consumption increased in significance. Today, writes Krutch, '' 'Scorn not the common man,' says the age of abundance. 'He may have no soul; his personality may not be exactly the same as his neighbor's; and he may not produce anything worth having. But, thank God, he consumes.' '' [21]

Naturally, this view of advertising is extrinsic. And just as naturally it quarrels, not with what advertisers tell us, but with what they *mean* by the telling, although thinkers like Krutch do not center on the political or economic assumptions that advertising represents in its celebration of the success of technological capitalism. Like all humanists, the writer included, he is concerned about people. And it is hard to confront with much moral annoyance a statement like this: "One thing seems clear. When man's first duty comes to be consumption, he suffers a strange loss of dignity, and not only he but the coming generation comes to be valued chiefly in terms of its potentiality as a voracious consumer." [22]

A generation has one-half come of age since those words were written, and we have seen the youngsters who were ten at that time grow out of the children's market, into the 'teen age market, on to the young adult market and finally into one of the differentiated male and female adult markets, like "young swinger," "Playboy-type," "bachelor girl," "young married," "new parent," "black business man," "executive type" and others. Each has its appropriate mode of consumption, its appropriate costumes, make-up, home and work settings, its methods of transportation, food habits and sexual mores, all of which are closely geared to patterns of consumption. Do consumers demean themselves to play these roles?

One may search, as O'Hara has,[23] to note differential pressures from different corners of society, by different methods of communication to different people, and discuss in various ways the pressures that advertisers exert upon the people involved in the mass culture industries and contemporary schooling. True, the press is freer of advertisers' pressure than radio or television, and the movies are less dependent than any other arm of mass communications upon it, except that the cinema industry's progress depends, in some measure, upon the effectiveness of its own advertising.

O'Hara, Berelson, Steinberg, Siepmann, Emery, Skornia and others who have attempted to characterize mass communications in our time (and whose works are too familiar to list here) all miss an essential logical point in their differing discussions of the variable pressures that mass communicators suffer— for better or worse—at the hands of commerce and the institution of advertising. This point centers on the fact that *all* mass communications in our culture are the *result* (not separate entities) *of the same commercial forces* that also created advertising. It was not a whim of history that joined the first newspaper with the first printed advertisement. They were both cut from the same historical clay, and both are inevitable, complementary components of the techno-structure of our world.

The great persuasive force of advertising is not specific; it is general.[24] It is not locatable in individual conduits of communication; it *is* an uber-conduit of communication. It uses, in various ways, and with various types of results, the press, films, radio, television, billboards, skywriting, supermarkets, electric signs and handbills to create a cultural climate whereby goods and services may be channeled in certain ways to certain markets to meet certain needs, some of them stimulated by these instruments of communication, not necessarily directly by advertisements.

One amusing but typical example of the process comes to mind. A contemporary sex novel on the best-seller list that the writer recently read (in response to a uxorial suggestion that he would abhor it; and he did) constituted a virtual lexicon of contemporary urban consumption. Set in New York City, telling the rather pathetic story of the sex lives of four young ladies under thirty, this weak imitation of Schnitzler's *La Ronde* contains more information about the various sex hygiene and contraceptive devices upon the market at present than even a gynecologist probably needs to know. In fact, attention to consumption potential of female genitalia—even to the extent of keeping it warm in winter—provides about the only originality discernible in the book. It is also a tout for expensive restaurants and stores in New York, something of a cookbook and menu guide, and it dabbles in interior decorating and available amusements in the big city. The volume might serve as a consumer's guide for almost any middle class, white, silly young female in town—and as something of a realistic rule-book for the sexually predatory male. It is, in short, a minor triumph of unpaid-for (one presumes) advertising.

On a more serious level, neither *Time* magazine, *The New York Times, The Wall Street Journal* or the *Chicago Tribune* may be evaluated as cultural artifacts without considering their overall roles in the friendly persuasion of consumerism. The short spots we see on television are, naturally, paid commercial persuasion; but the potent medicine is brewed in the longer video segments blandly called ''programming'' and are as likely, sometimes, to emerge from network news departments as entertainment factories. Hollywood movies help to create consumer culture, and films from all over the globe depict life styles for us to emulate, places for us to travel and objectives for us to imitate, if only in fantasy. American advertising is far bigger than Madison Avenue. It is also bigger than Wall Street, Hollywood Boulevard and Broadway. And let us not forget that our schools, from kindergarten to professional academy, adjust the young to our way of life and probably succeed better at making them consumers than at teaching reading and spelling.

Our purview, therefore, now transcends even Krutch's doubts concerning whether life as a consumer allows modern man the dignity he finds, or once found, in other cultures not devoted as avidly as ours is to fabricating consumers. Our vista is not only of society but of much history: not only of a few thousand men devoted to attracting the public to this or that product, but of millions of us in the contexts of our values, our recreation, our work, our style of living, mating and dying, as well as the continual noisy denial by many of everything these peculiar culture traits mean.[25]

Written, as these words are, at a moment of financial recession, inflation and (perhaps) impending profound disorientation of American industry (out of which the future of technological culture probably will be forged), one is impelled to refer discussions which derive *from* history back *to* history. Many of us have been, in the past, asked by our society to be far more than mere consumers. And many have fulfilled these requests, sometimes at the cost of their lives. We may yet be asked as citizens to become less *as* consumers, and much, much more *than* consumers in order to make peace with technology and modernity. This change, should it come, will require all the friendly persuasion the institution of advertising can muster. We may, some day, thank God for it.

Conclusion

Advertising has occupied a peculiar corner of American culture for a long time, because it is the subject of widely ambivalent emotional and cognitive dispositions. On the one hand, it is seen as a necessary lubricant of commerce. On the other, it is construed as annoying legerdemain, economic waste and cultural dross. Both points of view have meaning in contemporary life, and evidence exists that both are true—up to a point. The argument that centers upon them today is futile by virtue of the justifications to which both camps go to construe contemporary advertising (and salesmanship) as something which it is *not*. Justifications and techniques of the behavioral sciences, in one camp, are met by excess and irrelevant aesthetic and artistic rhetoric, in the other.

Advertising deserves a legitimate place in the technological capitalistic marketplace that can, in the construction offered in this chapter, satisfy champions of Keynesian economics and a planned economy (perhaps *especially* individuals so oriented) as well as those of more conservative economic dispositions. The question, mainly concerning the management of demand, of whether the marketplace *as we know it* will continue to function in its predicted ways is another matter with deep ramifications, not necessarily lethal, for the future of cultural persuasion by the advertising.

Most advertising is kitsch; some of it is amusing; some briefly brilliant; much is trash. But most criticism of the content of advertising stems from extrinsic dispositions towards the apparent useless success of advertising in contemporary industry, rather than intrinsic, thoughtful criticism of the output itself. Compared to much other American kitsch (and to public works and self-conscious attempts at American fine arts), a lot of advertising does not come off badly in respect to vitality, originality, spirit, technical excellence and—to the chagrin of many—popularity. The currently accepted American notion of class art, unfortunately, does not deal realistically with the way societies in the past have found to express their geniuses. And a good deal of resistance exists to the notion that a capitalist market-place and materialistic incentives are *not* totally incompatible with art of any type, fine or popular.

The persuasion of advertising has been charged with having raised in the USA a nation of consumers. While this may have been true in some measure, most of us have managed to find objectives in life richer and more rewarding than consumption, although without question, it has been one of the main cultural imperatives of the past two generations. And the future may well see the decline of the present great age of American consumption. Whatever the fate of our society (unless it is extinction), advertising in its present ubiquitous forms, a facet of many parts of culture, will probably play a major role in it.

NOTES

[1] See E. S. Turner, *The Shocking History of Advertising* (New York: Ballantine Books, Inc., 1953). Starting with the first British periodicals in the early seventeenth century, Turner tells the story of this aspect of salesmanship with clarity and charm. But there is little *shocking* about the account, despite all of its color; nor does it deserve to be published (as my edition was) as one of a series of books on deceptions, frauds and confidence schemes. The excesses of advertisers it covers are little worse than the excesses of schoolmasters of the same periods, or of physicians, dentists, theatrical producers and politicians. The shocking history of *mankind* displays that some people are liars and others are apparently infinitely gullible, and that the two groups often pair off together neatly.

[2] Readers may have seen announcements of the sales of Hershey products in local stores, paid for, I understand, by cooperating merchants and food distributors and circulated no further than local newspapers or throw-aways. A soap bearing the Hershey name, made in Hershey, Pennsylvania by a firm unrelated to the chocolate manufacturer, has also been advertised. Spokesmen for the Hershey chocolate organization have stressed that they have nothing against advertising; they simply feel that the company has little to profit from it, preferring to stimulate sales by other devices and attempting to attract as much attention as possible at the point of sales. Hershey bars, incidentally, have recently begun to be advertised in Canada. They are also, at last, to be advertised shortly in the United States, I am told at the present writing.

[3] See John Brooks, *The Fate of the Edsel and Other Business Adventures* (New York: Harper and Row, Publishers, 1963), pp. 17–75.

[4] Martin Mayer's *Madison Avenue, USA.* (New York: Harper and Brothers, 1958) is certainly *not* a blast at the advertising industry. If anything, Mayer twisted himself into benign attitudes when reporting some of the phenomena he observed in the big agencies, the overall attempt in his book being to correct common misconceptions about this aspect of marketing in America. His general thesis, that the sins of the advertiser are no greater (if no smaller) than those of the rest of our commercial community, is justified. His suggestions, positing a theory of the psychological utility of advertising (pp. 308–324), tip the scales of reason too far, I think, although the general tenor of his entire analysis—now unfortunately dated—is fair.

[5] Here is a thorny problem of ethics and prompts consideration of how variable ethics confuse people, even when the ethical structures themselves are quite simple. Magicians believe it is ethical to misrepresent their behaviors and props in the interest of entertainment, but that it is unethical to share with a non-magician the truth—that is, how their tricks are done. To substitute shaving cream for whipped cream on a television commercial is considered by federal auditors unethical, even if the whipped cream melts under studio lights, and shaving cream makes a pudding dessert look real. Yet such a substitution is freely permissible in a television drama. Variations between backstage ethics and public ethics (not sheer greed) lay at the roots of the great television quiz scandals in the late 1950's, and still admit of numerous unsolved curiosities in mass communications.

[6] See Vance Packard, *The Hidden Persuaders*. Recall that this volume was a run-away best seller in its day, but seemed to do no harm whatsoever to any aspect of the advertising industry in the United States. I imagine that it was probably read widely, and with masochistic glee, by advertising men and women, considering their usual proclivities for self-castigation.

[7] The most ardent opponent of astrology, witchcraft, ESP and other superstitious nonsense I have met was my friend, the late magician, John Mulholland, who would not countenance even the slim doubt in me that mind-reading *might* possibly occur or that any factual basis for the occult might exist. The reason, of course, was that Mulholland was perfectly competent at any moment to read my mind with astounding clarity and therefore knew that mind-reading is impossible, precisely *because* he could accomplish it so cleverly.

[8] David Ogilvy, *Confessions of an Advertising Man* (New York: Dell Publishing Co., 1963) is an interesting and literate example of how a clever huckster explains his own success in respectable terms. To Ogilvy's credit, he has the common sense, as a displaced Briton to snoot a bit at the vulgarities of American life, but his "secrets of success" give away the clue that he probably believes his own persuasion in spite of his intelligence.

[9] See J. K. Galbraith, *The New Industrial State* (Boston: Houghton Mifflin Co., 1967), pp. 202–210.

[10] *Ibid.,* p. 209.

[11] Galbraith makes the excellent point that such prestige now depends upon the output and consumption of goods instead of yesterday's symbols of prosperity: the hyper-affluence of the capitalist class, and/or ownership and use of real estate or land. Even today, however, atavists like the Georgist economists continue the fiction that land is the focal commodity in our economic system. And various mythologists still concentrate upon the power of colorful, mysterious, manipulating capitalists like Howard Hughes. Japan's experience during the past generation provides an interesting microcosm in perspective, however, of how a nation has recently and quickly centered its economy both on the production and *ownership* of consumer goods after centuries of activities largely in other economic areas. Advertising, of course, has been intimately related to the recent Japanese experience.

[12] *Ibid.,* p. 210.

[13] See Paul A. Robinson, *The Freudian Left* (New York: Harper and Row, Publishers, 1969), for an excellent study of how psychological and economic theories from Hegel to Marx to Freud found their way into the radicalism of Wilhelm Reich, Geza Roheim and Herbert Marcuse, primarily, although other similar thinkers are also discussed.

[14] Through the back door of highbrow culture, of course, advertising, over the years, crept into the galleries in such manifestations as "pop art," usually wearing the disguise of satire. University art galleries to this day exhibit pop art as "camp" or "spoof," unaware that considerable aesthetic and psychological gratification may be discovered in certain types of American package design, poster art and advertising layout work—particularly in the juxtaposition of shapes, forms and words. Nor is this gratification necessarily amusing, or any more or less amusing than other clear visual statements are.

[15] Far be it from me to grow sentimental about old Burma Shave signs, but I do not think that it is an indication of my increasing antiquity to note here that I miss them.

[16] Fairfax M. Cone, "What's Bad for TV is Worse for Advertising" in David M. White and Richard Averson, *Sight, Sound, and Society* (Boston: Beacon Press, 1968), p. 265.

[17] Of course, we would miss those ads which offer an orientation function, that is, tell us what movie is playing at the local popcorn palace, what is on sale at the supermarkets, etc. But, above and beyond this, I hope I am not hurting anyone's feelings by noting in passing that, these days, I enjoy the advertising matter in *The New York Times Magazine, The New Yorker,* and many similar upper-middle-brow fashionable publications more than the legitimate content. I may also be exceptional and the victim of foul taste, because I also prefer the kitschy copy and illustrations in mail order catalogs (especially the Haband Company, Spencer Gifts, Greenleaf Studios, Brecks of Boston, Walter Drake, etc.) to doctoral dissertations, commission reports, and educational research; but I imagine I am not alone.

[18] Advertising is frequently criticized because it is dishonest, which is naturally true of some of it. It is possible, however, that dishonest advertising, irrelevant sales claims, the bandwagon approach, testimonials, and the rest of the tricks of the trade help to sensitize many of us to the inevitable deception that I, personally, have seen in most marketplaces and bazaars around the world,

not necessarily in technological-capitalistic countries. In my experience as a teacher, also, I have noticed that children at about junior high school age are often highly critical of the faulty logic in advertising, beginning, for themselves, an informal kind of consumer education or marketplace sophistication distinctive of modern Americans.

[19] Pauline Kael, *Going Steady* (Boston: Little Brown and Co., 1970), p. 115.

[20] See Joseph Wood Krutch, *Human Nature and the Human Condition* (New York: Random House, 1959), pp. 21–39. Advertising's relationship to education, a matter no less serious than it was a dozen years ago, is Krutch's central and most poignant theme. If I fault Krutch's ongoing criticism of "modernism" (a term he has used in a book title), it is merely because he credits too little the frequent spontaneous antitheses that arise in American life and thought that modify the virulence of our fads in thinking and life styles. But he is a hard humanist to deny.

[21] *Ibid.*, p. 39.

[22] *Ibid.*, p. 38.

[23] See Robert C. O'Hara, *Media for the Millions* (New York: Random House, 1961), pp. 81–88.

[24] Even the best specific stories about advertising, like the creation of *Lestoil* or the genius stroke that gave us *Alpha Bits,* are simply colorful examples of general cultural trends. The late, lamented *Lestoil* was the natural culmination, in its day, of the cleanliness cult that had been created for industry by advertising, among other forces. The whole breakfast cereal world, which *Alpha Bits* upset unmercifully (and curiously), is a facet of culture devoted originally to using surplus grains and by-products from other types of food production. It was created in its early days mostly by clever advertising and good marketing that developed a need for a product which I, personally, have never found much of a use for, except to feed to my gerbils.

[25] Hippies, teeny-boppers, SDS radicals and Black Panthers are as much by-products of technological culture as canned cat food and Elmer's Glue.

Daniel Henninger:

Survival Tactics: No Fooling . . . Youngsters Analyze TV Commercials

PREPARING AN ARTICLE some time ago on television commercials aimed at children, I watched five hours of programs one Saturday morning. It was about noon, I think, that a GI Joe doll, making its 59th commercial assault that morning, finally got my mind in his sights and sent a nearly fatal bazooka round into my cerebellum. I recovered. But there are some vocal persons and groups who believe that TV advertising is in some way permanently damaging the minds of

(Mr. Henninger is a staff writer for the *National Observer*. Reprinted with permission from *The National Observer,* copyright Dow Jones & Company, Inc., 1974).

our children; they either want the number of commercials directed at children reduced, or they want such advertising eliminated completely.

Robert Choate, who became well-known for his criticism of nutritional deficiencies in ready-to-eat breakfast cereals, told a congressional committee recently that "advocating any product to any child should be assumed an unfair business practice unless proven otherwise." In Choate's opinion, we should be teaching children about "the practices of the market place *before* he or she gets burned."

The day Choate was saying that, I was sitting in a sixth-grade classroom at Benjamin Franklin Elementary School in Indiana, Pa., watching 11- and 12-year-olds defend themselves quite well against the Ad Monster. Using a video-tape recorder; these kids were taping a program called "Advertising: Don't Be Fooled."

On signal from the student director, a young cameraman switched on the Sony Videocoder and a sound girl pointed the stage microphone at the announcer, who brushed his hair out of his eyes and said: "Hello, and welcome to our program. We have prepared a program . . . to teach you some lessons about advertising. But first a message from one of our sponsors."

The camera crew changed and set up for the "Winky Dink Guitars" commercial.

"Hi! I'm the new teen-age sensation, Winky Dink," said Gena, strumming her toy guitar. "Buy a Winky Dink Stinky folk guitar and play just like me."

A "fan" ran up to Winky Dink: "Oh Winky Dink, can I have your autograph?"

"Sure," said Winky Dink, "and you can be famous just like me."

Another camera set-up and another announcer: "That advertisement was an example of the Good Names technique. A sponsor hopes you will buy his product because it will make you popular or famous."

For the next 45 minutes a succession of camera crews taped their classmates demonstrating advertising's selling secrets. As the kids played out Bad Names, Plain Folks, Don't Be Left Out, and other ad techniques, I thought of the millions of dollars spent annually on the production of TV commercials, on market research, on all the sophisticated hocus-pocus we watch nightly on the tube as 30-second spurts of sell. And here were sixth graders using the magic of television to expose Madison Avenue's magicians.

One boy did a beautiful parody of Euell Gibbons, the naturalist who currently is hawking one of the "natural" cereals. The youngster walked on camera holding a twig in his hand and a pine branch between his teeth. After taking the pine out of his mouth, he told us that this here new natural cereal reminded him of the "taste of acorns." Abruptly, a goofy-acting kid jumped on camera, shouting about his favorite "crispy sweets" cereal. "Euell" leaned back and said: "Now who would you believe, an old nature lover like me or this stupid kid?"

Some of the students conducted door-to door surveys among their neighbors on the use of heavily advertised classes of products, such as aspirin, shampoo, tooth paste, and soap. Then they called physicians, dentists, and other community experts to find out which products they recommend, since so many advertisers give the impression they've got most of the nation's medical community behind their product.

Doug and Bill taped a report on their pain-reliever survey. A chart indicated the following preferences among their neighbors: Anacin, 5; Alka-Seltzer Plus, 3; Bufferin, 3; Bayer, 13; Excedrin, 4; and neighbors with no opinion, 5. Parallel to the neighbors' column were the results of their inquiries to seven doctors: All had no opinion; none would recommend a specific pain reliever. The boys pointed out that the Government regulates the amounts of pain relievers permissible in these products (the school nurse told them).

The room was silent and still during the tapings, but a restrained bedlam broke out between "commercials," with questions flying nonstop at Winnie Bernat, the infinitely patient teacher who conceived the grade-school ad seminar. During a class break she found time to talk about the class, something she started four years ago, before children's advertising became the popular issue it is today.

An education magazine's article on advertising techniques gave her an idea: Why not teach the techniques to her students? She clipped magazine ads to illustrate the techniques. At the school she turned on the classroom's television during a commercial break and asked the students to write down the techniques used in the commercials. As might be expected, these McLuhanized kids caught on quickly.

They regularly told her of ads they'd seen using the ad techniques she had explained. A lot of them brought in cereal-box prizes, cheaply made toys that rarely matched their advertised promise.

The ad classes have expanded each year. As part of this year's project, several students took examples of cereal-box advertising to the lower grades. The message was: Is it worth having to eat all that gunk just to be disappointed with a junky toy?

Mrs. Bernat gives her sixth graders much credit for making the current course so extensive. The kids suggested door-to-door surveys, and they suggested making their own commercials.

The week following my visit Mrs. Bernat planned to bring in examples of honest advertising, lest her students get the idea that all advertisers are "stretching things," as one of them told me. (There are studies showing that by the eighth or ninth grade many youngsters disbelieve all TV advertising.)

Eventually Winnie Bernat's students will "market" their taped ad show to other classes at the school. To do so they'll create handbills advertising the program, broadcast "radio" commercials over the school's public-address system, and personally "sell" the program to each teacher before they can show it. The catch is they've got to sell the show without using the subtle advertising techniques explained in their program.

A thought: If Ben Franklin's sixth graders successfully sell their program with honest, straightforward advertising, maybe we could ship in planeloads of advertising executives to have the kids show them how it's done.

Richard L. Strout:

The Capitol Gallery Case:
Is the Press Betraying Itself?

A CHAIN OF EVENTS began last August which led, to my considerable surprise, to my being thrown out of the press galleries of Congress after 50 years.

Basically the issue is, I believe, whether it is proper for a working newsman to participate for pay in a weekly, three-man Voice of America panel discussion program called "Issues in the News." This is broadcast in English to all parts of the world. I did this four times last year at $55 a time.

The following unsolicited letter from Francis H. Russell, former Ambassador to New Zealand, was sent to Gene Bernhardt, '74 chairman of the five-member Standing Committee of Correspondents, that imposed the anti-VOA rule. Mr Russell presently teaches at the Fletcher School of Diplomacy, Tufts University. He likes the program.

> Those of us who treasure the American free press and its image abroad can only assume that the Standing Committee of Correspondents did not know what it was doing when it ended Richard Strout's 50 years of membership because from time to time he takes part in the VOA program "Issues in the News."
>
> In my 15 years as an American representative abroad there was nothing that so vividly conveyed to the world the American concept of the relationship of press and government as that program. Every Saturday afternoon a constantly rotating group of three or four eminent U.S. journalists and commentators such as Marquis Childs, Peter Lisagor, Roscoe Drummond and Richard Strout would hold a conversation on the important international and national issues of the day,

(Mr. Strout is a Washington reporter for *The Christian Science Monitor*. This article is reprinted by permission from *The Bulletin* of the American Society of Newspaper Editors April, 1974).

speaking in the living rooms of the world just as frankly and tren-
chantly as they did at home. The Congress, the White House, the
Supreme Court, big business and big labor were as likely to be criticized as approved, or half and half.

No other country, not even Britain, gave as fine an example of the
government using its facilities to present its free press in action as the
U.S. did in this program. Were we Americans abroad proud!

Occasionally we wondered if JFK or LBJ or RMN or members of
Congress knew what the VOA was conveying about them and
whether, if they did, the program might be axed. But it never occurred
to us, I have to admit, that a committee of the press itself would attempt this act. If you are not to have press representatives of the distinction I have mentioned speaking to the world, then who?

Needless to say nobody wants members of the press who cover
Congress to use their position to sell toothpaste or write speeches for
Congressmen. But if the press hasn't the IQ to draw a line between a
presentation to the world of the U.S. press at its best and commercial
moonlighting, we're leaning on an awfully weak reed.

There is no personal rancor in this dispute. I am sure that the Standing
Committee is acting in good faith. The Committee on Rules and Administration, U.S. Senate, of which Sen. Howard W. Cannon (D. Nev.) is presently
chairman, delegates to the five-member Standing Committee of Correspondents, periodically elected, the decision as to who gets, or doesn't get,
gallery cards. In some cases (particularly for a young reporter) a gallery card
might make the difference in getting a job.

The American press has been under attack and the Standing Committee
wants to help keep it unsullied. Last summer it ordered new accreditation
application forms printed and distributed to all current members. I got mine
August 17. It contained this pledge:

"Do you agree not to accept payment for publicity, advertising or promotion work for any individual, corporation or organization while a member of the
Press Galleries, including payment for appearances on radio-television programs sponsored by Members of Congress or the Federal Government?"

I wrote on my application form:

"I have been on panels of Voice of America, and get paid for it; no
propaganda."

My reply wasn't satisfactory. I and several others who protested the new
interpretation of the Standing Committee's authority explained our position at a
committee meeting, October 1.

Our group made these points:

(a) the VOA ought to be supported, particularly when and if it takes an independent line, like the BBC; (b) that the Periodical Gallery (maintained for
magazines, in distinction to that for newspapers) does not have such a rule; (c)

that the White House Correspondents' Association has no such rule and that (d) anyway, it was a pretty silly business and would get the Committee laughed at.

In questions put to us the committee raised these points:

(a) Members of Congress have hired reporters to appear on panel shows and the committee could not crack down on this supposed abuse without including the Executive Branch, too; (b) that if reporters felt they were doing a public service by going on the VOA panel show, why didn't they do it free? (c) actions of the committee were not controlled by what other professional groups did.

After an appropriate interval the committee unanimously voted against us. A nice note from William J. (Bill) Eaton, then chairman of the committee, said it wasn't personal. [Eaton is with the Chicago Daily News. The other four members of the Standing Committee at the time were: Patrick J. Sloyan, Hearst Newspapers; Gene Bernhardt, UPI; Shirley Elder, Washington Star-News, and Leo Rennert, McClatchy Newspapers.]

Another reporter and I exhausted our remedies by carrying the matter unavailingly to Michael L. Reed, legislative assistant of Speaker Carl Albert (who shares with Senator Cannon the nuisance-job of looking after the press galleries).

The episode surprised me. I find myself out of character: I never before even wrote a letter-to-the-editor. There has been a lot of publicity, most unfavorable to the committee, and generally taking the position of how-silly-can-you-get? My name has been dropped from the 1974 Congressional Directory. I go to hearings much as before. I received an unsolicited letter from Rep. Wayne Hays (D. Ohio) who turns out to be chairman of the Joint Committee on Printing, saying that he will see to it that my name is restored in the 1975 Directory. Thanks, Congressman.

I can't take the matter very seriously; the greatest discomfort I have is in being treated as some kind of a martyr by well-meaning sympathizers. But there are a couple of points which, I think, are important.

Who shall police the press?

My judgment is, after being around a while, that the present unwritten three-way police system works pretty well (at least in Washington) without need of outside supervision. The reporter himself may be biased, but he wants to be right, he puts his scoop ahead of his prejudices; in other words, professional pride is involved. Secondly, he has a boss who is watching him. (In my case, I would drop the gallery card business at once if my paper objected.) Thirdly, there is a fairly tight professional circle here in Washington, and I cannot believe that a corrupt reporter would get very far without hearing from his peers.

Who shall have access to press facilities?

A number of cases here recently make me wonder if freedom of the press isn't being betrayed by the press itself, or by its earnest and sincere guardians. A court, for example, had to step in and slap down the Periodical Correspondents' Association which tried to bar a writer from *Consumer Reports*. Then again, Robert Sherrill, the correspondent of *The Nation,* and a writer for Alternative Press Syndicate were barred from presidential press conferences, and have filed suit. It turns out that their applications for White House cards were barred by the Secret Service for "reasons of security." (This is pretty funny if you have read Sherrill's careful pieces in *The New York Times* magazine.) Now comes this stupid business of barring reporters who take government radio-TV pay. (The Committee of Correspondents says it is all right to appear on Meet the Press, or even on one of the Public Broadcasting news shows, though the latter are largely financed by government money. It is the VOA which is dangerous—though not to the Periodical Gallery.)

Should the press boycott VOA?

For me this is the real issue, though perhaps I cannot communicate it. I don't think the VOA as an international medium compares with the BBC. The managers cannot understand that the best way of selling America abroad, the best propaganda, is just to try to be fair, give the facts (even on disagreeable subjects like Watergate) and achieve credibility. My shortwave brings in Moscow and the stuff is so distorted it is funny. I have children living abroad—one in the Middle East, the other the Far East—and they generally prefer BBC to VOA for the reasons stated. As Ambassador Russell says, this half-hour, once-a-week VOA "Issues in the News" can be of great help, however, and it seems to me that the press should encourage, not hamper it. The payment is minute compared to commercial shows. Some 1,200 fellow reporters signed the cryptic pledge and many tell me they didn't know it involved VOA. A hot lot of investigatory journalists they are.

Here's a cheerful note at the end. B. P. McDonough, who says he owns Dromoland Castle, County Clare, Ireland, has sympathetically observed my plight and has invited me to this tourist attraction for "six days and five nights with all accommodations (brochures enclosed)." Now that's a letter I like! All these other letters just take time to answer and offer commiseration; Mr. McDonough crashes through with something concrete. In a postscript he offers to pay $250 to any legal costs I incur. Will I see you in Dromoland? Mr. McDonough's offer includes "Mrs. Strout and/or your girlfriend."

I thanked him warmly, though I explained at my age I had better stick to my wife.

William B. Blankenburg and Richard L. Allen:

The Journalism Contest Thicket:
Is it Time for Some Guidelines?

SHORTLY AFTER the turn of the century, in a memorandum that began with the word "incidentally," Joseph Pulitzer proposed to give money for "annual prizes to particular journalists or writers for various accomplishments, achievements and forms of excellence." The Pulitzer Prizes were first presented in 1917 and remain today the most prestigious journalistic awards.

Since then contests and prizes for journalists have proliferated beyond count. *Editor & Publisher* listed 107 major contests in late 1973, but did not include state and local competitions or strictly parochial awards. Prize money totaled over $100,000. As well as can be determined, 70 percent of these contests were sponsored in whole or in part by nonjournalistic interests.

Little criticism has been aimed at contests, probably because they reflect favorably on both winner and sponsor, and there are no indentifiable losers. Contests are *positive* evaluations of the press. Presumably no one is hurt.

Yet there are doubts. Last year's report of the APME Professional Standards Committee raised some questions: "Why are all those people offering all that money to recognize outstanding newspaper work? Are they sincerely interested in raising our level of professionalism? Probably not, your committee believes. More likely, the hope is that such contests will stimulate stories about certain things—hi fis, swimming pools, etc."

One result of last year's doubts is this year's survey of managing editors by the University of Wisconsin School of Journalism and Mass Communication at the request of the Professional Standards Committee.

The findings are reported in detail later, but here are some capsule conclusions:

1. On the whole, contests are well regarded—most newspapers enter contests and most eventually win something.

Mr. Blankenburg is an associate professor of journalism at the University of Wisconsin in Madison. Mr. Allen is a former graduate student there. A condensed version of this paper appeared in the *APME News* of the Associated Press Managing Editors Association (Sept., 1974). This paper is printed here by permission.

2. The main virtue of contests is recognition for individual journalists and newspapers.
3. The main problems of contests are the taint of commercial sponsorship, doubtful motives of sponsors and participants, and the quality of judging.
4. Although practically every newspaper has policies restricting conflicts of interest, hardly any regulate participation in contests.
5. Two-thirds of the responding editors favor the idea of the APME composing ethical guidelines on contests.

The survey sample of 175 was drawn at random from an APME membership list. Only newspapers having circulations above 20,000 were polled. The first mailing went out on March 8, 1974, and a duplicate followup was sent to nonrespondents on March 30. At the time the survey was closed on April 15, 114 questionnaires had been returned, or 65 percent. (Nine more questionnaires arrived later and were not included in the numerical analysis, but were reviewed for their comments.) Those respondents who wished to remain anonymous are not identified by name in this report.

Table 1 tells where the responses came from according to geography and circulation.

TABLE 1
Responses by Region and by Circulation

	Region				
Circulation	Midwest	South	East	West	Total
100,000 and above	12	6	10	8	36
50,000 to 99,999	2	9	8	4	23
20,000 to 49,999	25	10	12	8	55
Total	39	25	30	20	114

The popularity of contests was apparent in the response to several questions. Two-thirds of the editors have a favorable general opinion of contests and over half actively encourage staff participation, and only one said he discouraged participation.

What is your general opinion of journalistic contests?

Very favorable	8.8%
Favorable	59.6
Unfavorable	7.0

Very unfavorable   2.6
Neutral or no response   21.9
(Percentages here and elsewhere may not
total 100.0% because of rounding error.)

Does your newspaper encourage or discourage staff participation in journalistic contests?

Encourage   53.5%
Depends on contest   28.1
Discourage   .9
Neutral or no response   17.6

Has your newspaper or staff entered any news or editorial contests during the last year?

Yes   91.2%
No   8.8

If Yes, has your newspaper or staff members won any of those contests?

Yes   81.6%
No   11.4
No response   7.0

The editors who won contests were also asked to indicate how many they had won during the previous year. Of those naming awards, 43.5 percent reported four or more winning entries. Only 25.9 percent had captured only one prize. Table 2 shows the rate of success by circulation size.

TABLE 2

Number of Contests Won "Last Year" by Size of Newspaper

| | Circulation | | | |
Contests won	100,000 and above	50,000 to 99,999	20,000 to 49,999	Total
One	16.7%	22.2%	34.1%	25.9%
Two	23.3	22.2	27.0	24.7
Three	3.3	5.6	8.1	5.9
Four or more	56.7	50.0	29.7	43.5
Total	100.0%	100.0%	100.0%	100.0%

It is apparent from the table that larger newspapers win more prizes than smaller newspapers. This is understandable because responses to another question indicated that larger newspapers are more likely to enter contests. However, there was no particular difference of general opinion of contests among those who had won and those who had not.

About 40 percent of the editors had themselves been judges of contests during the previous year. Those editors who had judged contests during the past year showed a significantly higher opinion of the quality of judging than those who had not. The former judges also had a higher general opinion of contests.

On the whole, the editors liked contests, but they liked some better than others. (The Cigar Institute award for the best picture of a prominent cigar-puffer was widely disdained.) The editors were asked to rate the worthiness of 15 contests, and they appear in Table 3 in descending order of perceived value.

TABLE 3
Evaluation of Specific Contests

Rank	Contest	Very much worthwhile	Generally worthwhile	Neutral	Not especially worthwhile	Not at all worthwhile	No response
1.	Pulitzer Prize for Meritorious Public Service	78.1%	17.5%	1.8%	0.0%	0.0%	2.6%
2.	Sigma Delta Chi Awards for Distinguished Service in Journalism	62.3	27.2	7.9	0.0	0.0	2.6
3.	APME Public Service Awards	49.1	39.5	8.8	.9	0.0	1.8
4.	Your state's AP Association Contest	36.0	43.0	8.8	3.5	.9	7.9
5.	Your state's UPI Contest	18.4	30.7	21.1	1.8	1.8	26.3
6.	A local or regional press club contest	21.1	36.0	20.2	4.4	4.4	14.0
7.	Edward J. Meeman Conservation Awards for environmental writing	8.8	26.3	44.7	4.4	0.0	15.8

Rank	Contest	Very much worthwhile	Generally worthwhile	Neutral	Not especially worthwhile	Not at all worthwhile	No response
8.	American Bar Association "Gavel" Awards for newswriting on the law	13.2	34.2	31.6	9.6	7.0	4.4
9.	Freedoms Foundation Awards for articles and cartoons	8.8	36.0	32.5	11.4	5.3	6.1
10.	John Hancock Awards for business and financial writing	3.5	15.8	41.2	16.3	10.5	9.6
11.	American Meat Institute "Vesta" Awards for reporting about food	.9	7.0	27.2	20.2	34.2	10.5
12.	Schick Safety Razor Co. Awards for best pro football story of the year	0.0	3.5	32.5	19.3	37.7	7.0
13.	American Osteopathic Assn. Awards for reporting and interpreting osteopathy	.9	2.6	27.2	21.9	40.4	7.0
14.	American Furniture Mart Awards for reporting on home furnishing	0.0	2.6	26.3	25.4	40.4	5.3
15.	Koss Corporation Awards for series on hi-fi and home electronics	.9	1.8	19.3	20.2	48.2	9.6

The contests selected for evaluation by the editors were arbitrarily chosen to provide a range of quality and sponsorship. In cases where the percentages are high for nonresponse and neutrality, the contests were perhaps not well known. However, it is apparent from the ranking that the most favored contests are those sponsored by journalistic organizations. Lowest are those sponsored by commercial organizations and associations that may have public-relations motives.

Although there is a doubtful side to contests, a large majority of newspapers have done little about it. Only 15.8 percent of the respondents said their newspapers had written or unwritten policies regarding participation in competitions, and several of those policies were simply to encourage entries by staff members. This is in distinct contrast to concern over other areas of potential conflict, as shown in Table 4.

TABLE 4

Percentage of Newspapers Having Policies on Certain Activities

Policy on:	Yes	No	No response
Accepting gifts from advertisers, PR firms, or news services	79.8%	17.5%	2.7%
Active membership in political or other organizations that might indicate a conflict of interest	78.1	20.2	1.8
Accepting travel expenses in connection with news events	70.2	28.1	1.8
Engaging in outside employment or freelancing	66.7	29.8	3.5
Accepting complimentary tickets or passes to athletic or entertainment events	40.4	57.9	1.8
Participation in journalistic contests	15.8	81.6	2.6

What, exactly, is good and bad about contests? The editors offered many comments, and they were also given two sets of statements, favorable and unfavorable toward contests, about which they could state a position. The results appear in Table 5. The ambiguities of contests are readily apparent: Contests are a good source of PR for the newspaper, yet too many are self-serving for the sponsors. Contests provide independent appraisal, yet standards should not be set by outsiders, nor do contests adequately suffice as a form of criticism.

TABLE 5

Percentage Agreeing and Disagreeing on Certain Aspects of Contests

"Favorable aspects"	Agree	Disagree	Neutral no response
Contests provide independent appraisal of journalistic performance	66.7%	14.0%	19.3%

"Favorable aspects"	Agree	Disagree	Neutral no response
Contests encourage better work by staff members	47.4	26.3	26.3
Contests are a good kind of recognition for staff members	80.7	3.5	15.8
Contests are a good source of public relations for the newspaper	74.6	6.1	19.3
Contests are a potential source of supplementary income for staff members	11.4	53.5	35.1

"Unfavorable aspects"	Agree	Disagree	Neutral no response
Contests do not provide sufficient reward for the work entailed	16.7	35.9	47.4
Nonjournalists should not set standards for performance in contests	59.6	13.1	27.3
Contests do not suffice as a form of criticism	67.5	8.8	23.7
Too many contests are self-serving means of publicity for the sponsors	88.6	.9	10.5
Contests are usually not carefully judged	39.5	17.5	43.0

Because contests are so well entrenched and so few newspapers have policies regarding participation, it is somewhat surprising to find 65 percent of the responding editors agreeing that an APME code of ethics should contain advice on contests. Here is the question:

If the APME formulates a code of ethics . . . should the code include a section on journalistic contests?

Certainly	24.6%
Probably	40.4
Probably not	23.7
Certainly not	.9
Don't know	10.5

It is not just those who have low opinions of contests who feel that an APME code should touch upon contest ethics. Table 6 compares opinions on contests with those on a contest code (the "certainly" and "probably" categories have been combined):

TABLE 6

Opinions on Contests Compared With Opinions on a Contest Code

	Opinion on Contests		
Opinion on a Contest Code	Favorable	Unfavorable	Neutral or no response
Favorable	66.7%	54.5%	64.0%
Unfavorable	25.6	36.4	16.0
Don't know	7.9	9.1	20.0

Relatedly, the proportions of editors favoring a code do not vary greatly according to circulation-size. About 72 percent of the editors of the 100,000-plus newspapers favor a code while the editors of the middle- and small-sized newspapers give it about 61 percent support.

However, there are some differences by region. Editors of Western newspapers split evenly on the question of a code. Southern editors favor a code by 76 percent while Eastern and Midwestern editors gave it 66.7 percent support.

Editors' Comments

In addition to checking off answers to the questionnaire, slightly more than half of the responding editors added comments on contests and suggested ways to improve them.

Typical of the general observations was that of John W. Eure, managing editor of the Roanoke *World-News:* "The value, indeed acceptability, of contests varies widely; the chief factor is the sponsorship. We look askance at those sponsored by a commercial firm or trade association and having to do with a product or service of the firm or association, though we do not ban participation outright. We look with more favor on the contests sponsored by professional organizations—the bar or medical societies, though the distinction is by no means clear and easily defended.

"Contests sponsored by newspaper organizations are in another category. We encourage entries, believing they can contribute to staff morale and the paper's public relations (if we win). I have strong reservations about competence and care in the judging of such press association contests, having done a good bit of this judging myself in the past."

The editors' comments can be roughly sorted into three groups: on the principle of contests, on the mechanics, and on the question of an APME contest code.

The Merits of Contests

As for the merits of contests, some of the comments were quite succinct. Kenneth E. Berg. of the Mankato (Minn.) *Free Press* has a one-word policy: "TRY." Mike Nickel of the Hayward (Calif.) *Daily Review* siad, "I like them when we win." Harry Maier, Sheboygan (Wis.) *Press,* wrote: "Just too many contests."

Morale and public relations were among the major virtues of winning prizes, according to several editors. "I can see two excellent reasons for competing," said Elvin Henson of the Jacksonville (Fla.) *Journal,* who has been a Pulitzer juror. "If you win, you gain the impression of quality and this should improve staff morale. . . . If you are a regular winner, your paper gets a reputation for quality, and this makes recruiting easier."

So it is not surprising that one editor said his policy was "to get into as many as possible." But Jack Hagerty of the Grand Forks (N.D.) *Herald* was more restrained: "We would have nothing against entering such contests as the Penney-University of Missouri women's page contest, Inland Daily Press Association contests, etc., if we thought we were doing a job outstanding enough to warrant entry. So far, we are not satisfied enough with our own performance, however, to do so."

"Contests are fun things and do more good than harm," was the conclusion of an Eastern editor. Like many others, he noted that a potential for harm exists in self-serving commercially sponsored contests: "Contests by business or pressure groups are taboo and I don't think we ever entered one."

"It depends on the contest," said Ben J. Bowers, executive editor of the Roanoke *Times*. "Pulitzer yes, American Furniture Mart-type, no."

Joe Smyth of the *Delaware State News* discourages entry into contests other than those sponsored by newspaper associations. "No self-respecting journalist should participate in special-interest contests sponsored by trade associations and commercial firms to promote their professions or products," he wrote. "It's frightening to see how many respected newspapers allow themselves to be used for the promotion of products and other special interests, in return for a brass plaque."

Why, then, do editors permit entry into competitions they deplore? Sometimes it's management's choice, not theirs. Jack Foster, assistant M.E. of the Dayton (Ohio) *Daily News,* reported that management selects and prepares entries: "Since the contests exist, we enter a few high-prestige contests for promotional purposes—if we win—and to do a little ego-stroking for reporters. My personal belief is that contests are meaningless, poorly judged and do a disservice to journalism. I know two reporters whose egoes were so greatly enlarged by winning contests that it ruined their careers. If it were in my power, I would ban newspaper contests. I doubt that very many would agree, unfortunately."

And sometimes an editor's policy doesn't seem very effective. The editor of a major metropolitan paper said, ''We do not recognize contests sponsored for a commercial nature—Cigar Institute, Milk Foundation, etc.'' Yet the list of awards won by his newspaper in 1973 includes those sponsored by the Milk Foundation, a city builders' association, Associated General Contractors of America, American Bar Association, state department of mental health, state medical society, and the American Society of Planning Officials.

Three levels of sponsorship can be perceived. In the first tier are journalistically·sponsored contests, such as the Sigma Delta Chi and APME Public Service Awards. In the third tier are foundation- and corporation-sponsored competitions, such as those of the American Osteopathic Association and the Koss Corporation, whose motives are very much in doubt. (See Table 3.) The problem of evaluating sponsorship seems most difficult in the middle tier, which includes such events as the John Hancock competition for business and financial writing and the Missouri-Penney awards.

Of the middle tier, one editor said, ''Others, although linked to specific-interest groups, make a genuine effort to find and reward material which is public-educational and which provides genuine public service in a forward, positive way.''

Yet another problem was noted by several editors. It goes deeper than sponsorship: the question of benefit for the subscriber.

''The best judge of a newspaper is Joe Citizen, who either buys it or doesn't,'' wrote Ronald E. Rakos of the Woodbridge (N.J.) *News Tribune*.

Sid Hurlburt, Newburgh (N.Y.) *Evening News,* elaborated: ''We must be wary of contests becoming a not-very-subtle form of payola and our news judgment being warped by the desire to publish what will be a 'suitable' entry for a contest promoted by a special interest.''

Elwood M. Wardlow of the Buffalo *Evening News* observed, ''Both editors and reporters can fall victim to unbalanced judgment if they give high priority to winning prizes as opposed to serving the reader a unified, complete and balanced product.''

Said Thomas W. Jobson of the Asbury Park (N.J.) *Press,* ''In this day and age our products should speak for themselves without a lot of plaques hanging in the showcase. Readers aren't that naive—they want information they can trust—not a slice of baloney.''

Quoting Charlotte Curtis of the New York *Times* when she spoke at the Penney-Missouri awards dinner, George V. Hanson of the Racine (Wis.) *Journal Times* agreed: ''The responsible reporter and editor should report and edit in terms of what is of interest to their community, not in terms of another city. . . . If a paper is a hit with the readers in its own community, you are a winner whether anyone gives you a prize or not. If the paper bores your readers a prize is meaningless.''

Contests should be no more than a ''spin-off of journalistic effort,'' according to Richard P. Hronek of the Boise *Idaho Statesman*. ''If, in retrospect, a reporter's work 'fits' the provisions and entry rules of some contest, then his work should be entered. We do not and would not encourage our people to write a story with the idea of winning a specific contest.''

The Mechanics of Contests

Contest procedures evoked more comments than any other area. Problems (and some opportunities) were noted in regard to entry forms, judging, categories, award money, and publicity.

Paul Murphy, assistant to the executive editor of the Philadelphia *Bulletin,* commented, ''Good Lord, the thicket of rules is overwhelming . . . If I were king of the hill, I'd require:

—Nothing mounted, and no scrapbooks (except where great volume of an exhibit might necessitate it). Full-page tearsheets *or* photocopies of entered material, with the entered items outlined or circled . . .

—Simple entry blank asking for identity of author and newspaper; category in which it is entered; classification as to circulation . . .; date of publication, and signature of editor. . . .

—Rules to allow (but not require) an accompanying statement about highlights of the entry, problems in getting the picture or the story, and anything else which might help judges.''

By the way, the New England Associated Press News Executives Association (NEAPNEA) contest requires that stories be submitted without heads and without illustrations, and must be pasted to the letterhead of the submitting member. At least one editor urged that entries be standardized to reduce eye-appeal in contests based on writing. One editor proposed that the APME compose a ''plan for holding a meaningful news contest'' that could serve as a model for sponsors.

Jack Barkley, editor of the Kokomo *Tribune,* agreed that story background should be included with entries. Moreover, he is concerned with categories: ''What really is a news story, a feature, etc.? Few contests allow, much less ask for, a statement from the entrant about such things as deadline pressures, difficulty in reaching sources, number of people who may have assisted in gathering information, etc. Are these perhaps many, many aspects of what really makes a good newsman click and the story he or she produces left out of all contest judging? I think so.''

Circulation categories are frequently used to stratify entries in contests, and the dividing lines are not always the best, according to some editors. Buddy Baker, assistant to the publisher of the 64,000-circulation Cocoa (Fla.) *Today,* remarked, ''Many contests use a 50,000-and-over dividing line for the top category: this lumps the nation's medium-size dailies in with the 200,000-plus giants.''

Size categories also yield some peculiar consequences when it comes to judging, according to Kenneth E. Berg, editor of the Mankato *Free Press:*

"We have been consistently judged *higher* by judges from larger newspapers, but *lower* by judges from smaller newspapers. I can only surmise that the larger ones thought we were doing *better* than they expected, and the smaller ones *less* than we should."

The editor of a medium-sized daily in a sparsely settled Western state commented, "Our competition here is so limited that I detect a desire by those judging the contest to spread the awards around a little just to make everyone feel good."

On the other hand, another Westerner complained of the opposite result: "In our area contests have been dominated by one particular metropolitan paper which flooded entries and won the majority of prizes, then used its track record to advertise its own product—this left a bad taste with many in the business and downgraded the contest, in my opinion."

As expected, the process and quality of judging were heavily criticized.

Too often, several editors said, whim and whimsy rule the judges' decisions. Said Jack Barkley of the Kokomo *Tribune,* "I fear teams of judges use entirely different values in judging. And, I fear, much of the blame for this is inadequate ground rules being laid down for the judges."

"The system of judging is incredibly bad," wrote Darrell Sifford of the Charlotte *News.* "More care needs to be taken in selection of judges and they should be compensated adequately for the time they take. Now the difference between a winning and losing entry may be nothing more journalistic than whether or not the judge had a fight with his wife before he sat down to judge."

Speaking of wives, a New England editor explained that photos are voted on at the annual NEAPNEA convention "by both editors (the experts) and their wives (the REAL experts)." The writing awards, however, are judged by "outsiders" and the Sevellon Brown Award for public service was named by Arthur Deck of Salt Lake City, president of ASNE.

The consensus recommendation is for judging by peers—other professional journalists. "I deplore judging of newspaper awards by flacks or other non-journalists," said René Cazenave of the San Francisco *Examiner.* "I arranged for the present judging of the Los Angeles and San Francisco Press Club awards by all-journalist or journalism-professor boards of the opposite clubs." One Midwestern editor would also exclude "college professors, without media experience, who judge everything on textbook guidelines."

Still, one New York state editor commented, "I strongly oppose the suggestion that journalists alone can or should be the judges of what 'should' be done, or what is positive and helpful to the public."

The use of outside judges has some attractions—and some critics. Ronald E. Rakos of the Woodbridge (N.J.) *Tribune,* wrote: "If there is a contest, it should be judged by people who know what the hell goes on in this state. I'd be in favor of a permanent panel of judges made up of retired New Jersey newspaper editors, managing editors, city editors, etc., but not including those who have left the business for PR, etc.''

As one who has been a judge of contests in other states, Thomas W. Jobson of Asbury Park commented: ''I know we try to do our best—but studying clips and tearsheets often, mostly always, doesn't give you the long haul opinion of an entry. At best, it's a shotgun decision, done from a remote point— cursory and superficial.''

A few editors were concerned with the self-selection of contestants, and Al Williams of the Scranton (Pa.) *Tribune* suggested a modification: ''I think some journalistic group should be responsible for checking newspapers in various regions of the U.S. and should be responsible for making nominations for writing awards, I feel the same people enter journalistic contests every year; and many excellent writers do not.''

Like Darrell Sifford, Dick Rasmussen of the Stockton (Calif.) *Record* suggested monetary compensation for judges, and one editor asked whether entry fees shouldn't be generally required.

The most frequently cited rewards for winning a contest were ''pride'' and ''morale'' and ''PR for the paper,'' but there were some additional comments here, too. Buddy Baker of *Today* had some practical suggestions: ''We prefer plaques to trophies because they usually are more attractive and are more easily and effectively displayed in a 'trophy case.' In addition to awards, mini-critiques by the judges should be provided. Even though the award may not include a cash prize, this provides ego income for the winners; these comments also make for effective in-paper promotions propaganda.''

One newspaper, the *Idaho Statesman,* makes sure there is a monetary reward for its staff. According to M. E. Richard P. Hronek, winners of recognized contests receive a premium, which is added to their weekly paychecks. Amounts vary.

Elvin Hanson of the Jacksonville *Journal* argues that ''strictly promotional contests nearly always offer cash awards; so should the strictly journalism contests.'' Actually, the proportions of cash awards given by journalistic and nonjournalistic sponsors is not very different, according to an analysis done by the authors of this report. As near as we could tell from the *E&P* list of contests, 47 percent of journalistic and 68 percent of nonjournalistically sponsored contests offer cash prizes. The average amount among those who specified cash awards is $1656 for journalistic contests and $1756 for the nonjournalistic.

Publicity for the winning newspaper is an obvious reward, but it is often applied selfishly, according to one New England editor: ''I think newspapers err in not carrying news reports about, for instance, the Sevellon Brown award given by NEAPNEA because it was won by some newspaper in their area other than their own. But they do not hesitate a bit to publicize the Emmy, Oscar and all sorts of other awards. We seem to prefer to publicize what other media are doing in the award line rather than what newspapers do.''

Ronald E. Rakos of the Woodbridge *News Tribune,* who describes himself as "an anti-contest person," sees more value in education than prizes. "If I had my way I'd (1) run a two-day improve-your-newspaper seminar and forget about the ego-trip newspaper contests; or (2) run a contest with the seminar, but wouldn't make the contest the main event."

Bruce Manning of the Jacksonville *Times-Union* agrees in principle: "I feel that most bona fide news contests fail to achieve real benefit for newspapers and their staffs because they (the contest operators) don't let the non-winners see what copped the prize. We are losing, insofar as professional contests are concerned, a good educational tool for upgrading and motivating, when we neglect to reproduce and widely distribute the winning entries. A losing entrant never sees what beat him. Those who didn't enter never see what it is that can win. For a few mickles more of effort we could get a muckle of benefits from news contests."

Bill Schrader, editor of the Bloomington *Herald-Telephone* would have the criticism extend to "all entries, not just those that are judged winners. If contests were handled in this manner something could be gained by both the winners and the losers."

Frank Leeming, Jr., assistant to the executive editor of the Philadelphia *Inquirer,* hazarded what he called a "way-out" suggestion: "Maybe there's a place for a sort of sweepstakes winner where you could break the contests down into major ones, i.e., Pulitzer, SDX, Headliner, Polk, Hancock, and minor ones and assign points to the winners of each and come up at the end of the year with a grand winner, either newspaper or reporter/photo/wire service. It's wild and will never be done, but it would be fun."

Comments about a Code

One of the purposes of the survey was to determine whether editors were interested in having the APME include guidelines on contests if the organization composed a general code of journalistic ethics. As noted earlier, 65 percent of the respondents favored ("certainly" or "probably") such an inclusion. Several added comments, positive and negative.

An editor who strongly opposed such a code was Darrell Sifford, who said, "The decision is each newspaper's—not the APME's."

Another negative vote came from Ed Johnson of the Gainesville *Sun,* who said, "The success or failure of the offensive contests will depend upon the professionalism of the eligible entrants, not the judges, and not the sponsors. Most of us are inclined to take the other contests—the worthwhile ones—too seriously. And a few of us don't know the difference."

"I think we have any number of important things to be concerned about in our profession other than contests," wrote Louis G. Gerdes of the Omaha *World-Herald.*

Judith W. Brown, editor of the New Britain (Conn.) *Herald,* asked, "Is it possible or even necessary to try to regulate everything?'' However, she noted that the APME should ''probably'' have a code on contests.

Like several other editors who favor a code on contests, Howard Kleinberg of the Miami *News* isn't sure the problems can be eradicated: ''There really is no way the contests can be controlled. No one will ever manage to get ALL newspapers to restrict their entries. . . . If all newspapers would agree, the special-interest contests would dry up, but I'm afraid that will never happen.''

A first step that APME could take, according to several editors, would be to evaluate contests according to their merits. ''I would like to see as extensive a list as possible from APME or other professional group about current contests,'' wrote an Ohio editor. He would like to know which contests are based on good journalism rather than promotion and which are judged by working journalists. Frank Leeming of Philadelphia added that such a list should be circulated annually.

The next step, wrote Roy L. Barron, Kankakee *Daily Journal,* would be to ''endorse such contests as AP, UPI, or by other editorial organization sponsorship.'' Les Trautmann of the Staten Island *Advance* would also ''set up a code urging nonparticipation in contests not run by journalistic organizations.''

''It is easy to determine which contest is run for publicity purposes and which are on the up and up,'' wrote Robert J. Boyle of the Pottstown (Pa.) *Mercury*. Richard L. Stegeman of the East St. Louis *Metro-East Journal* agreed: ''Really, it ought to be a simple enough problem to sort out.''

But others weren't so sure it would be easy, no matter how desirable. Richard B. Tuttle of the Rochester *Democrat and Chronicle* observed, ''The John Hancock award for business writing has a good reputation, I believe, based on a slight knowledge of previous winners, but was it really established for clearly noncommercial reasons? What about Missouri-Penney? Certainly a fine reputation connected with a fine journalism school. But how and why did it get started? Where should the line be drawn?''

Joseph W. Dunn, Jr. of the Norfolk *Virginian-Pilot,* who favors a code, remarked, ''I don't know how APME realistically can adopt a policy on contests *per se* without investigating each and every one—that's a tremendous job. but one that ought to be undertaken if APME is to evolve such a policy.''

The final word goes to Joe Shoquist of the Milwaukee *Journal:* ''The whole contest mess needs to be evaluated by someone who will do it impartially.''

Ralph D. Barney:

The Ways of the Corrupters

A SERIOUS PROBLEM for the concept of ethics in communications is posed by the environment within which the communicator, whether he is a journalist, advertiser or author, operates.

By its very nature, a "free" society which has a rather high capability for self-determination shapes the ethics of the public institutions which operate within it. Communicators are 1) continually under assault by those who would alter the communicator's ethical determinants in service of their own self interests, and 2) constantly under scrutiny and subjected to the judgment of a variety of interest groups.

For our deliberations here, the public institutions with which we are most concerned are the institutions that have emerged as the disseminators of information, with the assumed responsibility—collectively—of providing sufficient information to the society that it will be able—again, collectively—to make rational decisions. These institutions range from the spectrum of newspapers through television, radio, books, movies and others of the "public" mass media to the more specialized forms of "private" mass media, such as mass mailings of persuasive literature and other "campaigns" of persuasion conducted through a variety of media.

Because the ethics of those who serve as the middleman in the dissemination is the topic here, our focus will primarily be on the ones who prepare information for the public media, those who serve as intermediaries between the persuaders and the targets of the persuasion. The persuaders are those whose overt intent is to influence the public decision-making process.

The persuaders are obviously concerned with their own vested interests, whether they be material or ideological.

A major function they may almost automatically set for themselves, then, is to modify the behavior of communicators in favor of their own interests. That is, the persuader often offers rewards to the journalist with the hope—or knowledge—that he will provide the credible third person endorsement in the media that serves the persuader's interest.

Dr. Barney, a co-editor of this volume, is an associate professor in communications at Brigham Young University. This brief essay was written especially for this book.

On the other hand, the communicator's audience, or at least the organized segments of the audience, bring threatening pressure in other efforts to modify the performance of the communicator.

Though each of these groups work at destroying the ethical structure the journalist may have erected around himself, they differ in their assaults.

The persuader in the first instance may be a "friend" privately offering gratification, praise and rewards. Such onslaughts gently chip away at the ethical sensitivities by explaining why they are permissible.

In the second instance, however, the monitor's attack is frontal and public, designed to mobilize waves of assault forces and to put the journalist to flight by discrediting him in the eyes of his audience, forcing a public or semi-public recantation and surrender (ie., pushing the journalist into the posture of no longer dealing with the topic, or of reversing his field). In some instances, but probably not often, for obvious reasons, the persuader and the monitor are the same person.

A major concern here is that the larger audience of the journalist, the truly silent majority, has little capability for organizing itself to assist the journalist in formulating and clinging to his ethic. Yet, that audience—in a self-determining society—should be the single greatest consideration of the ethical journalist. It is that audience to whom he must ultimately account for his utterances, though the intermediate accounting procedures (demanded by the omnipresent persuader and monitor) undoubtedly complicate the process.

Therefore, the communicator, or the journalist, must choose often between the ethical line he infers for the benefit of his readers, in the absence of broadly based direction or pressures, or follow a line pressed upon him by organized forces with the vested interests.

The only thing the journalist can look to his audience for is its ability to respond to cumulative information if he keeps faith long enough and persists in serving what he views is the audience interest. Sometimes this appears a futile hope.

Thus, it might be said there is a singular lack of pressure for audience-oriented ethical behavior on the part of the journalist. Perhaps, as a result, few people feel as lonely as the journalist with a strong personal ethical code.

On the other hand, there is a series of pressures constantly exerted to channel the journalist into pathways that divert him from his audience responsibilities and into the service of the persuaders, or into silence by the monitors.

Such pressures are not mythical, but are very real. Each offer of an amenity on the part of a persuader is a pressure that is countered by nothing more, immediately, than the conscious ethical integrity of the journalist. Likewise, each threat of consequences is countered immediately by nothing more than the ethical integrity of the journalist.

In cases in which ethical integrity has not yet been developed to the degree it can withstand the pressures, there will be a singular victory for the persuader at the expense of the journalist's audience.

For example, an energetic promoter for a popular radio station in Honolulu some years ago dangled an almost irresistible carrot before the noses of high school newspaper editors in the islands to stimulate publicity for a popular music group the station was presenting in live concert.

The carrot was an invitation to the editor to attend a special, and exclusive, reception for members of the musical group. The pressure took the form of a requirement—enclosed with the invitation—that the editor bring, as a condition of admittance, proof he had run stories in his newspaper promoting the concert. The reception became, then, a payoff to editors who served the vested interests of the promoter-persuader.

Such a promotion took unfair advantage of a very real desire on the part of immature editors to be able to attend a reception and to become acquainted with a group of celebrities, while at the same time capitalizing on the weaknesses of undeveloped ethical character by these editors.

Such an example serves to dramatize the potential for corrupting the young, but further exploration produces instances in which more sophisticated carrots break down the ethical characters of more sophisticated journalists, or are at least designed for that purpose.

The carrot of expense-paid trips to distant and exotic lands is a common one in the travel industry. It is no secret that the airline offering the junket hopes to reap a reward of favorable publicity by the journalist, but in at least one instance an airline lined up an itinerary for a journalist and asked for a commitment—in writing—to a certain number of stories to result from the trip. The journalist declined in this instance, but the promoter of the radio station concert mentioned above defended the story requirement of high school editors by noting that airlines "always expect" the writers who receive their services to produce a number of favorable stories on return home. Such, the promoter said, is the "price that must be paid" for receiving benefits.

The travel and entertainment industries are not alone in making concerted efforts to produce favorable information flow for themselves, however. They provide only some of the more dramatic examples.

Additional examples may easily be found in any area in which the persuader is in a position to offer emolument to a journalist. In politics, journalists have been put on payrolls (clandestinely, perhaps through family members, or even openly as consultants); in business, reporters sometimes are made privy to, or secret participants in, business opportunities that will enrich them; in sports the team often picks up the traveling expense of the reporter, and in almost any area a reporter may be rewarded by access to information if he minimizes the problems for his formal news sources.

This is not meant to be a catalog of ways in which journalists' ethics may be compromised, nor should it be assumed that such practices are universal in the profession. It does serve to demonstrate, however, that it can be very comfortable and rewarding to be subservient to the persuader.

On the other hand, on a case-by-case basis society appears almost not to care whether the communications it receives are ethically sound. On the contrary, special interest groups spend a great deal of time and effort attempting to persuade and demonstrate to the journalist that he is—by acting ethically in his view—indeed being unethical.

Probably the best single example in recent history is the series of continuing disclosures by Bob Woodward and Carl Bernstein, the *Washington Post* reporters who doggedly developed information about Nixon Administration involvement in the Watergate breakin and subsequent coverup. Countering fairly widespread coverage given by the nation's press to the Woodward-Bernstein stories were consistent and unrelenting attempts by the Administration and its spokesmen to muster the support of the "silent majority" into pressures that would have effectively discouraged pursuit of Watergate-related information. A highly developed sense of responsibility to the people—one that the reporters themselves perhaps were only partially aware of—and the growing sense of knowing that the information was there and that they were on the right track kept the two reporters working on the story in the face of substantial public discouragement. If there had been a combination of unfruitful investigation and a rising up of the "silent majority," including other journalists who felt such pursuits were ill-conceived, the investigation could easily have been abandoned. Thus, in a sense, the truth of the Watergate matter could conceivably have been irrelevant to the reality of pressure by monitors.

Such instances, as have been cited above, despite the brevity of their discussion, should point to a central need emphasized either implicitly or explicitly throughout this volume. A journalist must decide early, in moments of considerable introspection and from a background of a relatively great amount of knowledge, what his philosophical and ethical stance will be toward the society he will find himself serving. That the society is an increasingly pluralistic one places more pressures upon him and will understandably contribute to his confusion and, perhaps, indecision.

However, the early ethical foundation a journalist constructs for himself becomes crucial to the superstructure he must surely grace it with as he becomes involved with the forces who would like to mold him, and who will devote considerable of their resources to the attempts.

It is not unlike other molding processes in which the softer, more pliable the clay, the more likely the casual passerby is able to make an impression. The more set the clay, the less likely a casual impression can alter its shape.

Thus, as a journalist finds himself in the middle of the battle before he has donned his ethical shield the more likely he is to be either wheedled into a compromising position or to be put to full rout by the monitors of the world.

It will be left to others to discuss the value of being flexible, and therefore impressionable (or teachable). Suffice it here to say that some minimum "set" is needed if the neophyte journalist is likely to be able to weather without yielding completely to the blandishments of the persuaders.

BIBLIOGRAPHY

Abelson, Raziel, *Ethics and Metaethics: Readings in Ethical Philosophy*. New York: St. Martin's Press, 1963.

Agee, Warren (ed.), *Mass Media in a Free Society*. Lawrence: University of Kansas Press, 1969.

————, The Press and the Public Interest. Washington: Public Affairs Press, 1968.

Aristotle, *Nichomachean Ethics,* trans. J. A. K. Thomson. Baltimore: Penguin Books, 1955.

Ashmore, Harry S., *Fear in the Air: Broadcasting and the First Amendment: The Anatomy of a Constitutional Crisis*. New York: Norton, 1973.

Baker, Samm S., *The Permissible Lie: The Inside Truth About Advertising*. Cleveland: World Publishing Co., 1968.

Bagdikian, Ben H., *The Effete Conspiracy and Other Crimes By The Press*. New York: Harper & Row, 1972.

Banner, William A., *Ethics: An Introduction to Moral Philosophy*. New York: Scribners, 1968.

Barnes, Hazel, *An Existentialist Ethics*. New York: Random House, Vintage Books, 1971.

Barron, Jerome A., *Freedom of the Press for Whom? The Right of Access to Mass Media*. Bloomington, Ind.: Indiana University Press, 1973.

Baynes, Ken (ed.), *Scoop, Scandal and Strife: A Study of Photography in Newspapers*. London: Lund Humphries, Publishers, Ltd. and New York: Hastings House, 1971.

Becker, Carl L., *Freedom and Responsibility in the American Way of Life*. New York: Alfred A. Knopf, 1945.

Berdyaev, N. A., *Destiny of Man*. New York: Scribners, 1937.

Berle, Adolph A., *Power*. New York: Harcourt, Brace and World, 1969.

322

Berlin, Isaiah, *Two Concepts of Liberty.* Oxford: Clarendon Press, 1958.

Berns, Walter, *Freedom, Virtue, and the First Amendment.* Baton Rouge: Louisiana State University Press, 1957.

Bernstein, Carl and Bob Woodward, *All the President's Men.* New York: Simon and Schuster, 1974.

Blanshard, Brand, *The Impasse in Ethics.* Berkeley: University of California Press, 1945.

Bloom, Melvyn H., *Public Relations and Presidential Campaigns:* A Crisis in Democracy. New York: Crowell, 1973.

Bockle, Franz (ed.), *The Manipulated Man: Religion in the Seventies.* New York: Herder and Herder, 1971.

Boorstin, Daniel J., *The Image: A Guide to Pseudo-Events in America.* New York: Atheneum, 1973.

Boyd, Forrest, *Instant Analysis: Confessions of a White House Correspondent.* Atlanta: John Knox Press, 1974.

Bradley, F. H., *Ethical Studies.* London: Stechert, 1904.

Broad, C. D., *Five Types of Ethical Theory.* New York: Harcourt Brace, 1930.

Brown, Lee, *The Reluctant Reformation: On Criticizing the Press in America.* New York: David McKay, 1974.

Brucker, Herbert, *Communication is Power.* New York: Oxford University Press, 1973.

Buell, Victor, *Changing Practices in Advertising Decision-Making.* New York: Association of National Advertisers, 1973.

Buxton, Edward, *Promise Them Anything: The Inside Story of the Madison Avenue Power Struggle.* New York: Stein and Day, 1972.

Cirino, Robert, *Don't Blame the People.* Los Angeles: Diversity Press, 1971.

———, *Power to Persuade: Mass Media and the News.* New York: Bantam Books, 1974.

Cline, Victor B., *Where Do You Draw the Line? An Exploration into Media Violence, Pornography and Censorship.* Provo: Brigham Young University Press, 1974.

Columbia Broadcasting System, *Point of View: Equal Time.* New York: CBS, 1960.

Commission on Freedom of the Press, *A Free and Responsible Press.* Chicago: University of Chicago Press, 1947.

Coons, John E. (ed.), *Freedom and Responsibility in Broadcasting.* Evanston, Ill.: Northwestern University Press, 1962.

Crawford, Nelson A., *The Ethics of Journalism.* New York: Alfred A. Knopf, 1924.

DeGeorge, Richard T., *Soviet Ethics and Morality.* Ann Arbor: University of Michigan Press, 1969.

Dennis, Everette E. and William L. Rivers, *Other Voices: The New Journalism in America.* San Francisco: Canfield Press (Harper & Row), 1974.

Dewey, John, *Human Nature and Conduct.* New York: The Modern Library, 1957.

———, *Individualism Old and New.* New York: Capricorn Books Edition, 1962.

———, *Theory of the Moral Life.* New York: Holt, Rinehart and Winston, 1960.

Doig, Ivan and Carol Doig, *News, A Consumer's Guide.* Englewood Cliffs, N.J.: Prentice-Hall, 1972.

Duscha, Julius and Thomas Fischer, *The Campus Press: Freedom and Responsibility.* Washington: American Association of State Colleges and Universities, 1973.

Edwards, Verne E., *Journalism in a Free Society.* Dubuque: W. C. Brown, 1970.

Efron, Edith, *The News Twisters.* Los Angeles: Nash Publishing Co., 1971.

Ellul, Jacques, *Propaganda: The Formation of Men's Attitudes*. New York: Random House, 1973.

Emery, Michael C. and Ted C. Smythe (eds.), *Readings in Mass Communications: Concepts & Issues*. Second Edition. Dubuque: W. C. Brown, 1974.

Epictetus, *Moral Discourses*. New York: Dutton, 1910.

Epstein, Edward Jay, *News from Nowhere: Television and the News*. New York: Random House, 1973.

Ewing, A. C., *Ethics*. New York: The Free Press, 1965.

Farrar, Ronald T. and John D. Stevens, *Mass Media and the National Experience*. New York: Harper & Row, 1971.

Feldman, Samuel N., *The Student Journalist and Legal and Ethical Issues*. New York: Richard Rosen Press, 1968.

Fletcher, Joseph, *Situation Ethics: The New Morality*. Philadelphia: The Westminster Press, 1966.

Flippen, Charles C. (ed.), *Liberating the Media: The New Journalism*. Washington: Acropolis Books, 1974.

Ford, W. C., *Jefferson and the Newspaper, 1785–1830*. New York: Columbia University Press, 1936.

Friendly, Fred, *Due to Circumstances Beyond Our Control . . .* New York: Random House, 1967.

Garrett, Thomas M., *An Introduction to Some Ethical Problems of Modern American Advertising*. Rome: Gregorian University Press, 1961.

Georgetown Law Journal, *Media and the First Amendment in a Free Society*. Amherst: University of Massachusetts Press, 1973.

Gerald, James Edward, *The Social Responsibility of the Press*. Minneapolis: University of Minnesota Press, 1963.

Gerbner, George *et al.* (eds.), *Communications Technology and Social Policy: Understanding the New "Cultural Revolution."* New York: Wiley, 1973.

Goldwater, Barry, *The Conscience of a Majority*. Englewood Cliffs, N.J.: Prentice-Hall, 1970.

Gordon, George N., *Persuasion: The Theory and Practice of Manipulative Communication*. New York: Hastings House, 1971.

———— and Irving A. Falk, *The War of Ideas: America's International Identity Crisis*. New York: Hastings House, 1973.

Griffiths, Thomas, *How True: A Skeptic's Guide to Believing the News*. Boston: Little, Brown & Co., 1974.

Harrison, John M. and Harry Stein (eds.), *Muckraking, Past, Present and Future*. University Park, Pa.: Penn State University Press, 1973.

Hartmann, Nicolai, *Ethics* (3 vols.). New York: Macmillan, 1932.

Haselden, Kyle, *Morality and the Mass Media*. Nashville: Broadmann Press, 1968.

Henning, Albert F., *Ethics and Practices in Journalism*. New York: Ray Long and Richard R. Smith, 1932.

Herzog, A., *B.S. Factor—Theory and Technique of Faking It*. New York: Simon and Schuster, 1973.

Hobbes, Thomas, *Leviathan*. New York: E. P. Dutton and Co., 1950.

Hohenberg, John, *The Professional Journalist* (Third Edition). New York: Holt, Rinehart & Winston, 1973.

Hornby, Robert, *The Press in Modern Society*. London: F. Muller, 1965.

Howard, John A. and James Hulbert, *Advertising and the Public Interest*. Chicago: Crain Communications, 1972.

Hulteng, John L., *The Opinion Function: Editorial and Interpretive Writing for the News Media*. New York: Harper & Row, 1973.

———— and Roy P. Nelson, *The Fourth Estate: An Informal Appraisal of the News and Opinion Media*. New York: Harper & Row, 1971.

Huxley, Aldous, *Brave New World Revisited*. New York: Harper & Row, 1965.

Irwin, William H., *Propaganda and the News*. New York: McGraw-Hill, 1936.

Jaspers, Karl, *Man in the Modern Age*. Garden City, N.Y.: Doubleday & Co., Anchor Books, 1957.

Johannesen, Richard L., *Ethics and Persuasion: Selected Readings*. New York: Random House, 1967.

Johnson, Michael L., *The New Journalism: The Underground Press*. Lawrence: University of Kansas Press, 1971.

Johnson, William O., *Super Spectator and the Electronic Lilliputians*. Boston: Little, Brown, 1971.

Kant, Immanuel, *Foundations of the Metaphysics of Morals*. Indianapolis: The Bobbs-Merrill Co., 1959.

Key, Wilson B., *Subliminal Seduction: Ad Media Manipulation of a Not So Innocent America*. Englewood Cliffs, N.J.: Prentice-Hall, 1973.

Kingsbury, Susan, Hornell Hart and Associates, *Newspapers and the News*. Westport, Conn.: Greenwood Press, 1970.

Klein, Ted and Fred Danzig, *How to be Heard: How to Make the Media Work for You*. New York: Macmillan, 1974.

Kohler, Wolfgang, *The Place of Value in a World of Facts*. New York: New American Library (Mentor Books), 1966.

Kovesi, Julius, *Moral Notions*. London: Routledge & Kegan Paul, 1967.

Krasnow, E. G. and L. D. Longley, *The Politics of Broadcast Regulation*. New York: St. Martin's Press, 1973.

Krieghbaum, Hillier, *Pressures on the Press*. New York: Thomas Y. Crowell, 1972.

La Piere, Richard, *The Freudian Ethic*. New York: Duell, Sloan and Pearce, 1959.

Larsen, Otto N. (ed.), *Violence and the Mass Media*. New York: Harper & Row, 1968.

Le Duc, Don R., *Cable Television and the FCC: A Crisis in Media Control*. Philadelphia: Temple University Press, 1973.

Lee, Richard W. (ed.), *Politics and the Press*. Washington: Acropolis Books, 1970.

Leroy, David J. and Christopher Sterling (eds.), *Mass News—Practices, Controversies and Alternatives*. New York: Prentice-Hall, 1973.

Levy, L. W., *Legacy of Suppression*. Cambridge: Harvard University Press, 1960.

Liebert, Robert M., J. M. Neale and Emily Davidson, *The Early Window: Effects of Television on Children and Youth*. New York: Pergamon Press, 1973.

Lindstrom, Carl E., *The Fading American Newspaper*. Garden City, N.Y.: Doubleday, 1960.

Locke, John, *An Essay on Human Understanding*. Oxford: Oxford University Press, 1931.

Lofton, John, *Justice and the Press*. Boston: Beacon Press, 1966.

Lynes, Russell, *The Tastemakers*. New York: Harpers, 1955.

Mabbott, J. D., *An Introduction to Ethics*. Garden City, N.Y.: Doubleday & Co., Anchor Books, 1969.

MacDonald, Glenn, *Report or Distort*. New York: Exposition Press, 1973.

MacDougall, A. Kent (ed.), *The Press: A Critical Look from the Inside*. Princeton, N.J.: Dow Jones Books, 1972.

MacDougall, Curtis D., *Interpretive Reporting* (Sixth Edition). New York: Macmillan, 1972.

MacIntyre, Alasdair, *A Short History of Ethics*. New York: Macmillan, 1966.

Machiavelli, Niccolo, *The Prince*. New York: New American Library, 1961.

Markel, Lester, *What You Don't Know Can Hurt You: A Study of Public Opinion and Public Emotion*. Washington: Public Affairs Press, 1972.

Mass Media and Violence. (A report to the National Commission on the Causes and Prevention of Violence. Washington: U.S. Government Printing Office, Nov., 1969).

Mayer, Martin, *About Television*. New York: Harper & Row, 1972.

Meerloo, Joost, *The Rape of the Mind*. New York: World, 1956.

Melody, William, *Children's Television: The Economics of Exploitation*. New Haven: Yale University Press, 1973.

Merrill, John C. and Ralph L. Lowenstein, *Media, Messages, and Men: New Perspectives in Communications*. New York: David McKay, 1971.

Merrill, John C., *The Elite Press: Great Newspapers of the World*. New York: Pitman Publishing Corp., 1968.

————, *The Imperative of Freedom: A Philosophy of Journalistic Autonomy*. New York: Hastings House, 1974.

Mill, John Stuart, *On Liberty*. Indianapolis: The Bobbs-Merrill Co. (Library of Liberal Arts), 1956.

Mills, C. Wright, *The Power Elite*. New York: Oxford University Press, 1956.

Milton, John, *Areopagitica*. Ed. by G. H. Savine. New York: Appleton-Century-Crofts, 1951.

Moore, G. E., *Principia Ethica*. New York: Putnam, 1907.

Mott, Frank L., *Jefferson and the Press*. Baton Rouge: LSU Press, 1943.

Mueller, John E., *War Presidents and Public Opinion*. New York: John Wiley & Sons, 1973.

Newman, Edwin, *Strictly Speaking: Will America Be The Death of English?* New York: Bobbs-Merrill, 1974.

Nietzsche, Friedrich, *Beyond Good and Evil*. Several editions, the first in 1886.

————, *The Birth of Tragedy* (1872).

————, *On the Genealogy of Morals* (1887).

Nilsen, Thomas R., *Ethics of Speech Communication*. Indianapolis: The Bobbs-Merrill Co., 1974.

Nowell-Smith, P. H., *Ethics*. Baltimore: Pelican Books, 1954.

Padover, S. K., *Thomas Jefferson on Democracy*. New York: Penguin Books, 1939.

Phelan, John (ed.), *Communications Control: Readings in the Motives and Structures of Censorship*. New York: Sheed & Ward, 1969.

Pool, Ithiel de Sola (ed.), *Talking Back: Citizen Feedback and Cable Technology*. Cambridge: MIT Press, 1973.

Rembar, Charles, *The End of Obscenity*. New York: Random House, 1968.

Rivers, William L., *The Mass Media*. New York: Harper & Row, 1975.

————, *The Opinionmakers*. Boston: Beacon Press, 1965.

―――― and Theodore Peterson and Jay Jensen, *The Mass Media and Modern Society,* San Francisco: Rinehart Press, 1971

―――― and Wilbur Schramm, *Responsibility in Mass Communication.* New York: Harper & Row, 1969.

Russell, Bertrand, *Human Society in Ethics and Politics.* New York: New American Library of World Literature, 1962.

Rutland, Robert A., *The Newsmongers: Journalism in the Life of the Nation, 1690–1972.* New York: Dial Press, 1973.

Sahakian, William S., *Ethics: An Introduction to Theories and Problems.* New York: Barnes & Noble Books, 1974.

Sartre, J.-P., *Existentialism.* New York: Philosophical Library, 1947.

Schiller, Herbert L., *Mass Communications and the American Empire.* Boston: Beacon Press, 1971.

Schwartz, Tony, *The Responsive Chord.* Garden City, N.Y.: Anchor, 1973.

Servan-Schreiber, Jean-Louis, *The Power to Inform.* New York: McGraw-Hill, 1974.

Shayon, Robert L., *Open to Criticism.* Boston: Beacon Press, 1971.

Skornia, H. J., *Television and the News.* Palo Alto: Pacific Books, 1968.

Small, William, *Political Power and the Press.* New York: W. W. Norton & Co., 1972.

――――, *To Kill a Messenger: Television News and the Real World.* New York: Hastings House, 1970.

Spencer, Herbert, *The Data of Ethics.* New York: Hurst, 1923.

Spinoza, Baruch, *The Ethics: The Road to Inner Freedom.* New York: The Wisdom Library, 1957.

Steinberg, Charles S., *Mass Media and Communication* (Second Edition). New York: Hastings House, 1972.

Stevenson, Charles L., *Ethics and Language.* New Haven: Yale University Press, 1944.

Strouse, James C., *The Mass Media, Public Opinion, and Public Policy Analysis.* Columbus, Ohio: Charles E. Merrill, 1975.

Tocqueville, Alexis de, *Democracy in America.* New York: Alfred A. Knopf, 1945.

Voelker, Francis H. and Ludmila A. Voelker, *Mass Media Forces in Our Society* (Second Edition). New York: Harcourt Brace Jovanovich, Inc., 1975.

Warnock, Mary, *Ethics Since 1900.* London: Oxford Univ. Press, 1966.

Wells, Alan, *Picture-Tube Imperialism?* Maryknoll, N.Y.: Orbis, 1972.

Whale, John, *The Half Shut Eye.* New York: Macmillan-St. Martins, 1969.

Whitney, F. C., *Mass Media and Mass Communications in Society.* Dubuque, William C. Brown Co., 1975.

Widmer, Eleanor (ed.), *Freedom and Culture: Literacy Censorship in the 70's.* Belmont, Calif.: Wadsworth, 1970.

Wilhelmsen, Frederick D. and Jane Bret, *Telepolitics: The Politics of Neurotic Man.* Plattsburgh, N.Y.: Tundra Books, 1972.

Williams, Bernard, *Morality: An Introduction to Ethics.* New York: Harper & Row (Torchbooks), 1972.

Winick, Paul, *Taste and Censor in Television.* New York: Fund for the Republic, 1959.

Wolfe, Tom, *The New Journalism.* New York: Harper & Row, 1973.

Wood, James Playsted, *The Great Glut: Public Communication in the United States.* New York: Thomas Nelson, Inc., 1974.

INDEX